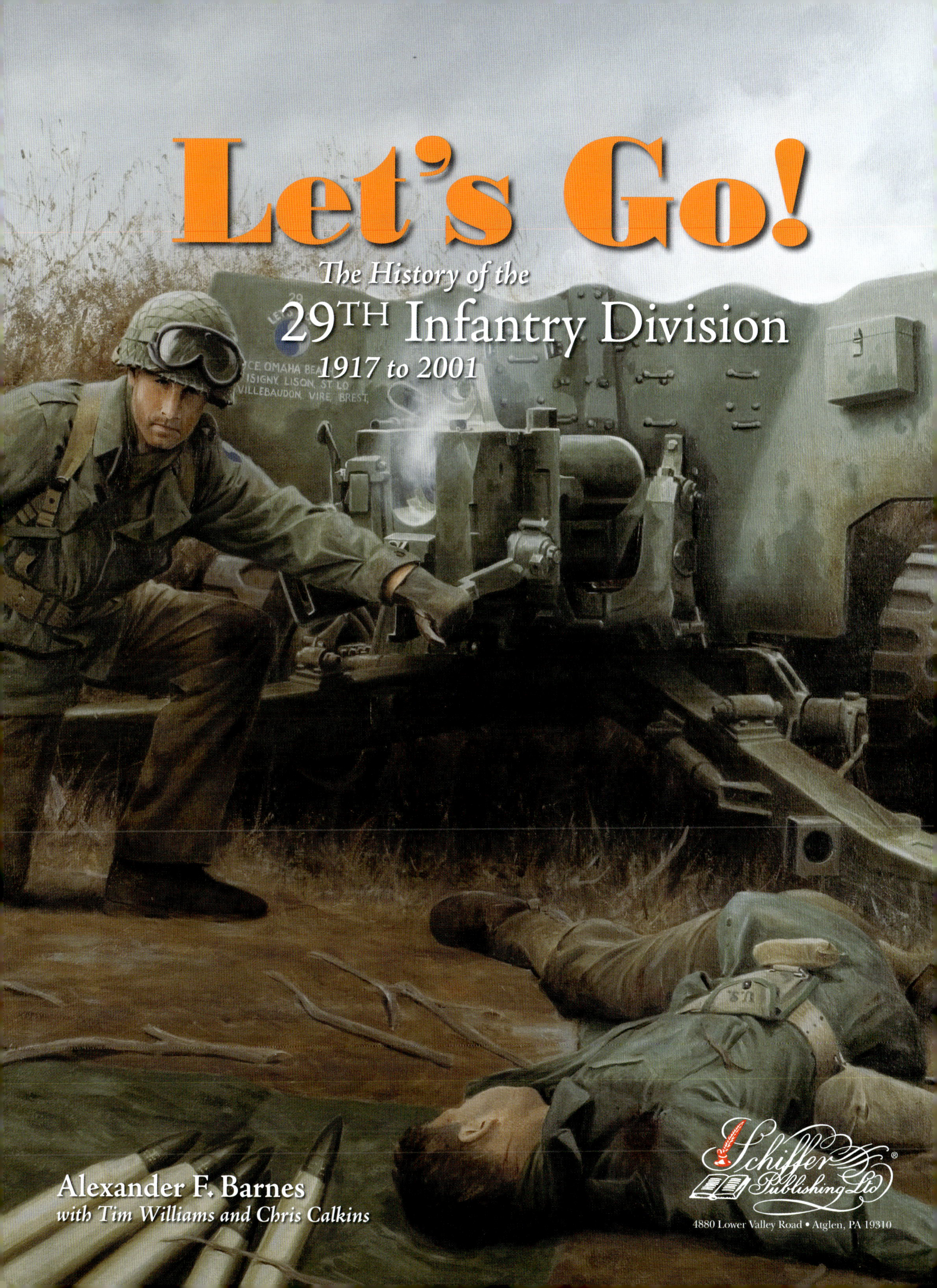

Let's Go!

The History of the 29TH Infantry Division *1917 to 2001*

Alexander F. Barnes
with Tim Williams and Chris Calkins

Schiffer Publishing Ltd®
4880 Lower Valley Road • Atglen, PA 19310

Library of Congress Control Number: 2014932896

Designed by John P. Cheek
Type set in Adobe Jenson Pro

ISBN: 978-0-7643-4636-1
Printed in China

Published by Schiffer Publishing, Ltd.
4880 Lower Valley Road
Atglen, PA 19310
Phone: (610) 593-1777; Fax: (610) 593-2002
E-mail: Info@schifferbooks.com

For our complete selection of fine books on this and related subjects, please visit our website at www.schifferbooks.com. You may also write for a free catalog. This book may be purchased from the publisher. Please try your bookstore first.

We are always looking for people to write books on new and related subjects. If you have an idea for a book, please contact us at proposals@schifferbooks.com
Schiffer Publishing's titles are available at special discounts for bulk purchases for sales promotions or premiums. Special editions, including personalized covers, corporate imprints, and excerpts can be created in large quantities for special needs. For more information, contact the publisher.
Title page painting *Courtesy National Guard Bureau and Larry Selman..*

This book is dedicated to the soldiers of all eras who served in the 29th Infantry Division. Without them, there would be no story to tell.

Acknowledgments

Color photography of uniforms and artifacts courtesy of Alison Hutton.

This project would never have been possible without the help of some great editors, tireless historians, and even better friends: Charles G. "Chuck" Thomas; James "Sluggo" Ebertowski; John Simmons; Matt Fidler; and MAJ (ret) Richard "Digger" Dell. All gave freely of their own time to ensure the accuracy and readability of the book you are holding. John and Chuck also contributed some extremely valuable pieces of their personal collections to ensure the completeness of this work. Other important contributors were Major General (ret) Ken Bowra; Steve MacGeorge; Scott Stevens; LTC Mike Swanson; COL Paul Griffin; Henri-Paul Enjames; COL Michelle Rose and her brother, SFC John Cameron Mills; Clark Burdine; Colin Romanick; SFC James Long; Wyatt Almond and the Inge family; SSG Brian Crawford; Paul Reijnders; CW3 Clay Deckert; CPT Jake Goodine; Ray Johnson; Adam Cogley; John Contratto; Jason Mikles; Allan Henderson; Ed Loyd; Airman Troy Williams; Larry Perecko; Joan Shkane; Jake Blair; Penny Koon Santilli; Jack Smith; Teena Gordon; Jon Quinn; Michael Albanese; Rogier VandeHoef; Steve Klima; David Williams; Pete Combee; Richard Killblane (Army Transportation Corps historian *extraordinaire* and author of *The Filthy Thirteen*; Dennis Whitehead; and CSM Carl Holcomb, Steve DeVito, and Jack Womer (authors of *Fighting with the Filthy Thirteen*). We also received significant help from two 29th Infantry Division Chiefs of Staff: COL Eric Barr and COL Bill Coffin.

We would also like to thank Molly Bompane at the U.S. Army Historical Education Center; Major Daniel Jones and SFC Thurman Felker at the 1/111th Field Artillery Headquarters; Luther Hanson at the U.S. Army Quartermaster Museum; Mr. Dwight Walsh at the Citadel Archives and Museum; Mr. M. Allyn Brooks-LaSure; the National Guard Educational Foundation; the Institute of Heraldry; and the great staff at the U.S. Military Academy at West Point.

There are also a number of folks who provided information about specific topics that were way outside of our knowledge profile: Carolyn Wilkins and Mike Moore taught us about horses and mules (and the differences between); Kevin Born made sure we got the patches right; LTC (ret) Lawrence B. (Larry) Smith served as the armorer to guide us through the intricacies of American military small arms; once again, John E. Patton escorted us through the paths of righteousness concerning the often-confusing Army regulations and rank structure of the 20th century; and Monty Winget kept our vehicle information correct with the camouflage side up and the rubber side down. A special thanks also goes out to Mike Woody, who kept the old computer alive long enough to reach the finish line.

We also received the help and encouragement of some truly fine soldiers: CW5 (ret) Rufus Montgomery, COL Sharon Leary, COL Greg Mason, COL (ret) Steve Bourgeois, CW5 (ret) John Birkner, LTC Robert Nay, and the Australian Army's finest, LTC Piers Cambridge, who is notable for his expertise in Australian beer and small arms.

Thanks are owed to Ian Robertson for his patience in answering questions, guiding us through the book design process again, and reminding us that there really comes a time when you just have to stop.

And most of all, a sincere thank you to our wives: Michele Barnes, Cheryl Williams, and Sara Calkins. They never once questioned why we were doing this—even when they truly wondered.

Foreword

Tracing its roots back to the earliest colonial militias, the National Guard is the oldest branch of the United States military. In one form or another, the National Guard has served in every one of its country's conflicts, including the French and Indian War, which took place before there was a United States. From the Revolutionary War through the Civil War—serving on both sides—and into the Spanish-American War, National Guard units, raised and supported by the individual States, served with character and distinction as part of the U.S. Army. It was not until 1903, however, that a more formal relationship was defined by the U.S. Government's Militia Act. Under this guideline, some federal funding was provided for National Guard units. To earn this funding, however, the states were required to meet certain personnel strength requirements.

Prior to the First World War, training periods for the National Guard were often marked more by elaborate departure and arrival ceremonies than by serious training for the modern battlefield. In this photograph, Colonel Harvey, commander of the Washington, D.C., Guard, awaits the return of his soldiers from training. *Courtesy Library of Congress.*

The relaxed atmosphere at a National Guard training site is apparent from this very early twentieth century picture. Innovations in military technology, such as machine guns, armored vehicles, submarines, fighter airplanes, and poison gas will soon sweep this away. *Courtesy Library of Congress.*

Looking more like politicians or businessmen than the senior leaders of their state's military forces, this assembly of Adjutant Generals pause for a group picture. After the end of the First World War, many of the Adjutant General positions would be filled by soldiers with actual wartime experience. *Courtesy Library of Congress.*

The Act also provided for greater control of the states' units by the Federal Government. Among its other mandates, the Militia Act included provisions for voluntary enlistment, standardized equipment, equal pay and rank for performance, and equal discipline and punishment for misbehavior. The U.S. War Department (precursor to the Department of Defense, established in 1947) also assigned Regular Army officers to work with the state units and created the Division of Militia Affairs, later renamed the National Guard Bureau. A few years later, another piece of legislation was passed that required all states to rename their military units as "National Guard." It also spelled out the qualifications required for officers and permitted them to attend Regular Army schools as part of their career progression.[1]

Many state units also maintained elaborate ceremonial uniforms reflecting both their units' lineage and their social strata. Unit names, such as the Richmond Light Infantry Blues, Petersburg Grays, Portsmouth Light Artillery, or the "Dandy Fifth" all bring to mind a certain pomp and ceremony. Seen here is Hurley Thacker, a young artilleryman, in his dress uniform for the Richmond Howitzers. *Courtesy Colin Romanick.*

Even collar emblems were ornate and colorful, as evidenced by this medical officer's insignia from the 4th Maryland Infantry.

Another example of the ornate style of the period is this hat plate from a Maryland uniform.

The history of the 29th Infantry Division in the twentieth century is perhaps a fitting analogy for both the history of the National Guard and of the United States Army during that same period. With lineage predating the Revolutionary War, the units of what would later become the 29th Division entered the new century as volunteer state militias until the provisions of the 1903 Militia Act led to the more formal structure. Before that time, units had been organized in their hometowns and counties, primarily as infantry, cavalry, artillery, or engineer units, and often based on what equipment the state or locality could afford to purchase or support. The vast majority of these Guard units were more adept at marching in parades and restoring civil order during local labor disturbances than they were at facing a well-equipped foe on the modern battlefield. That would change.

With a growing war in Europe and continued problems on the Mexican Border, raising troops for the Regular Army and the National Guard became of primary importance. Recruiters for the D.C. National Guard are seen here working the crowd, looking for young men eager to wear Army khaki. *Courtesy Library of Congress.*

As part of the deployment of almost every National Guard unit in the country to the Mexican border in 1916, the dress uniforms were put away, and in their place were the more practical olive drab and khaki uniforms. Upon arrival in France, this Virginia Doughboy's uniform will change again, as the campaign hat will be replaced by a steel helmet and the leather leggings with woolen puttees.

As a result of America's emergence on the global scene following victory in the 1898 Spanish-American War, these citizen-soldiers would be called by their president to serve as an essential part of America's military. Led by officers and NCOs, the majority of whom had first seen combat in the Boxer Rebellion, the Spanish-American war, and the Philippine Insurrection, these soldiers and units would serve along the Mexican border before the 29th Division had even come into existence. Upon the formal activation of the 29th Division in 1917, the assigned officers and men travelled to Camp McClellan, Alabama, to prepare themselves for war as best they could by creatively using whatever training materials they could find. Although originally designated as a regionally-based National Guard division, their ranks were quickly filled with volunteers and draftees from numerous other states. In time, they would make their way to France and serve bravely in the bloody Meuse-Argonne campaign. After the Armistice, the 29th was deactivated upon return to the United States and the units released once again to state control. Across the board, the combat units of the American Army were very quickly downsized and, similar to Rip Van Winkle, much of the American military took a twenty-year nap.

Symbolizing the inter-war era, this well-dressed National Guardsman and his equally well-dressed wife pose for a picture. Under magnification it is possible to see that the officer is wearing spurs on his boots and First World War service ribbons on his coat.

The thundering events of 1939 in Europe and the Pacific would serve to rouse the American military from its slumber, and once more, the 29th would train for war. Crossing the Atlantic for the second time in twenty-five years to serve in the European Theater of Operations (ETO), the 29th trained for so long in Britain that they would come to be thought of as a hometown unit by many British citizens. Their return to France would take place the morning of 6 June 1944 on a Normandy beach soon to be forever known as Omaha.

Looking much less stylish than the officer in the preceding picture, this American NCO celebrates the 4th of July in 1944 by sharing candy with some little girls in France during the Second World War. *Courtesy Library of Congress.*

Serving valiantly throughout the European campaign, the 29th would suffer many casualties before eventually celebrating Victory in Europe (V-E) Day in Germany. Returning to the States, the men and units of the 29th Division would undergo a number of transitional periods, as the unit was reformed and readjusted to meet the changing needs of the Army during the Cold War. Though not deployed as a full division in either the Korean or Vietnam wars, individual members would serve in both of these conflicts. In 1969, the 29th was inactivated as a division and its units were forced to give up their Blue and Gray patch as they were rolled into other organizations, such as the 28th Infantry Division and later the 58th and 116th (Separate) Infantry Brigades. In 1985, the 29th Infantry Division would once again unfurl its colors and reenter the Army's strategic planning. The 29th was activated for service as the first National Guard infantry division to be designated a "Light" Division. Operations "Urgent Fury" in Grenada, "Just Cause" in Panama, and the invasion of Kuwait by Iraq in the late summer of 1990 provided real-world events that helped focus its training. Though the 29th did not deploy to Desert Shield/Desert Storm as a division, many specialized individual units were activated, some serving in the Persian Gulf. With the completion of the Gulf War, the U.S. Army began a period of nation building and peacekeeping operations in Somalia, Haiti, the Sinai, and in the Balkan countries emerging from the breakup of Yugoslavia. The end of the twentieth century found the old units of the 29th deployed and supporting several of these operations. It was during the period while the 29th was preparing to send another rotation of soldiers to Bosnia that the terrorist attacks of 11 September 2001 on America took place, ushering in a new century and a new era of service to the nation by the 29th. While that epoch lies beyond the scope of this book, it is impossible not to acknowledge the service and sacrifices of the Blue and Gray Division in the Global War on Terror.

Wherever possible, the authors have attempted to let the soldiers speak in their own words, and trusted them to speak their minds freely. They did! We have also made use of the most common spelling of locations, particularly for the place names in France and Bosnia. As perhaps the definitive history of the 29th Infantry Division in the Second World War, we have followed Joseph Ewing's *29 Let's Go!* (1947) for the spelling of Pointe du Hoe, St. Lô, and other key locations. One other advisory note is important, as it relates to the 116th Infantry Regiment. Drawing lineage from the "Stonewall Brigade" of American Civil War fame, soldiers assigned to the 116th often referred to themselves as "Stonewallers" and their unit as the Stonewall Brigade, even when the unit was only regimental in size. Though some readers may find this and other lineage details confusing, inside an infantry division with as rich a history as the 29th, it makes perfect sense.

For those readers who are seeking even more in-depth details of the fighting in the Meuse-Argonne in 1918 or in Normandy in 1944, they can also look in the other very fine books listed in the bibliography. It is the authors' intent in this work to provide the history of the 29th Division from just prior to its birth in 1917 through the start of the twenty-first century. In doing so, full advantage has been taken of the many fine museum and private collections of 29th Division material in order to share with the reader the best illustrations and images we can of the campaigns, equipment, uniforms, and faces of the soldiers of the Blue and Gray Division. Originally formed using state guard units from New Jersey, Delaware, Virginia, Maryland, and Washington, D.C., the 29th would be reconfigured several times. By the time the 29th went ashore on D-Day, it was primarily a Virginia and Maryland unit, and it remains so today.

In every soldier's career, regardless of length, they will hear the bugle call them to duty many times. Sometimes it will call them to leave the safety of their muddy trench and advance into an artillery-shattered and mustard gas-filled clump of French forest. Other times they will hear it when the ramp drops on their landing

With victory near comes time for celebration. In this picture, taken in Germany in early spring 1945, a group of infantrymen take time to share a bottle. Note that the soldier with the bottle has also managed to find a German Army belt and buckle to wear with his uniform.

craft off the Normandy coast as they spearhead the liberation of Europe. Its call is clear in these dramatic events. However, it sounds far more often in less dramatic conditions, as when a young soldier has to leave his sleeping bag, pull on his cold combat boots, and walk out into a cold, snowy Bosnian morning to deliver a fairly hot meal to his fellow soldiers that have been standing guard on the bridge between two warring ethnic groups in the Balkans. Or its sound is heard during a combat engineer's endless sixteen- to twenty-hour shift, operating his heavy equipment to clear a stretch of road closed by trees uprooted by a hurricane. The engineer continues to work, knowing that until he clears the road, the trucks filled with ice and bottled water can't make their deliveries to the small Maryland towns that need them. It will be heard by the young officer who, on his own initiative, forces open a unit supply room, loads a truck with cots, and drives through the night so that American citizens forced to evacuate their homes because of a flood or hurricane won't have to sleep on the floor in an emergency shelter. All of these are interlocking pieces of the same puzzle; American soldiers serving their hometowns, their states, and their country. All of these are part of the Blue and Gray Division's traditions. Their service brings distinct honor upon themselves, their units, and the United States Army.

So, if the story of the 29th Division is one of valor and vigilance, selfless service and sacrifice, the implication follows that those places made so sacred by the soldiers of the 29th Division, such as the Meuse-Argonne, Omaha Beach, and St. Lô, may be haunted. Don't worry; if you visit these hallowed sites and encounter any ghosts, they will be friendly and ask nothing of you, except to remember them for their deeds and sacrifices. In keeping with the words engraved above the entrance to the Memorial Chapel at the Flanders Field American Cemetery in Belgium: "Greet Them Ever With Grateful Hearts."

Perhaps typifying the family aspect of National Guard membership and service is this picture of two brothers. Both captains (one a member of the 246th Field Artillery and the other in the 116th Infantry), they pose together at the end of their 1991 annual training at Fort Pickett, Virginia.

The various versions of the 29th Infantry Division patches worn by the soldiers of the Blue and Gray since the Second World War.

CHAPTER 1

From Home to the Rio Grande

In August 1914, the world went off its rails. What had started as an ugly little affair in the Balkans quickly evolved into the greatest war in history. One by one, the governments and royal families of Europe joined the conflict. When the final sides were chosen in this deadly game, it was Germany, the Austro-Hungarian Empire, Bulgaria, and Turkey (known as the Central Powers) against France, Russia, Belgium, and the British Commonwealth, most commonly referred to as the Allies. Italy eventually came in on the side of the Allied powers in exchange for British promises of Austro-Hungarian territory which the Italians believed to be a natural part of their country. By 1916, there was an unbroken line of trenches from the North Sea to the border of Switzerland stretching over four hundred miles. The Allies had made an early attempt to knock Turkey out of the war at Gallipoli and failed miserably. However, they were having greater success against the Ottoman Empire in the Middle East and on the Arabian Peninsula. Things were not going as well for the Allies in Africa. A small German force was keeping a much larger Allied force tied up in a "cat and mouse" campaign in the jungles and plains near Mt. Kilimanjaro and Lake Tanganyika.

The United States had so far managed to stay neutral and out of the war. In spite of his anger over the Germans' unrestricted

A truly unique picture; President Woodrow Wilson and Secretary of War Newton Baker informally review a unit of the D.C. National Guard in Washington, D.C. Soon Wilson would be dispatching these troops to the Mexican border, and then later to France. *Courtesy Library of Congress.*

Captain Louis Wilson of the Washington, D.C., National Guard, poses for a carefully staged photo taken prior to National Guard service along the border. In the prewar training periods, state guard units were often visited by high-ranking dignitaries and politicians; therefore, Captain Wilson has both his campaign hat and a more formal visor cap ready for wear. *Courtesy Library of Congress.*

submarine warfare, President Wilson was determined not to be drawn into the European fight. While the vast majority of Americans favored the Allies, there were still large numbers of pro-German sympathizers in the country. They were found primarily in the communities with large German-American populations and, perhaps not surprisingly, also among many Irish-Americans. The truth be told, the Irish were more anti-British than they were pro-German, but the effect was pretty much the same.[1] These groups were not alone; from the progressives of Wisconsin to the isolationists of Texas, many an elected politician took a stand against involving America in a war that pitted one set of kings and royalty against another set. Still other Americans believed that there was a conspiracy of industrialists that wanted America in the war with Germany to make a profit from selling weapons and supplies. At least for a while, it appeared that Wilson was listening. One of his re-election campaign slogans in 1916 was "He kept us out of the war."

The D.C. Guard got another chance to show off their skills and equipment while marching on Flag Day, 14 June 1916, when the Preparedness Parade traveled the main streets of the nation's capital. *Courtesy Library of Congress.*

However, political slogans aside, the president was not above getting involved in international politics when it concerned countries that he felt belonged in America's sphere of influence. By 1916, Wilson had dispatched Marines to Haiti and the Dominican Republic to "stabilize" their governments, and he also maintained American troops in Cuba and the Philippines.[2] Adding to the mix was the fact that the Americans were once again having issues with their neighbors directly to the south. In 1910, an insurrection against the dictator Porfirio Diaz had started another round of violence and bloodshed in Mexico. In 1914, the United States Navy, along with a few Marines, landed at the port of Vera Cruz. The purpose of this mission was to rescue some U.S. sailors and prevent a shipment of weapons from being sent to one of the participants in a Mexican power struggle. While this incursion alone was enough cause for concern, just two years later, on 9 March 1916, several hundred Mexican revolutionaries crossed the border and attacked the town of Columbus, New Mexico. With this attack, already fragile American-Mexican relations took a very drastic turn for the worse. At the heart of the problem this time was Francisco "Pancho" Villa. Villa had already earned a reputation for violence and ruthlessness for his part in the seemingly endless battles for control of the Mexican government. After the attack on Columbus, for most U.S. citizens, the name Pancho Villa became synonymous with large-scale banditry and brigandry. When Villa and his gang of raiders rode away from Columbus, they left behind ten American soldiers and eight civilians dead, as well as seven soldiers and two civilians wounded. Public outrage at the attack and pressure from the Army finally convinced President Wilson to dispatch the American military to pursue Villa into Mexico and punish him. The President summoned his Army leaders and after conferring with them, gave orders to Brigadier General John J. "Black Jack" Pershing to lead an expedition into Mexico. His guidance to Pershing was fairly simple and succinct: capture Villa and put an end to the raids along the border.

Commanding the American forces arrayed against Villa was Brigadier General John J. Pershing. Pershing, seen here on the left, walking with Major General Tasker Bliss, was the perfect choice for leading the American forces: tough and resilient but not rash; he would soon be selected to lead the American Expeditionary Force (AEF) to France. *Courtesy Library of Congress.*

In an attempt to rally his wavering countrymen to his side of the fighting in Mexico, Francisco "Pancho" Villa (seen here in the center) would lead his band of soldiers and revolutionaries across the U.S. - Mexican border. Their attack on the small town of Columbus, New Mexico, in the early morning hours of 9 March 1916 would be the catalyst for the "Punitive Expedition." *Courtesy Library of Congress.*

Closer view of the cavalry tunic clearly showing the "I" Troop, 6th Cavalry disk with crossed sabers. Along with the Mexican Campaign ribbon, this tunic also has a World War I victory ribbon.

Another view of the 6th Cavalry uniform, this time clearly showing the uniform's sergeant's stripes and how susceptible wool and felt are to insect attacks.

A heavily-worn U. S. Army M1912 tunic of a trooper of the 6th Cavalry. Note the rounded buttons indicative of the prewar era and the Mexican campaign ribbon that signified the wearer was a regular Army soldier who crossed the border chasing Pancho Villa.

Soldiers, as part of their annual training, perfect their skills disassembling, cleaning, and reassembling their 1903 Springfield rifles. *Courtesy Library of Congress.*

After becoming well-versed in the care of their rifle, Virginia Guardsman perfect their marksmanship skills. *Courtesy Library of Congress.*

Only six days after the attack, on 15 March 1916, Pershing led a force of 4,800 Regular Army soldiers with over 4,000 horses and mules into Mexico to capture Pancho Villa. In time, the campaign would come to be called the "Punitive Expedition." Pershing's initial forces were soon joined by some of the Army's latest transportation acquisitions: touring cars and cargo trucks. Angry at the U.S. Army's incursion into their territory, the Mexican authorities forbid Pershing from using the Mexican railway system to supply his troops. As a result, Pershing's forces soon became dependent on the logistical support provided by the cargo vehicles, as well as the motorized vehicles borrowed from the 1st Aero Squadron.[3]

As is so often the case in military operations, what seemed a fairly straightforward task (capture Pancho Villa) turned out to be a much more complicated and harder mission than expected. The state of Chihuahua—the area of Mexico where Villa had gone to ground—was poorly mapped, and the operational area was characterized by flat sandy deserts on one side and the Sierra Madre mountain range on the other. Along with the rugged terrain and long distances between towns, the weather was also a factor, including "anything from dust storms to sudden blizzards, and the temperature ranged from burning hot to freezing cold, sometimes veering ninety degrees in a single day."[4] Pershing established a base of operations at Casas Grandes and from there split his force into independent columns to chase down Villa and his men. In time, some of Pershing's forces would actually be more than 484 miles deep into Mexico. The 13th Cavalry would record the deepest penetration when they reached the Mexican town of Parral, a distance of over 516 miles from the U.S. border. To the infantrymen and cavalrymen of Pershing's force, it was to be an exercise in futility, as they marched and rode through the hot and dusty countryside. The few skirmishes between the Army and Villa's men were generally inconclusive. Although the American soldiers inflicted more casualties on the enemy, most of the enemy normally escaped; worst of all, Pershing couldn't capture Villa. The occasional run-ins between the Army and the forces of other Mexican "warlords" were equally bloody and inconclusive, and at times the Mexican forces got the best of the Army. Equally frustrating to the U.S. political and military leaders, some Mexican cross-border raids continued while the Army was chasing Villa's band deeper and deeper into Mexico.

Along with tactics and weapons training at Camp Ordway, Virginia, the Guardsmen also received their required inoculations. *Courtesy Library of Congress.*

One of the eight Curtis JN-2 airplanes assigned to Pershing's force is seen here as it prepares to take off on a scouting mission. The austerity of the Mexican desert, seen in the background, was typical of the terrain with which the expedition had to contend. *Courtesy Library of Congress.*

Another typical scene during any National Guard training; soldiers practice performing a "guard mount" under the watchful eye of their sergeant. *Courtesy Library of Congress.*

Certainly a glimpse of what twentieth century warfare would entail; National Guardsmen perform routine maintenance on some of their vehicles, including a scout car and an ambulance. The Punitive Expedition would prove to be the U.S. Army's first real use of motorized vehicles in a military campaign. *Courtesy Library of Congress.*

Chow time, a welcome break in the training day. Note the wide variety of hat styles and uniforms. *Courtesy Library of Congress.*

An ornate pin-back collar disk for the Maryland National Guard State Headquarters.

President Wilson eventually decided that the only way to maintain security of the border required the services of the National Guard units from Texas, Arizona, and New Mexico; he federalized them into national service 8 May 1916. By mid-June, Wilson had called out an additional 110,000 National Guard soldiers for border service. This expansion included National Guard units from almost every state in the union and brought into active duty "3 regiments, 13 separate squadrons, and 22 separate troops of cavalry....108 regiments and 7 battalions of infantry and 6 regiments, 12 battalions, and 17 batteries of field artillery."[5] For many of the National Guardsmen from New York, Pennsylvania, Maryland, Virginia, and other east coast states, the hot, dry environment of the Mexican border region was as foreign to them as if they had been sent to the moon. Temperatures in excess of 110 degrees greeted the 1st Pennsylvania Engineers and the Massachusetts artillery batteries that arrived in El Paso 4 July 1916. Prevented by United States law from crossing into Mexico to join the chase after Villa, the National Guard units had to be content in the role of border guards. They still had to remain alert, as raids across the border by Mexican gangs continued. In Texas, these raids during the summer of 1916 were particularly violent and bloody. And while small in scale and fairly infrequent, these raids were enough of a threat to keep the recently-federalized soldiers alert to the possibility of danger and the importance of taking their training seriously. If nothing else, the raids also took the soldiers' minds off of the dust, heat, and rattlesnakes that tormented them on a daily basis.

National Guard artillerymen seen here serving on the Mexican border and mounted on their horses, ready to move a field piece. At this point in Army history, except for the field piece itself and the colors of the uniforms, little had changed in basic artillery tactics or organization since the Civil War.

Although no Mexican raiders crossed the border today, something almost as deadly tried; a large rattlesnake has been caught, killed, and displayed by one of the soldiers.

A typical scene in an early twentieth century artillery camp: several artillerymen are attempting to get a mule under control while their comrades, sitting on the caisson, enjoy the show.

A familiar scene for army mechanics of all eras; a soldier poses with his rifle while taking a break from repairing a vehicle. Behind him, a truck has been pulled in for repairs at a maintenance facility with overhead cover. Note that the cots have been moved outside to make room for work during the day.

A closer picture of the collar of the M1917 111th Artillery uniform, highlighting the "VA" (Virginia) disk. Virginia provided a number of artillery batteries to the Mexican campaign.

By the time most of the Guardsmen arrived and sealed the U.S. side of the border, the mission of the Punitive Expedition forces inside Mexico had changed. From actively seeking out Pancho Villa, the mission was now more focused on patrolling and maintaining a defensive posture inside Mexico to protect the border towns from further attacks.[6] As the soldiers settled into a daily regimen of training and guard duty, they continued to struggle against the combination of boredom and the harshness of the heat, dust storms, and insects. To pass the time, they soon learned to entertain themselves with baseball games, boxing matches, sing-a-longs, and endless poker games. In many ways, the time on the border served as a preview for what many of them would encounter when they trained for another war in the not-too-distant future. In fact, the Mexican Expedition, as it was officially known, proved to be an excellent training ground for many of the National Guard officers and men who would be recalled to Federal Service in 1917 for duty in France.

Close-up of the 29th Division patch showing the two-piece construction and hand stitching used to secure it to the uniform. The "Blue and Gray" would not come to symbolize the Virginia, Maryland, New Jersey, Delaware, and D.C. Guardsmen until the following year at Camp McClellan, and 29th Division soldiers would not wear shoulder patches, such as this one, on their uniforms until November 1918.

A well-preserved M1917 wool tunic of a Corporal of Battery "D," 111th Field Artillery, displaying his Mexican Border Ribbon and a First World War period 29th Division patch. The tactics, techniques, and unit procedures learned during the 1916 deployment to the border would be the most realistic training many Doughboys would receive before going into action in France in 1917 and 1918.

The use of the National Guard soldiers led to some interesting and somewhat ironic occurrences. When the artillery batteries from Virginia, the Richmond Howitzers, the Norfolk Light Artillery Blues, and the Portsmouth Light Artillery reported into Camp Wilson in San Antonio, Texas, they were combined with a northern-based artillery unit known as the New Hampshire Battery and formed into a provisional artillery regiment. When the units compared Civil War lineages, it became apparent that the Virginia and New Hampshire men's predecessors had fought each other during the Civil War on at least seventeen occasions. Fortunately, none of that counted much for them now, and even less for their new commander, Regular Army Lieutenant Colonel Manus MacCloskey. He was a veteran of the Boxer Rebellion and had served in the artillery unit that broke open the gates to Peking. Taking over the provisional regiment in October, he drilled it in every aspect of field artillery operations, from cannon firing to horse-breaking. Under his careful tutelage, the Guardsmen became proficient field artillerymen. By December, the regiment was declared fit for duty; the fastest of any of the newly-formed units on the border.[7] Along with the field artillery units, Virginia contributed two infantry regiments, a cavalry squadron, and several companies of engineers and signal troops. All total, there were nearly four thousand Virginians deployed to camps in southern Texas near the Mexican border. Similar numbers were deployed from New Jersey, Maryland, and Delaware. Among the more unusual units arriving on the border was a squadron of Virginia cavalry. Not among the original levy of troop units from Virginia, the Richmond Light Infantry Blues were an independent state military unit; therefore, they were not included in the list of state units from Virginia to be federalized. Disappointed at being excluded from the troop list, the "Blues" volunteered their services, only to be told the Army had all the infantry units they needed. The history of the "Blues" would later report: "To the members of the old command this situation was intolerable." Rebuffed in their attempts to join the deploying force, the Blues found out there was a shortage of cavalry units. With little hesitation, the Blues turned their backs on their 125-year history as an infantry unit and converted themselves into the "1st Squadron, Virginia Cavalry." In this configuration, they were now a type of unit for which the U.S. Army had great need. They were mustered into Federal service 5 July 1916 and by October they, and their horses, were en route to Texas.[8]

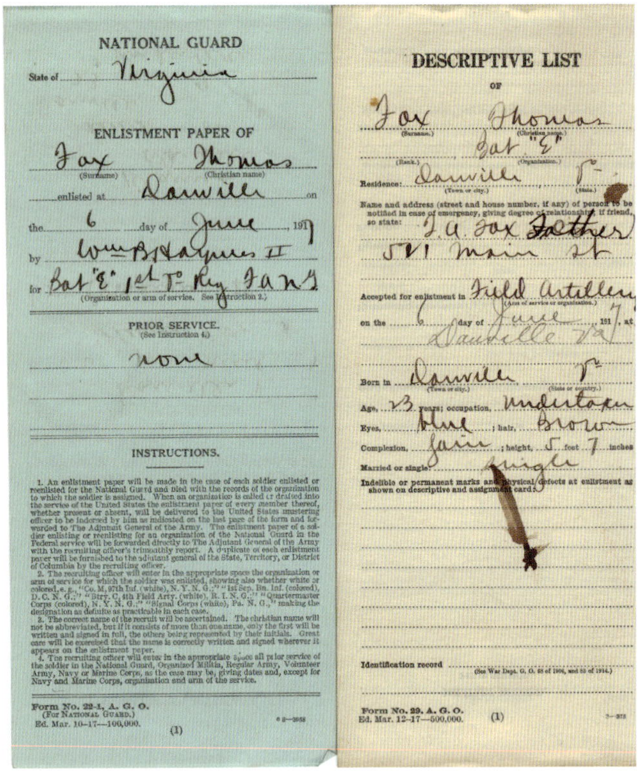

NATIONAL GUARD

State of Virginia

ENLISTMENT PAPER OF

Fox (Surname) Thomas (Christian name)

enlisted at Danville on the 6 day of June 1917 by Wm B Haynes II for Bat "E" 1st V. Reg F A N G (Organization or arm of service. See Instruction 2.)

PRIOR SERVICE. (See Instruction 4.)

none

INSTRUCTIONS.

1. An enlistment paper will be made in the case of each soldier enlisted or reenlisted for the National Guard and filed with the records of the organization to which the soldier is assigned. When an organization is called or drafted into the service of the United States the enlistment paper of every member thereof, whether present or absent, will be delivered to the United States mustering officer to be indorsed by him as indicated on the last page of the form and forwarded to The Adjutant General of the Army. The enlistment paper of a soldier enlisting or reenlisting for an organization of the National Guard in the Federal service will be forwarded directly to The Adjutant General of the Army with the recruiting officer's trimonthly report. A duplicate of each enlistment paper will be furnished to the adjutant general of the State, Territory, or District of Columbia by the recruiting officer.

2. The recruiting officer will enter in the appropriate space the organization or arm of service for which the soldier was enlisted, showing also whether white or colored, e. g., "Co. M, 97th Inf. (white), N. Y. N. G.;" "1st Sep. Bn. Inf. (colored), D. C. N. G.;" "Btry. C, 4th Field Arty. (white), R. I. N. G.;" "Quartermaster Corps (colored), N. Y. N. G.;" "Signal Corps (white), Pa. N. G.," making the designation as definite as practicable in each case.

3. The correct name of the recruit will be ascertained. The christian name will not be abbreviated, but if it consists of more than one name, only the first will be written and signed in full, the others being represented by their initials. Great care will be exercised that the name is correctly written and signed wherever it appears on the enlistment paper.

4. The recruiting officer will enter in the appropriate space all prior service of the soldier in the National Guard, Organized Militia, Regular Army, Volunteer Army, Navy or Marine Corps, as the case may be, giving dates and, except for Navy and Marine Corps, organization and arm of the service.

Form No. 22-1, A. G. O.
(For National Guard.)
Ed. Mar. 10-17—100,000.

(1)

DESCRIPTIVE LIST

OF

Fox (Surname.) Thomas (Christian name.)

(Rank.) Bat "E" (Organization.)

Residence: Danville (Town or city.), Va (State.)

Name and address (street and house number, if any) of person to be notified in case of emergency, giving degree of relationship; if friend, so state: J. A. Fox Father 521 Main St

Accepted for enlistment in Field Artillery (Arm of service or organization.)

on the 6 day of June 1917, at Danville Va

Born in Danville (Town or city.) Va (State or country.)

Age, 23 years; occupation, undertaker

Eyes, blue; hair, brown

Complexion, fair; height, 5 feet 7 inches

Married or single? single

Indelible or permanent marks and physical defects at enlistment as shown on descriptive and assignment card:

Identification record

Form No. 29, A. G. O.
Ed. Mar. 12-17—500,000.

(1)

Enlistment papers and unit data sheet for Thomas Fox. According to this paperwork, Fox joined Battery "E" of the First Virginia Field Artillery. At that time, Battery "E" was located in Danville, Virginia, which was also Fox's hometown. Fox would later serve in France as a Private First Class in Battery "E," 111th Field Artillery.

Soldiers from one of the Norfolk, Virginia, artillery batteries take time out from training for a picture while serving on the Mexican border. *Courtesy 1/111th Field Artillery.*

National Guard Artillerymen practicing crew drills while serving on the border. This is most likely a posed shot, indicated by the empty limber chest on the left and the absence of any shell casings on the ground. The gun they are drilling on is the M1902 3-inch Field Gun, the Army's first rifled, breech loading, recoiling field gun with an armored shield for crew protection. These cannons would be left in the States; when the units reached Europe, they received the famous French 75 in their place.

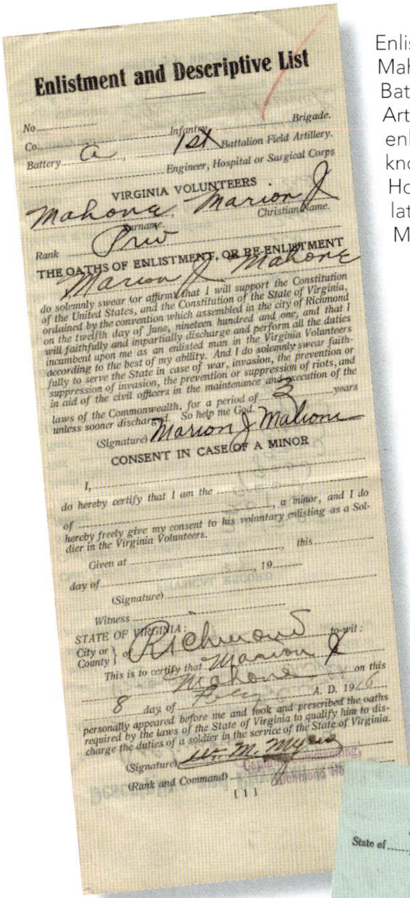

Enlistment and Descriptive List

No. ______ Infantry ______ Brigade.
Co. ______ 1st Battalion Field Artillery.
Battery a, ______ Engineer, Hospital or Surgical Corps

VIRGINIA VOLUNTEERS

Mahone, Marion J. Surname. Christian Name.

Rank Priv

THE OATHS OF ENLISTMENT, OR RE-ENLISTMENT

I, Marion J. Mahone do solemnly swear (or affirm) that I will support the Constitution of the United States, and the Constitution of the State of Virginia, ordained by the convention which assembled in the city of Richmond on the twelfth day of June, nineteen hundred and one, and that I will faithfully and impartially discharge and perform all the duties incumbent upon me as an enlisted man in the Virginia Volunteers according to the best of my ability. And I do solemnly swear faithfully to serve the State in case of war, invasion, the prevention or suppression of invasion, the prevention or suppression of riots, and in aid of the civil officers in the maintenance and execution of the laws of the Commonwealth, for a period of 3 years unless sooner discharged. So help me God.

(Signature) Marion J Mahone

CONSENT IN CASE OF A MINOR

I, ______ do hereby certify that I am the ______ of ______, a minor, and I do hereby freely give my consent to his voluntary enlisting as a Soldier in the Virginia Volunteers.

Given at ______, this ______ day of ______, 19___

(Signature) ______

Witness ______

STATE OF VIRGINIA: City or County } of Richmond, to-wit:

This is to certify that Marion J. Mahone on this 8 day of Feb A. D. 1916 personally appeared before me and took and prescribed the oaths required by the laws of the State of Virginia to qualify him to discharge the duties of a soldier in the service of the State of Virginia.

(Signature) W. M. Myers

(Rank and Command) Captain Commanding, Richmond Howitzers

[1]

Enlistment papers for Marion Mahone, recording his joining Battery "A," 1st Virginia Field Artillery. At the time of his enlistment, Battery "A" was known as "The Richmond Howitzers." Mahone would later serve in France in the 29th Military Police Company.

Another interesting picture of artillerymen in action. Note that, except for the hat, most of the soldiers are now dressed in the uniform styles they will wear in France. However, they are still following nineteenth century artillery tactics. Artillery pieces parked wheel to wheel like these would quickly draw a violent response of German counter-fire.

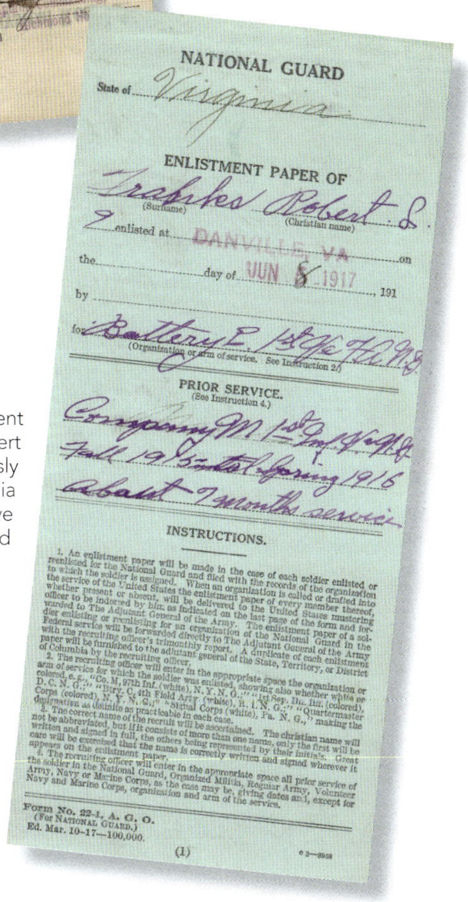

NATIONAL GUARD

State of Virginia

ENLISTMENT PAPER OF

Frankes Robert S. (Surname) (Christian name)

enlisted at DANVILLE, VA

the ______ day of JUN 8 1917 on ______, 191

by ______

for Battery E, 1st Va. F.A. N.G. (Organization or arm of service. See Instruction 2.)

PRIOR SERVICE. (See Instruction 4.)

Company M 1st Inf. Va. N.G. Fall 1915 until Spring 1916 about 7 months service

INSTRUCTIONS.

1. An enlistment paper will be made in the case of each soldier enlisted or reenlisted for the National Guard and filed with the records of the organization to which the soldier is assigned. When an organization is called or drafted into the service of the United States the enlistment paper of every member thereof, whether present or absent, will be delivered to the United States mustering officer to be indorsed by him as indicated on the last page of the form and forwarded to The Adjutant General of the Army. The enlistment paper of a soldier enlisting or reenlisting for an organization of the National Guard in the Federal service will be forwarded directly to The Adjutant General of the Army with the recruiting officer's trimonthly report. A duplicate of each enlistment paper will be furnished to the adjutant general of the State, Territory, or District of Columbia by the recruiting officer.

2. The recruiting officer will enter in the appropriate space the organization or arm of service for which the soldier was enlisted, showing also whether white or colored, e. g., "Co. M, 97th Inf. (white), N. Y. N. G.;" "1st Sep. Bn. Inf. (colored), D. C. N. G.;" "Btry. C, 4th Field Arty. (white), R. I. N. G.;" "Quartermaster Corps (colored), N. Y. N. G.;" "Signal Corps (white), Pa. N. G.," making the designation as definite as practicable in each case.

3. The correct name of the recruit will be ascertained. The christian name will not be abbreviated, but if it consists of more than one name, only the first will be written and signed in full, the others being represented by their initials. Great care will be exercised that the name is correctly written and signed wherever it appears on the enlistment paper.

4. The recruiting officer will enter in the appropriate space all prior service of the soldier in the National Guard, Organized Militia, Regular Army, Volunteer Army, Navy or Marine Corps, as the case may be, giving dates and, except for Navy and Marine Corps, organization and arm of the service.

Form No. 22-1, A. G. O. (For National Guard.) Ed. Mar. 10-17—100,000.

(1)

Another Battery "E" enlistment form, this time for a Robert Franks, whol had previously served in the 1st Virginia Infantry and would later serve in France in the 111th Field Artillery's Supply Company.

When the guard units deployed to the border, they brought all their equipment with them. In this rare picture, a field artillery unit of the Ohio National Guard prepares its observation balloon for use near El Paso, Texas. *Courtesy U.S. Army.*

Perhaps most importantly for the American Army, the officers and men in the units deployed to the border received hands-on, practical experience in campaigning. The Mexico Expedition had turned out to be an excellent training opportunity for individual National Guard soldiers as much as for their units. As will be seen later, some of them, like Samuel Gardner Waller and John Cutchins, would parlay this opportunity into extremely successful military and civilian careers. Similarly, many Regular Army officers, including such future general officers as General George Catlett Marshall, General John Leonard Hines, Major General Ralph Corbett Smith, Lieutenant General William Hood Simpson, and Major General Robert Lee Howze served in the campaign against Villa.

This damaged but still interesting photo provides a glimpse of a seldom discussed aspect of soldier life in the early twentieth century: shown here are three nurses and other hospital staffers at their crudely constructed clinic. From the Mexican border all the way to France, many female medical and support staff would share the discomforts of the male soldiers.

Standard procedure in good weather was for the sleeping tents to be rolled up to the middle pole during the day, transforming the space into company or battalion administrative offices. *Courtesy Library of Congress.*

An extremely dark, yet valuable, image showing General Pershing standing in front of his staff during the Punitive Expedition. Included in the picture are two future Army leaders: Lieutenant George S. Patton (fourth from right) and Major John L. Hines (third from right). Patton went on to a well-known career. Hines, not nearly as well known as Patton, would later command the 4th Division in France in 1918, be named Army Chief of Staff in 1924, and live to see his 100th birthday in 1968. *Courtesy Library of Congress.*

A closer view of the 5th Maryland uniform's state and regimental collar disks. Also note the early version rimless buttons used on the chest.

Carefully hand-carved 4th Maryland Infantry Regiment mess kit lid. The 4th Maryland would soon be part of the 115th Infantry Regiment, as was 2nd Lieutenant Paul Williams, the owner of this mess kit.

The M1912 wool tunic of a corporal in Company "G", 5th Maryland Infantry. Note the mix of older and newer style buttons, and that this uniform has corporal stripes on both sleeves. Soon the rapid expansion of the Army would introduce a cost-cutting measure by authorizing rank stripes for the duration of the war to be on the right sleeves only.

The last large-scale skirmish of the Mexican Expedition was fought at Carrizal 21 June 1916, between a force of Mexican soldiers led by General Felix Gomez and some U.S. cavalrymen from the 7th and 10th Cavalry Regiments. During the course of the battle, eleven U.S. troopers were killed and twenty-four were captured. The Mexican force suffered sixty-seven casualties, including General Gomez.[9] What outraged Pershing the most was that the Mexicans who attacked the cavalrymen were not Villa's followers, but were instead soldiers belonging to another Mexican leader (and soon to be President of Mexico), Venustiano Carranza. Knowing that any retaliatory attack on Carranza's other forces in the area would escalate to a full-scale war with Mexico, President Wilson refused Pershing's request to expand the expedition's mission to include attacks on the Carranzistas.

Eventually it became obvious to all concerned that the Expedition had reached the point of being about as successful as it was going to be, so the bulk of American forces were withdrawn by January 1917. Although Pershing would claim that the Expedition was a success, most people tended to see it as a draw. When there were battles, the American soldiers fought well, and some young officers used their exploits to build reputations as combat leaders. One of them, in particular, Lieutenant George S. Patton, proved himself to be a dynamic and courageous leader. While leading a patrol of 9th Cavalry troopers mounted in Dodge touring cars instead of on horses, Patton raided a ranch belonging to one of Villa's senior lieutenants, Julio Cárdenas. Patton, a future army general and armored warfare visionary, displayed the shooting skills he exhibited as a member of the U.S. 1912 Olympic Pentathlon team, as he personally shot Cárdenas and two of the other Villistas at the ranch. He then brought their bodies back to Pershing strapped across the hoods of the cars.[10]

Despite the occasional success against some of the other Villistas, Pancho continued to evade the Americans. In February 1917, after eleven months in pursuit, Pershing and the last of the Regular Army troops in his command crossed the border back into the United States.

Early version of collar insignia for the 1st Maryland Infantry Regiment.

The small town that was the site of Villa's first attack, Columbus, New Mexico, is now a bustling army post and supply depot. In the foreground, a large truck convoy is forming up to carry supplies across the border to Pershing's columns that are in pursuit of Pancho Villa and his men. *Courtesy Library of Congress.*

Three NCOs from the 1st Virginia Cavalry, identified (from left to right) only as Corporal Gray, Sergeant McC, and Corporal Abbott. The 1st Virginia Cavalry was comprised of men who had previously served in the Richmond Light Infantry Blues and voluntarily converted to cavalry in order to deploy to the Mexican Border.

A cavalryman from the 1st Virginia cares for his horse. When the 29th Division was formed, most of these former infantrymen/cavalrymen would serve in the 104th Ammunition Train.

Perhaps symbolic of the Punitive Expedition, an Army truck is towing a disabled automobile across a small stream. In spite of some mechanical problems, after the expedition was over, there were few doubters left to the value of having motorized vehicles providing logistics support. *Courtesy U.S. Army QM Museum.*

This picture of New York National Guard cavalrymen serving on the border provides a clear picture of the variety of individual equipment worn. Colonel G.A. Wingate (on the right) is equipped with a .45 automatic pistol in an M1912 cavalry holster, while the other soldier appears to have a Smith and Wesson .38 caliber revolver in a left-hand-draw leather holster. *Courtesy Library of Congress.*

The timing was good. Although re-elected as the man who kept America out of the war, Wilson would soon decide that America could no longer remain neutral. With increased submarine attacks and evidence of a German conspiracy to aid Mexico against the United States, even the pacifist members of his cabinet were now in agreement that war with Germany was necessary.[11] On 6 April 1917, the United States declared war on Germany and the Central Powers. Many of the National Guardsmen who had served on the Mexican border had barely returned to civilian life before they again found themselves in uniform. The former Light Infantry Blues, now known as the 1st Virginia Cavalry, arrived home in Richmond in mid-March 1917, but the soldiers were not released from active duty. Instead, they were immediately assigned to patrol rail yards, bridges, dams, and other vital infrastructure against sabotage by "enemy agents." Some units of the Maryland Guard that had returned from the border in October 1916 were reactivated. They were then deployed throughout the state to guard "railroad tunnels and bridges, munitions plants and grain elevators." [12] Other Maryland units were dispatched to Virginia, Pennsylvania, and New York to perform similar duties. As the historian of the 115th Infantry Regiment later noted: "This kind of warfare was very agreeable to the men. The duty given them was light and the experience was more like a summer vacation."[13] All that was about to change and summer vacation would soon be over. President Wilson was going to make "the world safe for democracy," and to do that, he would need every soldier the United States could produce.

The Mexico Expedition Medal was awarded for service on the Mexican border between 14 March 1916 and 7 February 1917.

A unique picture of a Virginia cavalryman and his horse. The note on the back indicates this is a picture of the March 1917 return from the Mexican border of Company "A", 1st Virginia Cavalry Regiment, and that the photograph was taken at the 17th and Broad Street intersection in Richmond, Virginia.

CHAPTER 2

The 29th Division is born at Camp McClellan

Although the United States's entry into the First World War did not catch the American Army completely by surprise, it was still woefully unprepared. With the exception of a few Regular Army and National Guard units that had been deployed to the Mexican border as part of the Punitive Campaign against Pancho Villa, the vast majority of what would become the United States Army was still wearing civilian clothes and was untrained when war was declared 6 April 1917. The last time U.S. troops were in any shooting war had been more than fifteen years previous during the Boxer Rebellion in China, when the U.S. provided 3,125 soldiers and 295 Marines as part of an eight-nation force of 54,226 men. The Philippine Insurrection was the other, and it lasted from February 1899 until July 1902. At its peak, 126,000 Regular Army and National Guard troops had served in the Philippines. The fighting in these wars had taken place almost exclusively against untrained and poorly-armed foes. Now, however, they had to prepare for combat against a well disciplined and highly professional German Army, thought by many to be the best organized and best equipped military force in the world.

With the declaration of war, many Americans began to talk boldly about what the "Yank" soldiers would do to the Kaiser and his "Huns." Wiser heads in the War Department knew it was going to take a lot more than patriotic slogans to build an army capable of defeating the Germans on the Western Front. It would require building new organizations designed for dealing with the intricacies of modern warfare and it would take solid, focused training under tough conditions before the American troops would be ready for combat. The simple task of just transporting units with thousands of soldiers, animals, and equipment to France was going to be a major challenge. German warships, both surface raiders and U-boats, had been patrolling the Atlantic and devastating the shipping fleets of England and France since 1914.

After arriving in France in 1917 with a small headquarters contingent, General John J. Pershing, the American Expeditionary Force (AEF) commander, waged a continuous struggle against his French, British, and Italian counterparts to maintain a cohesive U.S. force. Frightened by recent German successes, the Allied leaders wanted to use the U.S. "Doughboys" as piecemeal replacements for their decimated armies. Always mindful of the terrible casualty rates of the European allies in their trench warfare tactics, Pershing steadfastly insisted that the U.S. soldiers would serve and fight as an independent American force. But what would that American force look like when it arrived in Europe?

Prior to the First World War, the American Army was small and based on regimental-sized units. Many of the infantry regiments based in the U.S. were stationed at small outposts scattered throughout the country. These units had worked well in the small-scale conflicts of the late nineteenth and early twentieth centuries. However, the conflict in Europe had dramatically changed how war was waged. The opposing forces in Europe had fielded massive armies with large artillery units, efficient machine guns, poison gas, and extensive logistics support. They even had airplanes capable of scouting, bombing, and fighting in the skies over Belgium and France. The trench line stretched four hundred miles from the North Sea, starting in Belgium and running through France all the way to the border of Switzerland. To provide the personnel that would become the American Expeditionary Force, the United States began the massive undertaking of drafting, enlisting, and training its citizens. By the end of the war, the total number of men serving in the Army, Navy, and Marine Corps was in excess of four and a half million; almost five percent of the U.S. population at the time. As a measure of comparison, this force was twice the size of the force raised by the northern states in the American Civil War.[1]

As early as 1913, under Chief of Staff Major General Leonard Wood, the U.S. Army had debated changing to a larger "divisional" configuration, but little more than discussion had actually taken place. Now, with war approaching, and after conducting a review of Allied combat formations, the American Army leadership, under the watchful eye of the now-Chief of Staff, Major General Hugh L. Scott, decided to restructure the Army using a divisional format. In this way, all of the necessary units needed to fight and survive on the modern battlefield were under the direct control of a division commander. Each division would have a headquarters element, two infantry brigades of two regiments each, an artillery brigade of three regiments, a machine gun battalion, an engineer regiment, a trench mortar battery, a signal battalion, and smaller headquarters, supply trains, and military police units.

The four infantry regiments would each have 3,700 men assigned. Inside the regiment, there would be three infantry battalions, each with a thousand men, a supply company, a headquarters company, and a machine gun company. When these units were added to the men in the artillery regiments and the other assigned units, an American division would eventually have over 28,000 soldiers.[2] A fully equipped and manned American division placed 17,666 rifles, 72 field artillery pieces, and 260 machine guns in the field. Overseeing and commanding this massive organization was a major general and 978 other officers.[3] With this large number of soldiers and weapons, American divisions were more than twice the size of the divisions fielded by their French and British allies and their German enemies. That said, anyone who has spent time in the military, or has studied military operations, understands that for many reasons, no unit is ever at full strength for very long. Nonetheless, the units the Americans were bringing to France were intentionally designed to dominate their operational area.

Combining four divisions with some cavalry and other non-divisional support units would create an Army Corps that was prepared to conduct combat operations in a front line sector. Doctrinally situated behind the four combat divisions were a "depot" division to provide materiel and equipment support and a "replacement" division assigned to provide replacement soldiers.[4]

Obviously, to maintain command and control, each of the new divisions would require a numerical designation. A simple but very effective system was devised in which Regular Army divisions were numbered from one to twenty-five, National Guard Divisions would be twenty-six to fifty, and National Army Divisions, being formed mainly from draftees, started using the number seventy-six.[5]

The order in which the numbers were assigned to the Guard and National Army units is easily discerned by looking at a map of the United States. The majority of National Guard units in New England were assigned to the first National Guard division, numbered twenty-six, and would soon become known as the "Yankee" Division. The next number, twenty-seven, went to New

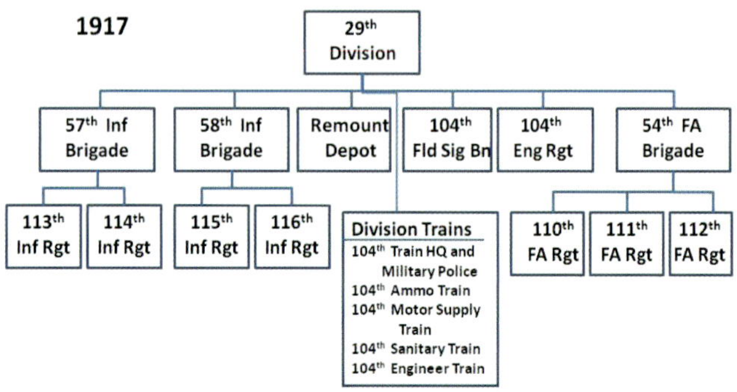

An indication of the extremely large size of the American Divisions in the AEF can be seen in this figure. With four infantry, three artillery and one engineer regiments as well as support units, there were more than 28,000 soldiers assigned to each division.

York State units. Pennsylvania was assigned number twenty-eight. The honor of being the "Twenty-Ninth Division" went to the units from Washington D.C., New Jersey, Maryland, Delaware, and Virginia. North and South Carolina were designated the Thirtieth Division, and the numbering continued across the country until it reached the Pacific Northwest, where Oregon and Washington were designated the 41st Division. Apart from this system, a division was also created with units from twenty-six states and designated the 42nd Division. This unit, at the suggestion of Brigadier General Douglas MacArthur, would soon receive the nickname "Rainbow Division," because its composition included so many states that it seemed to cover the country. The assignment of National Army division unit numbers followed the same pattern, starting in New England with the 76th Division, the 77th Division in New York, and so on.

General Charles G. Morton with his staff car at Camp McClellan. Morton would serve as 29th Division Commander from its beginning of training in 1917 to its inactivation in 1919.

A set of New Jersey collar disks. Though the Army would later standardize the disks in an attempt to simplify the procurement process, many soldiers continued to wear the disks of their home states. *Courtesy Michael Albanese.*

The new numerical designations for divisions also required assignment of new regimental numbers. The numbering would start geographically, just like the divisions. The first number assigned, the 101st Infantry Regiment, went to New England's 26th Division, along with the 102nd, 103rd, and 104th Infantry Regiments, and the 101st through 103rd Field Artillery Regiments. The 26th Division would also have the 101st Engineers, 101st Signal, 101st through 103rd Machine Gun Battalions, etc. At first, this renumbering caused great consternation among the members of National Guard units. It was feared they would lose their historical lineages, which in many cases stretched through the Civil War all the way back to the Revolutionary War.[6] Fortunately, most realized the awkwardness and impracticability of having several "1st Regiments" in the same division, i.e., 1st New Jersey, 1st Maryland, 1st Virginia, etc. The problem was also somewhat eased when it became clear that several state units would have to be consolidated in order to reach the regimental strengths required by the newer Army formations. By taking a new regimental number, there would not be an argument over which of the New Jersey regiments (1st, 2nd, or 4th) would keep their numeric designation. Following the organizational guidance, the first infantry regiment in the 29th Division would be the 113th. Though there would be some minor adjustments later, what follows is the initial alignment of the new units of the 29th Division and the designations of the old units from which they were drawn.[7]

57TH INFANTRY BRIGADE—COMMANDED BY BRIGADIER GENERAL CHARLES W. BARBER
113th Infantry Regiment—1st, 2nd, and 4th New Jersey Infantry Regiments
114th Infantry Regiment—3rd and 5th New Jersey, 1st Delaware Infantry Regiments
111th Machine Gun Battalion—2nd and 3rd New Jersey Infantry Regiments' Machine gun companies

58TH INFANTRY BRIGADE—COMMANDED BY BRIGADIER GENERAL HARRY HILL BANDHOLTZ
115th Infantry Regiment - 1st, 4th, and 5th Maryland Infantry Regiments
116th Infantry Regiment—1st, 2nd, and 4th Virginia Infantry Regiments
112th Machine Gun Battalion—4th Maryland, 4th Virginia Infantry Regiments' Machine Gun Companies

54TH FIELD ARTILLERY BRIGADE —COMMANDED BY BRIGADIER GENERAL WILLIAM. C. RAFFERTY
110th Field Artillery Regiment—Batteries A and B of D.C. Field artillery, Troops A, B, C, and D of the D.C. Cavalry, and Batteries A, B, and C from the Maryland Provisional Battalion
111th Field Artillery Regiment—1st Virginia Field Artillery Regiment
112th Heavy Field Artillery Regiment—1st New Jersey Field Artillery Regiment and Troops B and D, New Jersey Cavalry.
104th Trench Mortar Battery- Battery F of the New Jersey Field Artillery

104th Engineer Regiment—Companies A, B, and D and 1st Battalion New Jersey Engineers, as well as Infantry Companies from the 1st, 2nd, 3rd, 4th, and 5th New Jersey Infantry Regiments
104th Field Signal Battalion—Companies A, C, and HQ New Jersey Signal Corps and Company B of the D.C. Signal Corps
104th Train Headquarters and Military Police—Troops A and C, 1st Squadron New Jersey Cavalry and Troop A of the Maryland Cavalry
104th Ammunition Train—1st Squadron Virginia Cavalry and recruits
104th Engineer Train—from the 54th Depot Brigade and recruits
104th Motor Supply Train—from the 54th Depot Brigade and recruits
Remount Depot—1st Squadron Virginia Cavalry
104th Sanitary Train:
113th, 114th, 115th, and 116th Ambulance Companies—1st Maryland, 1st Virginia Ambulance Companies, and other units as needed.
113th, 114th, 115th, and 116th Field Hospitals—1st Maryland, 1st New Jersey, 1st Virginia Field Hospitals, and other units
110th Machine Gun Battalion (the Divisional Machine Gun Battalion)—Machine Gun companies from the 1st Delaware, 4th New Jersey, 5th Maryland, and 1st Virginia Infantry Regiments

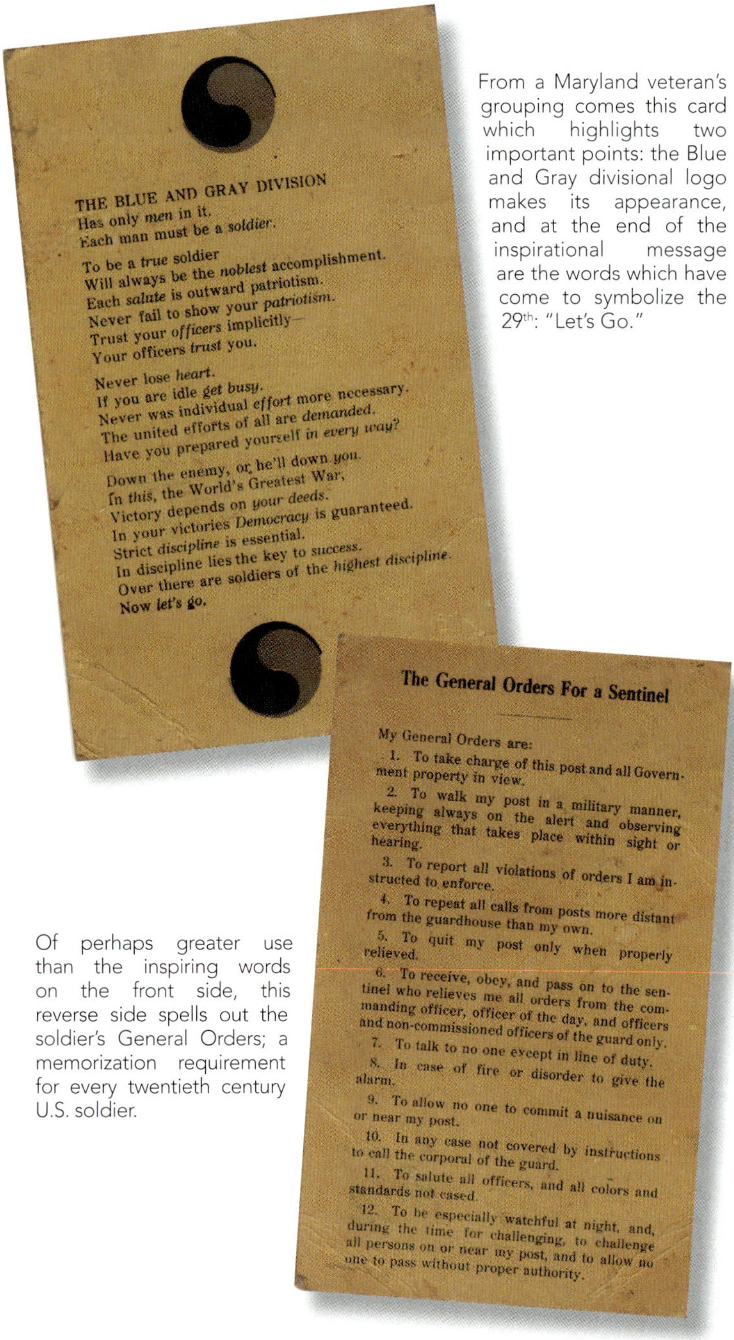

THE BLUE AND GRAY DIVISION
Has only *men* in it.
Each man must be a *soldier*.

To be a *true* soldier
Will always be the *noblest* accomplishment.
Each *salute* is outward patriotism.
Never fail to show your *patriotism*.
Trust your *officers* implicitly—
Your officers *trust* you.

Never lose *heart*.
If you are idle *get busy*.
Never was individual *effort* more necessary.
The united efforts of all are *demanded*.
Have you prepared yourself *in every way*?

Down the enemy, or he'll down *you*.
In *this*, the World's Greatest War,
Victory depends on *your deeds*.
In your victories *Democracy* is guaranteed.
Strict *discipline* is essential.
In discipline lies the key to *success*.
Over there are soldiers of the *highest discipline*.
Now *let's go*.

The General Orders For a Sentinel

My General Orders are:

1. To take charge of this post and all Government property in view.
2. To walk my post in a military manner, keeping always on the alert and observing everything that takes place within sight or hearing.
3. To report all violations of orders I am instructed to enforce.
4. To repeat all calls from posts more distant from the guardhouse than my own.
5. To quit my post only when properly relieved.
6. To receive, obey, and pass on to the sentinel who relieves me all orders from the commanding officer, officer of the day, and officers and non-commissioned officers of the guard only.
7. To talk to no one except in line of duty.
8. In case of fire or disorder to give the alarm.
9. To allow no one to commit a nuisance on or near my post.
10. In any case not covered by instructions to call the corporal of the guard.
11. To salute all officers, and all colors and standards not cased.
12. To be especially watchful at night, and, during the time for challenging, to challenge all persons on or near my post, and to allow no one to pass without proper authority.

From a Maryland veteran's grouping comes this card which highlights two important points: the Blue and Gray divisional logo makes its appearance, and at the end of the inspirational message are the words which have come to symbolize the 29th: "Let's Go."

Of perhaps greater use than the inspiring words on the front side, this reverse side spells out the soldier's General Orders; a memorization requirement for every twentieth century U.S. soldier.

Within the 29th division, soldiers from Maryland and Virginia totaled about fifty percent of the divisional strength, while New Jersey alone contributed almost forty percent.[8] After receiving their new numerical designation, the staff of the 29th debated what symbol should be used to represent the division. The Divisional Chief of Staff, Colonel George S. Goodale, settled the matter by deciding that a slightly reoriented version of the Korean "Tae Geuk" symbol would serve the purpose and the colors would be blue and gray to symbolize the northern and southern geographical origins of the division. It also paid respect to the original units of the division that could trace their lineage back to both sides of the Civil War.[9] Coincidentally, furthering the conciliatory spirit of the 29th Division was the training base to which its units were sent: Camp McClellan, a southern post named for Union General George B. McClellan. Camp McClellan, located near Anniston, Alabama, was established 18 July 1917, as one of the many training bases that were rapidly being constructed throughout the country to train America's Army for service in France. Like the other training sites, Camp McClellan was comprised of hurriedly-built buildings for headquarters, supply rooms, mess halls, latrines, and showers. The initial barracks were wooden-floored tents. In time, some wooden barracks were constructed to provide more permanent shelter, especially after the extremely harsh winter of 1917, when the "sunny south" suffered from freezing weather and heavy snowfalls. Eventually, there would be over fifteen-hundred buildings on the post, including a massive base hospital consisting of more than a hundred buildings. A similar training site was located near Petersburg, Virginia, and named after Robert E. Lee. Camp Lee grew so quickly in size that it became the third largest city in that state. Along with rapid growth, all of these sites shared one other key feature in common: ready access to a railhead. This was needed to allow rapid movement of large numbers of untrained troops into the training sites and equally large numbers of trained soldiers away from the sites on their way to the east coast seaports for loading onto ships taking them to Europe. In most cases, as at Camp

Private Hurley H. Thacker of Battery "A," 111th Field Artillery Regiment. Thacker had previously been a member of the "Richmond Howitzers." *Courtesy Colin Romanick.*

A panoramic image of Camp McClellan, showing the vast cantonment area occupied by the 29th Division. *Courtesy Library of Congress.*

An extremely interesting picture showing the tents of the 111th Field Artillery Regiment at McClellan. The longer tents in the middle ground appear to be the mess tents for the different batteries of the regiment. Private Thacker has marked his tent on the photograph with an X. *Courtesy Colin Romanick.*

Not all Virginians that were part of the war effort were in the Army. Others, such as Katherine Schultz of Richmond, shown here in 1917 in her Red Cross uniform, volunteered to care for sick or convalescing Doughboys. After the war, she would become Mrs. Hurley Thacker. *Courtesy Colin Romanick.*

A period photograph showing the mix of billeting for the soldiers of the 29th. On the left hand side are the unit mess halls, while the soldiers' tents are on the right.

A nice portrait of Sergeant John H. Osbourne of Headquarters Company, 111th Field Artillery Regiment. Though it is unusual to find portraits of the soldiers in heavy overcoat and gloves, the bitter winter of 1917 turned the "sunny south" into a snowy, cold training ground. Osbourne may have felt this uniform best reflected his appearance during the period. Osbourne, a veteran of the Mexican Border, was promoted to 1st Sergeant of the 111th's Headquarters Company 17 April 1919.

McClellan and Camp Lee, an actual rail spur was built right into the base.

By September 1917, trains were arriving at McClellan on a regular schedule and the troops were pouring in from their home states to be greeted by their new Division Commander, Major General Charles Gould Morton. Morton was an interesting selection to be the Commanding General of the 29th. Unlike many of the National Guard officers, Morton had a long career in the Regular Army and had served in the Philippines during the Spanish-American War. Also unlike most of the National Guard officers that the Guardsmen had served under, Morton was a firm disciplinarian. Under his stern guidance, the arriving units quickly received instruction in everything from how to properly wear the chinstrap on their campaign hats to the correct way to tie their shoelaces. He was also quite vocal about his intent to make the 29th Division more disciplined than any Regular Army unit. Later, as he began to prepare the division for its deployment overseas, he conducted a careful weeding out process to remove officers he felt did not meet his standard. The *History of the 29th Division*, published in 1921, noted that Morton relieved one officer for chewing gum and another for being "nervous" in his presence.[10]

A continuing problem Morton faced in training the division for duty in France was the rapid influx of new soldiers needed to completely fill the Table of Organization and Equipment for a 28,000-man division. Though he had received almost the entire National Guard of several states, it was not nearly enough to get to the required end strength. In September 1917, the 29th received 154 reserve commissioned officers into the unit. While many of these officers would stay with the 29th, some were parceled out to other units. The first levy of additional enlisted soldiers sent to join the 29th at McClellan included 1,000 draftees from New Jersey, Maryland, Virginia, Delaware, and Washington, D.C. While these "new" recruits were not volunteers like the original soldiers that formed the division, they were at least from the same states. Later, just before deployment to France, the 29th would receive another levy of 5,000 draftees drawn primarily from New York, New England, and the Midwest. Adding to the complexity of integrating these soldiers into the division, Morton also had to deal with the fact that 2,000 of these additional troops were not yet even citizens of the United States. That headache, however, lay in the future. For now, Morton's biggest challenge was getting his troops trained to a standard that would allow them to survive their first encounter with the enemy.

Another picture of Major General Morton; a stern taskmaster, he insisted his troops would become as disciplined as any Regular Army division. *Courtesy USARPAC.*

A group of Maryland National Guard soldiers from the 115th Infantry Regiment take a break from training at Camp McClellan. Of particular note here are the wide variety of work and fatigue uniforms, and in particular the fact that one, in the front row, has even brought his own beanie with him.

Three Virginia Doughboys from the 29th take a break from training at Camp McClellan to have their picture taken in front of their tent. Some soldiers of the 29th would spend more than nine months at McClellan.

One notable feature of Doughboy uniforms during the Mexican border and training phase was canvas leggings. Perhaps the most commonly worn leggings of the time period were this simple type that were meant for wearing above the shoe and easily laced up.

Shown here are other types of leggings used by the Doughboys, including the leather reinforced style for use with draft animals and two other styles for use by infantrymen. By the time American soldiers went into action in France, most of these had given way to the long woolen "puttees."

Morton took to his task with a flourish. He directed the newly-formed 104th Engineer Regiment to build a vast trench system that provided his troops the opportunity to train as closely as possible under conditions they would face on the western front. Taking advantage of the expertise of a French Army liaison officer, soldiers constructed their trench line with built-in observation posts, dugouts, and command posts. Unlike many of the other units that deployed to France before them, the soldiers of the 29th were given ample training on the rifle range to become proficient with their assigned weapons. This critically important training period was denied the earlier deploying divisions, such as the 26th and 42nd, in the rush to get them overseas. Therefore, these divisions found themselves conducting much of their weapons training in France under less than optimal weather conditions.[11] Reflecting later on the problems encountered with the nasty weather after his arrival in Europe, one Doughboy would note "sometimes it doesn't rain in France."[12]

A crudely-marked mess kit belonging to William E. Cottrell of Company "F", 104th Engineer Regiment.

Although taken at Camp Jackson, South Carolina, this unique photo shows clearly the extent to which the Army went to recreate the intricacies of trench warfare, even to the point of adding full-size camouflaged tank mockups. Visible in the background are other typical training "obstacles."

Another picture of the "tank," this time with a soldier posing next to it and giving a clear indication of the size of the mockup.

Unusual picture of two soldiers training in a vast array of barbed wire. Note the bright finish on the binoculars being held by the soldier on the right; such a finish would certainly draw fire from the Germans in the Meuse-Argonne.

As the training tempo picked up, two events happened that set the rumor mill operating at full speed. In the first, all of the Delaware troops were withdrawn from the division and sent to Camp Dix, New Jersey, where they were formed into a Pioneer Infantry Regiment. In the second and potentially more significant event, Morton and a few members of his staff received orders instructing them to sail to France to become familiar with the processes and procedures by which the 29th would operate upon arrival in the war zone. To the troops of the 29th, these actions seemed a clear indication that they too would soon be heading to France. However, as Christmas approached and no further information was forthcoming, the 29th settled down to see what the holiday season would bring.

Still holding his shiny binoculars, the Doughboy now poses in front of one of the dugout entrances in the training area.

Emblematic of the "girl they left behind," this stylish lady poses carefully in front of one of the "yard long" unit photographs that were mass produced for the soldiers to send home. *Courtesy Carolyn Wilkins.*

Unfortunately, what it brought most of all was a real black eye for the 29th Division. Due to the distance between Camp McClellan and most of the hometowns of the soldiers, it was announced that only twenty percent of the Division would receive holiday home leave. Shortly before the lucky leave recipients were to depart, it was announced that the twenty percent figure was a mistake and now only five percent were to receive Christmas leave. After that announcement was made, over fifteen-hundred Doughboys took off on what was at the time referred to as "French" leave, but today is more commonly called AWOL (Absent Without Leave). Needless to say, when Morton returned from his advance party trip to France, he wasn't pleased to find a camp full of homesick Doughboys and a number of other soldiers still on the run. After all, Morton saw himself as a general who had made his reputation on command, control, and appearance. These absentees were a shameful indication of a lack of discipline. Using all his resources, including letters to the families of absent soldiers, Morton went back to work rebuilding the division as he thought it should be. Reflecting on this, one of his soldiers would later comment that Morton was so concerned about the individual soldier's appearance that "he'd make you wear your blouse in hell."[13] It was also about this time that the 29th Headquarters released General Order 38, dated 14 December 1917, giving instructions that all wagons, trucks, and sidecars in the division were to be marked with the Blue and Gray symbol as a means of identifying unit equipment.

In time, however, some of the troops began to see past the discipline and pettiness and to appreciate that Morton had a tough job to do. The trenches and battlefields of France were an unforgiving environment, and Morton was determined to have the soldiers of his Blue and Gray Division as thoroughly ready as possible for what they were about to face. One of his Assistant Chiefs of Staff, a former Virginia National Guardsman named Captain John A. Cutchins, would later reflect that while quite worried at first about working for Morton, he was pleasantly surprised to find the general a firm, yet at times congenial boss. Cutchins also found Morton to be an insightful and thoughtful leader with a complete focus on providing the best-trained unit he could for America's war effort. Cutchins would have many opportunities in France to view Morton as both a combat leader and division administrator. As will soon be obvious, his opinion will remain generally positive, but always with a slight reservation due to some of Morton's methods.

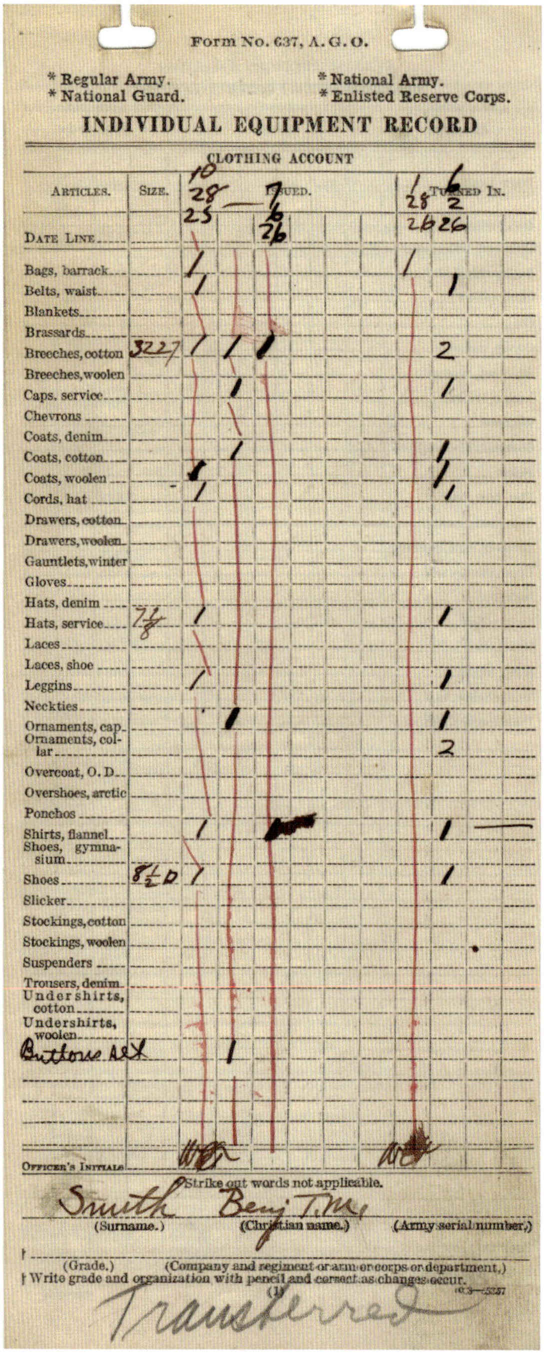
Form No. 637, A. G. O.

* Regular Army. * National Army.
* National Guard. * Enlisted Reserve Corps.

INDIVIDUAL EQUIPMENT RECORD

CLOTHING ACCOUNT

Articles. | Size. | Issued. | Turned In.

Date Line

Bags, barrack
Belts, waist
Blankets
Brassards
Breeches, cotton
Breeches, woolen
Caps, service
Chevrons
Coats, denim
Coats, cotton
Coats, woolen
Cords, hat
Drawers, cotton
Drawers, woolen
Gauntlets, winter
Gloves
Hats, denim
Hats, service
Laces
Laces, shoe
Leggins
Neckties
Ornaments, cap
Ornaments, collar
Overcoat, O. D.
Overshoes, arctic
Ponchos
Shirts, flannel
Shoes, gymnasium
Shoes
Slicker
Stockings, cotton
Stockings, woolen
Suspenders
Trousers, denim
Undershirts, cotton
Undershirts, woolen
Buttons set

Officer's Initials

*Strike out words not applicable.

Smith Benj. T. M.
(Surname.) (Christian name.) (Army serial number.)

† (Grade.) (Company and regiment or arm or corps or department.)
† Write grade and organization with pencil and correct as changes occur.

Transferred

A clothing record was maintained for each soldier at the company level. Note the hand-written addition at the bottom of the page: "button set." Some states provided buttons with state crests instead of the Army eagle. This clothing record is particularly interesting, because it not only shows "issues," it shows what clothing and equipment Benjamin Smith, a Virginia Guardsman, turned in when he was transferred to another unit.

A portion of a button set still on the original cardboard backing, clearly showing the State Crest of Virginia. As the war wore on, unique state-related collar disks and buttons such as these almost completely disappeared.

While most of the soldiers of the 29th expected Morton's return from Europe to signal their turn to cross the Atlantic had arrived, they were to be disappointed. As spring arrived in Alabama, the division was still there and still training. *The History of the 115th Regiment* reported that they had been at McClellan "nine long months. Had anyone known he was to stay there that long, he would probably have committed suicide."[14] Their disenchantment with the seemingly endless tour of duty at Camp McClellan manifested itself when one of the Guardsmen defaced a large sign set up by a visiting evangelist minister. Under the large printed question: "Where will you spend eternity?" the soldier wrote his answer "At Camp McClellan."[15]

GADSDEN THEATRE

Friday and Saturday Mar. 22 & 23
Matinee Saturday

29th Divisional Minstrels

IN 7 PARTS Featuring

BILL SMALL PREMIER END MEN HURLEY THACKER

Don't Fail to See Your Soldier Boys

SPECIAL MATINEE SATURDAY 2:15........................50c
NIGHT PRICES................25c, 50c, 75c, $1.00, $1.50

ALL SOLDIERS :-: ALL PROFESSIONALS
Fresh From Record Breaking Run in Birmingham

SEATS ON SALE AT VANCE DRUG STORE---PHONE 256

Perhaps indicative of how long the 29th spent training in Alabama, this playbill from a soldier show announces a minstrel show to take place in Anniston March 1918. Hurley Thacker's participation is noted, as well as the fact that he is one of the premier "End Men," a period name for comedian in a Minstrel show. *Courtesy Colin Romanick.*

Sadly, for some of the soldiers in the 29th Division, Camp McClellan would be all they would see of the war. When the American Legion Post in Rockingham County, Virginia, published its account of the local citizens' activities in the World War, it noted that of the fifty men from the county serving in the 29th Division, four had died while in service. Two of the four (Walter S. Arey and John S. Bradley) died of pneumonia and measles, respectively, while stationed at Camp McClellan. Of the nearly one thousand servicemen originating from Rockingham County, forty-six would die during the war. Of these, only sixteen were actually killed in action. The rest died of accidents, drowning, and disease, fifteen of them while still in training in the States.[16] Disease, in the form of the Great Influenza Epidemic of 1918, was going to play a major disruptive role when the 29th Division finally made it to France.

Typical image of a young Doughboy with his constant companion; the Army mess kit. Made of fairly soft metal, these mess kits would soon become adorned with a wide variety of flags, pictures, names, dates, and locations. *Courtesy Library of Congress.*

A well-worn postcard from Private First Class Harry Cable, Company "A", 112th Machine Gun Battalion, to his brother back in Baltimore to let him know that he was sending home a package.

For the soldiers, however, the question remained; when would they stop training and go overseas? Finally, for those who could interpret them, the signs of an impending departure were appearing. An advance party was dispatched to Europe in May to prepare for the 29th's arrival. On 28 May, a U.S. District Judge began the two-day process of officiating turning over seven hundred soldiers of the division into naturalized citizens. Along with recognizing the patriotism and service of these soldiers, the Act of Naturalization also had a pragmatic purpose. It ensured that, if captured, the newly-minted U.S. citizens could not be forced into serving in the enemies' armies; definitely an important point, because so many of the Doughboys had been born either in Germany or in the countries of the Austro-Hungarian Empire. On 1 June 1918, Morton himself gave an even clearer indication that the departure date was coming soon when he gathered all of the officers and NCOs on a small hill near his headquarters building. Explaining that this would be the last chance for all of them to be brought together in such a manner, Morton told them they would soon face combat, and inevitably casualties would result in sergeants having to assume officer leadership positions. He impressed on them the importance of doing their duty, especially in the absence of instructions from higher authorities. This also meant that it would be necessary for the sergeants and corporals to enforce the discipline needed during the strain of combat. He reminded them that the soldiers of the 29th Division were to be "led" into combat, not "driven." Whatever the soldiers of the 29th thought of their commander prior to this talk, those that heard it were convinced they were now ready to show the world that the Blue and Gray Division was a combat force with which to be reckoned. All that was needed now were enough ships to carry the 29th to France so it could take its rightful place among the other units of the American Expeditionary Force.

A Doughboy in training; Private Paul A. Klonowski from LaGrange, Illinois. Klonowski would later be assigned to Company "L", 116th Infantry Regiment, and serve with them in France. *Courtesy John Simmons.*

A postcard sent to Corporal Frank Greber of Company "C", 114th Infantry Regiment, from his friend, Gladys. The note on the reverse side includes information about a female friend of theirs that just married a sailor and ends with news that was probably not much comfort to the Doughboy corporal; Gladys also has a date tonight.

CHAPTER 3

"Over There": Fighting the "War to End All Wars"

Due to the large size of the division, the units of the 29th were sent by rail to several seaports on the east coast for their deployment to France. While at the ports, each Doughboy's equipment was checked and re-checked to ensure he had all of his required gear. As reported by a New Jersey soldier in the 113th Infantry, this meant each man carried a pack with a blanket, shelter half with poles and tent pegs, condiment can, bacon can, two sets of underwear, a pair of breeches, a shirt, four pairs of socks, a slicker or poncho, overcoat, mess kit, entrenching tool, toilet articles, and personal items. The soldiers in the 113th also noted with irony that the ship on which they would sail was formerly a German-owned vessel named *Princess Alice*, in honor of the Kaiser's daughter. Japan, one of America's allies in the First World War, had impounded the ship and renamed it the *Princess Matoika* before selling it to the U.S. By any name, the *Princess* was about to carry 4,500 soldiers to clash with her former owners. The 29th Division Headquarters, the 57th Infantry Brigade, and the 110th Machine Gun Battalion loaded aboard the *Pastores, Lenope, Wilhelmina*, and the newly-named *Princess Matoika* and sailed 15 June from Newport News, Virginia. That same day, in Hoboken, New Jersey, five more ships were loaded with the soldiers and equipment of the 58th Infantry Brigade: *Covington, George Washington, Dante Alighieri, Finland*, and the *DeKalb*.[1]

Looking much like soldiers of the earlier Spanish-American War period, these Doughboys are marching through the streets of Newport News on their way to the ship that will carry them overseas. Soon after arrival in France, the campaign hats and canvas leggings will be replaced by overseas hats or helmets and woolen puttees. Almost 300,000 Doughboys would sail from Newport News en route to France. *Courtesy USAMHI.*

The USS *Lenape* sailed for France from Newport News 15 June 1918 with a large contingent of 58th Brigade soldiers. *Courtesy USN.*

The USS *Finland* was another transport vessel carrying a large number of soldiers from the 58th Brigade to Europe. *Courtesy USN.*

A well-preserved uniform of a private in Company "F", 113th Infantry Regiment. This Doughboy not only managed to bring home his helmet and gas mask, but also his leather jerkin.

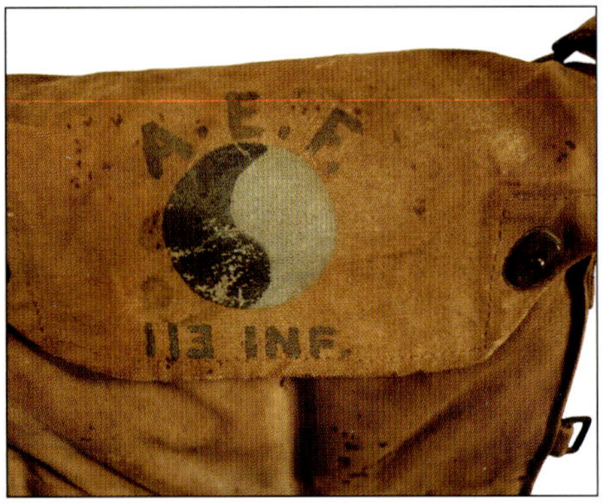

A closer view of the 29th Division's symbol painted on the gas mask carrier. It's possible to see from the worn areas that a gray circle was painted first, then the blue portion applied on top of it.

Puttees belonging to the 113th uniform, clearly showing their French maker's marks. These replaced the canvas leggings worn on the Mexican border and during the training period in the States.

A closer view of the National Guard and Company "F", 113th Infantry collar disks. The large-letter USNG is clearly visible on the right collar disk.

Another view of the same uniform, allowing better visibility of the jerkin that shows how two large buttons, perhaps from an overcoat, are used with leather loops to close the jerkin. The division patch, seen on the left shoulder of the uniform, is silk thread embroidered on a wool circle.

After leaving port, the ships from both ports headed eastward and merged into a large convoy that eventually had thirteen troop ships, as well as several escort vessels. Numbered among the transports, but not carrying any soldiers from the 29th on this voyage, was the British supply ship *Czar*. The *Czar* would later play an interesting role in history, when it was dispatched to Archangel to pick up and return the American soldiers serving in the North Russia expedition to the United States.

Among the other escort vessels determined to keep the German submarines away from the troop-laden transports were the U.S. Navy battleship USS *Texas* and several destroyers. Although the 115th's history later reported that the USS *North Carolina* was serving as an escort, that appears to be a mistake, and it's most likely the *Texas* was the only battleship in the convoy. Though troops of the 29th were the vast majority of soldiers on the ships, there were other units represented in the convoy. Among them was a contingent of African-American soldiers assigned to the 366th Infantry Regiment sailing on the *Covington*. Since the *Covington* was also carrying a large number of Maryland soldiers from the 115th, there were fears that racial problems could erupt between the groups. Happily that did not occur, and the history of the 115th Regiment would later comment on how much the Marylanders enjoyed listening to the 366th's regimental band during the voyage. It was noted, however, that a "tactful segregation was maintained between the white and colored officers."[2]

A clear and well-preserved photograph of the USS *Texas*, the battleship responsible for shepherding the first convoy of 29th Division soldiers to France. *Courtesy USN.*

The USS *Covington*, which carried the 115th Infantry Regiment to France. It would be her final voyage, as she was sunk by a U-boat during the return trip to the States. *Courtesy USN.*

A few of the books provided to the Doughboys of the 29th on their way to France. Along with the New Testament, the soldiers were provided a basic guide to speaking French and a pamphlet that explained the various rules to be followed while aboard ship.

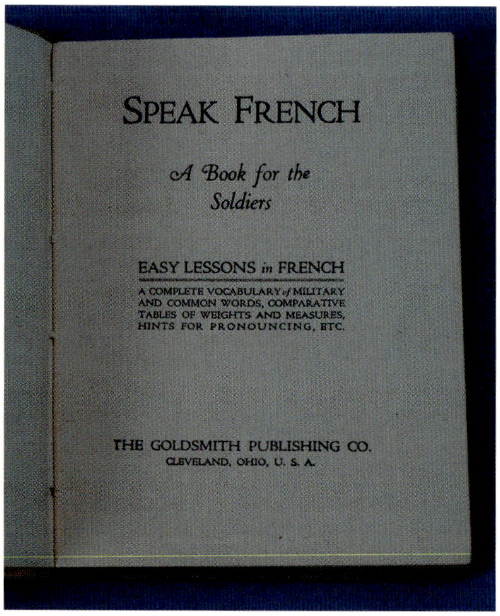

SPEAK FRENCH

A Book for the Soldiers

EASY LESSONS in FRENCH

A COMPLETE VOCABULARY of MILITARY AND COMMON WORDS, COMPARATIVE TABLES OF WEIGHTS AND MEASURES, HINTS FOR PRONOUNCING, ETC.

THE GOLDSMITH PUBLISHING CO.
CLEVELAND, OHIO, U. S. A.

The inside cover of "Speak French," the book that promised "easy lessons in French" for the soldiers. In spite of the lessons in these booklets, most Doughboys would soon develop their own version of an American/French vocabulary.

Of far more danger than fighting between the Doughboys was the deadly threat of German submarines. The greatest danger from the subs lay just off the coasts of America and Europe, as these were the prime hunting grounds for the underwater warships. When the American and British ships reached the relative safety of the middle of the ocean, the troops and Navy crews on board the transports were able to relax a bit. Nonetheless, they all knew that up ahead, off the coast of France and Britain, more U-boats would be waiting. During the course of the voyage, there were several encounters with German submarines, of which the U.S. Navy later claimed to have sunk three U-boats. In spite of this success, all of the land-loving soldiers waited with some anxiety for the first sight of land. After twelve days at sea, the large convoy finally approached the French coast, where it split into three elements, sending the *Princess Matoika*, *Wilhelmina*, *Lenope*, *George Washington*, *Covington*, and the *DeKalb* to Brest; the *Pastores* and *Finland* to St. Nazaire; and the *Dante Alighieri* went to Bordeaux. The soldiers of the 116th, arriving at St. Nazaire, were particularly aware of the danger of the voyage, as they sailed past the hulks of four damaged ships outside the harbor.[3] Similarly, the soldiers of the 115th were equally glad to arrive in Brest. Their passage aboard the *Covington* had been fairly uneventful, but during the journey through the Bay of Biscay they had encountered the roughest water of the entire voyage, and many of the men were seasick. Arriving in port at dinner time, a major in the officer's mess called attention to the event and asked the chaplain to lead them in a prayer of thanksgiving for their safe arrival in France.[4] For better or worse, the first units of the Blue and Gray were now in Europe.

On 19 June, four days after the initial ship departures, the 104th Engineers, 104th Engineer Train, and the 104th Signal Battalion embarked from New York City on the *Great Northern* and the *Northern Pacific*. Both ships docked at Brest 26 June, and the units aboard them were reunited with the infantry brigades of the division at their designated arrival camp, Camp Pontanezen. Built on the site of an old Napoleonic-era camp, Pontanezen was located just a few miles outside of Brest, and was the only deep water port available for use by the Americans in landing their forces. The facilities in the camp were capable of housing eighty thousand transient soldiers and fourteen thousand support personnel.

An interesting though faded shot of the harbor at Brest showing a number of warships and troop transports. The port of Brest would take on even greater significance in the history of the 29th Division during the Second World War.

The front gate of Camp Pontanezen. Of obvious interest here is the Camp's insignia shown on the right-hand side of the gate; a wooden duckboard or sidewalk, acknowledging the problems of ever-present mud brought on by the relentless rains.

The barracks and administration buildings of Camp Pontanezen. In some ways, the short time the 29th Division spent here proved to be a blessing. Many other units spent much more time at the camp and complained miserably about the conditions of the facilities and the constant mud.

The 104th Ammunition Train and Ordnance Repair Shop left New York City on board the *Medic* 29 June and disembarked in London 22 July. Joining them in England were the division field artillery units, who departed from New York City, Baltimore, and Philadelphia in late June and arrived at the port of Liverpool in mid-July. Also sailing for England were the Field Hospitals, Ambulance Companies, and Military Police. These units sailed aboard the *City of Exeter*, *Keemun*, *Demosthenes*, *Melita*, *Aquitania*, and the *Louisville*.

As the 29th Division history later rather succinctly recounted: "The troops had sailed from four different ports in the United States and landed in two old world countries."[5] For the record, the 29th Division was the twenty-fourth American division to arrive in France: the first unit of the 29th arriving in Europe 26 June and the last 22 July 1918.[6]

It was not a minute too soon. The German summer offensive was in high gear, and among the Allied leadership fear of an enemy breakthrough ran high. Although not even close to being ready for frontline combat duty, it was decided that the 29th could be used in a quiet sector to relieve an earlier arriving and therefore more completely trained unit. That unit could then, in turn, be thrown into the battle. Due to this urgent need, the 57th and 58th Infantry Brigades of the 29th, unlike some of the previously arriving units, did not spend much time in Pontanezen. They were hurriedly placed in the famous French "40 men, 8 horses" railcars and transported from the port to a staging area in preparation for duty at the front.

A close-up of the 112th Field Artillery uniform's disks. It's clear in this picture that the soldier carefully sanded down the "A" to show he was a member of a different battery. This is a result of the difficulty in obtaining the correct disks for each unit and why the Army eventually went to basic "US" and "branch" disks.

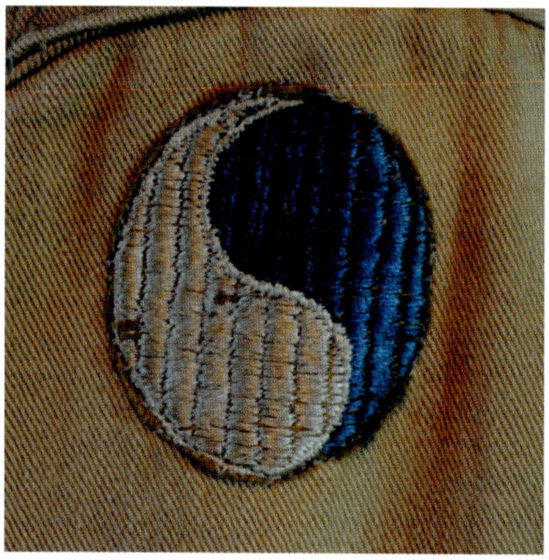

A picture of the 112th Field Artillery patch showing construction similar to other patches displayed here, but deliberately sewn "upside down."

A very faded summer weight uniform for a soldier in the 112th Field Artillery Regiment. Note that the 29th Division patch on the left sleeve has been reversed to move the blue portion to the top. This unauthorized adjustment was apparently common among the predominantly New Jersey units.

The field artillery units and ammunition train of the division were slowly brought over from England and moved to French artillery training camps in Brittany. Upon arrival at the training sites, the artillery units were hit by an extremely vicious wave of Spanish Influenza. Due to the flu most training had to be suspended, and the units were quarantined in their camps. By mid-September, seventeen soldiers of the 111th Field Artillery Regiment had died and many more were suffering from the effects of the global pandemic. Equally hard hit were the French railroad crews that were to carry the artillery units to rejoin their 29th Division comrades in the Meuse-Argonne campaign. As a result, even after the artillerymen had recovered enough to complete their training, there was not enough transportation to carry them to the front.

A close-up of Faris's Field Artillery Chief Mechanic's rank patch on the right sleeve, which also shows wear damage.

Close-up view of the collar disks on Faris's uniform. The "G" below the large "T" indicates that Faris served in Company "G" of the 104th Ammunition Train. The 104th Ammo Train would spend most of the war at artillery training camps in Brittany; therefore, Faris's World War Victory ribbon does not have the small bronze stars reflecting multiple campaign participation.

The commercially-purchased uniform of Chief Mechanic Esron McG Faris of the 104th Ammunition Train. The delicate nature of some of the divisional patches is evident here; almost all of the gray thread has disappeared, leaving only the blue.

It was not only the 29th Division's artillery men that were suffering; the flu was playing havoc with the rest of the AEF, as well. It struck with such ferocity that Pershing was forced to cannibalize several of his divisions to keep others up to strength. Yet, as bad as things were in France, it was worse in the States. The flu had spread to more than twenty of the training camps in America, and ships arriving in France were offloading numbers of dead or seriously ill Doughboys. An Ohio Doughboy wrote his mother from France that "Spanish influenza has killed many of the boys and a lot of the people over here…quite a few died on the boat."[7] In the two months prior to the Armistice, there were 1,817 Doughboy burials in the port of Brest alone, with most dying from the flu while on the ships to France.[8] Things were so bad in November 1918 that General Peyton March, Army Chief of Staff, was forced to send Pershing a telegram informing him that influenza had brought stateside training to a halt.[9]

It would not be until 9 November, when sufficient transportation resources were again available, that the 54th Field Artillery Brigade started to move to the front lines. Passing by Paris during the night of the 10th, the artillerymen began to hear rumors that the Armistice was being signed. It was confirmed the next morning, when they arrived at the front and encountered some New England National Guardsmen of the 26th Division walking around without helmets or gas masks.[10] Because of the flu and problems with the French transportation infrastructure, the 54th Field Artillery Brigade and 104th Ammunition Train never served directly with the infantry regiments of the 29th Division during the war.

The summer-weight M1912 tunic of Corporal P.W. Fore of Company "G" of the 104th Ammunition Train.

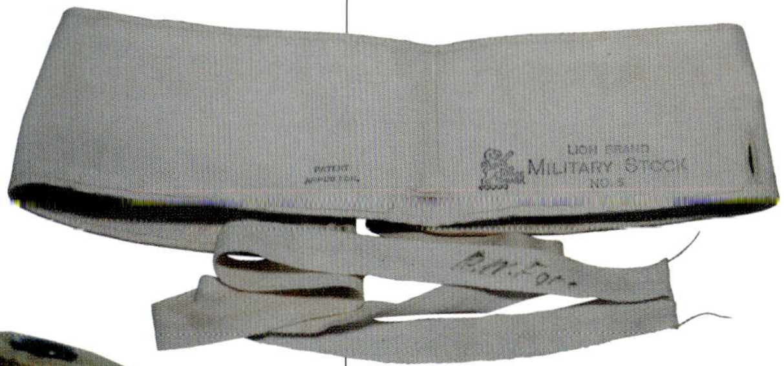

A rarely seen collar protector used by Fore to reduce neck irritation from the stiff uniform collar. The British trademark may be indicative of the fact that the 104th Ammunition Train spent some time in Britain before entering France.

A close-up shot of the 104th Ammunition Train collar disks belonging to Corporal Fore. Note that Fore has a National Army U.S. disk instead of a National Guard U.S. disk, most likely reflecting a shortage of the "NG" version.

Details of Corporal Fore's carefully-embroidered 29th Division patch; the blue and gray threads have been carefully sewn onto a khaki-colored wool patch, then affixed to the uniform.

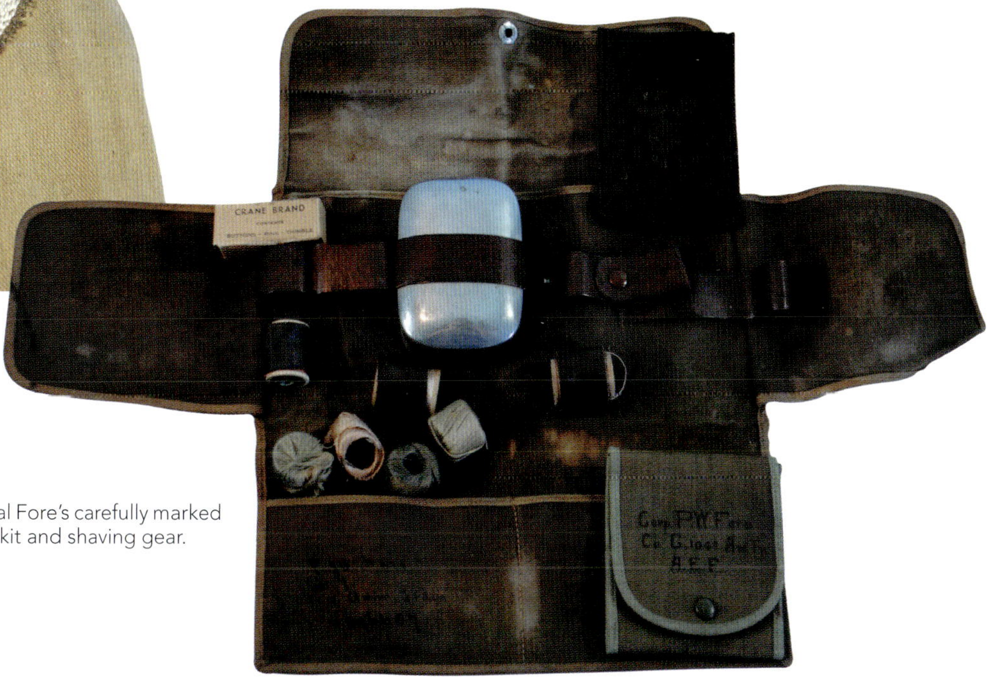

Corporal Fore's carefully marked sewing kit and shaving gear.

The somewhat haphazard and hasty deployment of the 29th Division upon arrival in France was not what Pershing and his AEF staff had intended for these units. In fact, their original plan for training American units after arrival in France had been well thought out. It was designed to work arriving units into shape, starting at the lowest individual maneuver level: the battalion. The training program provided for a month in small unit instruction at the battalion level, followed by another month at the battalion level in a relatively quiet trench sector. Thereafter, the battalions would rejoin their division for a month of large-scale unit training. Concurrently, a series of schools would be available to provide instruction in leadership, artillery tactics, and general staff work, as well as many other essential subjects for modern warfare. Enlisted men who had shown aptitude towards leadership would also be given the opportunity to attend some basic officer commissioning courses to add them to the officer ranks. Throughout this training program, seasoned officers from the French and British armies were attached to the American units to provide the benefits of their practical experience in fighting the Germans.

For the 29th, however, as we have seen, much of this preliminary training was necessarily bypassed due to the German advance, so almost immediate duty in a "quiet sector" would have to suffice. The arrival of the infantry brigades at their initial training site near Vaux-sous-Aubigny, known as the 10th Training Area, was also cause for some concern. As the 29th Division Quartermaster later reported: "With an entire infantry brigade…coming in at the rate of one battalion every four hours, the transportation problem presented a critical situation. Troops were detrained immediately and the baggage was at once unloaded and placed in the railyard so that the [rail] cars could be moved away quickly..."[11]

Upon arrival in France, many officers in the 29th were surprised to find themselves separated from their units and sent to schools while their men proceeded to the initial frontline training areas. Lieutenant Colonel Samuel Gardner Waller, serving as the executive officer of the 116th, was among those officers sent to school and would not rejoin his regiment until August. Those officers returning to duty on the Divisional staff after this individualized training were surprised again by being welcomed back by General Morton with a strong chewing out. Apparently, Morton was inclined to believe officers might have grown slack in school, and therefore he felt the need to remind them of the discipline he expected in the 29th Division. When Captain John Cutchins returned to the 29th from the Staff School at Langres, Morton not only chewed him out, he warned him that his predecessor on the 29th staff had been relieved because he didn't "look intelligent." Cutchins wasn't sure what to make of this information, but he noted that the relieved officer went on to have an extremely successful career in another division.[12] Morton never stopped attempting to mold the division in his own image, and later on, even in the midst of the Meuse-Argonne Offensive, he continued to relieve officers as he saw fit. The AEF General headquarters responded to one such relief request with a letter pointing out the obvious fact that some officers deserved to be given a second chance, and that for others, there was "sufficient machinery in existence for the elimination of officers who have fully demonstrated their inefficiency and whose conduct is reprehensible. Such officers should not be saddled upon the Services of Supply, but their cases should be acted on at the Divisional or Corps Headquarters."[13]

A period map of the sector occupied by the 29th Division during its training period in Alsace. The front lines are indicated by the dotted line and the Fontaine railhead, serving as the logistical hub for the division, is clearly marked.

A field post office during the Meuse-Argonne campaign. This picture provides interesting contrast to the neat administrative office seen in chapter one. It is important to note that the duties of a mail orderly could be dangerous; of the twelve assigned to the 114th Infantry, nine were killed or wounded during the performance of their duties.

Along with moving to a quiet sector of the front line as a forward training area, the Doughboys of the 29th were exposed for the first time to the use of the 24-hour clock. Using this timekeeping method, where 9 a.m. was written as 09:00 and 9 p.m. was 21:00, the soldiers were in sync with the French railroad system, which had long used this method to prevent confusion over morning and evening train schedules.[14] On a happier note, the 29th division was also assigned its own Army Post Office number (APO 765), which meant that the mail-hungry soldiers could now receive letters and packages from home.[15]

With a new way to tell time and with hopes of mail from home, the 29th moved towards the front. The evening of 25 July, they began to take over a section of the front line in the Alsace region of France. It's ironic that this region, whose ownership was much disputed by France and Germany, was now considered a "quiet sector" and used by both sides for training new units. Some of the initial skirmishes of the First World War had taken place in this very area. The soldiers of the 29th were soon billeted in the same town where the first clash between French and Germans had taken place. The 29th's arrival permitted another National Guard division (the 32nd) to redeploy and move to a more active area of the war. The 32nd Division, primarily composed of Guardsmen from Michigan and Wisconsin, would soon earn a well-deserved reputation as an excellent fighting unit and was later selected to serve in the occupation of the German Rhineland after the Armistice. But that lay in the future; for now, the 32nd was charged with handing over the sector to the 29th and moving out to join the rest of the AEF engaging the Germans.

By 30 July, the regiments of the 29th Division were manning the front lines in Alsace. The 29th heard actual gunfire for the first time as they witnessed the airplanes from a French squadron shoot down a pair of German observation balloons. The nearby town of Fontaine had been set aside to serve as the logistical hub for support to the units of the 29th. There was a problem, however. The Fontaine railhead was under enemy aerial observation and therefore subject to German artillery fire or aerial attack. To minimize the risk of these attacks, only seven trucks were allowed near the railhead at any one time. The rest were concealed from enemy observation by staging them in the tree line on the road leading to Fontaine. The movement in and out of the supply point was strictly controlled by a military policeman stationed on top of a warehouse and visible to the waiting trucks. From his observation point, the MP would signal to the hidden trucks how many were to come forward for loading or unloading. Eventually the Germans caught on to the deception, so the Doughboys soon learned to vary the delivery time and schedule every few days.

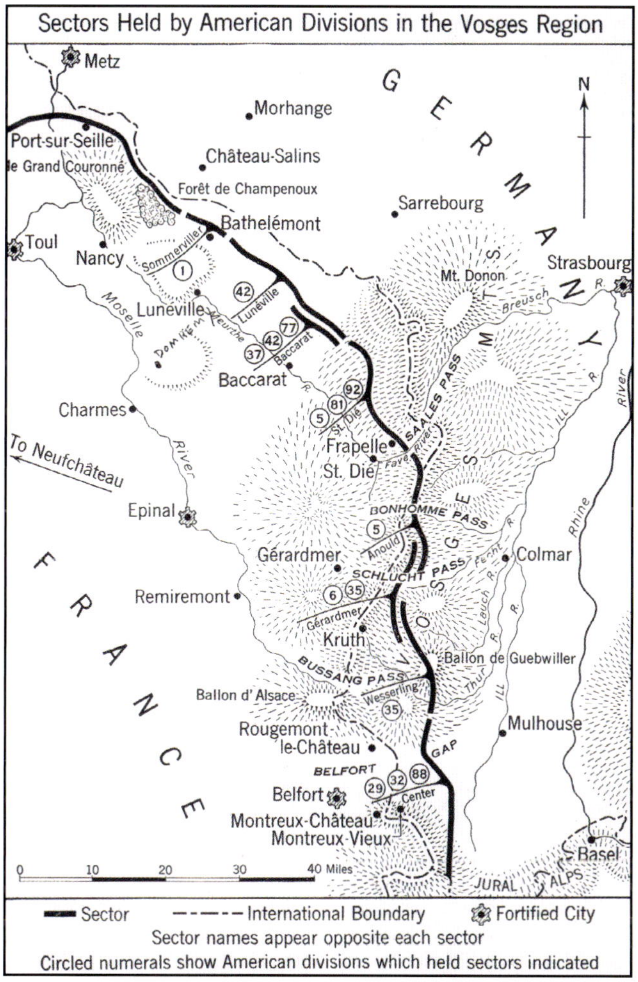

The Vosges region served as a training sector for many of the new arriving American divisions. The sector, defended by the 32nd, 29th, and 88th divisions, was located on the far right of the line near the fortified city of Belfort. *Map courtesy USAMHI.*

A nicely engraved mess kit cover for Private E. L. Daymude from Co "K," 115th Infantry. Interestingly, the "Bois de Holzberg" carved into the cover appears to represent the 31 July trench raid by the Germans against Company "K" of the 115th in the Alsace. During this raid, the 115th suffered its first combat casualties of the war.

For the majority of the division in Alsace, the first few days remained fairly quiet and the historian for the 113th reported that, at this time, the "worst enemy were the rats—dugouts, shelters, and barracks were infested with them."[16] The soldiers of the 29th were about to be introduced to a much worse enemy, however, as the Germans soon decided to welcome the new occupants of the sector with a trench raid.

Approaching the American lines under the cover of darkness, the Germans attacked Company "K" of the 115th at 04:45 a.m. on 31 July. Reacting quickly to a German volley of grenades, the Marylanders rallied and drove them back into no-man's land. Although three Doughboys were killed in this attack, the Germans were unable to take any of the 115th as prisoners. Four days later, it was the 114th's turn to be raided. This time, the Germans were more successful and managed to capture a corporal and three privates.[17] On 7 August, while clearing a section of the front line to improve field of fire, the 104th Engineers were attacked and suffered several casualties.

Close-up view of the collar disks for the 104th Engineers uniform. Note the small "NG" centered on the U.S. disk; one of many National Guard collar disk variations.

A close-up of the 104th Engineers, 29th Division patch. As seen in other examples, the gray silk threads of the patch are more susceptible to the ravages of insects and time.

Summer-weight M1912 uniform belonging to an unidentified soldier in Company "E", 104th Engineers. The 104th Engineer Regiment was formed originally with engineers and infantrymen from New Jersey Guard units.

The 29th Headquarters was determined to give something back to the Germans, and as a result, a schedule of machine gun barrages was set up to take place once a night in each of the division's sectors. This activity soon elicited a German response with their own artillery and machine gun fire. The "quiet sector" was starting to heat up, and the soldiers of the 29th realized that they were now truly part of the war. It was during this period that Captain Cutchins commented on one of the more unusual sights he had seen during the war. He observed two teams of Doughboys playing baseball while wearing their gas mask carriers around their shoulders in case of attack, though still a relatively safe distance from the front lines. Adding to the strangeness of the scene, Cutchins recounted that some French observers in a large balloon nearby seemed to be watching the game from their vantage point, as were several German aircraft that were scouting the area.[18] Cutchins also made note of the fact that French officers who served with U.S. forces were amazed at the American habit of completing a meal in thirty minutes or less. Having served with French units previously, he was well aware that French meals, even in unit mess halls, often consisted of five or six courses that often took more than an hour. Cutchins determined that the basic reason for this was because the French food was much better than the American fare, and therefore worth the extra time to enjoy it. He also noted the French officers assigned to the 29th as liaison officers often "rebelled" against the constant Doughboy menu of corned beef hash and canned salmon.[19]

The Commander of the AEF, General John J. Pershing is seen here with Major General Charles G. Morton during Pershing's 20 August 1918 visit to the 29th Division in the Alsace. *Courtesy US Army Signal Corps.*

General Pershing himself paid a visit to the 29th on 20 August 1918 and spent considerable time with the 29th's Division Commander, General Morton, and his staff. As the population of this area of Alsace was known to have mixed loyalties, depending on their German or French ancestry, it was presumed by the staff of the 29th that Pershing's visit was a bit of deception on the part of the Allies to give the impression that the next offensive might be taking place in that region. Strangely enough, as the preparations for the St. Mihiel offensive progressed, it was feared that security for that operation had been compromised to the degree that George Marshall was obliged to write an alternate operations plan for moving the attack to the Alsace region.[20]

Any review of the unit histories of the 29th reveals that the soldiers were convinced they were under constant observation by German spies in the area. Spies or not, the Germans picked the day after Pershing's visit to pound the soldiers of the 113th with an hour and a half artillery barrage. They followed it up with a trench raid by 120 of their soldiers, who managed to capture three Americans and wound several others. During this action, the soldiers from the 104th Field Signal Battalion were recognized for their heroism in repairing broken field telephone lines under heavy fire.

On 25 August, it was the 116th's turn to be raided, but this time the Germans got the worst of the fight and were driven off. The 58th Infantry Brigade Commander, Brigadier General Harry H. Bandholtz, recognized the importance of this skirmish and told them "You damned Virginians fought like hell." By the end of August, it was time to do more than fight off the raids or conduct nightly machine gun firing against the Germans.[21] A hundred soldiers were selected from the 115th to conduct a raid on the German lines. Moving to the rear, they practiced their raiding techniques and prepared to exact some revenge on the Germans. When they returned to the front, they moved quietly through the 116th's sector and by 3 a.m. were in "no-man's land," waiting for the cover of an artillery barrage. The barrage commenced as planned at 4:41, but as the raiders moved forward to a gap in the German barbed wire, a short round from the American artillery landed among the raiders and ignited some of the explosives they were carrying. In spite of these casualties, the Doughboys pressed on and reached the German trenches, where they engaged the Germans in hand to hand fighting. When the "withdrawal" flare was fired, the Americans broke off the engagement and retreated back across no-man's land under heavy fire from the now-alert and very angry German soldiers. Although the raiders failed to capture any of the enemy, they had managed to cross to the German lines, conduct an attack, and return to safety. In so doing, the raiding force suffered more than fifty casualties, including several dead and missing. It was now obvious to all that this trench raiding was serious business and the 29th needed to improve.

The 113th was selected to conduct the next raid. This time, the unit drew its men from the various scout platoons in the regiment. In addition to performing rehearsal raids in a rear area, some of the raiders also spent daylight hours observing the section that they would be attacking. As before, the American raiders

The 29th Division patch from Sergeant Davis's tunic showing the details of the silk embroidery on the wool background patch.

A closer view of Sergeant Davis's collar disks. As an early cost cutting measure, the Army moved the unit numerical designations to the "US" disk, thereby allowing the 104th Engineers, 104th Signal, 104th Ammo Train, etc., to use the same "US 104th" disk.

A view of Signal Sergeant Davis's tunic stripes. The 104th Signal Battalion was originally manned with signalmen from New Jersey and Washington, D.C., signal companies.

Well preserved, British-made M1918 tunic and wool shirt of Signal Sergeant William D. Davis of Company "C", 104th Field Signal Battalion. To save wool, the pockets on the M1918 tunics have been moved to inside the uniform.

Sergeant Davis's well worn wool shirt, showing not only his rank, but also, quite uniquely, a 29th Division patch, his red honorable discharge stripe, and an overseas stripe. Repairs are evident on the collars, indicating Sergeant Davis occasionally wore collar disks on this shirt.

approached the front during darkness and slipped out into the desolate area between the two forces. When a rolling barrage from the French supporting artillery began, the raiders moved behind it in relative safety. Upon reaching the enemy positions, they were surprised to find that the barrage had demolished much of the trench structure and they were therefore forced to work their way from shell hole to shell hole in hopes of finding a German to capture. One of the scouts, "Heinie" Bley, a private in Company "I" who "spoke German like the Kaiser himself" managed to find a dugout full of Germans.[22] After speaking to them in their own language and determining that they were not coming out to surrender, "Heinie" tossed in all of the grenades (smoke, gas, and explosive) he was carrying and ended the conversation. After that, the raiders realized they needed to return to their own lines and hurriedly made their way back, just as the German artillery started to pound the area. General Morton himself was waiting to greet the returning soldiers and congratulate them in person. The accolades were well deserved; although the raiders had captured no prisoners, they had successfully attacked the German lines, caused a number of casualties, and returned safely with only three men wounded.

The night of 13 September, when a heavy and extremely accurate artillery barrage by German long-range guns pounded their positions, it added to the Doughboys' belief that German sympathizers were providing the locations of the American units. This attack caught the 113th Infantry in their billets behind the lines and caused more than sixty casualties in that regiment's Company "L" alone. The accuracy of the German artillery in hitting the Doughboys in the town of Montreux-Vieux was interpreted two ways at the time: as either evidence of spies in the their midst, or more optimistically, the Germans were now realizing they were going to lose the war and were destroying the towns in Alsace that they would never occupy again. To the survivors of Company "L", it didn't matter much either way; they wanted revenge. Their time was coming soon.

To the north, the first great American offensive, soon to be known as the St. Mihiel campaign, had started. St. Mihiel and subsequent campaigns were going to be Pershing's opportunity to showcase the capabilities of the American Army. Unfortunately, before the 29th received orders to move north and join the AEF, they had to endure another week of persistent German air raids and gas attacks. As the 29th later reported of their time in the "quiet" sector, they suffered 923 casualties. Of these, 586 were from gas attacks.[23]

At last, on 23 September 1918, the 29th was relieved at the front by the American 88th Division. The 88th was a National Army division made up primarily of draftees from North Dakota, Minnesota, Iowa, and Illinois.[24] The 88th had originally been scheduled to relieve the 29th in Alsace in late August. However, upon arrival in the region, the division was so short of helmets, gas masks, and other essentials that they could not be put into the line.[25] Now, a month later, they were equipped and ready. The 29th handed over the sector and eagerly began to march towards the rest of the American Army. Moving mainly at night and mostly in the rain, the Blue and Gray infantrymen finally reached the rear assembly area of the American First Army and, as planned, became part of the AEF reserve force for the upcoming Meuse-Argonne Offensive.

While the 29th was practicing raids and honing their combat skills under the aggressive guns and airplanes of the German Army in the Alsace region, the rest of the AEF was busy conducting the St. Mihiel offensive. St. Mihiel was the first almost entirely American campaign of the war. In impressive fashion, the AEF moved from that campaign directly into staging positions to begin the massive Meuse-Argonne campaign. The day after the AEF had secured the St. Mihiel salient, most of the supporting artillery units started their movement to new firing positions. They were now set up between the Meuse River and the western edge of the Argonne Forest to provide direct support for the attacking forces. The infantry units that had been held in reserve at St. Mihiel also began to move into position. Over the next two weeks, the soldiers of Pershing's First Army, following the operational plan developed by Colonel George C. Marshall, executed a complex deployment of infantry, artillery, and logistics units to the new staging areas. Compounding the overall complexity of this movement was the French road network, which was extremely limited in capacity. Only three roads in the area of operation were capable of handling heavy equipment. A considerable degree of difficulty was added by the fact that the deployment had to take place at night to mask the units' shifting. In accordance with Marshall's plan, more than 800,000 troops were on the move. This total included the 200,000 French soldiers leaving the sector and the 600,000 American Doughboys moving in. Impressively, of the fifteen American divisions poised to start the battle, seven had just fought at St. Mihiel, three others had moved from Soissons, another three from near the town of Vesle, one from Bar-le-Duc, and one had come directly from a training area.[26] The resulting entanglements caused by having this many moving pieces on the French road system was predictable and aggravating for the participants, but in time most of the units reached their designated staging areas.

The AEF's right flank rested on the Meuse River, while the left was bordered by the Argonne Forest. The Argonne had been systematically fortified by the Germans, and the hills, gullies, ravines, and dense underbrush were considered impervious to attack. Adding to these natural defenses were the strong points and machine gun pits the Kaiser's troops had prepared within the forest. The high ground on both flanks gave the German forward artillery observers perfect vantage points from which they could direct heavy fire on the advancing Americans. For several years the Germans had occupied the area and had put their time to good use, building an "in depth" defensive system that maximized interlocking fires and provided reinforced fighting positions for their soldiers and machine guns. At this point in the war, the Allied armies had developed a healthy respect for the efficiency and effectiveness of German troops and their machine guns. Even with declining morale and rumors of revolution taking place back in Germany, the average German soldier was not inclined to give up without a fight. There was little doubt that the coming offensive would be met with as much vigor as the Germans could muster. Making the attack even more difficult was the fact that the geography of the region had dictated a compression of the three German lines of defense, so they were emplaced in an area only eighteen miles deep. According to German defensive doctrine, these three lines should have been arrayed in an area almost sixty miles deep. Due to the nature of the terrain, along with attacking uphill, the Doughboys were going to have to fight their way through a densely-packed German defense sector for most of their advance.

Pershing's plan called for the American First Army to attack northward while supported by the French Fourth Army. Their main objective was to capture the rail line between Carignan-Sedan-Mézières, a key segment of the rail system running through Luxembourg to Metz. This objective was almost thirty miles from the starting point. The First Army's operational front was fifteen to twenty miles wide, with the Meuse River on the east and the dense Argonne Forest and Aire River on the west. An area known as the "Heights of the Meuse" looked down on the right side of the American attack and the Argonne Forest was on the high ground that overlooked the American left flank. Against the German defenses, the American First Army mustered its 600,000 men for an attack that would begin with nine divisions on line and another five in reserve. Once the attack commenced, the American soldiers leading the assault would be supported by 189 tanks, 2,700 pieces of artillery, and more than 800 aircraft.

A sign of the daily increasing strength of the American forces is seen in the disposition of the divisions. The AEF was organized with a three-Corps front: I Corps (35th, 28th, and 77th Divisions with the 92nd in Corps reserve); V Corps (79th, 37th, and 91st Divisions with the 32nd in reserve); and III Corps (33rd, 80th, and 4th Divisions with the 3rd Division in reserve). Behind these three Corps was the overall First Army reserve, consisting of the 1st, 82nd, and making their first appearance in a main campaign, the Blue and Gray Doughboys of General Morton's 29th Division.[27]

The night of 25 September, the majority of the American assault troops moved into their pre-attack positions. After a three-hour artillery barrage, the Americans went over the top into the pre-dawn darkness. Moving swiftly through the mud and barbed wire in front of them, they achieved tactical surprise and made steady progress while the Germans scrambled to reinforce their front lines. Pershing was pleased with the early advances and reported that his troops had taken over 10,000 prisoners in the initial assault. As he later wrote:

> In the chill rain of dark nights our engineers had to build new roads across spongy, shell-torn areas,

Map of the opening phase of the Meuse-Argonne campaign showing the approximate locations of the AEF's divisions. By the time the campaign ended with the signing of the Armistice, almost a million American soldiers had been involved. *Map Courtesy USAMHI.*

> repair broken roads beyond No Man's Land, and build bridges. Our gunners, with no thought of sleep, put their shoulders to wheels and drag-ropes to bring their guns through the mire in support of the infantry now under the increasing fire of the enemy's artillery. Our attack had taken the enemy by surprise, but quickly recovering himself, he began fierce counter-attacks in strong force, supported by heavy bombardments with large quantities of gas.[28]

The other Allies may have looked derisively at the earlier American success in the St. Mihiel campaign, but there was no doubt that that AEF was now tackling a tough job. However, as the American advance continued over the next few days, the Germans took advantage of the better road systems and railroads behind their lines to speed more units to the defense. The Germans, while realizing the seriousness of the situation, feared a morale disaster among the front line troops if their soldiers' scheduled furloughs were cancelled. They did, however, direct that no special trains were to be used to take the soldiers home on leave, in order to focus transportation on supplies and reinforcements for the Meuse-Argonne front.[29]

The Germans' quick response soon stabilized the front and the American forces now found themselves in a slow, grinding campaign with mounting casualties. With the French Army's supporting attack on the far right making little progress in their advance, the 29th was summoned from its place in the American First Army Reserve and ordered to move to Verdun 3 October.[30] In this phase of the campaign, the 29th was now attached to the French XVII Corps. Crossing the Meuse on a bridge near the village of Charny, the Blue and Gray were on the east side of the Meuse River and the American 33rd Division, comprised primarily of National Guardsmen from Illinois, was on their left flank. The movements from Alsace to Verdun and then to the Meuse had been long and difficult. The long and arduous effort was clearly reflected in the Guardsmen's uniforms and shoes. The historian for the third battalion of the 116th later reported that the trousers of many of the troops in his battalion were hanging in shreds and the British-supplied field shoes were just as bad. The quartermasters in the regiment attempted to provide fresh uniforms, but could only manage to replace twenty pairs of the most ragged trousers each night during unit resupply operations.[31]

After making a fourteen-kilometer march the night of 7 October, General John Palmer's 58th Infantry Brigade, consisting of the 115th and 116th Infantry regiments and the 112th Machine Gun Battalion, reached their starting positions. At 5 a.m. the next morning, they followed a hundred yards behind a rolling artillery barrage and crossed the no-man's land to their front. Moving swiftly, the Doughboys captured the German positions on Malbrouck Hill and with it many machine guns, artillery pieces, and approximately 1,500 enemy soldiers. During this advance, two soldiers from Company H of the 115th (2nd Lieutenant Patrick Regan and Private Henry Costin) led an attack on a German machine gun nest that would earn them each the Medal of Honor. The attack cost Private Costin his life, and when it was over, a badly-wounded Lieutenant Regan was surprised to find that he had captured thirty Austrians and four machine guns with an unloaded pistol.[32] Not far away, near the Bois-de-Consenvoye, Sergeant Earl D. Gregory of the 116th Infantry was also taking the fight to the enemy. Moving out alone in front of his trench-mortar squad, Gregory captured a German machine gun, 75mm field howitzer, and twenty-two enemy soldiers. He too would be awarded the Medal of Honor in recognition of his bravery.

A carved canteen of a Company "C", 116th Infantry soldier, Corporal O.C. Shelor. Based on a picture in the 29th Division's history written by John Cutchins, carved canteens and mess kits, as well as dog tags, were used to identify grave locations for soldiers killed in action. This practice, at least among 29th Division soldiers, may explain why so many of these carved items can be found today.

One interesting commentary on the relative inexperience of the Doughboys making the attack was directed to a staff officer by an older Regular Army sergeant who had been appointed an officer in the 29th Division: "dere are men today leading companies what don't know how to make out a morning report."[33] Knowledgeable about U.S. Army standard reports or not, the soldiers of the

29th showed far more enthusiasm and skill when it came to the important soldier skills of marksmanship and engaging the enemy.

The other infantry units of the division soon joined in the attack, and by the time German reinforcements finally stabilized the line, the 29th Division was holding a seven kilometer-long front. The ground gained during this period had a direct effect on the American advance on the other side of the Meuse, as German artillery batteries situated in the 29th's sector had been firing across the river at the U.S. III Corps' units.[34] With this area now in American hands, the flanking artillery fire was eliminated and III Corps was able to advance.

Always a welcome sight; a mobile kitchen moves forward to deliver meals to the front. Unfortunately, congested and muddy roads restricted movement during the Meuse-Argonne campaign and the Doughboys faced many hungry days. *Courtesy USAMHI.*

A nicely colorized portrait of Sergeant Howard E. Madsen of Company "D", 115th Infantry. Madsen, shown here with his decorations, was awarded the Distinguished Service Cross for gallantry in action at the Bois De Consenvoye. *Courtesy John Simmons.*

AMERICAN·EXPEDITIONARY·FORCES

UNITED★STATES★ARMY

DISTINGUISHED SERVICE·CROSS

★CITATION★

Sergeant Howard E. Madsen, Co. "D", 116th Infantry

DISTINGUISHED HIMSELF BY EXTRAORDINARY HEROISM IN CONNECTION WITH MILITARY OPERATIONS AGAINST AN ARMED ENEMY OF THE UNITED STATES AT Bois de Consenvoye, France ON 22 Oct 1918 AND IN RECOGNITION OF HIS GALLANT CONDUCT I HAVE AWARDED HIM IN THE NAME OF THE PRESIDENT THE DISTINGUISHED SERVICE CROSS

AWARDED ON 6 Dec 1918

John J. Pershing
COMMANDER-IN-CHIEF

Sergeant Madsen's Distinguished Service Cross Citation. The action at Bois De Consenvoye was particularly important, as it cleared the way for the 33rd Division to maintain their advance on the 29th's flank. *Courtesy John Simmons.*

Getting supplies forward to the fighting units—already a serious problem—was made worse when German artillery knocked out one of the pontoon bridges being used by the 29th to provide logistical support. As the 113th would later report, "we had no breakfast, no dinner, and no prospects of supper. The kitchen had gotten stuck in a shell hole…under these conditions permission was granted to eat the reserve rations."[35] The lack of rations became a common complaint in most of the American units during the campaign. Many divisions reported that their front line infantrymen had gone several days without receiving rations and soldiers were straggling away from their units in search of food. Some were reduced to looking through packs of dead or captured German soldiers, searching for something to eat.[36] As the campaign continued, the straggling became worse and began to seriously affect the fighting ability of some units. Whether due to Morton's strict discipline or the good fortune of operating in a fairly constricted battle space, the Guardsmen of the 29th do not appear to have been inclined to straggling as some other units did.

On 11 October, the 116th resumed its attack by moving out at 6 a.m. under the cover of a dense fog. German artillery observers, however, managed to see them moving and directed heavy and accurate artillery and machine gun fire on the Virginians of the 116th. Suffering heavy casualties, the 116th held on until darkness fell, at which time they returned to their starting positions.

Private Paul Klonowski from Company "L", 116th Infantry, seen previously while training at Camp McClellan, poses for another portrait, this time in France. *Courtesy John Simmons.*

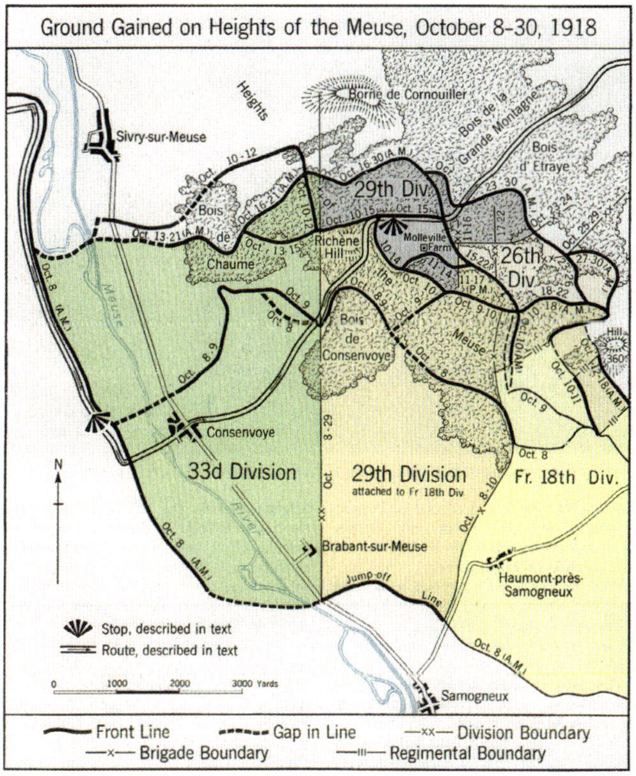

The 29th and 33rd Divisions' operational sectors on the eastern side of the Meuse River. By the end of the war, the 29th had suffered more than 5,500 casualties, most of which were from this relatively small area of operation. *Map courtesy USAMHI.*

After interrogation, an American officer poses with a rather calm looking German prisoner. By the mid-point of the Meuse-Argonne campaign, prisoners such as this one were becoming more common and many seemed relieved to be out of the war alive. *Courtesy USAQM Museum.*

During this period, John Cutchins and other members of the 29th division staff spent a significant amount of time interrogating the German prisoners being brought in by the forward units. He tended to divide them into several categories: older men drafted into the army, young students, regular soldiers from non-Prussian units ("more agreeable"), and the hard-core Prussians. While none of his interrogations unearthed any information that was particularly earthshaking, he was amused by the opinion of one German officer who admitted, while discussing the American soldiers his unit had taken prisoner, that the Germans were quite surprised to discover that the average Doughboy didn't "seem to give a damn who their brigade or division commander was."[37] This finding matches closely what another German officer wrote in a report to his commander: "Remarkable, even among the good American troops, is the indifference as to the aims of the war. They know not for what they fight. After they serve for some length of time at the front, it may be quite possible, therefore, that they will become less eager to fight."[38] Indifferent or not to war aims, Cutchins was forced to break up a fist fight between his soldiers and German prisoners that apparently started because the Germans said the Americans were such bad soldiers that they didn't even know how to salute properly.[39] That insult had set the Doughboys off. Obviously, after having General Morton as their commander for over a year, the soldiers of the Blue and Gray took their saluting abilities pretty seriously.

On 12 October, the 113th and 114th regiments attacked the Bois d'Ormont and soon were heavily engaged in the densely packed woods. Encountering strong resistance, the 114th suffered heavy casualties and were driven from the woods. With the help of the 113th, the 114th attacked again and managed to regain a portion of the forest, holding it while under continuous attack from German aircraft and a heavy gas barrage. In this fight, the 114th suffered 118 dead and over 800 wounded.

Another view of Private Smart's canteen cup, showing a crudely-drawn 29th Division symbol. The simplicity of this carving, when compared to the earlier 4th Maryland carved mess kit cover, reflects the full spectrum from simple to extremely ornate carving that can be found on soldiers' equipment.

A hand-carved canteen cup belonging to Private W.E. Smart, a private in Company "I", 114th Infantry Regiment.

An unidentified sergeant from Company "M", 114th Infantry, poses for a formal portrait. The 114th suffered heavy casualties during the fighting near the Bois d'Ormont and a subsequent gas barrage.

Knowing that his frontline troops were taking a beating, Colonel William R. Pope, Regimental Commander of the 113th, was determined to get food and hot coffee to his soldiers. He assembled the regimental cooks and gave them the mission: the mess sergeants from Companies "F" and "I" of the 113th were to lead their sections to the front and get food to the hungry men fighting there. Almost immediately the cooks ran into heavy German artillery fire, and the attempt had to be delayed until next morning. Trying again, the little band set out and quickly lost their bearings as they moved forward. To their unhappy surprise, they soon realized that they were now actually in front of the units they were seeking. And they were even more unpleasantly surprised to be caught in the middle of a battle between Company "E" and some German machine gun nests. The German machine guns quickly riddled the cooks' wagons and demolished their kitchen trailer. Having come this far, however, the cooks refused to give up. They kept moving until they found a kitchen from another unit. Using borrowed equipment, they prepared another meal and another batch of hot coffee, finally delivering it to their soldiers in the front lines.

While the 29th was engaged in their fight with the Germans and Austrians on the east side of the Meuse, on the west side of the river, the other divisions of the American First Army were continuing their own bloody struggle. On 9 October, I Corps captured the town of Fleville and V Corps advanced into open country north of Gesnes. III Corps, working its way up the west bank of the Meuse, continued to face heavy opposition. By 10 October, the Argonne Forest was almost completely cleared of German forces. Continuous advances by the Americans west of the Meuse now brought V Corps up against the next German line of defense, known as the "Kriemhilde Stellung." The Kriemhilde had been well fortified by the Germans and was considered the "strongest natural line in France"; like the Giselher and Freya Stellungs, it too was named by the Germans for a Wagnerian opera witch.[40] As the weather worsened, the fighting continued to its fullest intensity. Whenever there was even the slightest letup in the action, the staff units of the First Army tried to recover their many stragglers and replace their casualties with new soldiers.

The problems inherent in supporting a division-sized unit under these conditions were readily apparent to a 29th Staff officer, who wrote of the difficulties of "feeding 27,000 or more men and 10,000 or more animals even under normal conditions...under the orders of a corps commanded by a foreign general and composed of different nationalities, speaking a different language and operating over a country which had been a battleground for four years." He also pointed out the difficulties of maintaining an ammunition supply for a division in combat, describing the difficulties encountered in moving a ton of ammunition from the factory, across the country, through the various army and corps boundaries, and then delivering it forward to the unit, only to be expended in a matter of hours or minutes.[41] Likewise, when the senior quartermaster officer for the 29th Division wrote his after-action report for the Meuse-Argonne, he described in detail the struggles and ultimate success of one night-long convoy with which he traveled the nearly impassible muddy roads under constant artillery and gas attack, enduring miles-long traffic jams to get the required supplies to the 29th's units. He noted that one such supply convoy required twenty-four hours to make the six-mile round trip. He concluded with a simple statement which is perhaps a fitting tribute to all the logisticians in the American Army: "Where would the fighter be if not for the machinery that permitted him to keep fighting?"[42]

A stretch of road typical of the Meuse-Argonne campaign. Attempting to resupply forward units while traversing these roads and under constant enemy shell fire would prove to be a stern test of the AEF's logisticians. *Courtesy Charles G. Thomas.*

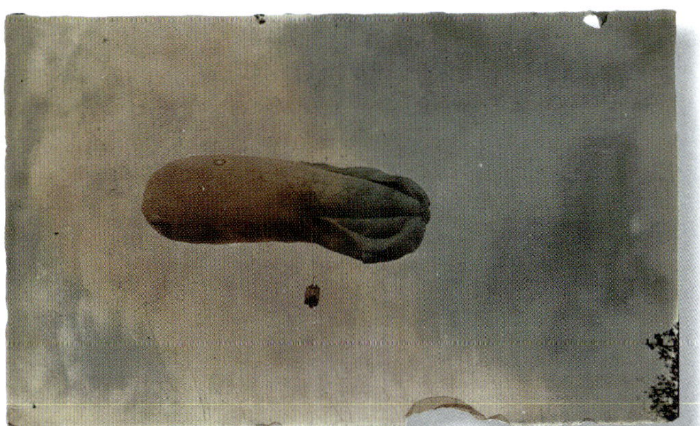

A damaged but nonetheless interesting picture of an American observation balloon taken during the Meuse-Argonne campaign. With almost 3,000 artillery pieces operating in support of the American attack, these observers were critical for accurately adjusting artillery fire.

For the fighters of the 29th Division, the offensive continued in their sector the morning of 15 October with an attack in conjunction with the Illinois National Guardsmen of the 33rd Division on their left. The 115th and 116th Regiments attacked side by side after an artillery barrage. The short duration of the barrage was more by necessity than choice, as artillery ammunition had become increasingly hard to obtain.[43] During the next two days, all four infantry regiments of the 29th were engaged in clearing out the enemy strong points in their sectors. For most of this time, the 113th and 114th were actually under direct control of the French 18th Division. During this period, they suffered an intense gas attack so persistent that some men were forced to wear their gas masks for over two hours. In addition, many low-lying gullies and ravines became so contaminated by the pools of gas settling in them that they had to be avoided completely. By 17 October, after ten days of almost continuous combat by the 29th Division, there was a short lull in the battle. Even the weather improved temporarily, as the sun made an appearance for the first time in many days. The morning of 19 October, the Germans attempted a counterattack against the 116th, but it was easily beaten back. The regimental historian noted that the Germans seemed "badly confused as to the exact location of the American lines."[44] Perhaps this was finally a sign, at least in the 29th Division's sector, that the Germans were running out of first-rate troops and were resorting to their less well trained and reserve units.

A photograph taken in the Meuse Valley during the September-October fighting. It is unique because it appears *not* to be raining. This campaign was marked by bad weather and wet conditions, in addition to relentless German artillery and machine gun and gas attacks. Additional elements that make the picture interesting are the lean-to shelters, extra equipment, and the German bayonet, as well as the pistol and holster stuffed into the back pocket of the Doughboy second from the left. *Courtesy USAMHI.*

A closer view of Corporal Caraway's 29th patch. It appears that the wool base to which the blue and gray sections are sewn is made of the same material as the tunic, indicating this was probably a postwar purchase in the States. It is interesting to note that this New Jersey Guardsman has also chosen to have the blue portion sewn on top of the gray as a reflection of his northern origins or sympathies.

Beautifully preserved 29th Division uniform; shown here is a privately purchased coat belonging to Corporal Lawrence Caraway of Company "I", 114th Infantry Regiment.

First-rate troops or not, the soldiers of the Blue and Gray Division had developed a healthy respect for the fighting qualities of the German soldier. They also were quite aware that, to make up for manpower shortages, the Germans increased the number of machine guns in every infantry company to the point that they were actually machine gun units. So when the infantrymen of the 29th received orders to resume the attack 23 October, they knew it would be a challenge. This time, both brigades of the division were to attack on a three-regiment front, with the 115th making a covering attack to protect the flank of the 116th Regiment. As the units moved to the "parallel of departure" (more commonly known to modern soldiers and historians as the "line of departure"), a German gas barrage swept the area where the 113th's Machine Gun Company was assembling and knocked them out of action. Nevertheless, the rest of the division had to press on with the attack as planned.

From 5:30 to 6:15 a.m., the American and French Artillery provided a rolling barrage. Previous experience in this sector had shown that some of the German machine gun emplacements were so close to the American lines that artillery barrages tended to miss them. Therefore, Lieutenant Colonel William S. Bowen, the assistant Chief of Staff for Operations, had the Doughboys withdrawn from the front line trenches. This allowed the barrage to start on the American lines and move forward. In spite of this additional support, it was still a rough day's fight for the 29th. That said, the day's results were impressive: an advance of over half a mile on an 800-yard front. The battle continued past midnight, as the Doughboys struggled to organize their new front line and clean out bypassed pockets of German soldiers. Over sixty German machine guns were captured by the time the objective had been secured.

On 24 October, the Intelligence section in the division reported that a barrage plan had been recovered from a captured German artillery officer and it listed the four German artillery regiments the 29th was facing in this sector. Unfortunately, the Intelligence team was also obliged to report that the German map that accompanied the plan had been kept by an American officer as a souvenir, so the exact location of these units remained unknown.[45]

The New Jersey Guardsmen of the 113th had a particularly difficult fight and were pulled off the line after being relieved by soldiers of the 114th. Some of the men were so weak that they required several rest breaks just to move to the rear. This proved fortunate, as one of the assembly areas towards which they were moving was heavily shelled by the Germans just prior to their arrival. Had they been on time, there was little doubt they would have suffered even more casualties. As it was, they were finally able to reach the rear and unload their rifles for the first time in weeks. They even managed to find the field kitchen of an engineer unit that shared breakfast and hot coffee with them.[46]

While the German infantry counterattacks proved to be weak and ineffective, their artillery continued to be extremely effective. For the next few days, the big guns continued to bombard the 29th's front line units with heavy doses of artillery and gas. The randomness of the danger from the artillery strikes began to wear on the American soldiers, and many began to believe that there was no safe area anywhere in the Meuse-Argonne region. They were right. After being relieved from frontline duty and seeking shelter from the persistent rain, two Co "I", 116th Infantry Doughboys took cover in a small shed. At three o'clock in the morning, an apparently random German shell demolished the shed, killing Private Earl Airhart while he slept and seriously wounding his friend, Private John Hughes. The same day, George Webster, a Mexican Border veteran working as a cook for the 116th Regimental Band, was killed by another random artillery blast.[47] Yet the 116th continued to stick it out and fight. The 3rd Battalion of the 116th would later report that in twenty-one days of combat, they "never failed to take an objective, never gave any ground to the enemy, never lost a prisoner…[and] captured 618 prisoners from the enemy." They could also boast of the capture of more than seventy enemy machine guns.[48] These accomplishments came at a cost: sixteen dead and seventy-four wounded in Company "I" alone. Numbered among the dead was their Company Commander, Captain Robert Conrad. Similarly, Company "K" was reduced in size from over 200 soldiers to one officer and 111 men. The 29th was fighting hard, but the Division was paying a heavy price.

A clear image of an extremely youthful-looking sergeant, John Hickson, Jr. of Halifax, Virginia, from Company "L", 116th Infantry Regiment.

A close up of the collar disks, showing how the owner sanded down the "116" to the shinier base metal to make sure it would stand out. Also shown here is the sergeant's hat, made of the same material as the tunic and displaying an officer's crossed rifles pin.

A privately-purchased uniform. This well-preserved coat belonged to a sergeant of Company "D", 116th Infantry. The company was primarily raised from the Warrenton and Front Royal region of Virginia and was originally commanded by Samuel Gardner Waller.

Another view of the 116th uniform, this time showing the sergeant's stripes and the elaborate bullion wound stripe on the right sleeve cuff.

A close view of the construction of the two-piece 29th Division patch on the 116th uniform.

Interestingly enough, the matching trousers of the 116th uniform have had Indian Wars era buttons added to the legs.

The persistent problem created by ever-present lice forced the American units to run their sterilizing machinery on a regular basis. This sterilizer appears to be mounted on a rail car, while others were truck or horse-cart mounted. *Courtesy USAMHI.*

On 28 October, the 29th Division received word that they were being relieved by the 79th Division and withdrawn from the front lines. By the evening of 29 October, most of the division was off the line and heading for the rear. It was also announced that the 29th was being transferred to the newly-formed American Second Army in preparation for operations soon to begin on the western side of the Meuse. The units hiked away from the fighting area until they finally encountered "a long column of buses manned by Chinese Colonials [who] took the weary, lousy, dirty veterans to Buery with sixteen men to a truck. After a six-hour bus ride they climbed out and were assigned to billets, where they quickly sunk into a well-earned rest in the hay of the cow sheds."[49] As well as providing rest for the troops, the 29th staff again attempted to arrange for new uniforms for them. They also set up delousing stations to help rid the soldiers of the "cooties" which had accompanied them through the campaign. The delousing was only partially successful in ridding the men of the persistent lice that tormented them, leading many of the 29th's soldiers to comment that it was probably a French louse that caused Napoleon to always be portrayed with his hand in his shirt.[50]

As for General Morton, the attitude of the men towards him and his strict discipline had changed only slightly. As one officer on his staff wrote: "He was rather thoroughly hated when we went into battle, for he was quite a martinet. When we came out of the battle, he at least had the respect ...of the men. He was the strangest combination I ever saw...unquestioned courage with the attributes of a bully."[51] The same officer also wrote that Morton was "absolutely ruthless, destroying a man's career without a moment's hesitation," and that the commander of the 115th Infantry, Colonel Milton Reckord, was the only colonel in the division to retain his command throughout the war. Cutchins would also note later that, while he disapproved of Morton's methods and he believed "the same results could have been gotten by less ruthlessness and more consideration, [Morton] must be credited with a high sense of duty...and a glowing patriotism."[52]

As the 29th rested and gathered its strength for the next mission, the fighting on the west side of the river continued. With

Colonel Milton Reckord, Commander 115th Infantry Regiment. The history of the 115th Infantry Regiment in the World War was written by two of the regiment's chaplains and dedicated to Colonel Reckord, who was "Always just, kind in treatment, calm in excitement, brave in danger, wise in decision, quick in action." Reckord would later command the 29th Division from 1934 to 1942. *Courtesy National Guard Historical Foundation.*

reinforced and now somewhat rested divisions, the final American advance on the Meuse-Argonne front started 1 November. Heavy artillery barrages preceded the attacks and, as Pershing would report, "the enemy broke before the determined infantry, which by its persistent fighting of the past weeks and the dash of its attack had overcome his will to resist."[53] The Doughboys of V Corps punched a hole in the middle of the enemy defenses, which would cause the Germans to withdraw their forces behind the Meuse entirely. On 5 November, III Corps crossed the river in strength and suddenly, it seemed that the war might be winding down. That same day, I Corps units were directly across the Meuse from the city of Sedan. This advance marked a distance of twenty-five miles from the original start point of the offensive; an impressive feat, particularly when measured against the strength and depth of the German defenses in the area.

On 6 November, Marshal Foch requested that six American divisions be withdrawn from the fighting to prepare for supporting another French attack. Pershing agreed to provide the requested units, but also insisted that the American troops be commanded by General Robert Lee Bullard as part of the newly-formed Second Army. This new attack was to begin 14 November, and would include the six American divisions and twenty French divisions under General Charles Mangin. Along with the 29th, the other American divisions were the 3rd, 4th, 28th, 35th, and 36th.[54]

By early November, rumors of peace talks were filtering all the way down to the individual soldiers in the trenches, with some of the soldiers even beginning to think that they might survive the fighting. However, the war continued. Earlier, in mid-October, German Field Marshal Paul von Hindenburg had sent a powerful message to the German Army: "The diplomatic negotiations to end the war have begun. Their result will be the more favorable the more we succeed in maintaining a high state of discipline in the army, in holding the ground gained and injuring the enemy. The battle must be conducted in the immediate future on the basis of these principles."[55] With such orders as these, it is small wonder the German soldiers fought so intensely during the last days of October 1918. But now, even stirring words were not enough. Bulgaria had dropped out of the war and the Turks were being defeated in the Middle East. In Germany, the Kaiser had relieved the Army's leader, General Erich Ludendorff, and replaced him with General Wilhelm Groener. The German Navy had mutinied, and Bolsheviks/Workers Councils were now taking over large German cities as part of the revolutionary movement sweeping the country. German delegates had already been dispatched to meet with Allied representatives to ask for an Armistice. The Kaiser abdicated his throne 9 November. Nevertheless, the night of 10 November, the Marines and soldiers of the 2nd Division, assigned to V Corps, attacked across the Meuse, near the town of Mouzon, under heavy fire. The next morning (11 November), the 89th Division crossed the Meuse and captured Stenay. In preparation for the next offensive, bridges were immediately constructed at Pouilly and Stenay by the American engineers. Right up to the last minute before 11 a.m., when the Armistice was set to begin, the fighting continued in earnest. Marine Captain John Thomason, Jr. made that point later by saying "they weren't using blank ammunition the morning of the Armistice when I scampered across those fire-raked pontoons of the Meuse."[56] Fortunately, the 14 November assault was no longer necessary, as the Armistice had been signed and was going into effect at 11 a.m. Though the Armistice ended the fighting, it did not end the war. The real end of the war would not occur until June 1919, with the signing of the Treaty of Versailles.

Nothing but smiles in the back of this truck; the war is over and they know it. Now the only real question is "When are we going home?" *Courtesy USAQM Museum.*

Taken just a few days before the Armistice, this picture of engineers that have just finished building a bridge in the Argonne shows a full range of emotions. Rumors were already circulating that the war was about to end, and some of these Doughboys are beginning to think they might survive the war after all. Others, not as optimistic, are keeping their helmets on and their gas masks handy. *Courtesy USAQM Museum.*

Pershing would later express his regret that the American offensive ended before the Germans really acknowledged their defeat. He was right. On 11 November 1918, German General Karl von Einem sent a message to his soldiers:

> Undefeated and tested again and again in numerous battles, you are terminating the war in enemy country. What you have accomplished in the face of an enemy force many times superior to ours in number, belongs to history. You can be certain to possess my undying gratitude and the gratitude of the fatherland. With unbroken ranks, each one staunchly in his place, proudly as we left in 1914, so we want to return to our native soil."[57]

Convinced that the Armistice had let the Germans off the hook, Pershing, with some foresight, would remark: "They never really knew they were beaten in Berlin. It will all have to be done all over again."[58] The Doughboys of the 29th, not having their commander's strategic vision, were just happy that it was over. They had proven their worth during the Meuse-Argonne campaign, and 5,568 casualties was a hefty price to pay for the four miles of France they had liberated. They had made the world safe for democracy and now they were going home.

An unidentified member of a 29th Division Machine Gun Battalion poses for a formal portrait in a very elaborate studio. *Courtesy Rogier Vandehoef.*

Basel Cromwell, a private in Battery "B," 111th Field Artillery Regiment, poses for his portrait in a more austere studio than his comrade shown in the previous picture.

Even the Doughboys of 1918 were not immune to the glamour of Hollywood. This 115th Infantry Regiment soldier's wallet has been decorated with a picture of the famous motion picture actress Theda Bera.

Inside view of the 115th wallet showing the commonly carried small comb, file, thread, and sewing needles.

The large certificate awarded to Doughboys wounded in battle. This example was awarded to Private First Class James W. Simmons of Headquarters Company, 115th Infantry Regiment.

CHAPTER 4

Homeward Bound...Eventually

The 29th Division was going home, but not just yet. Under the conditions of the Armistice, the U.S. Army was required to dispatch some units to serve as part of an Allied occupation force administering the German Rhineland. This force would not only serve as a buffer between Germany and the battered countries of Belgium and France, but also control the bridges across the Rhine that the German Army used to move soldiers and supplies to the Western Front during the war. The occupation army's zones stretched in layers from north to south: Belgium, Britain, United States, and France. These four zones would serve as administrative centers for receiving and inspecting war reparations material that Germany was being forced to provide to the victorious Allies. Ultimately, Pershing would dispatch eight divisions to Germany and two to Luxembourg to serve as the American contingent in the occupation. The divisions in Germany would be under the command of the U.S. Third Army and their headquarters would be located in the German city of Coblenz.

Almost coincidental to the signing of the Armistice was the formation of the Third Army. For a while, it appeared that the 29th Division would be one of the chosen occupation divisions. The rumor mills were running full blast amongst the soldiers of the 29th, debating whether or not they would make the march into Germany. It was even reported in *The New York Times* that the 29th had been selected. In the 54th Artillery Brigade, some of the soldiers believed that, because they had missed out on the fighting, "the best [they] can hope for is a crack at the Army of Occupation..."[1] On 14 November, it became obvious to all that the 29th was not going to be part of the occupation. On that date, they received official orders to hand over their best draft animals to the 3rd Division. Recognizing that the Meuse-Argonne campaign had severely damaged the health of every division's horses and mules, Colonel George Marshall directed that the divisions selected for occupation duty should have the best equipment and healthiest pack animals available. Each division had, on average, ten thousand draft animals on its Table of Organization and Equipment to transport everything from kitchen equipment to artillery pieces, so the need for healthy animals was clear. In spite of the age-old standard military practice of dumping a unit's undesirable equipment (and even personnel at times) onto another unit, the 29th Division played it straight and gave up the best they had. The commander of the 3rd Division, MG Robert L. Howze, later sent an acknowledgement, thanking the 29th for the "sportsmanlike spirit and soldierly manner in which the 29th Division had obeyed so exactly an order which afforded so great a temptation to do otherwise."[2]

Almost certainly a uniform issued after arrival back in the States due to the generic US and Infantry disks and the still clearly legible size "40" label inside the collar.

An M1917 tunic displaying a wool on wool version of the 29th Division patch with a very dark blue half in contrast to the gray.

Closer view of the patch clearly showing the hand stitching used to attach the patch to the uniform.

Sergeant stripes from the same 29th Division uniform. In all likelihood, these stripes, the collar disks, and the division patch are the only remnants of the soldier's original uniform.

A scene familiar to American soldiers of all generations; an Army truck with soldiers packed in the back for transport from their billets to either work or a recreation site. The tail gate on the truck has been carefully painted with the warning "Load not to exceed 3 tons."

The 29th's morale soared briefly 13 December, when the 104th Trench Mortar Battery received orders to prepare for redeployment back to the States. They were sent to the port of St Nazaire in February and boarded the USS *Mongolia*, a Navy-chartered troopship. They were back in New York City by early March. Unfortunately, this was the only unit of the 29th to receive an early "port call." The rest of the division was moved to the 11th Training Area near Bourbonne-les-Bains to practice their combat skills. It was becoming obvious that they would have to endure a European winter before it would be their turn to go home. Being good soldiers, the units of the 29th made their best attempt to ignore the rain, sleet, and snow while performing endless drills. The more astute among them did see the "irony in maneuvers against [a pretend] enemy, after having met successfully in battle an actual enemy."[3] The 29th Division staff, realizing they would remain in France for the foreseeable future, began to work on the three things they thought would keep the division disciplined and content: "interesting work, comfortable quarters and healthful amusements."[4]

With the typically inclement European winter weather, the Doughboy's favorite pastime of playing baseball was out of the question. That said, the 29th quickly produced and fielded some very good football teams. Rising through the standings after competing against teams from other divisions, the 29th's consolidated team lost to the 36th Division in the First Army Championship game on a very muddy field by a score of three to nothing. The 36th's team would go on to lose the AEF Championship game to the Third Army's 89th Division team coached by George "Potsy" Clark. Clark would later gain fame as the coach of the National Football League's Detroit Lions. Ironically, the quarterback for the 89th Division's AEF Championship football team was an officer and recent West Point graduate named Charles Gerhardt, a name that would become very familiar to the 29th Division during the next war.[5]

One of the problems inherent to the large size of the American divisions was the equally large number of billets/barracks they required. Therefore, every available house or farm in the area became home to the Doughboys. Here, a group of Doughboys take time for a picture with their hostess.

Another view of the baseball game between the artillerymen and the Divisional All-Stars. *Courtesy of USAMHI.*

An unidentified soldier from the 29th Division poses for a picture with his hand on his .45 pistol. Although his unit is also unknown, he is most likely from a New Jersey unit, as indicated by his patch having the blue section mounted over the gray.

Two 112th Field Artillery Regiment Doughboys: Private Ritz Walters, a middle-weight boxer for the 29th Division; and his trainer, Private Teddy Raymond (on the left). The 112th was a predominately New Jersey regiment. *Courtesy of USAMHI.*

On 3 April 1919, the weather cleared enough for the 54th Artillery Brigade's baseball team to play the 29th Division All-Star team. Unlike earlier games played in the Alsace, gas masks were not required for the athletes and spectators, nor was there any danger from German airplanes. *Courtesy of USAMHI.*

Not all of the Doughboys went to Paris or Monaco on leave after the end of hostilities. This group of 104th Ammo Train soldiers visited Lamalou-les-Bains, a small town in southern France well known for its scenic view of lakes, rivers, and mountains.

The same group from the previous picture has now moved to another part of their hotel for a second group picture. The women in the photograph are perhaps either the proprietors or members of the staff of the Hotel Villa de Rosiers. The picture is dated 1 April 1919.

In addition to sporting events and maneuvers, the soldiers of the 29th were given their first opportunity to be real tourists. Among the favored sites to visit were Aix-les-Bains, Grenoble, and Nice. They also were quick to take advantage of the facilities and activities offered by the various American welfare agencies: the Red Cross, YMCA, Knights of Columbus, and the Jewish Welfare League. The YMCA alone established twenty or so of their huts in the 29th Division's area and the Doughboys that visited them were given the opportunity to occasionally converse with one of the female canteen workers. As the 29th's history reported, "While there may be conflicting opinions as to the advisability of having sent woman workers to France…it will be difficult to find any member of the 29th Division who has anything but words of praise and gratitude to them for the very real help and the many hours of companionship they provided."[6] In spite of all the efforts to keep them busy and productive, the Doughboys were impatient to return home. In the 115th, the Maryland soldiers were especially wistful after a movie named "Miles of Smiles" was sent over from the States. Commissioned by the *Baltimore Sun* newspaper, the movie consisted of film footage of the families and friends of the men in the 115th and was replayed many times throughout the regimental area. The homesickness was so pervasive that the standard Doughboy question "When do we eat?" had been replaced by "When are we going home?"[7]

These 29th Division Doughboys were luckier than most, having found both a musical group and several American ladies to dance with at the Hotel Mas in Lamalou. *Courtesy of USAMHI.*

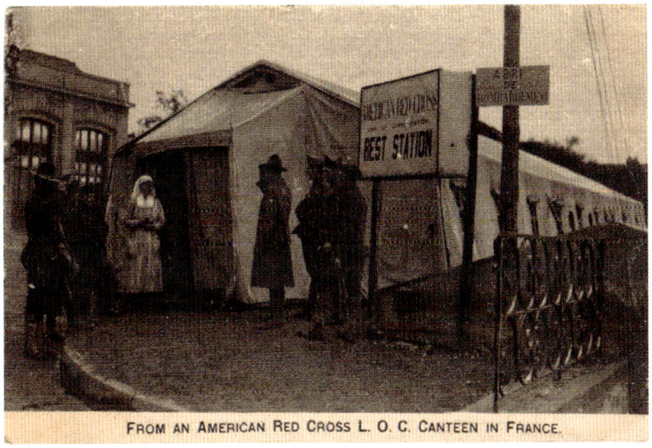

Service organizations such as the Red Cross, YMCA, and Knights of Columbus were an important part of keeping the Doughboys entertained and out of trouble. This Red Cross postcard is particularly interesting, since it shows a mix of soldier uniforms, including some who have managed to keep their campaign hats.

Canteen cup belonging to Private John D. Clark of Company "A", 115th Infantry Regiment.

Neatly carved mess kit plate belonging to Maryland native Willis R. Jones of the 115th Infantry.

Carefully engraved mess kit plate belonging to Private James C. McNeil of Company "F", 110th Field Artillery. The 110th was formed originally from National Guard units in Maryland and the District of Columbia.

Indicative of the soldiers' preoccupation with food were the large number of food-related portraits. Here, an unidentified Doughboy poses in what appears to be a photographer's tent studio with his mess kit and canteen cup.

Enjoying some free time at one of the local recreation centers and still making up for missed meals, a Doughboy loads up on doughnuts. *Courtesy Library of Congress.*

An unidentified cook from the 104th Ammo Train stops to pose for a picture outside the mess tent.

After suffering many a hungry day in the Meuse-Argonne campaign, every Doughboy had an increased appreciation for receiving meals on a regular basis from unit kitchens equipped with butchers such as these. Soon, however, the most pressing question became "When are we going home?"

While the vast majority of the 29th were practicing their soldier skills, playing football, or travelling through France on guided tours, there were some soldiers that were still soldiering on. The soon-to-be Lieutenant Colonel John Cutchins, of the 29th's headquarters staff, had been assigned to the Allied Peace Commission almost as soon as the fighting stopped. Before long, he was travelling back and forth between France, Belgium, and the American Occupation zone in the Rhineland. Cutchins was serving as a member of an Allied team attempting to determine the proper amount of war reparations the Germans would have to pay. In the meantime, Lieutenant Colonel C. R. W. Morison of the 115th Infantry led a detachment of more than a hundred soldiers into Germany to serve as commandant and staff of a camp for Russian prisoners of war. The fear that repatriated Russian POWs would immediately join the Bolshevik forces had led the Allies and the Germans to continue to maintain the prison camps. Now under Allied management, these camps would remain open until something could be figured out to do with the Russians.

Another detachment, drawn from the 114th and 115th Regiments, had an equally interesting assignment. During the war, a large number of Polish citizens had joined the French Army, and by war's end, were concentrated in a fighting force known as "Haller's Army." With the emergence of Poland as an independent nation, it was time to transport these troops home. It was doubly important to get them there quickly, as Poland was being viewed as the eastern barricade to prevent the spread of Bolshevism from Russia. The soldiers of the 29th served as escorts for some of the trains carrying the Polish soldiers through occupied and unoccupied Germany to ensure a nonviolent passage. American soldiers from the Third Army, headquartered in Coblenz, would also participate in both of these types of missions and found them equally challenging, as well as somewhat dangerous.[8]

The Armistice has been signed and the shooting is over, but fear of the "Bolshevik tendencies" of Russian prisoners of war keeps them still under armed guard by the German Army. Soon these Russians, and many others like them, will be turned over to American Army detachments for repatriation back to Russia. *Courtesy Charles G. Thomas.*

With the slow advent of spring, the 29th realized the time was finally drawing near for their departure from France. In keeping with his tradition of personally decorating and thanking his units prior to their departure, General Pershing visited the 29th Division at Fresnes 24 March 1919, on a particularly rainy day. Arriving at the designated parade ground—a relatively flat area that was quickly turning into a shallow lake from the constant rain—Pershing surprised the men by wading through the mud and water in his highly polished boots to where they were standing. He then conducted an inspection in ranks of both assembled infantry brigades and seemed to make eye contact with every soldier on the parade field. He also made

An extremely unusual picture taken in Gardelagen, Germany. The Sergeant with an "X" on his collar is displaying two patches on his left sleeve: the Third Army and the 29th Division. Though double-patched uniforms are fairly common for Army of Occupation units, the 29th was not part of the Army of Occupation. Therefore, this unusual combination would indicate that these soldiers are part of one of the *ad hoc* detachments sent by the 115th Infantry Regiment to Germany to administer the Russian prisoner of war camps.

a point of talking to each man who displayed a wound stripe on his right sleeve. After the inspection, the AEF Commander decorated the regimental and division flags. During this portion of the ceremony the sun made its first appearance of the day. After all the regimental flags had been decorated, each regiment's national flag was raised and the consolidated band of the 29th Division played the "Star Spangled Banner." Pershing also awarded a number of individual medals to deserving soldiers. When the last medal had been presented, the infantrymen passed in review for Pershing and the senior staff. Pershing then gathered the entire formation around him and thanked them for their service. Shortly thereafter, he left to perform a similar ceremony with the 54th Artillery Brigade and the other 29th Division units. As happy as the soldiers were to be recognized and to have their service appreciated by their highest military commander, they were even happier to know that this was Pershing's way of saying goodbye.[9]

Less than two weeks after their farewell visit from General Pershing, one regiment would receive another honor, and with it

Captain Thomas Armstrong of the 104th Field Signal Battalion receives the French *Croix de Guerre* from General John Pershing 24 March 1919 at Fresne, Haute Marne, France. *Courtesy of USAMHI.*

A closer view of the collar disks shows that this soldier personalized his insignias by removing almost all of the black coating, leaving only the letter for Company "D" with the original finish.

This version of the 29th Division patch from the Company "D", 116th Infantry Regiment uniform, shows a very nicely machine-embroidered pattern of blue and gray thread onto a wool disk, then sewn onto the tunic itself.

A well-preserved M1917 uniform belonging to an unidentified soldier from Company "D", 116th Infantry Regiment.

The 116th Infantry Regiment was honored 4 April 1919 at the AEF Headquarters in Chaumont with a review by General Pershing and the Commander of the British forces, Field Marshal Sir Douglas Haig. *Courtesy of USAMHI.*

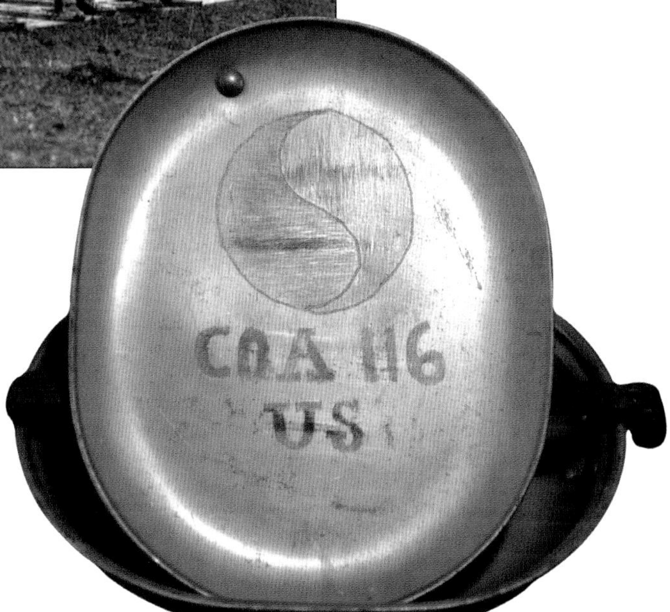

A carved mess kit plate from Company "A", 116th Infantry Regiment.

another chance to see Pershing. The 116th Infantry Regiment was selected to be part of an award ceremony at the AEF headquarters in Chaumont. This time, the awards would be presented by British Field Marshal Sir Douglas Haig to deserving members of the AEF. Following Pershing's Headquarters Band, the 116th passed in review for the commanders of the British and American forces, as well as several of their subordinate Army commanders. The 116th was particularly pleased when it learned later of Haig's compliments on their appearance and performance.[10]

After the review was over, Field Marshal Haig congratulated an officer of the 116th on the appearance of the regiment. Of particular note here are the wound stripe on the right sleeve of the American officer and the spurs on Field Marshal Haig's boots, indicative of his cavalry background. *Courtesy of USAMHI.*

A short while later, the division moved to Le Mans for final inspections and inventory of unit property, individual soldier's equipment, and administrative records. It seemed to the 29th that the wait for their turn to move to the port was interminable. In a way, the delay worked in their favor. Many of the problems experienced by earlier home-bound units had been solved. Other divisions, such as the 27th, had suffered through repeatedly unnecessary inspections and shakedowns while preparing to board the home-bound ships. This petty bureaucracy and needless harassment brought the departing units' morale to an all-time low. Encountering the problem during an inspection tour, George Marshall was able to get to the underlying cause. He discovered that many of the officers relieved from combat units for incompetency had been reassigned to these rear echelon billets, where their poor leadership skills allowed them to hide behind regulations and "orders."[11] There was also a tendency among the combat unit officers to go along with the process for fear that by protesting, they might actually make things worse. Neither of these attitudes were acceptable to Marshall, and his willingness to personally call upon the highest ranking officers in the AEF soon fixed many of the more aggravating problems. By the time the 29th was scheduled to depart, the redeployment process was much improved.

Two soldiers operating a standard Army clothing sterilizer and de-lousing machine. In spite of their best efforts, soldiers of the 29th would later report that some of the French "cooties" still made it aboard home-bound ships.

A very colorfully camouflaged helmet of a 29th Division Doughboy. This example is unique, in that the owner managed to carefully integrate his divisional symbol into the paint scheme. *Courtesy Scott Stevens.*

Looking surprisingly somber for a group of Doughboys soon to be headed home, the band of the 111th Field Artillery poses outside their billets in France. *Courtesy 1/111th Field Artillery.*

Not looking any happier than their comrades in the band, these soldiers of Headquarters Company, 111th Field Artillery regiment, also pose for a unit picture. Behind them, the windows are filled with other soldiers, perhaps waiting their turn for a unit photograph. *Courtesy 1/111th Field Artillery.*

The 29th's turn finally arrived, and with it came an increased emphasis on delousing the entire division to ensure that no "cooties" made it onto the ships going home. After that, it was a short journey via the French railcars that the 29th men had come to refer to as "side door Pullmans" to the seaport of St. Nazaire. By early May, most of the division was on the seas and headed for the east coast of the United States. First to sail was the Division Headquarters and the units of the 57th Infantry Brigade. This included the 113th and 114th Infantry Regiments and the 111th Machine Gun Battalion, which were loaded on the *Powhatan, Calamares, Floridian, Iowan,* and *Madawaska*. The Headquarters and the 114th were taken to Newport News, while the other units in this group went to ports in the vicinity of New York City.

Typical examples of the reading material the Doughboys of the 29th gathered as they were waiting their turn to go home. Along with joke books and tourist guides, they were also given pamphlets, such as "Keeping Fit to Fight," which warned them to "Keep away from the Whores."

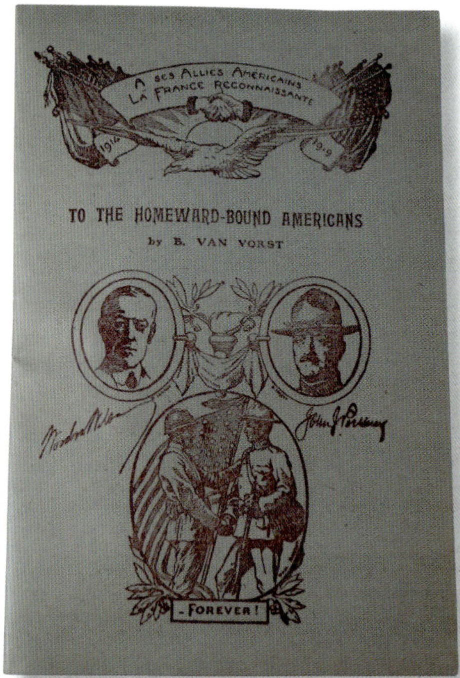

Inside one of the small booklets for the home-bound soldiers was this graphical depiction of the "forever" quality of American-French friendship. Unfortunately, by the time the 29th was deploying back to America, many members of the AEF were becoming disenchanted with their French friends due to the "price gouging" they suffered from local merchants.

Another scene familiar to soldiers of every era: "hurry up and wait." The members of a home-bound unit are loading onto a barge that will carry them out to a larger vessel for the voyage back to the States. As a side note, this appears to be a well disciplined unit, as indicated by the uniformly identical appearance of their packs with helmets and gas masks.

Members of the 112th Field Artillery Regiment march through the streets of a French town en route to their ship. The 112th sailed 12 May 1919 aboard the *Orizaba*. *Courtesy National Archives.*

Interesting shot of an America-bound ship taking on both coal and a contingent of Doughboys prior to departing Brest.

Due to their size and draft, some of the larger ships could not dock at the piers, so it was necessary to ferry the home-bound soldiers out to them. In this 1919 dated picture, a ferry is loaded to the brim with Doughboys en route to their designated ship. *Courtesy USN.*

Soldiers of the 104th Ammo Train pass time on the deck of the USS *Virginian* en route to Newport News, Virginia. The *Virginian* would arrive 25 May 1919 after a stormy thirteen-day voyage.

Heavily laden soldiers of the 29th Division board the ship that will take them back to the States.

A photograph of the USS *Artemis,* the ship that would carry the 115th Infantry Regiment back to Newport News, Virginia. The overcrowded ship carried four thousand soldiers home safely. True or not, and probably more so as a result of that crowding, the Maryland Doughboys quickly circulated the rumor that the *Artemis* was a converted cattle ship.

To keep the troops entertained during the long voyage back to the east coast, unit bands gave concerts wherever they could find deck space. Doughboys lucky enough to be on ships transporting nurses or American service organization females were able to dance with the ladies during calm seas. That the life boats' capacity are still marked "51 Personen" would indicate that this was one of several German ships confiscated by the U.S. and converted to troop transports.

Doughboys compete to be the first to spot land as their ship approaches America. Note that many are in shirtsleeves, indicating that this was taken probably in late spring or the summer of 1919.

A few days later, the 58th Infantry Brigade sailed from St. Nazaire on the *Manchuria*, *Artemis*, and *Matsonia*. The trip for the 115th was particularly notable because the *Artemis*, according to Maryland Doughboy lore, had previously been a cattle boat and was seriously overcrowded with more than four thousand Doughboys. In typical troopship fashion, an experience shared by all twentieth century U.S. servicemen deploying by ship, the entire day was seemingly spent waiting in the chow line. As soon as one meal was finished, the soldiers would immediately head to the back of the line, knowing that by the time they reached the front, it would be time for their next meal. Their ships arrived in Newport News slightly more than a week later. Among the last to leave France were the soldiers of the 54th Field Artillery Brigade, the 110th Machine Gun Battalion, and the 104th Ammo Train. These units were spread among the *Tiger*, *Orizaba*, and *Virginian*.

The summer-weight uniform for a Private First Class in Company "B", 115th Infantry Regiment. This uniform was most likely issued to the soldier after his return to the States, just before the unit was deactivated.

Closer view of the collar disks on the 115th summer uniform. The large-letter USNG disk is easily discernible, as is the Company "B", 115th disk.

Detailed view of the 29th Division patch from the 115th summer uniform. The intricate weave of the silk thread is easy to see in this photo, as is the khaki disk on which the 29th's symbol has been sewn. It is highly likely that this patch, the two overseas stripes on the left sleeve, the rank, and the collar disks are the only remaining components of the uniform this soldier wore in France.

Close up view of the 115th uniform's "Private First Class" crossed rifles patch on his right sleeve.

The Machine Gun Company of the 114th Infantry Regiment poses together for the last time 11 May 1919, just five days after their arrival at Newport News, Virginia. Shortly after this photograph, the unit would travel to their New Jersey home and be deactivated.

A close up detail from the previous picture; perhaps indicative of the severity of the fighting the 114th experienced at the Bois d'Ormont 12 October 1918, a very high percentage of the soldiers in the picture display wound stripes on their right sleeves.

A column of soldiers from the 111th Field Artillery Regiment parade before their family and friends. It's interesting to note in this shot, taken 25 May 1919 in Newport News, Virginia, that the soldiers of the 111th are still wearing their heavier wool tunics instead of lighter weight summer uniforms.

Upon arrival, the troops of the 115th were marched through Newport News' recently built "Victory Arch" to nearby Camp Stuart for final processing. The history of the 115th also records that the regiment was issued new lightweight "cotton uniforms" at Camp Stuart. This may explain why so many of the surviving 29th Division uniforms today are the lighter style, instead of the more commonly worn heavy wool uniforms. From Stuart, it was a short train trip for the 115th north to Baltimore, then on to Camp Meade for out-processing. Other 29th Division units headed to Army camps near their homes for their demobilization processing: the soldiers from Virginia and some New Jersey units went to Camp Lee, while other New Jersey units went to Camp Dix, New Jersey. During a week's stay at these camps, the men received a physical and turned in their military equipment. Now ready to be discharged, they drew their final pay and railroad fare to return home. Each soldier was allowed to retain a full set of uniforms, gas mask, and helmet.[12] After a final inspection and company formation, they were released from active duty and went home.

The M1912 uniform of Paul A. Klonowski. In the previous chapter, Klonowski is pictured in a M1917 wool tunic, indicating the uniform displayed here was probably issued to him and the other members of the 116th upon return to the States. Note that he has added a 1-4 September 1950 29th Division Reunion badge and smaller 29th Division pin next to his marksmanship badge. *Courtesy John Simmons.*

Typical of the "Welcome Home" items worn by 29th Division family members and friends, this pin honors the service of the 115th Infantry Regiment. Later, many of these same tokens would be worn by the soldiers at their reunions.

Another welcoming home pin for the 29th Division; it is unknown whether this pin was made for northern-based units of the division or was merely a manufacturer's mistake in placing the blue portion of the symbol on the right side, rather than properly on the left.

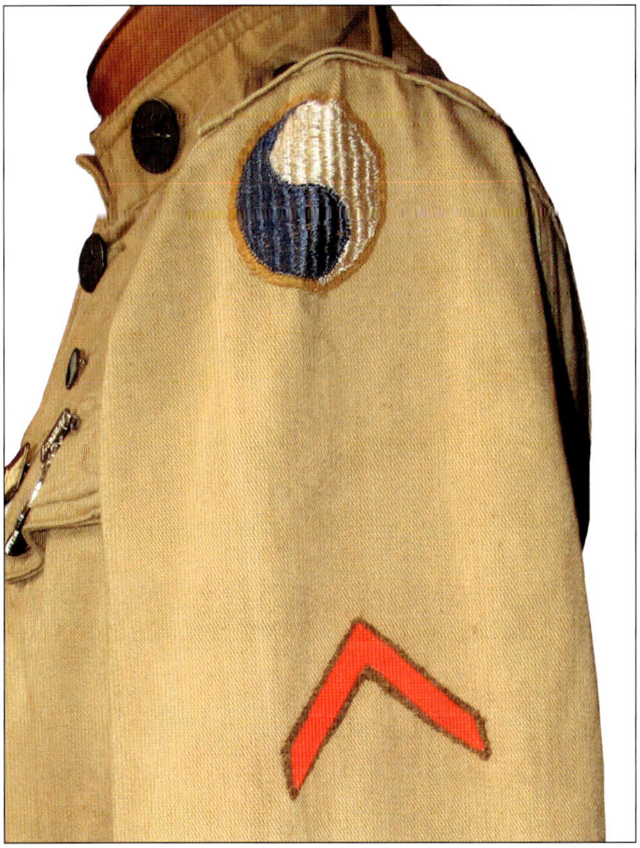

Another view of Klonowski's uniform showing the Company "L" disk, embroidered 29th patch, and the felt on wool discharge stripe. *Courtesy John Simmons.*

A view of Klonowski's British-made helmet with a painted 29th Division symbol. *Courtesy John Simmons.*

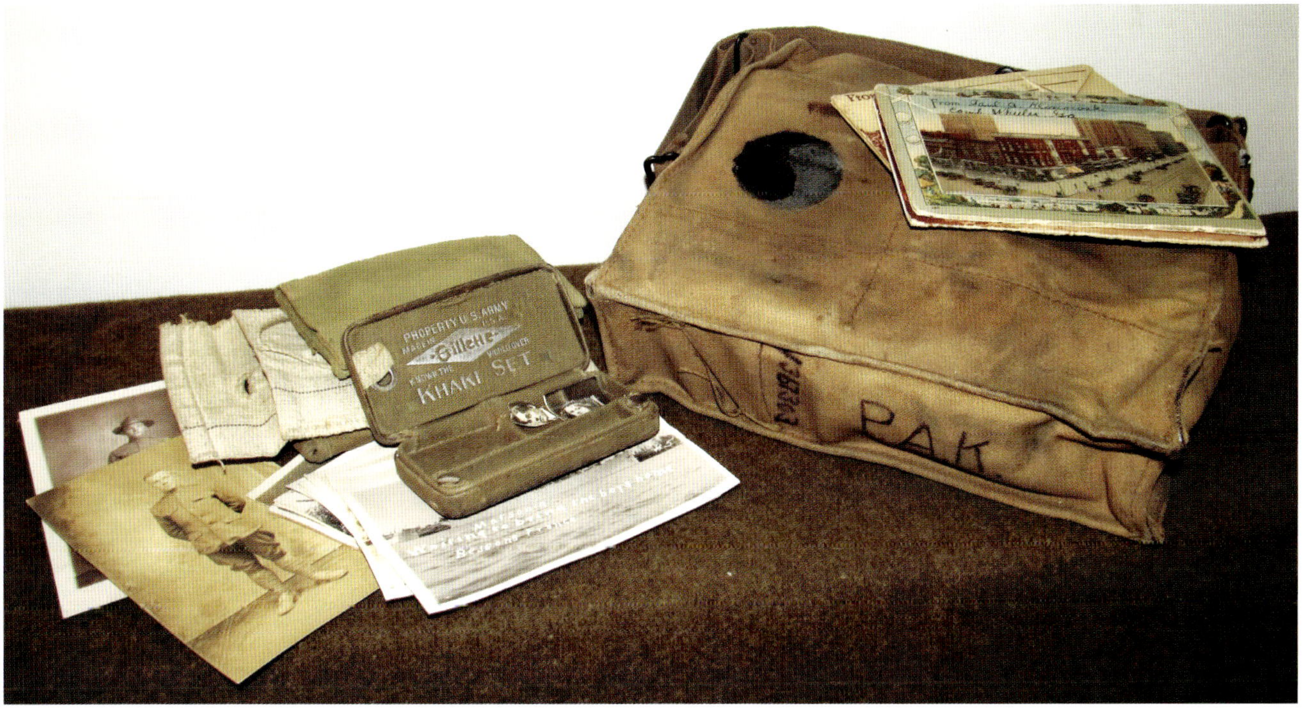

Some of the souvenirs Private Klonowski brought back from his time in the Army: a number of pictures, postcards, a shaving kit, a painted gas mask pouch, and even a picture of the USS *Matsonia*, the ship that carried the 116th back from Europe. *Courtesy John Simmons.*

There was no demobilization, however, for General Morton. Upon arrival in the States, he and the other Regular Army officers assigned to the division received orders to report to their next duty stations. For Morton, his new assignment was going to be a nice change from the rainy French weather; he was headed westward to take command of the Department of Hawaii.

A young girl posing with a 29th Division soldier, proudly showing off her "Welcome Home 29th Division" pennant.

An unidentified 29th Division soldier from Petersburg, Virginia, poses for his "back home" picture. He is wearing what appears to be a newly-issued summer uniform and has managed to find a campaign hat to accent his uniform. Although most soldiers appreciated the difficulties of wearing the campaign hats while on front line duty, many preferred them to the overseas hat.

Another "Welcome Home" pennant. This time, Jersey City welcomes back the "Hun Smashers" of the 29th and provides an alternative version of the division's patch; once again, the blue is on top, but now has been turned backwards as if seen in a mirror. *Courtesy John Simmons.*

A closer view of the collar area displays the Company "H" and "VA" collar disks, as well as another example of the "Welcome Home" pin.

Another example of an M1912 summer-weight uniform. Most likely the soldier sewed the 29th Division patch, red "Honorable Discharge" stripe, and the two overseas stripes himself, as they are crudely, yet firmly attached to the uniform.

A close-up view of the "Liberty Loan" woven style of yet another variation of the 29th Division patch.

A 29th Division Doughboy from Virginia poses for a "back home" portrait that has been transferred to a tin backing. Though faded and cracked, the soldier's overseas stripe and "Honorable Discharge" red stripe higher on his sleeve are clearly visible.

A Doughboy from Petersburg, Virginia, has his picture taken now that he is home. He has chosen to pose in a campaign hat and, for the first time, full length trousers are beginning to be authorized for wear with the uniform.

Home from the war, Germer Wright, a mechanic in the 113th Infantry Regiment, poses for a formal portrait. It appears that he, like many of the New Jersey Doughboys, has the blue side of his divisional patch on the right in the higher position. *Courtesy Charles G. Thomas.*

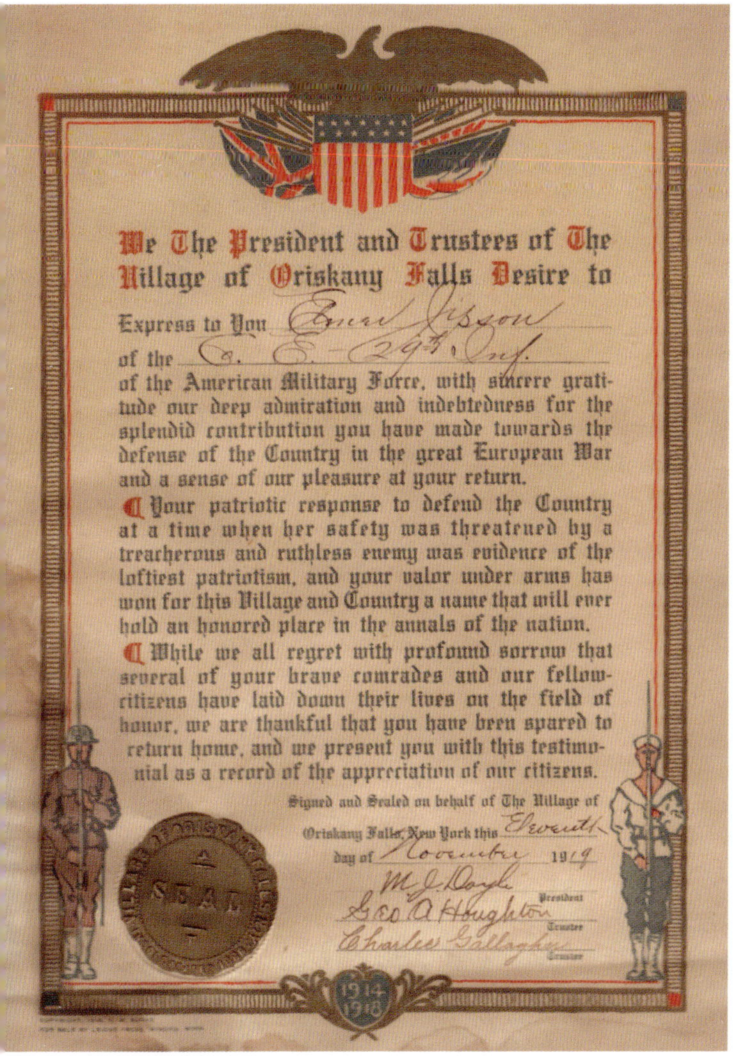

We The President and Trustees of The Village of Oriskany Falls Desire to Express to You [illegible] of the Co. E - 29th Inf. of the American Military Force, with sincere gratitude our deep admiration and indebtedness for the splendid contribution you have made towards the defense of the Country in the great European War and a sense of our pleasure at your return.

Your patriotic response to defend the Country at a time when her safety was threatened by a treacherous and ruthless enemy was evidence of the loftiest patriotism, and your valor under arms has won for this Village and Country a name that will ever hold an honored place in the annals of the nation.

While we all regret with profound sorrow that several of your brave comrades and our fellow-citizens have laid down their lives on the field of honor, we are thankful that you have been spared to return home, and we present you with this testimonial as a record of the appreciation of our citizens.

Signed and Sealed on behalf of The Village of Oriskany Falls, New York this Eleventh day of November 1919

M. J. Doyle, President

Geo. A. Houghton, Trustee

Charles Gallagher, Trustee

SEAL

1914 1918

Not all of the Doughboys in the 29th Division were originally members of the National Guard. Many of the replacements received at Camp McClellan and in France were draftees from other states. This certificate of appreciation from the town of Oriskany Falls, New York, was presented to a member of the 104th Ammunition Train.

Home at last; this infantry lieutenant poses for a portrait showing the Victory medal that was awarded to citizens of New Jersey "who served in the Great War." Also of interest here are his "Liberty Loan" style 29th Division patch and the barely visible wound stripe on his right sleeve cuff. *Courtesy Charles G. Thomas.*

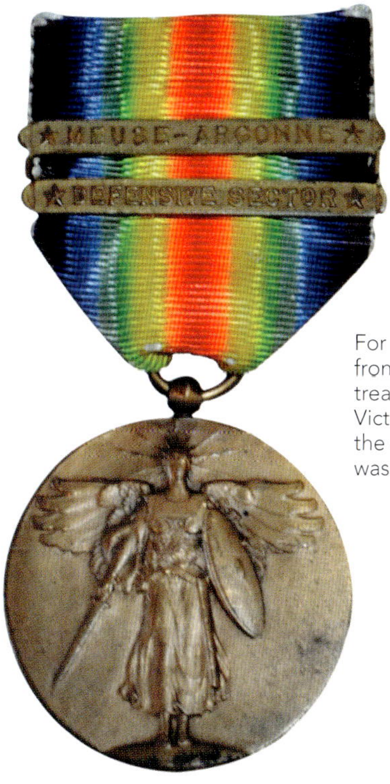

For soldiers of the 29th Division and other front line units of the AEF, one of the most treasured keepsakes of the war was their Victory Medal and the bars on it, indicating the campaigns for which the individual soldier was credited in the official unit records.

CHAPTER 5

The Interwar Period (1919 to 1941)

While the victorious American troops had returned from France to parades and cheering crowds, the American government performed the standard practice at the end of any war; the rapid drawdown and reorganization of the military to cut costs. Along with most of the other National Guard and National Army Divisions, the 29th was deactivated as a Federal unit. After this deactivation, National Guard units were returned to the control of each state's Adjutant General and Governor. Some of the regiments in these divisions reverted to their original prewar numerical designation (i.e., 1st Maryland and 1st Virginia), while others retained their wartime regimental number, as in the case of the 116th Infantry Regiment and the 111th Field Artillery.

The National Defense Act of 1920 provided for an all states combined National Guard strength of 436,000 soldiers,

The cover of the extremely rare 1923 "Year Book of the Virginia National Guard." *Courtesy John Simmons.*

Interwar collar disk set belonging to a Virginia soldier in Company "D", 116th Infantry Regiment. Of all the regiments assigned to the 29th Division, the 116th would be one of the very few to maintain the same numerical designation throughout the twentieth century.

The uniform of Captain Cecil C. Vaughn III. Vaughn had served in the Headquarters Company, 116th Infantry Regiment, during the First World War, and by 1923, he was serving on the staff of the 91st Infantry Brigade. The manufacturer's label inside the coat indicates that it was made in Norfolk, Virginia. *Courtesy John Simmons.*

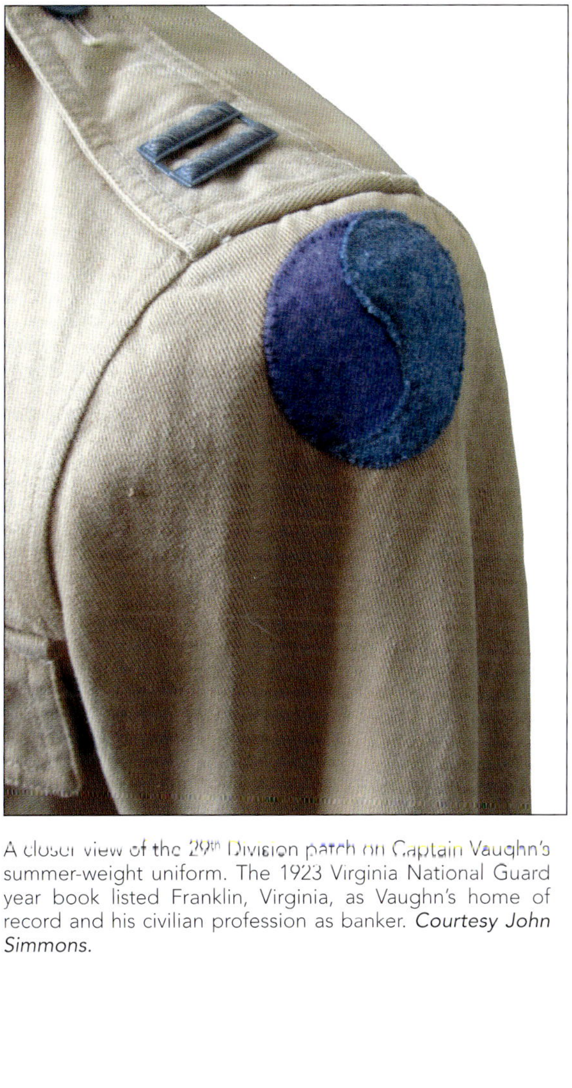

A closer view of the 29th Division patch on Captain Vaughn's summer-weight uniform. The 1923 Virginia National Guard year book listed Franklin, Virginia, as Vaughn's home of record and his civilian profession as banker. *Courtesy John Simmons.*

From the 1923 Virginia National Guard Year book; pictures of the staff officers of the 91st Infantry Brigade. Of primary importance here are number 1, Brigadier General Samuel Gardner Waller; and number 2, Captain Cecil C. Vaughn III. *Courtesy John Simmons.*

Enlisted collar disk for the Maryland 5th Infantry Regiment. The 5th Regiment would be redesignated the 175th Infantry Regiment 1 January 1941.

During the early twentieth century, many National Guard armories were designed and built to resemble medieval castles. This example was constructed in 1918 for use by the Hyattsville, Maryland, unit. It was followed by many others in Maryland, particularly during Governor Ritchie's administration. *Courtesy Library of Congress.*

A postwar formation of Guardsmen marching with rifles and full packs. Though the campaign hats have returned as headgear and rank stripes are again visible on the left sleeves, puttees have remained the standard leg wrap for the soldiers. *Courtesy Library of Congress.*

but during the 1920s and 1930s, the actual strength was closer to 180,000.[1] The Regular Army did not escape reduction and reorganization either. Along with most of the divisions, some twenty-seven infantry regiments were deactivated. Many of the regiments remaining had a battalion removed, so that of the thirty-eight regiments in the regular Army, fourteen had only two battalions apiece instead of the normal three. Internal battalion structures also changed, as headquarters companies were reduced in size to detachments, while the rifle and machine gun companies were reduced to having only two platoons from four. Ironically, the most robust units remaining in the Army during this period were those assigned to the American Forces in Germany (AFG). The AFG's three infantry regiments, associated artillery, and support units were almost fully manned. Their expertise in combat skills and high visibility as the American force in the Rhineland tended to give them an elite status within the U. S. Army. Not only were the soldiers provided almost unlimited training ammunition, they were stationed in a country where "Prohibition" had not dried up the supply of alcoholic beverages as it had in the States. The benefits of service in the AFG were not to be taken lightly, and once assigned there, the troops did their best to remain a part of that force.[2]

Another collar disk, this time for the 1st Virginia Infantry Regiment.

Officer's collar insignia with the letters "V" and "A" for Virginia individually superimposed over the U.S.

With the Army's 1923 reactivation of the 29th Division, the 104th Observation Squadron was added to the Maryland National Guard to provide aerial reconnaissance. Seen here is the unit crest for the 104th. *Courtesy Charles G. Thomas.*

THE VIRGINIA GUARDSMAN

VOL. VII. RICHMOND, VA., MONDAY, AUGUST 1, 1927. No. 19.

ASHLAND'S NEW ARMORY

CAPTAIN DANFORTH ASSI... 4TH F. A., FORT McINT... TEXAS

A SUMMER IDYLL

An August 1927 issue of *The Virginia Guardsman*. Among other stories, the paper reported on the building of a new armory in Ashland and provided information about schooling available for officers. Similar to the previous picture, the U.S. in the paper's banner has been overlaid with "VA" for Virginia.

On 31 July 1923, the Army reorganized and reactivated the 29th Division, keeping it a National Guard organization. It was now composed of units from the District of Columbia, Maryland, Pennsylvania, and Virginia, with the divisional headquarters in Washington, D.C. The Virginia contribution consisted of the 1st Virginia Infantry (later redesignated the 176th Infantry), 116th Infantry, 111th Field Artillery, and several smaller units, including the 29th Tank Company and 29th Signal Company. Additionally, the 246th Coast Artillery Regiment combined the various coastal artillery companies that had existed during the war into one non-divisional regiment. Maryland's largest contribution was the 58th Infantry Brigade, comprised of the 1st and 5th Maryland Infantry Regiments. Maryland also added an aviation unit (the 104th Observation Squadron) in recognition of the key role aviation would play in future conflicts. The 104th was formed from a private flying club that met in the Baltimore area. Although initially they had no uniforms or aircraft, most of the club members were former Army aviators with combat experience from the First World War. With the help of General Reckord, who was now serving as the Adjutant General of Maryland, they were quickly awarded federal recognition, and in July 1921, received their first aircraft, Curtiss JN-4Ds. The 104th was redesignated the 104th Observation Squadron 25 January 1923.[3]

During the interwar period, it was not unusual for a number of units to change names and numbers for both state and federal requirements. Adding to the confusion was the fact, as mentioned earlier, that while most Virginia units kept the numerical designations they had received during the war, most Maryland units switched back to their prewar designations. While these name and numbering changes may seem confusing, it is important to remember that by the 1930s, the 29th Division was almost exclusively a Virginia and Maryland unit.

A panoramic image of the 1st Coastal Defence Command of the Virginia National Guard taken at Fort Monroe in 1922. This unit would later be absorbed into the 29th Division.

A series of Maryland collar disks reflecting the variety worn from 1917 into the late 1930s.

The distinctive unit insignia for the 114th Infantry Regiment. After the First World War it reverted to the 3rd New Jersey Infantry until 1921, when it was again redesignated the 114th Regiment. Though it would never again serve in the 29th Division, the crest retained the 29th Division symbol as a sign of its previous affiliation and wartime service.

Well-preserved portrait of a Virginia National Guardsman from Petersburg, Virginia. The high-collared tunic seen here would soon be replaced by the newly-designed uniform coat with lapels.

The Petersburg Greys (Company "G", 183rd Infantry Regiment) take a break from training at Camp Trinkle, named for Virginia's Governor Elbert Lee Trinkle, to pose for a picture, most likely in 1922. It's interesting to note that the soldiers have set aside the helmet and returned to wearing the campaign hat for field duty.

In 1923, Company "G" poses again, this time joined by the unit cooks, seen standing in the back row at the far left and far right. If not for the enlisted soldiers wearing "puttees," this group could easily be mistaken as a prewar photograph.

Elbert Lee Trinkle, the Governor of Virginia, poses for a picture on the steps of the Virginia Capitol building in Richmond with Colonel Herain W. Smith, his National Guard assistant. *Courtesy Library of Congress.*

The well-worn uniform of an unidentified lieutenant assigned to the 116th Infantry Regiment. The World War Victory medal is adorned with clasps that reflect the officer's participation in the Meuse-Argonne campaign and the Alsace Defensive Sector.

A close-up view of the high quality, embroidered silk-thread on wool backing 29th Division patch on the officer's uniform.

1st Lieutenant Richard H. Ryan and a "match quality" 1903 Springfield rifle. Ryan was a member of the 1st Virginia Regiment and would later command the "Petersburg Greys." Of particular note in this picture is the leather "Sam Browne" belt converted for field wear. *Courtesy LTC (ret) James Ryan.*

A well-preserved portrait of a 116th Infantry Regiment officer that was most likely taken during the early 1920s, before the high collars were replaced by lapels on the dress uniforms.

A 116th Infantry Regiment soldier's worn, yet still serviceable campaign hat. Note that the unit crest, fastened to the hat with a screw post and round washer, reflects the 116th's motto which it earned in France during the war: "Ever Forward."

Ryan's English-made "Sam Browne" belt. This belt is clearly visible in several of the pictures of Ryan in this chapter.

During the interwar period, the Army began to field new infantry weapons, such as the 81mm Mortar, the .30 caliber machine gun, the 37mm anti-tank cannon, and various types of submachine guns to the Regular Army units. This resulted in greatly increased firepower in an infantry unit, despite reductions in the total number of assigned soldiers. Within National Guard units, however, the bolt action rifle and bayonet remained the basic weapon for their soldiers, as the newer weapons were reserved almost exclusively for Regular Army soldiers. For many National Guard units, the interwar period would be remembered as a period

One of the enduring symbols of the American soldier of the twentieth century; the two-man shelter half, better known as a "pup tent." In this 23 July 1921 image, a group of Virginia Guardsmen stand ready for tent inspection during annual training at Camp Meade, Maryland. *Courtesy Library of Congress.*

Calvin Coolidge, 30th President of the United States, poses with a group of senior National Guard officers in 1924. It is interesting to contrast this group with the picture of the Adjutant Generals seen in the Foreword. Standing in the front row, second from right, is Milton Reckord, Adjutant General for Maryland. *Courtesy Library of Congress.*

Taken in the 1920s, this picture of a formation of National Guardsmen standing at attention clearly shows the wide assortment of clothing styles and shades of color worn by the soldiers of the period.

of true austerity, as money for the Guard was simply not available. This is understandable to a degree. While the "Roaring Twenties" were a period of great economic growth for the U.S., no one in the U.S. Government or in the general population was overly concerned about maintaining a large military force. The "War to End All Wars" had been fought and won, so very few in power at the national level saw any need to provide continued support to the military. Nonetheless, National Guard units remained an important part of each state governor's administration. This became clear in January 1928, when Virginia Governor Howard M. Gore called out the soldiers of the 104th Ammo Train, now once again serving as the "Richmond Light Infantry Blues," to restore peace in Gloucester County, Virginia, where a dispute between independent oystermen and large oyster "farming" organizations threatened to become violent. The Guardsmen accomplished their mission and were withdrawn when a compromise was reached between the two sides concerning access to the oyster fields and the technologies used for harvesting the shellfish.[4]

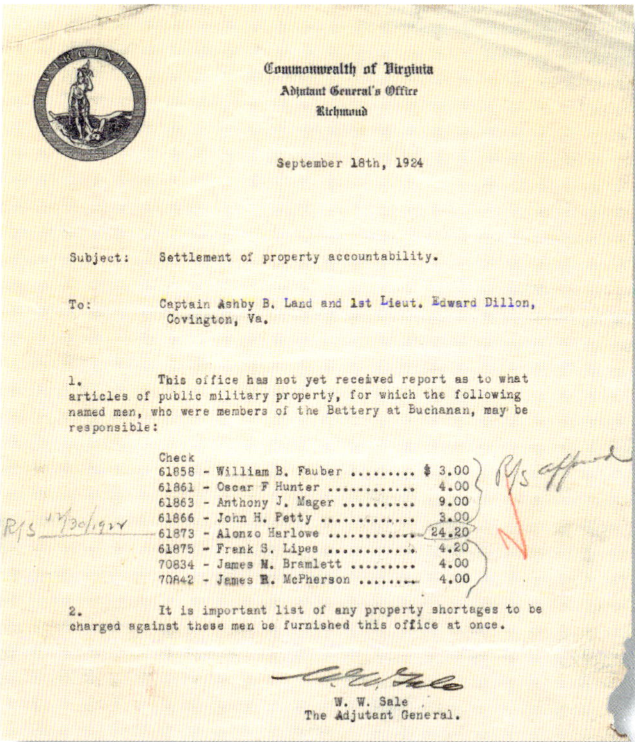

Commonwealth of Virginia
Adjutant General's Office
Richmond

September 18th, 1924

Subject: Settlement of property accountability.

To: Captain Ashby B. Land and 1st Lieut. Edward Dillon, Covington, Va.

1. This office has not yet received report as to what articles of public military property, for which the following named men, who were members of the Battery at Buchanan, may be responsible:

Check
61858 - William B. Fauber .... $ 3.00
61861 - Oscar F Hunter 4.00
61863 - Anthony J. Mager 9.00
61866 - John H. Petty 3.00
61873 - Alonzo Harlowe 24.20
61875 - Frank S. Lipes 4.20
70834 - James M. Bramlett 4.00
70842 - James R. McPherson 4.00

R/S 4/30/1924 R/S approved

2. It is important list of any property shortages to be charged against these men be furnished this office at once.

W. W. Sale
The Adjutant General.

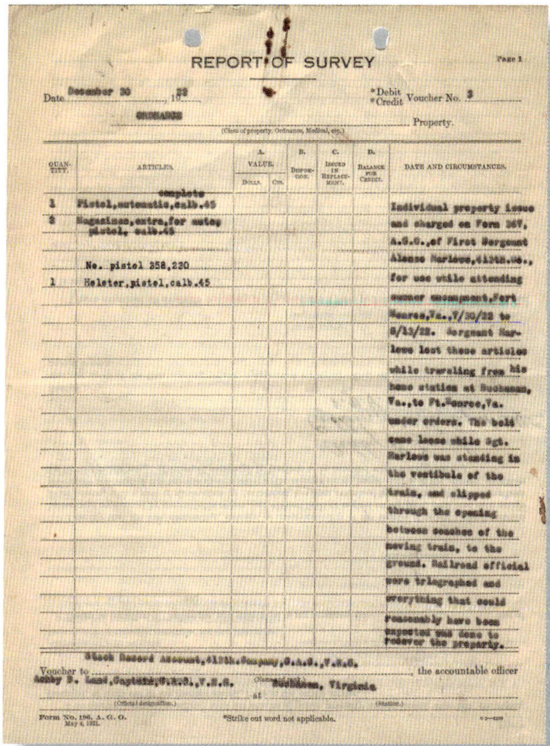

REPORT OF SURVEY — Page 1

Date December 30, 1922 — *Debit *Credit Voucher No. 3

ORDNANCE Property. (Class of property, Ordnance, Medical, etc.)

QUANTITY	ARTICLES	A. VALUE Dolls.	Cts.	B. Disposition	C. Issued in Replacement	D. Balance for Credit	DATE AND CIRCUMSTANCES
1	Pistol, automatic, calb.45 complete						Individual property issue and charged on Form 367, A.G.O., of First Sergeant Alonzo Harlowe, 4?th Co., for use while attending summer encampment, Fort Monroe, Va., 7/30/22 to 8/13/22. Sergeant Harlowe lost these articles while traveling from his home station at Buchanan, Va., to Ft. Monroe, Va. under orders. The belt came loose while Sgt. Harlowe was standing in the vestibule of the train, and slipped through the opening between coaches of the moving train, to the ground. Railroad official were telegraphed and everything that could reasonably have been expected was done to recover the property.
3	Magazines, extra, for autog pistol, calb.45						
	No. pistol 358,230						
1	Holster, pistol, calb.45						

Voucher to Stock Record Account, 4?th Company, C.A.C., V.N.G., the accountable officer
Ashby B. Land, Captain, C.A.C., V.N.G. at Buchanan, Virginia
(Official designation.) (Station.)

Form No. 196, A. G. O. May 4, 1921. *Strike out word not applicable.

A Report of Survey filed against First Sergeant Alonzo Harlow for losing his .45 pistol, holster, and two magazines from a moving train while en route to his unit's annual training at Fort Monroe in 1922. The narrative describes the incident and provides information that everything possible was done to recover the weapon.

Follow-on documentation from 1924 with a hand-written annotation indicating that Sergeant Harlowe's Report of Survey explanation was accepted by the Virginia Adjutant General. Note that resolution of this case took almost two years.

Also typical of the 1920s, Guardsmen in a variety of uniforms and headgear load their equipment in the back of a truck in preparation for either annual training or to prevent a civil disturbance. *Courtesy Library of Congress.*

On Black Thursday, 24 October 1929, the Stock Market crashed and the country was dropped almost overnight into what became known as the "Great Depression." One result was that the pay from membership in a state Guard unit quickly became an important source of income to many Americans as they struggled to find work to support their families. Another effect of the Depression was an increased number of labor strikes seeking better working conditions and higher wages. Given the large number of men that were now out of work, some industrial plant owners reached the obvious conclusion that it would be both easier and cheaper to bring in non-union labor to replace striking workers. Predictably, this led to some very violent confrontations between strikers, management security forces, and strike-breaking workers. Governor Pollard of Virginia mobilized the entire 116th Infantry Regiment for duty in November 1930 and deployed them to Danville to maintain the peace. A labor dispute between the owners of the Riverside Cotton Mills and the United Textile Workers of America union had turned violent. Striking mill workers prevented non-union workers from entering the mills by setting up a "human barricade." In retaliation, management had some of the strikers evicted from their company-owned homes. As the tensions rose, cars were overturned and the situation was rapidly deteriorating. At this point, the Governor ordered the 116th, commanded by Colonel H.L. Opie, to Danville to prevent further violence.[5] After more than two months of state duty, the 116th was relieved by the 246th Coast Artillery. The artillerymen remained on duty only for a short while, as the strike was broken when the union ran out of funding to feed the striking mill workers and their families.

A short while later, another phenomenon of the Depression appeared almost in the 29th's backyard. In 1924, in a more prosperous time, Congress had passed the World War Adjusted Compensation Act of 1924, which provided a bonus for veterans

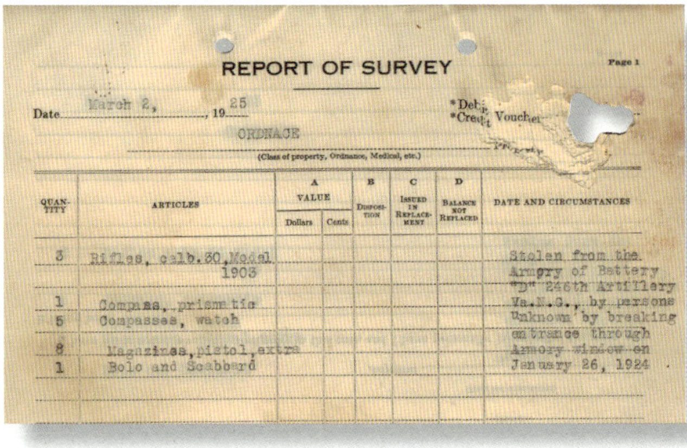

REPORT OF SURVEY

Page 1

Date March 2, 1925 *Debit *Credit Voucher

ORDNACE (Class of property, Ordnance, Medical, etc.)

Quantity	Articles	A Value Dollars	Cents	B Disposition	C Issued in Replacement	D Balance not Replaced	Date and Circumstances
3	Rifles, calb.30, Model 1903						Stolen from the Armory of Battery "D" 246th Artillery Va.N.G., by persons Unknown by breaking entrance through Armory window on January 26, 1924.
1	Compass, prismatic						
5	Compasses, watch						
8	Magazines, pistol, extra						
1	Bolo and Scabbard						

Another Report of Survey; this time dated 1925 and concerning the loss of three rifles and various other equipment from the Battery "D" armory as a result of a burglary.

Colonel Milton Reckord, standing third from right, is presented the Distinguished Service Medal by Secretary of War Newton Baker in a ceremony 20 February 1920 in Washington, D.C. *Courtesy Library of Congress.*

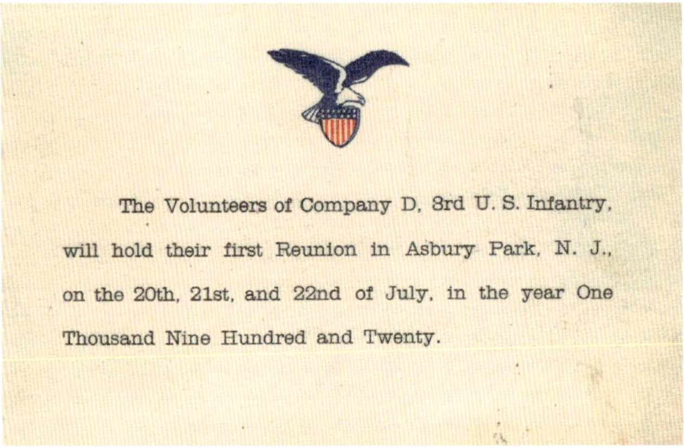

The Volunteers of Company D, 3rd U. S. Infantry, will hold their first Reunion in Asbury Park, N. J., on the 20th, 21st, and 22nd of July, in the year One Thousand Nine Hundred and Twenty.

Reunion invitation sent to the former members of the 3rd New Jersey Infantry Regiment in 1920. During the war, the soldiers of the 3rd New Jersey served in the 114th Infantry Regiment of the 29th Division.

A section of a 1924 panoramic photograph taken at Tobyhanna, Pennsylvania, showing all of the headquarters officers for the 111th Field Artillery Regiment. The commander, Colonel William H. Sands, seated third from the left, will lead the 111th, as well as all artillery units of the 29th Infantry Division throughout the Second World War.

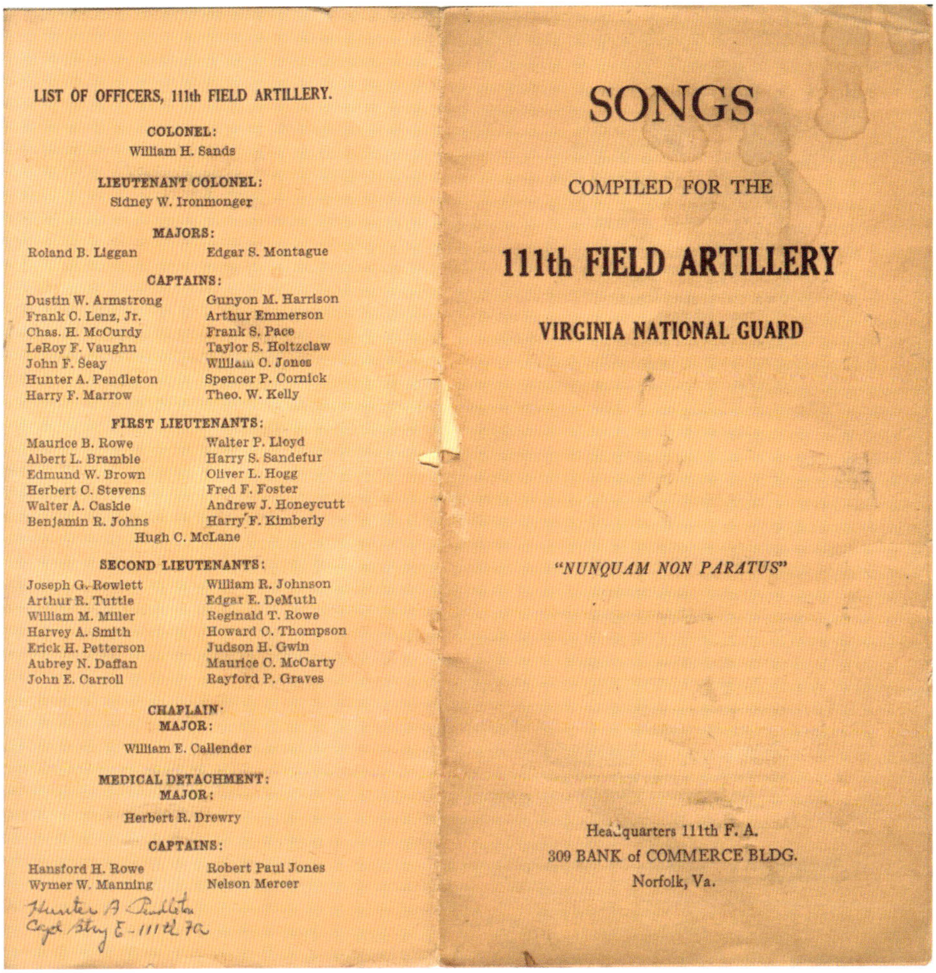

LIST OF OFFICERS, 111th FIELD ARTILLERY.

COLONEL:
William H. Sands

LIEUTENANT COLONEL:
Sidney W. Ironmonger

MAJORS:
Roland B. Liggan — Edgar S. Montague

CAPTAINS:
Dustin W. Armstrong — Gunyon M. Harrison
Frank C. Lenz, Jr. — Arthur Emmerson
Chas. H. McCurdy — Frank S. Pace
LeRoy F. Vaughn — Taylor S. Holtzclaw
John F. Seay — William C. Jones
Hunter A. Pendleton — Spencer P. Cornick
Harry F. Marrow — Theo. W. Kelly

FIRST LIEUTENANTS:
Maurice B. Rowe — Walter P. Lloyd
Albert L. Bramble — Harry S. Sandefur
Edmund W. Brown — Oliver L. Hogg
Herbert C. Stevens — Fred F. Foster
Walter A. Caskie — Andrew J. Honeycutt
Benjamin R. Johns — Harry F. Kimberly
Hugh C. McLane

SECOND LIEUTENANTS:
Joseph G. Rowlett — William R. Johnson
Arthur R. Tuttle — Edgar E. DeMuth
William M. Miller — Reginald T. Rowe
Harvey A. Smith — Howard C. Thompson
Erick H. Petterson — Judson H. Gwin
Aubrey N. Daffan — Maurice C. McCarty
John E. Carroll — Rayford P. Graves

CHAPLAIN·
MAJOR:
William E. Callender

MEDICAL DETACHMENT:
MAJOR:
Herbert R. Drewry

CAPTAINS:
Hansford H. Rowe — Robert Paul Jones
Wymer W. Manning — Nelson Mercer

Hunter A Pendleton
Capt Btry E - 111th FA

SONGS

COMPILED FOR THE

111th FIELD ARTILLERY

VIRGINIA NATIONAL GUARD

"NUNQUAM NON PARATUS"

Headquarters 111th F. A.
309 BANK of COMMERCE BLDG.
Norfolk, Va.

Front and back covers of a pamphlet designed to help the artillerymen of the 111th sing their favorite songs. Included among the songs are "The Red Guidon," "Dixie," "The Artillery Song," and a number of First World War hits. The address listed as the headquarters of the 111th Field Artillery in Norfolk is the same address that will serve as the 29th Infantry Division headquarters when General Sands is the division commander from 1946 to 1954.

of the First World War: $1.25 for each day served overseas and $1.00 for each day served in the States, with the caveat that the payment would not be made until 1945. Each qualified veteran that applied received a certificate with value equal to the soldier's promised payment. Now, worried about feeding their families and seeking early payment of the bonus they believed they had earned through their service during the First World War, some 17,000 veterans, known as the Bonus Army, marched across the country to Washington, D.C., in the spring of 1932. The organizers called it the Bonus Expeditionary Force as a spin on the American Expeditionary Force name they had served under in France. Many of these veterans had been unemployed and out of work since the beginning of the Depression. To members of the Bonus Army, the 1945 redemption date on the bonus was too far off—they needed the money now.[6] Numbered among the Bonus Army were several 29th Division veterans, including William T. Calder, who would become one of the elected leaders of the Virginia contingent to the BEF. Calder had served as the Supply Sergeant for Battery "D" of the 112th Field Artillery Regiment during the war. Joining him in the march was B.E. Chalkley, former cook in the 111th Field Artillery's Headquarters Company.

While there were many people in the country that supported the bonus marchers, there were an equal number who disagreed with both their request and their actions. Feelings were particularly strong in Maryland and Virginia. This was due in part to their geographic location as neighbors of the bonus marchers' Washington, D.C., destination. Among those on the side opposing the march was Samuel Gardner Waller, a former officer from the 116th Infantry Regiment now serving as the senior National Guardsman in Virginia; the State Adjutant General.

A 183rd Infantry disk for a Virginia guard unit. In 1922, the 1st Virginia Infantry was redesignated the 183rd Infantry and remained so until 1929, when it reverted back to the 1st Virginia. In 1941, the 1st Virginia was renamed again to the 176th Infantry Regiment. The 183rd would be reborn in 1961 as the 1st Reconnaissance Squadron, 183rd Armor Regiment.

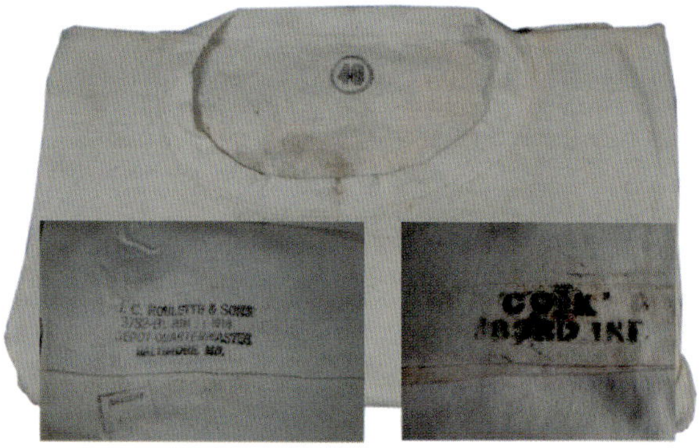

A unit-issued undershirt dated 1918 and clearly marked for Company "K", 183rd Infantry.

A clear indication of importance of Adjutant General S. Gardner Waller (third from left); here he fills in for the Governor of Virginia while placing a wreath on the tomb of George Washington at a ceremony celebrating the 150th signing of the Constitution. *Courtesy Library of Congress.*

Interwar 29th Division patch showing the high-quality weaving typical of the period.

Waller, a lawyer by profession, had significant local governmental experience, having been elected to four terms as the mayor of Front Royal. As seen earlier, he had also served on the Mexican Border and in France. His outstanding service during the war had been very well recognized and rewarded; Waller had risen quickly through the ranks until appointed by Virginia Governor John Garland Pollard to be the State Adjutant General. At first, Waller appeared to be sympathetic, or at least neutral, towards the marchers when he was quoted in a Richmond paper as saying that the marchers had been well-behaved and disciplined as they passed through Virginia.[7] The longer the marchers stayed in Washington, however, the stronger feelings grew on both sides. It soon became apparent that there could be no compromise to solve the problem. Still looking for a way to peacefully disperse the marchers and get them out of Washington, some D.C. officials met with Waller in hopes of getting his support to move some of the marchers out of town via Virginia-provided vehicles. Waller would not agree to this, even when informed that neighboring Maryland had already agreed to provide some transportation. Waller made it clear that Virginia could not afford the costs that would arise from moving the marchers south and west out of his state. Shortly thereafter, the Governor of Virginia, under advisement from Waller, decided that Virginia would close its border to the marchers unless they could demonstrate that they had enough money to pay for further transportation out of Virginia.

In the end, it didn't matter. The behind-the-scenes political activity to push a "bonus pay now" bill through Congress had failed, thereby ensuring that the marchers wouldn't receive their money early. That failure resulted in a decision by the marchers to the effect that they weren't going anywhere, and they would stay in their camps until Congress changed its mind. The few that did want to leave and attempted to pass through Virginia were rounded up by state troopers and escorted back to D.C. Shortly thereafter, President Herbert Hoover decided that the only way through the impasse was to send in the Army and forcibly evict the Bonus Army from their camps. The U.S. Army Chief of Staff, General Douglas MacArthur, personally took charge of the operation. Leading Regular Army troops, he soon had the marchers cleared out. MacArthur then directed the destruction of their camps. With Virginia's border effectively sealed, the marchers moved through Maryland until they ended up in Pennsylvania, where they attempted to set up more camps near Johnstown.[8] Surviving records do not reflect what happened to the 29th Division vets that participated in the Bonus March. Chances are they returned to their homes in Virginia and continued to suffer through the hard times of the Depression with many of their fellow citizens. While the marchers were being dispersed, another 29th Division veteran, and now a Colonel in the Virginia National Guard, John Cutchins, was interviewed in a Richmond newspaper and also took a strong anti-march stance. It was Cutchins' opinion that the Government should spend its efforts on fixing the economy, rather than dealing with the issues of the bonus marchers.[9]

Gun Chief Corporal Herman Lukehard supervising his crew while standing on a caisson of the 111th Field Artillery. Lukehard, a Richmond, Virginia native, had served in the 116th Infantry Regiment's Machine Gun Company during the First World War.

Another picture of Corporal Lukehard (far right) with members of his gun crew. Note the 111th Field Artillery crests on their campaign hats.

Master Sergeant Ward P. Burdine receives an award from Albert Cabell Ritchie, Governor of Maryland. Note the 115th Regimental crest on Burdine's helmet and the wearing of collar disks on the wool shirt. Ritchie served as Maryland's Governor from 1922 to 1935. *Courtesy Burdine Family Collection.*

Now in motion and led by a soldier carrying their guidon (far right), three horse-drawn cannons of Battery "B," 111th Field Artillery regiment take part in an exercise. *Courtesy 1/111th Field Artillery.*

An interesting set of 1902-style Sergeant stripes worn by Master Sergeant Burdine. The stripes are white, indicating infantry, and were rendered obsolete by the Act of 1920, which introduced a single color stripe for all Army branches. That said, due to the large quantities of these stripes still in the supply system, they remained in use as late as 1938. Also seen here are a set of National Guard "hash" marks (each stripe indicating three years of service) and a two-piece felt 29th Division patch. *Courtesy Burdine Family Collection.*

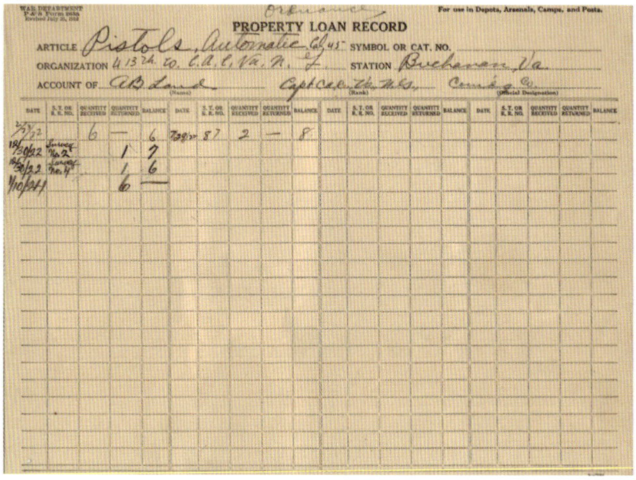

WAR DEPARTMENT

Ordnance

For use in Depots, Arsenals, Camps, and Posts.

PROPERTY LOAN RECORD

ARTICLE Pistols, Automatic Cal .45 SYMBOL OR CAT. NO.

ORGANIZATION 413th Co. C.A.C. Va. N.G. STATION Buchanan, Va.

ACCOUNT OF A.B. Land (Name) Capt. C.A.C. [illegible] (Rank) Comdg. Co. (Official Designation)

DATE	S.T. OR R.R. NO.	QUANTITY RECEIVED	QUANTITY RETURNED	BALANCE	DATE	S.T. OR R.R. NO.	QUANTITY RECEIVED	QUANTITY RETURNED	BALANCE	DATE	S.T. OR R.R. NO.	QUANTITY RECEIVED	QUANTITY RETURNED	BALANCE	DATE	S.T. OR R.R. NO.	QUANTITY RECEIVED	QUANTITY RETURNED	BALANCE
2/3/22		6	—	6	[illegible]	87	2	—	8										
12/30/22	Survey No. 2		1	7															
12/30/22	Survey No. 4		1	6															
1/10/24			6	—															

From 1922, a seldom-seen document; the original property book page for .45 caliber automatic pistols showing the transactions annotated by the unit property accountability officer.

On 5 June 1933, the National Guard of the United States was created and designated as a "Reserve Component" of the United States Army. The newly redefined National Guard would consist of the units from all of the States, the District of Columbia, and the Territories (Hawaii, Puerto Rico, Guam, American Virgin Islands, etc.). As a result of this legislation by Congress, all National Guard officers and men were sworn into their units at their current ranks. The ultimate result was that all of the Guardsmen were now considered part of the overall National Guard of the United States, as well as their own state. This greatly simplified many of the administrative processes that had to be performed when Guard units were to be activated for Federal duty.

The Regular Army was going through changes of its own during this period. Organizational and equipment changes continued to shape its operational capabilities during Douglas MacArthur's tour of duty as the Army Chief of Staff from 1930 to 1935. His vision for the Army of the future included smaller, more mobile units with greater firepower than their First World War predecessors.

A set of U.S. and Infantry collar disks from a Maryland member of the 29th Division. The gilt finish and very intricate background pattern, easily visible in this photograph, dates these disks to the period between the early 1920s to the mid-1930s.

Captain Robert Buford Rose (center) and two lieutenants pose with the regimental trophy Company "C" received for its "General Proficiency in Field Training." In the 1930s, Rose would command a battalion in the Richmond Light Infantry Blues.

William Thornton, one of the newest members of the 29th Infantry Division, poses with his rifle while still wearing his civilian clothes. Thornton would later serve as a Seabee in the Second World War.

An interesting grouping of collar disks for the 29th Division Headquarters: red/white for medical, blue for the 88th Infantry Brigade, green/yellow for military police, and yellow/white for Signal. The Washington, D.C., National Guard still use this National Capital image for their shoulder patch. *Courtesy Allan Henderson.*

Garrison hat worn by Lieutenant Colonel Rose, as seen in the previous picture. During this period, the "Blues" were part of the 1st Virginia Infantry Regiment.

"Expert" marksmanship badges for Rifle and Pistol that were earned by a member of the 115th Infantry Regiment.

Award presented to members of the Virginia Guard units after they completed six years of "Faithful" service.

Inevitably, these changes filtered down into the National Guard throughout the 1930s. In the 29th Division, some of the changes were far reaching and provided much needed modernization. In 1932, the 111th Field Artillery exchanged their horses for motorized vehicles to serve as the prime movers for their artillery pieces. Similarly, the tank company in the division turned in their First World War era tanks and received more modern armor. Most importantly, the 29th was now equipped with wireless radios, a major advance in tactical telecommunications technology.

The new equipment proved useful almost immediately, when the Virginia units were called to emergency state duty in response to natural disasters. Units in Virginia employed both the new trucks and new radios in recovery operations after a violent hurricane struck the Hampton Roads area in 1936. Using the organic communications now available at the tactical unit level, local commanders were able to keep General Waller, Virginia's State Adjutant General, apprised of the on-going recovery operations. In turn, Waller was then able to keep the Virginia governor informed of all the ongoing efforts. During this period, the 29th Division was commanded by Milton Reckord who, in addition, was serving as the Adjutant General of Maryland.

Many of the national level government policies aimed at spending money to create work and jobs to fix the Depression-shattered economy enabled the military services to obtain new

Ryan's award for fifteen years of faithful service in the Virginia National Guard. As can be seen, the award reflects the lineage of both the 1st Virginia and the 176th Infantry Regiments.

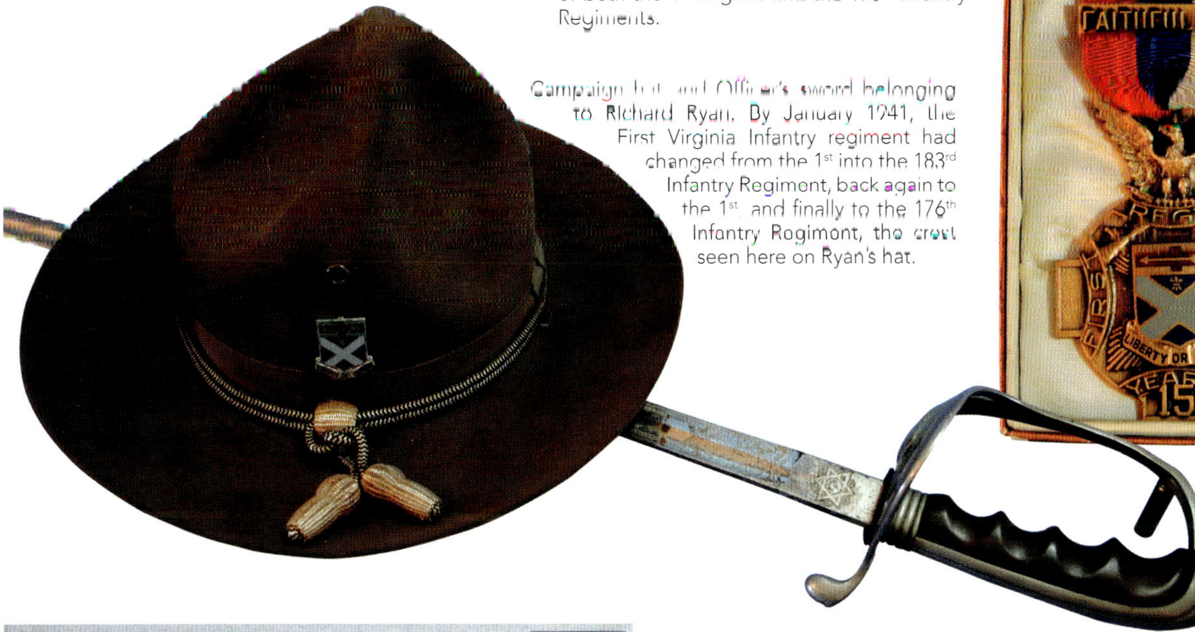

Campaign hat and Officer's sword belonging to Richard Ryan. By January 1941, the First Virginia Infantry regiment had changed from the 1st into the 183rd Infantry Regiment, back again to the 1st, and finally to the 176th Infantry Regiment, the crest seen here on Ryan's hat.

Sec. 562, P. L. & R.
U. S. POSTAGE
PAID
Richmond, Va.
Permit No. 512

The VIRGINIA GUARDSMAN

TWENTY NINTH DIVISION — NINETY FIRST INFANTRY BRIGADE

VOL. 13 — RICHMOND, VA. — JAN.-FEB., 1935 — Nos. 4 AND 5

1ST INFANTRY REGIMENT — 183RD INFANTRY REGIMENT — 111TH FIELD ARTILLERY — 246TH COAST ARTILLERY

29TH TANK COMPANY — 110TH HOSPITAL COMPANY — 29TH SIGNAL COMPANY — 110TH AMBULANCE COMPANY — STATE STAFF AND STATE DETACHMENT — 1ST COMPANY NAVAL MILITIA

CAPTAIN HENRY G. DICKERSON
Service Company, First Infantry, Virginia National Guard

FOR THE OLD DOMINION

The January-February 1935 issue of *The Virginia Guardsman*. Displayed on the cover are the crests of the four main units of the Virginia National Guard and a listing of the smaller units. Among the contents is a report on the upcoming summer training for the 29th Infantry Division at Fort Indiantown Gap, Pennsylvania. The author was Colonel William Sands, at the time commander of the 111th Field Artillery and later 29th Infantry Division Commander.

An ornate and well-worn cigarette case decorated with the unit symbol for the Richmond Light Infantry Blues. During the First World War, most of the "Blues" would serve in the 104th Ammo Train. After the war, they would be reorganized and become part of the 1st Virginia Infantry.

Flanked by two versions of unit crests is a newer version collar disk for the now "renumbered" 5th Maryland Infantry Regiment, reflecting its new designation as the 175th Infantry Regiment. The flanking unit crests for the 175th clearly show both the numerical and Maryland lineage of the unit. *Courtesy Allan Henderson.*

equipment and increased the number of men in uniform. That policy "was abetted by the troubled state of Europe. At first the growth was slow, so that by 1939 the infantry had risen 17,000 [soldiers] from its 1932 low. That year the overall policy changed. Whereas before 1939 the Army had been recognized as no more than a cadre, afterwards there was official recognition that an army-in-being was needed, and $1,000,000,000 appropriated to implement its creation."[10] There were other changes: tank companies were shifted from the divisions and concentrated in separate armored units. Large numbers of trucks were added to the units' Table of Organization and Equipment in recognition of the mobility and combat capability they provided. While most of the new equipment went to the Regular Army, some did find its way to the Guard, and the receiving units began to study intently how to best employ their new equipment.

Master Sergeant Ward P. Burdine of the 115th Infantry Regiment is seen here in a circa 1939 photograph. He is wearing a 115th crest on his campaign hat and is once again using the canvas leggings that would remain in service for field use until the appearance of the "Combat Boot" during the Second World War. *Courtesy Burdine Family Collection.*

Even with another World War approaching, there were still many vestiges of the First World War to be seen in National Guard supply rooms; this M1910 Haversack has been marked for use and accountability by Company "C", 115th Infantry Regiment.

For many veterans, the 11 November 1918 Armistice ending the fighting in the First World War remained an important date. During the 1920s and 1930s, it was often celebrated with dances and patriotic gatherings, as evidenced here by this 1931 dated postcard.

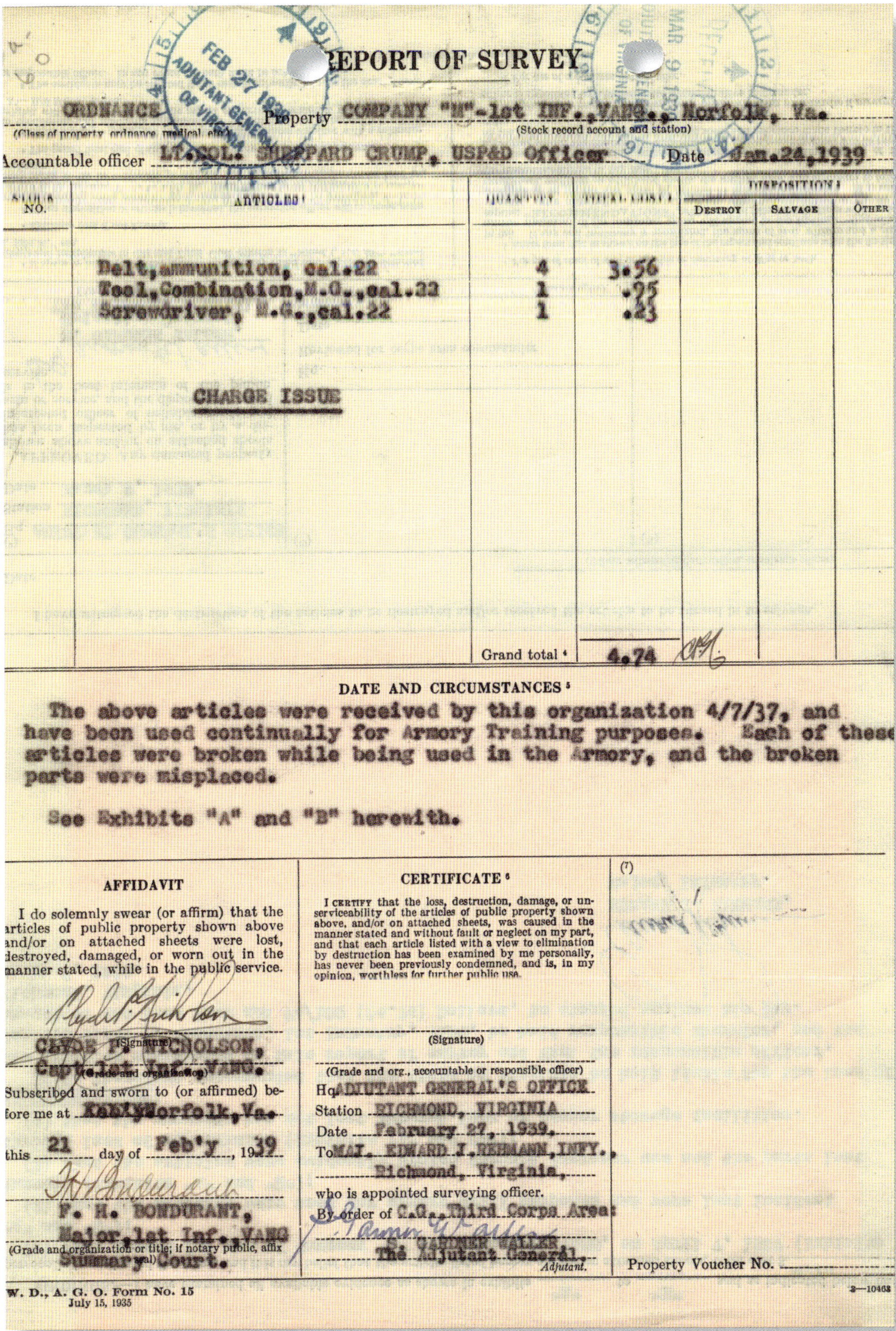

REPORT OF SURVEY

ORDNANCE Property COMPANY "M"-1st INF., VANG., Norfolk, Va.
(Class of property, ordnance, medical, etc.) (Stock record account and station)

Accountable officer LT.COL. SHEPPARD CRUMP, USP&D Officer Date Jan.24,1939

STOCK NO.	ARTICLES	QUANTITY	TOTAL COST	DISPOSITION: Destroy	Salvage	Other
	Belt, ammunition, cal.22	4	3.56			
	Tool, Combination, M.G., cal.22	1	.95			
	Screwdriver, M.G., cal.22	1	.23			
	CHARGE ISSUE					
	Grand total		4.74			

DATE AND CIRCUMSTANCES

The above articles were received by this organization 4/7/37, and have been used continually for Armory Training purposes. Each of these articles were broken while being used in the Armory, and the broken parts were misplaced.

See Exhibits "A" and "B" herewith.

AFFIDAVIT

I do solemnly swear (or affirm) that the articles of public property shown above and/or on attached sheets were lost, destroyed, damaged, or worn out in the manner stated, while in the public service.

CLYDE P. NICHOLSON, (Signature)
Capt. 1st Inf., VANG. (Grade and organization)

Subscribed and sworn to (or affirmed) before me at Norfolk, Va.
this 21 day of Feb'y, 1939

F. H. BONDURANT,
Major, 1st Inf., VANG
Summary Court.
(Grade and organization or title; if notary public, affix seal)

CERTIFICATE

I CERTIFY that the loss, destruction, damage, or unserviceability of the articles of public property shown above, and/or on attached sheets, was caused in the manner stated and without fault or neglect on my part, and that each article listed with a view to elimination by destruction has been examined by me personally, has never been previously condemned, and is, in my opinion, worthless for further public use.

(Signature)

(Grade and org., accountable or responsible officer)

Hq. ADJUTANT GENERAL'S OFFICE
Station RICHMOND, VIRGINIA
Date February 27, 1939.
To MAJ. EDWARD J. REHMANN, INFY.,
Richmond, Virginia,
who is appointed surveying officer.
By order of C.G., Third Corps Area:
S. GARDNER WALLER,
The Adjutant General,
Adjutant.

(7)

Property Voucher No.

W. D., A. G. O. Form No. 15
July 15, 1935

2—10463

An interesting 1939 Report of Survey that charged an officer $4.74 for misplacing "articles" after they were broken during training. Indicative of the budgetary issues of the times, this documentation had to be reviewed by the Accountable Officer, Lieutenant Colonel Sheppard Crump (later Adjutant General of Virginia), and signed by the current Adjutant General, Major General S. Gardner Waller. The investigation was conducted by Major F. H. Bondurant, who had served as a company commander in the 112th Machine Gun Battalion in the First World War.

The continuous experimentation, looking to develop the right mix of vehicles, weapons, personnel, and tactics, led senior Army leaders to the decision that the basic structure of the infantry division needed revamping. The leadership settled on having three infantry regiments assigned to a division. With the added firepower provided by the new weapons, the end result was a much smaller and more mobile division, with offensive capability equal to or exceeding its much larger predecessor. By 1939, the Regular Army's infantry divisions had been converted to this new organizational structure. However, most of the National Guard divisions were still configured in the old four-infantry regiment structure when they entered Federal service in 1940. As will be seen, events were on the horizon that would soon cause that to change.

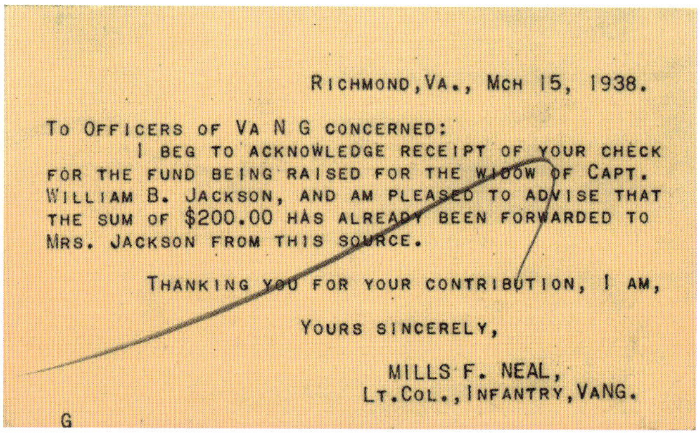

RICHMOND, VA., MCH 15, 1938.

TO OFFICERS OF VA N G CONCERNED:

I BEG TO ACKNOWLEDGE RECEIPT OF YOUR CHECK FOR THE FUND BEING RAISED FOR THE WIDOW OF CAPT. WILLIAM B. JACKSON, AND AM PLEASED TO ADVISE THAT THE SUM OF $200.00 HAS ALREADY BEEN FORWARDED TO MRS. JACKSON FROM THIS SOURCE.

THANKING YOU FOR YOUR CONTRIBUTION, I AM,

YOURS SINCERELY,

MILLS F. NEAL,
LT. COL., INFANTRY, VANG.

G

Evidence of the close-knit character of the National Guard units; this postcard, sent from Lieutenant Colonel Mills Neal to Lieutenant Colonel Sheppard Crump of the Virginia Adjutant General's office, is thanking him for the money raised on behalf of a soldier's widow.

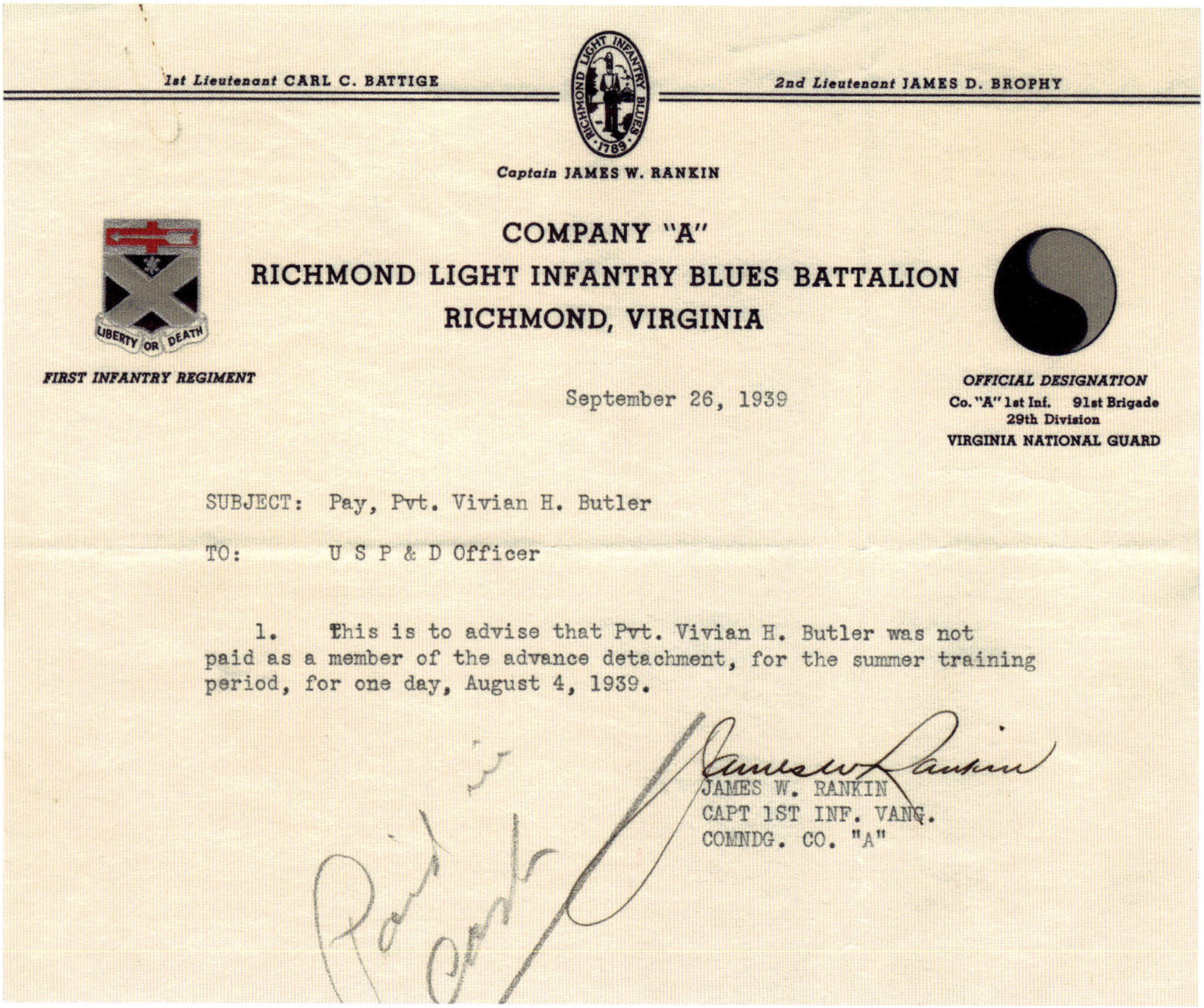

1st Lieutenant CARL C. BATTIGE — *2nd Lieutenant* JAMES D. BROPHY

Captain JAMES W. RANKIN

COMPANY "A"
RICHMOND LIGHT INFANTRY BLUES BATTALION
RICHMOND, VIRGINIA

FIRST INFANTRY REGIMENT

OFFICIAL DESIGNATION
Co. "A" 1st Inf. 91st Brigade
29th Division
VIRGINIA NATIONAL GUARD

September 26, 1939

SUBJECT: Pay, Pvt. Vivian H. Butler

TO: U S P & D Officer

1. This is to advise that Pvt. Vivian H. Butler was not paid as a member of the advance detachment, for the summer training period, for one day, August 4, 1939.

JAMES W. RANKIN
CAPT 1ST INF. VANG.
COMNDG. CO. "A"

Letter on official letterhead from a unit commander in the 1st Virginia Infantry to the state's military finance office to rectify a pay problem for one of the soldiers in the unit. Note the annotation "Paid in Cash" written on the letter and the fact that the letter is dated 25 September 1939, meaning the Second World War had already started in Europe.

Presented to soldiers of the Virginia National Guard for six years faithful service, the front of this medal has the seal of the state of Virginia and the U.S. and Virginia flags on the reverse.

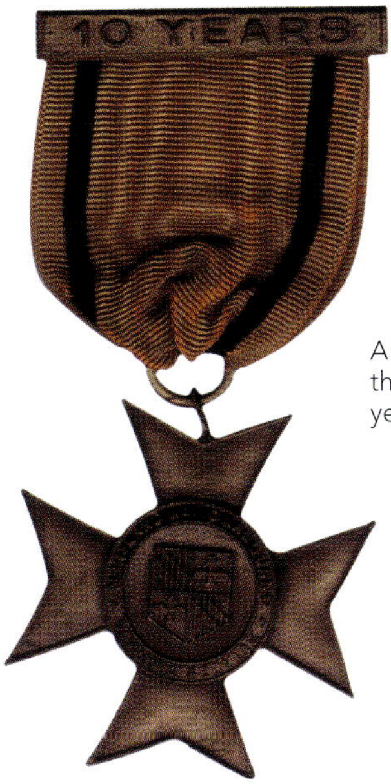

A medal presented to members of the Maryland National guard for ten years of faithful service.

An extremely ornate and embroidered early-version shoulder patch for wear by a Maryland National Guardsman on his dress uniform.

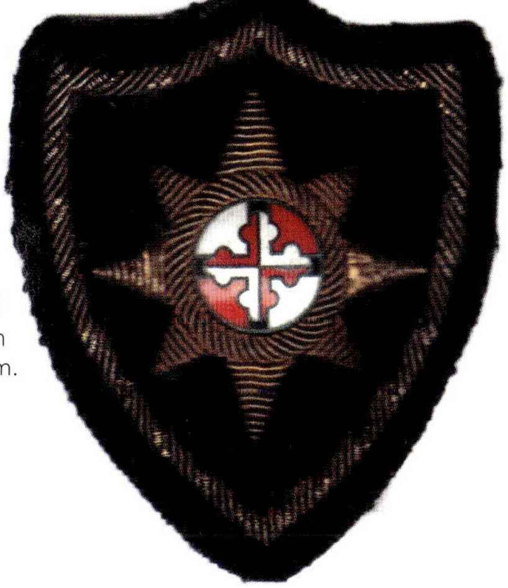

Following an age-old army tradition of marking their area, the cannoneers of Battery "B," 111th Field Artillery Regiment have created, using rope and rocks, an image of their unit insignia during annual training at Fort Indiantown Gap, Pennsylvania, in 1936. *Courtesy 1/111th Field Artillery.*

Another reflection of the Blue and Gray lineage of the 29th Division, a National Guard major enjoys showing two elderly Civil War veterans around his 75mm self-propelled gun.

CHAPTER 6

Mobilization (1941 to 1942)

In 1939, Europe plunged into its second major conflict of the century, causing the American government to once again begin the slow painful process of mobilizing its own armed forces. The problems and pitfalls encountered in mobilizing the United States' military might are, for the most part, beyond the scope of this book. However, as mentioned earlier, there were some organizational changes in the basic structure of the U.S. Army Infantry Division, as well as problems associated with the mobilizing of the National Guard units that must be described in order to understand how they affected the 29th Division.

During the First World War, the number of soldiers in the state guard units being mobilized was found to be insufficient to meet the personnel demands of the newly designed divisions of the Army. At the start of the Second World War, the same proved true. Therefore, the twenty or so divisions formed from National Guard units would, once again, require augmentation from either volunteers or draftees.

When the 29th Infantry Division was federalized, the soldiers were still wearing First World War-style helmets and were equipped with vehicles mounting the M1917A1 .30 Caliber water-cooled heavy machine gun, as seen in this parade of 176th Infantry Regiment troops and vehicles.

There was another interesting aspect of the Guardsmen of this era when compared to the First World War version. They were significantly larger: "The average recruit was five feet ten inches tall and wore size ten shoes, while the average draftee of the earlier generation was five feet seven and a half inches in height and wore slightly over size seven shoes."[1] Another major difference was also size-related: this time the size of the force that was required to fight the war. The United States was going to need a much larger military force to fight the Germans and Italians in Europe and the Japanese in Asia and the Pacific. In fact, before the war was over, more than sixteen million Americans had served in the military and over eleven million of them were in the Army.[2]

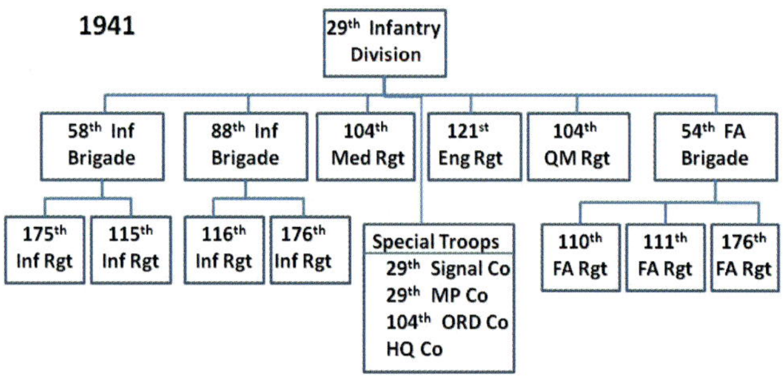

When the 29th was activated in February 1941, it reported to Fort Meade, Maryland, still configured like a First World War division, with four infantry and three field artillery regiments. Within a short period they would have a new commander, Major General Leonard Gerow, who would be responsible for converting the 29th to the new "triangle" configuration.

In contrast to the overall size of the soldiers and the total force, the size of the division became smaller. In the Second World War, the basic infantry division was designed on a new doctrinal principle for combat operations that became known

An image of the 29th's Fort Meade barracks area taken from the Divisional headquarters. The mud in the foreground and the unpainted building nearby would indicate this was taken fairly soon after the 29th arrived. Soldiers would later refer to the post as "Fort Mud."

Private First Class Willis Robertson, a member of the Medical Detachment of the 176th prior to the regiment being transferred from the 29th Infantry Division. After the war, Robertson lived on High Street in Petersburg, Virginia, in the same building that Robert E. Lee used as a headquarters during the Civil War siege.

Unit crest for the 176th Infantry Regiment. After the 29th was "triangularized," the 176th was assigned to other duties and did not serve with the 29th Division during the war. *Courtesy Allan Henderson.*

as "triangularization." Triangularization was based on a simple tactical concept: combat units were to be organized into three modular elements. This committed one element to conduct the attack and another to conduct a decisive maneuver in support of the attack. The third element would remain as a reserve to either support the attacking force or exploit any breakthrough. This same concept was applied at all levels of infantry units. There would be three squads in a rifle platoon, three rifle platoons in a company, and so on. This pattern followed all the way up to the division, where there were now three infantry regiments instead of the previous four.[3]

Just as happened in the First World War, when the Guard units were mobilized, the new structure completely changed how the units were organized in their own states. Units with historic lineages and habitual relationships were once again swept away or transferred to other organizations. All this lay in the future for the men of the Blue and the Gray; when federalized, the 29th Division reported to active duty still in the older, pre-triangularization structure.

During the 1930s, a great deal of thought and discussion had gone into planning how the United States would mobilize its armed forces should the need arise again. The "Protective Mobilization Plan of 1937" laid out a road map, where one of the key first steps would be to federalize all of the National Guard units. The Guard units would then be the trained force that could defend the country while the Regular Army was expanding in size and training a draftee force large enough to defeat the enemy. Included in the plan were some initial training center locations and rudimentary programs of instruction for training soldiers.[4]

By August 1940, the war in Europe and Asia had reached the boiling point, thus leading the U.S. Congress to authorize the induction of the National Guard into federal service. At the same time, it began the process of drafting men for the Army and the Navy. By the fall of 1941, there were thirty-four Army divisions

An aerial view of the 29th Infantry Division's area on Fort Meade cut either from a magazine or postcard and found in a soldier's scrapbook. Fort Meade would be home to the 29th for almost eighteen months.

Major General Milton Reckord, 29th Infantry Division Commander from 1934 until 1942. Reckord's military service started before the First World War and continued until 1966, when he retired at the age of eighty-six. The faded inscription appears to be addressed to William "Billy" Sands, the 29th's premier artilleryman. *Courtesy NGEF.*

Starting in 1937, the Army changed to a two-piece collar disk style. This example, with a screw-post fastener and a superimposed "MD" for Maryland, is typical of the US disk that would have been used before the unit was called to active duty.

undergoing training in the United States: twenty-seven infantry, five armored, and two cavalry. Among the last of the Guard divisions mobilized, the 29th was brought into active service 3 February 1941. After initial assembly at their armories, the soldiers of the Blue and Gray Division were then sent to Fort Meade, Maryland, for training. Though Fort Meade had been designated by the Army as a permanent facility 5 March 1929—hence the name "Fort Meade" instead of "Camp Meade"—the first impressions of the post were not favorable and it was jokingly referred to as "Fort Mud." One young officer later recalled "Everything had a flayed look; unpainted wooden barracks sprouted in rows out of vast, rutted, sandy fields, and cleared vegetation was bulldozed into huge piles all under a dull gray-glass sky that threatened snow."[4]

The 57th and 58th Infantry Brigades, so integral to the 29th's performance in the Meuse-Argonne, were deactivated as part of an army-wide removal of brigade staffs and structures from divisions. The troops from these staffs were spread among the other units in the division.

The shoulder patch that was worn by some Maryland Guard units in the early 1940s. Note the black and yellow version of the 29th Division patch, providing the background for the red and white cross representing Maryland.

Another picture of the barracks in the 29th Infantry Division's area, this time from a 115th Infantry Regiment soldier's collection. The building in the forefront shows a building number "T657." The "T" indicates it is a temporary building, certainly a misnomer, since some of these 1940 "temporary" structures are still standing and remain in use at U.S. Army posts today.

Another view of the 29th Infantry Division barracks complex at Fort Meade. Though the barracks are still unpainted, it appears that most of the ever-present mud has been cleaned up.

Unit crest and one-piece collar disk for the 115th Infantry Regiment. *Courtesy Allan Henderson.*

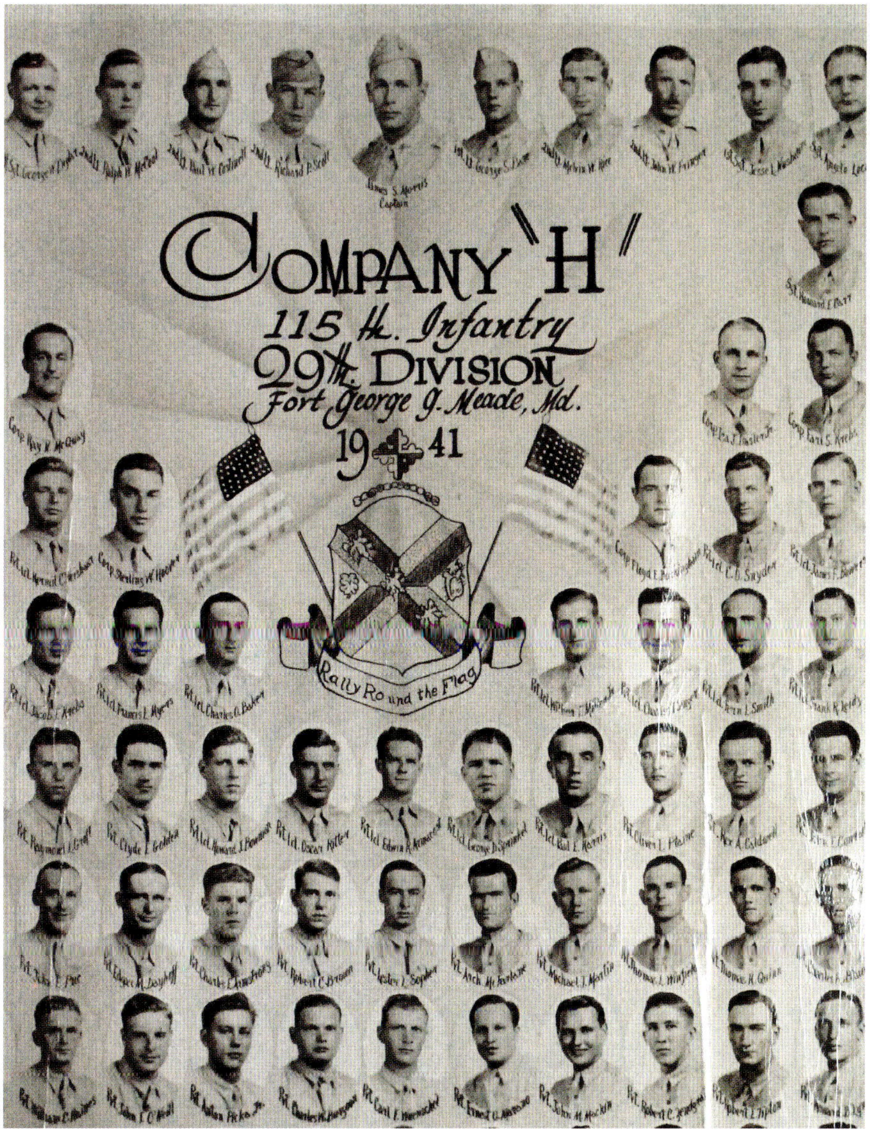

Perhaps fortunate to be among the last of the Guard divisions called to active duty, the 29th escaped some of the well-intentioned, but ultimately very destructive "harvesting" of cadres to support or fill out other units. The 30th Infantry Division, originally comprised of Guardsmen from the Carolinas, was harvested so many times that by the time they deployed to Britain, they had lost and replaced almost twelve thousand soldiers. Similar problems were also affecting the draftee divisions, and quite possibly were the causes of some of the initial performance problems displayed by these units in combat. As it was, "Whether by luck, or happenstance dictated by its place in the mobilization queue, the 29th escaped the most deleterious effects of personnel stripping."[115]

A unit photograph of the officers and men of Company "H", 115th Infantry Regiment taken at Fort Meade. Company "H", commanded by Captain James S. Morris, would be part of the D-Day assault on Omaha Beach. *Courtesy Teena Gordon.*

Wearing a fatigue uniform, this soldier is being coached in marksmanship while firing a bolt-action Springfield rifle. Before long, the Springfield would be replaced by the new standard for U.S. infantrymen, the M1 Garand. *Courtesy USAQM Museum.*

Unit collar disk for the 110th Field Artillery Battalion. On this multi-part disk, the U.S. has had the numbers for the 110th Field Artillery regiment and the Maryland "MD" added. *Courtesy Allan Henderson.*

In hindsight, it's interesting to note that during the period after being drafted, or their unit's mobilization, and prior to the Japanese attack on Pearl Harbor, many soldiers doubted a "state of emergency" actually existed. As a result, their morale was extremely low. A survey of soldiers and units across the Army, later known as the "Railey Report," indicated that a great number of soldiers believed their equipment was inadequate, their officers were unskilled or incompetent, and they wanted to go home. From his vantage point as the Commander of the 29th, Milton Reckord was not convinced, and when visited by the survey team was uncooperative. Keeping in mind that during this period Reckord was both the 29th Division Commander and the Adjutant General of Maryland, it's easy to understand why Reckord would view unfavorably any report that implied there were problems with National Guard units.

While the 29th was training for war, back home in Virginia, General S. Gardner Waller, still serving as Virginia's Adjutant General, was busy as well. Under his direction, Virginia established the equivalent of another State Guard that would take on the responsibility for protecting Virginia while the National Guard was deployed. This new formation was known as the Virginia Reserve Militia (VRM), and their mission was "To furnish immediate local protection against saboteurs and raiding parties, destroying them or serving as a holding force, pending the arrival of better equipped troops."[6]

Each county or city in the state was directed to recruit and maintain a unit which would be designated a "company." The company would have three officers and fifty enlisted men. A unique requirement of the VRM, probably reflecting the fact that most military vehicles were already designated for use by the Regular Army, was that each soldier in the unit had to own a car or truck that could transport an entire squad. Also reflecting the wartime shortages caused by the requirement to field the national military force, VRM members had to provide their own weapons and ammunition.

To the north, the Governor of Maryland had come to the same conclusion; a state guard was needed to replace the federalized National Guard units. Even prior to Pearl Harbor, Governor Herbert O'Conor signed into law an emergency measure that called for the activation of the "Maryland State Guard." After the Japanese attack 7 December 1941, the Maryland units of the State Guard were called out to protect reservoirs, bridges, industrial areas, and sewer plants. Interestingly enough, the funding to pay these new units came not from military budgets, but from the state gasoline tax fund. More lavishly equipped than their Virginia neighbors, the Maryland State Guard units wore U.S. Army uniforms, had military police insignias, and were armed with bolt action Springfield or Enfield rifles. In spite of several accidental shooting incidents at the Kent Narrows Bridge and the Havre de Grace Bridge, the Maryland guard units remained on duty throughout the war, making their own contribution to the war effort.[7]

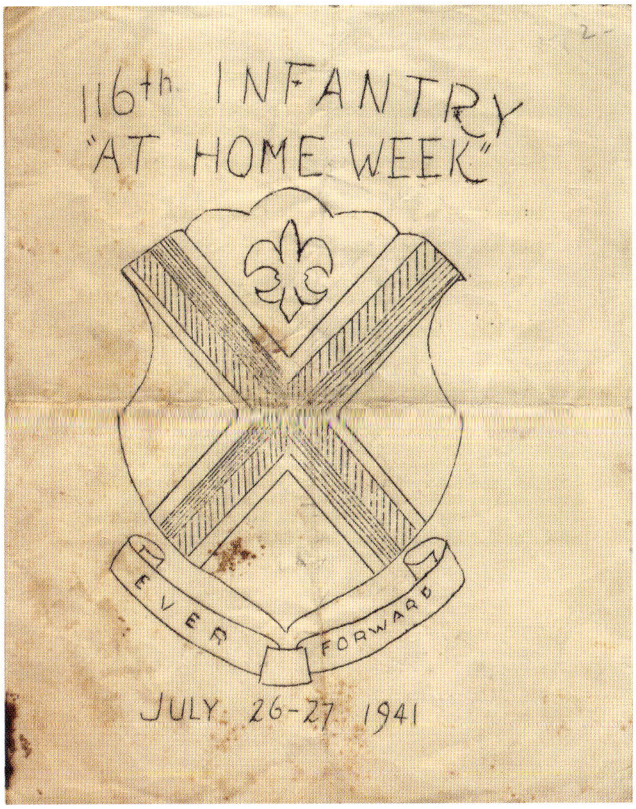

A locally-reproduced program listing the schedule of events that would take place on the 116th's "Family Visit" weekend. Along with a number of religious services, family members would be given a chance to inspect the barracks, enjoy a band concert, and review a regimental parade.

An aerial shot of Camp A. P. Hill, Virginia, showing the "tent city" occupied by the 29th Infantry Division during their time there. An interesting comparison with this picture is the "tent city" photo of the 29th at Camp McClellan shown in chapter two. *Courtesy National Archives.*

A group of soldiers from the 176th Infantry in a variety of work and fatigue uniforms stand in line waiting for chow. This photo and the next were most likely taken at Camp A.P. Hill in Virginia during maneuvers.

This soldier, wearing a campaign hat with a 111th Field Artillery crest, takes time for a picture while standing in the middle of his unit's "tent city."

The distinctive unit crest for the 111th Field Artillery. With the reorganization, this regiment was reduced to battalion size while still retaining the same unit crest. Other soldiers from the regiment were used to create the 227th Field Artillery Battalion, a 155mm Howitzer-equipped unit.

Before being reassigned, some members of the 176th Infantry Band showcase their musical skills at an event held by the 29th.

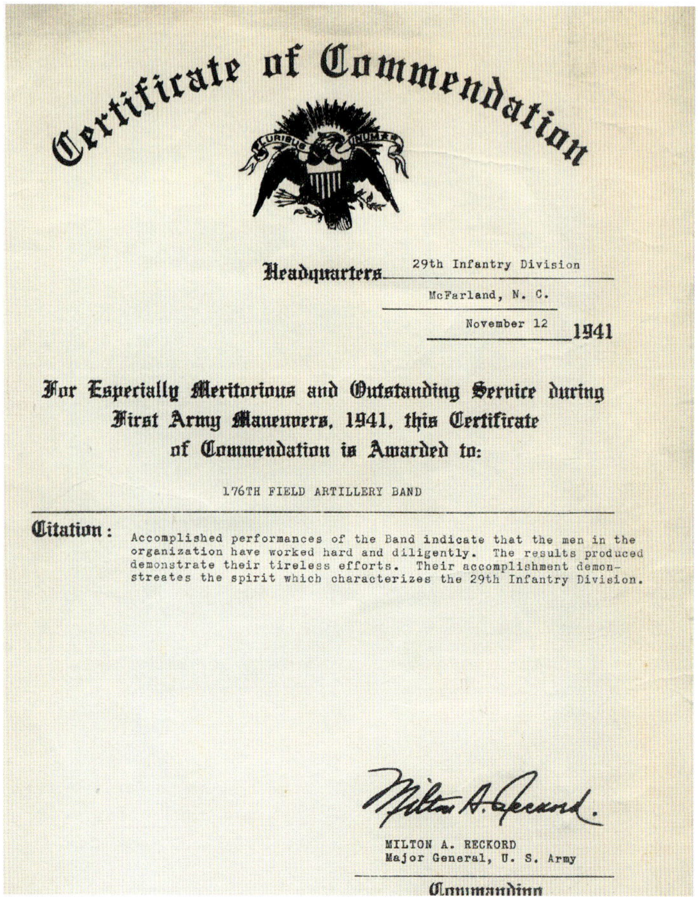

Certificate of Commendation

Headquarters 29th Infantry Division
McFarland, N. C.
November 12 1941

For Especially Meritorious and Outstanding Service during First Army Maneuvers, 1941, this Certificate of Commendation is Awarded to:

176TH FIELD ARTILLERY BAND

Citation: Accomplished performances of the Band indicate that the men in the organization have worked hard and diligently. The results produced demonstrate their tireless efforts. Their accomplishment demonstreates the spirit which characterizes the 29th Infantry Division.

Milton A. Reckord

MILTON A. RECKORD
Major General, U. S. Army
Commanding

As a testament to their musical abilities, the 29th Division Commander, Major General Milton Reckord, awarded the 176th Field Artillery Band a letter of commendation for their performance during the 1941 First Army maneuvers.

Meantime, the 29th's training was getting more intense and more complicated, as the division participated in the "Carolina Maneuvers" under the command of the First Army. The 29th made a strong showing in the large scale exercise that stretched over several states. For their performance, the Blue and Gray were declared the victors over their opponents, the Pennsylvania National Guardsmen of the 28th Infantry Division. While many of the senior Army staff were pleased with the overall results and evaluations conducted during the maneuvers, one participant from a Virginia unit recalled the exercise as "a huge, uncomfortable, motorized camping trip."[8]

After mobilization, along with required military education and combat training, National Guard soldiers spent a great deal of time defending coastal areas from possible enemy attacks. This soldier, with equipment reminiscent of the First World War, is guarding Fort Story, near Virginia Beach, Virginia. *Courtesy Library of Congress.*

Ulric "Rock" Rothgeb, a Virginia native and member of Company "G", 116th Infantry Regiment, poses for a picture at Fort Meade. Rothgeb would later be wounded twice and earn a Bronze Star for bravery in action near St. Lô.

Here are examples of four slightly different versions of the 116th Infantry Regiment crest. As with shoulder patches, there were almost as many variations of unit crests during this period as there were manufacturers, each quickly producing large numbers for the rapidly-growing United States Army. *Courtesy Allan Henderson.*

Shortly after their return from the exercise and just before the Division's one-year call up was due to expire, the Japanese attack on the Pacific Fleet in Hawaii brought everything into much clearer focus. No one doubted anymore that there was a national emergency. When units from the division were sent to guard industrial sites and transportation nodes in Pennsylvania and Virginia, just as their fathers and uncles had done during the early days of the First World War, it was taken seriously. In January 1942, the 116th was chosen to play the role of beachhead defenders in an exercise against the 1st Infantry Division in the Cape Henry area. The purpose of the exercise was to give the soldiers of the 1st Division, nicknamed the Big Red One, some practical experience in amphibious warfare. Consequently, the 116th would spend two very cold and wet days defending the Virginia coast from the 1st Infantry Division. Ironically, the next time the 116th Infantry Regiment and the 1st Infantry Division (including the newly-promoted Norman Cota) would be on a beach together, it would be in Britain, when the two divisions practiced their amphibious landing skills in final preparation for spearheading the Normandy invasion.[9]

Another picture of Rock Rothgeb (on the right), this time with his friend, Henry Glasgow. Glasgow would later be killed during an artillery barrage in France.

A picture of Company "G", 176th Infantry Regiment, with Captain Richard H. Ryan identified in the center. While training at Fort Meade, the 176th Infantry would be detached from the 29th Infantry Division and sent to Fort Benning; Captain Ryan would be reassigned to the Army Air Force.

Major General Leonard Gerow, a native of Petersburg, Virginia, would take over command of the division in February 1942 and lead them across the Atlantic to Britain. By the time of the D-Day landing, Gerow had moved on to be V Corps Commander. *Courtesy USAMHI.*

A short while later, Major General Leonard Gerow replaced Major General Reckord as 29th Infantry Division Commander. The Army had determined that age sixty-two was the cut-off point for commanding a division, so on 20 February 1942, Reckord relinquished the command he had held since 1934. Among Gerow's first duties was to reorganize the division into the new "triangular" structure. In this new configuration, the number of soldiers assigned was reduced from 22,000 to 17,000.[10] Of immediate significance, the 29th had to give up the 176th Infantry Regiment, while the quartermaster, engineer, and signal units were greatly reduced in size. The 104th Observation Squadron was also detached from the division and assigned other duties.

As a result of the change in structure, the 29th was now reduced to three infantry regiments: the 115th Infantry Regiment, 116th Infantry Regiment, and the 175th Infantry Regiment. In place of the previous three regiments of field artillery, the 29th now had

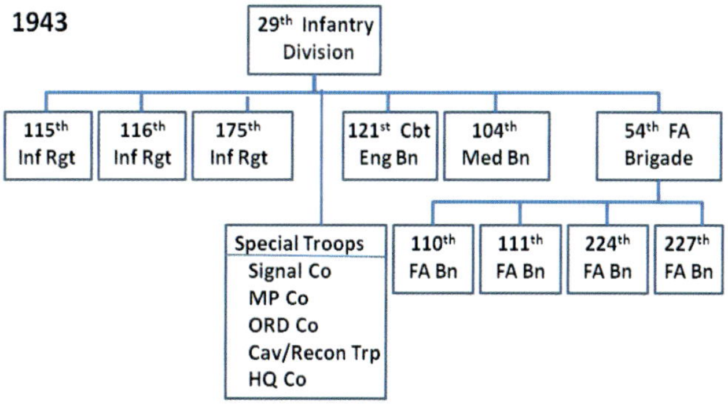

Schematic of the new 29th Infantry Division after it has been triangularized. By this point in time, the artillery regiments were reduced to battalions, the 176th Infantry and 176th Field Artillery had been reassigned elsewhere, and the total number of officers and enlisted soldiers assigned was reduced to 15,000.

Distinctive unit crests for the three infantry regiments remaining after the 29th was reconfigured: the 115th, 116th, and the 175th. The cactus seen on the 115th Regiment crest reflects the unit's Mexican border service. *Courtesy Allan Henderson.*

A typical example of a multi-piece collar disk for the 175th Infantry Regiment. As the war progressed and metal became harder to obtain, the Army switched over to simpler one-piece machine-stamped "U.S." disks.

Those soldiers assigned to the 29th Infantry Division, but not yet assigned to a specific unit, would wear a unit crest that was a duplicate of the division patch. Here the two are shown side by side to provide a size and color comparison.

Officers and men of Battery "A," 111th Field Artillery, commanded by Captain John Wales. On D-Day, this battery lost all four of its 105mm howitzers in overloaded DUKWs. As such, they were unable to provide artillery support until they were re-equipped 13 June. Wales would end the war as a major and serve as the battalion executive officer.

Official mail from Company "H", 176th Infantry, sent from Fort Meade to Richmond. In March 1942, the regiment would be detached from the 29th Division and assigned to other duties.

the 110th, 111th, 224th, and 227th Field Artillery Battalions. Other units now assigned to the division were the 29th Signal Company, 729th Ordnance Company, 29th Quartermaster Company, 29th Reconnaissance Troop, 121st Engineer Battalion, and the 104th Medical Battalion. On 12 March 1942, the reorganization was complete and the division could then begin their training in preparation for their eventual deployment overseas.

As part of the structural changes, the 176th Field Artillery Regiment was removed from the division completely, as previously noted, and the 110th and 111th Field Artillery Regiments were deactivated as regiments and converted into the new four field artillery battalions. Three of these battalions were equipped with twelve 105mm howitzers each and organized into three firing batteries. The fourth battalion, now designated the 227th Field Artillery Battalion, was to be equipped with twelve 155mm howitzers and organized to provide "general support" artillery fire for divisional operations. Habitual relationships between the infantry regiments and the field artillery battalions were also established. The 110th Field Artillery was linked to the 115th Infantry, the 111th Field Artillery to the 116th, and the 224th to the 175th Infantry. These infantry and artillery combinations were now considered "Regimental Combat Teams."

At the same time, as the many organizational changes were taking place, there were a number of equipment upgrades for the division. The artillery units were issued the new six-wheel-drive, two and a half ton cargo capacity trucks that they would use throughout the war. With the addition of all of the other assigned trucks, weapons carriers, and jeeps, a field artillery battalion in the 29th Infantry Division had over a hundred vehicles assigned. Artillery cannoneers were also issued the new M1 carbine that would become the standard self-defense weapon for artillery crewmen.[11]

Though the 29th had escaped the worst of the manpower harvesting, it was inevitable during this transition to the new structure. A large number of soldiers were sent to other units, including some to the 37th Infantry Division and others to coastal defense artillery units in Bermuda. At this time, the anti-tank and cannon platoons were also removed from the division artillery units and transferred into the newly-created independent Tank Destroyer Battalions. By the time the reorganization was complete and all of the personnel movements finished, the new end strength for the 29th division was set at 15,500. In effect, the "new" 29th Infantry Division was only slightly more than half the

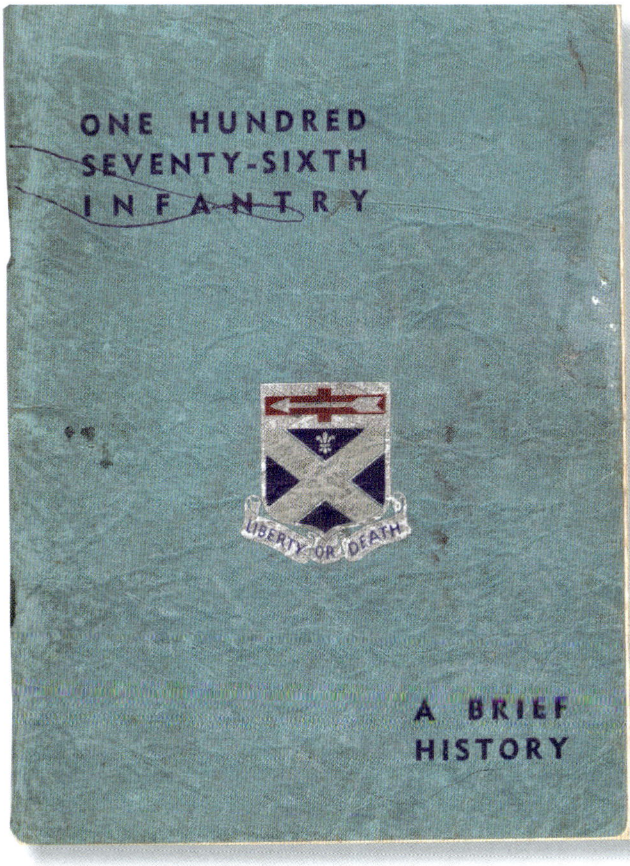

A small booklet, dated July 1943, provided to soldiers of the 176th Infantry Regiment. By this time, the 176th had been detached from the 29th Infantry Division and transferred to Fort Benning, Georgia.

size of the 29th Division that had deployed to France in 1918. Along with the troop reductions, what impacted the 29th the most was the number of well-trained personnel that were being transferred to other gaining units. Their loss required the 29th to establish its own divisional training center at Fort Meade in an attempt to regain the lost expertise. Along with the establishment of the internal training program, the 110th, 111th, 224th, and 227th Field Artillery Battalions were sent to an artillery training site at Cape Cod, Massachusetts. While there, they received extensive training using old French 75mm guns. When they rejoined the division at Fort Meade, they finally received their assigned field pieces: the 105mm M2A1 and 155mm M1 howitzers.

During the summer of 1942, the 29th once again took part in large-scale maneuvers in the Carolinas. This time, there was no feeling among the soldiers that they were on a "camping trip." The nation was at war and the soldiers took the exercise seriously. Many of the safety restrictions of the previous year had been eliminated, thus allowing much more realistic training, including

A Company "G", 116th Infantry Regiment soldier, Richard Inge, takes time out from training to pose with his sweetheart and future wife, Rosa Martin Inge. *Courtesy Inge Family.*

Company "G", 115th Infantry Regiment, takes a break in training at Fort Meade to pose for a unit picture. Captain Randolph Millholland, seen seated in the center with his hands in his lap, would later command the 29th Ranger Battalion in Britain, then an infantry battalion in France and Germany.

Studio portrait of an unidentified member of the 116th Infantry Regiment.

Typical "herringbone twill" fatigue hat worn and decorated by a Virginia guardsman during the mobilization and training period at Fort Meade.

an exercise that involved advancing under live artillery fire. New equipment was being issued on a regular basis, and the division began to receive the vehicles and radios called for by their Table of Organization and Equipment; the Army's basic guideline for all of the quantities and types of soldiers and equipment possessed by a specific kind of unit.

In August, the division was sent to Camp Blanding, in Florida. While there, they were issued the new style M-1 helmet.

Battery "B" of the 111th Field Artillery poses for a unit picture at Fort Meade in August 1941. Battery "B" would have the only remaining 105mm howitzer of the 111th Field Artillery Battalion available for use by the afternoon of 6 June 1944. *Courtesy 1/111th Field Artillery.*

A closer view of a section of the previous picture, showing three of the battery NCOs and the guidon. The First World War helmets the unit was wearing at this time are shown at their feet. The 29th would retain these helmets until just before they deployed to Britain in September 1942. *Courtesy 1/111th Field Artillery.*

A copy of the 1940 version of "The Soldier's Handbook." This pocket-sized guide to the Army provided simple information on everything from the "Articles of War" and "Rules of Drill" to map reading and personal hygiene. It not only had a section on National Guard Regulations, it also offered advice on avoiding venereal diseases.

At the same time, they were shocked to receive orders directing them to dispatch all of their artillery to Fort Sill. This was followed by an order to send an infantry regiment to Fort Benning to serve as school cadre there.[12] Just when it appeared that the 29th was going out of business, Gerow received another set of orders that countermanded the previous orders. These new orders now directed him to prepare the division for immediate overseas deployment. With some alacrity, the 29th Division staff began a hurried roundup of all men on furlough and even managed to recall the advance party that had gone to Fort Sill.

This time, it was for real: the 29th Division was going back to Europe. Loaded aboard the giant ocean liners *Queen Mary* and *Queen Elizabeth*, the Blue and Gray were soon on their way once again for British ports and European soil.[13]

This well-preserved Fort Meade "sweetheart" pillow is an example of one of the favored items that American soldiers liked to purchase at their local post exchanges and send home to wives or girlfriends.

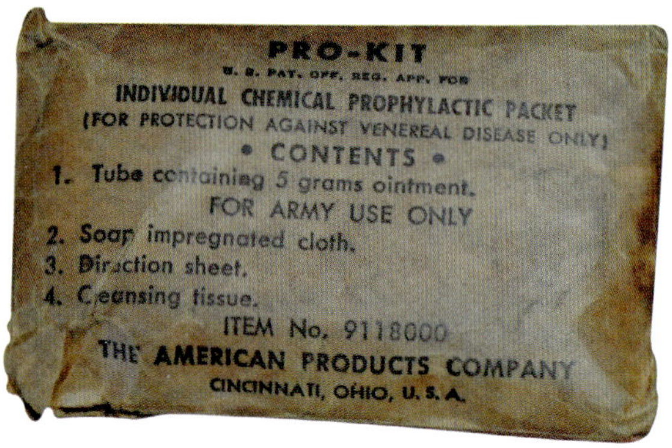

No aspect of the soldier's life was left to chance. For the soldiers who did not use prophylactics, seen here at the top of the picture (marked on the back "WAR TIME PACKAGE 3 for 50 cents"), the Pro-Kit was provided to prevent the spread of venereal disease.

Although much more uniform in appearance than the divisional patches that appeared after the First World War, there were still a number of variations due to 1940s manufacturing techniques. These three examples show the typical differences in color shadings, weaves, and textures.

The well-worn footlocker used by Brigadier General William H. Sands. Sands would command the 29th's artillery for the entire war and would later command the division from 1946 to 1954. *Courtesy 1/111th Field Artillery.*

A gathering of some of the officers of the 111th Field Artillery battalion just prior to the deployment to Britain in September 1942. Captain Frederic E. Consolvo (standing second from left) would later be killed in action in France. *Courtesy 1/111th Field Artillery.*

CHAPTER 7

Arrival in Britain and D-Day to St. Lô

When describing the history of the 29th Infantry Division in the Second World War, there is always a tendency to immediately rush forward to the Normandy landing as if that were the opening act in the play. It certainly wasn't. After departing the States, the 29th was destined to spend a great deal of time and sweat "rehearsing" in Britain before they boarded the ships carrying them to the beaches of Normandy. Nor could the landing even be considered the climax of a theater production; it was only the first act of a much longer epic. After the D-Day landing on Omaha Beach, it was the 29th's destiny to remain in battle for nearly a year longer. They would suffer casualties, seemingly for every yard of French soil they liberated and German soil they captured. With that in mind, what follows in the next two chapters is the story of the 29th's experiences from their arrival in Britain through the end of the war and to their return to the States.

An unscientific poll might show that, with the exception of the Battle of Gettysburg, there are more books written about every possible aspect and personality of D-Day than any other battle in American military history. That stands to reason; those two battles are certainly defining moments in the American soldiers' pantheon of honor and history. Having said that, it is essential to understand that the 29th did much more than just make their heroic assault on Hitler's "Fortress Europe" in Normandy. The soldiers of the Blue and Gray Division lived, fought, and died in a number of battles after D-Day and, at times, suffered staggering losses. In fairness, these must be described as well, as they too contribute to the 29th's legacy.

Even before the 29th Division reached European soil, they were unfortunate witnesses and unwilling participants in a military tragedy. Almost half of the division (including the entire 116th Regimental Combat Team and detachments from other units) had sailed from New York City on the evening of 27 September 1942 aboard the *Queen Mary*. On 2 October, the giant ship was within a day's sail of its destination—the port of Greenock in Scotland—when it was met by the British escort ships that were sent to protect it on the last leg of the journey. While performing an anti-submarine maneuver, the British light cruiser HMS *Curacao* misjudged both the direction and the twenty-five knot speed of the liner. The *Curacao* cut in front of the *Queen Mary* and was rammed by its sharp bow. Being more than eighteen times the size of the escorting ship, *Queen Mary* sliced the cruiser in half without much effort. Members of the 116th Infantry Regiment, sworn to secrecy at the time, later recounted that they hardly noticed the collision.[1] Although the incident went almost unnoticed on the *Queen Mary*, the affect on the *Curacao* was catastrophic. The cruiser sank quickly, taking over three hundred British sailors to their graves.

The Army wasted no time moving the arriving troops from Scotland down to their new homes in southern England. Soon after debarkation, the Guardsmen found themselves on trains to Tidworth Barracks, near the city of Salisbury. There, they were joined a week or so later by the rest of the division that had made their transatlantic voyage aboard the *Queen Elizabeth*. Even though the entire division was now in Britain, it still wasn't quartered together. At the time, Tidworth was also home to some units of the 1st Infantry Division that were preparing to take part in the invasion of North Africa. As the units of the 1st departed, more elements of the 29th Infantry Division moved to Tidworth, until finally, all of the Blue and Gray were assembled in one location.

Prewar image of the *Queen Mary*. Carrying almost a third of the 29th Infantry Division, she would complete the transatlantic voyage in seven days. Her sister ship, the *Queen Elizabeth*, would transport the rest of the division a week later.

For many soldiers of the 29th, there was a negative aspect to having the entire division together. General Gerow was now able to commence an extremely strenuous physical fitness program for the entire division that would soon challenge even the fittest soldiers in the unit. Seven days a week, training programs with 25 to 40-mile marches around the local countryside soon brought the men to the edge of their endurance. Since the division had arrived in Britain with only a portion of their required weapons and equipment, the majority of the training had to be oriented more towards physical fitness than to improving combat skills. Over time, Gerow's constant demands on speed marching and long hikes started to break down the soldiers, rather than build them up.[2] Their only relief from training was a once-a-month 48-hour pass that allowed them to visit local cities and make friends among the British population.

Private First Class Richard D. Inge of Company "G", 116th Infantry Regiment, poses for a picture in Britain. *Courtesy Inge Family.*

Major General Leonard T. Gerow, 29th Infantry Division Commander from February 1942 to July 1943. A veteran of the Mexican Border campaign and the First World War, Gerow would later command V Corps during the Normandy Invasion. At the end of the war, Gerow would be rated by General Eisenhower as one of his best senior American Commanders. *Courtesy USAMHI.*

A soldier from Company "G", 116th Infantry enjoying a picnic and social gathering with some of the locals near his base. Annotated on the back "May 16 1944," this picture is especially poignant since the 116th's attack on "Fortress Europe" would take place just three weeks after this picture was taken. *Courtesy Inge Family.*

Richard Inge, now wearing an HBT (herring-bone twill) one-piece work suit, poses for another picture "somewhere in Britain." The damage to the 29th Division symbol on his helmet may be from a censor's attempt to obscure the unit information when Inge sent this photo home. *Courtesy Inge Family.*

Closer view of Rothgeb's collar disks, showcasing the U.S. disks with the attached 116th regimental numerals. These three-piece disks would soon be replaced by plain U.S. disks that were stamped from a single piece of metal, making them universally applicable, not to mention easier and cheaper to produce.

Rothgeb's garrison hat. Rothgeb has removed the framework that stretches the crown in order to give it a more dramatic appearance.

Technician 5th Grade (Tech-5) Ulric "Rock" Rothgeb's dress uniform. Clearly visible are the distinctive 116th unit crests and 29th Infantry Division patch. Four-pocket dress coats, such as this one, would soon be replaced by the much more popular "Ike" jackets.

Along with complaints regarding the exhausting and potentially injurious training program, the soldiers' biggest gripe was about the food they were being given in their unit chow halls. One 115th Infantry vet would later tell his family that he would never again eat canned corned beef as a reaction to the food the soldiers ate in England.[3] For other soldiers, it was the constant menu of brussels sprouts and dehydrated eggs that most irritated them.

In December 1942, a provisional Ranger Battalion was formed from volunteers in the 29th Division. Selected to command the new battalion was Major Randolph Millholland, a Maryland National Guardsman and the former commander of Company "G" of the 115th Infantry Regiment. Millholland would go on to have a long and highly prestigious career in the 29th Division and in the Maryland National Guard. Both he and the Ranger battalion will receive more extensive coverage later. For now, it is sufficient to say that members of this special battalion will certainly go on to prove to be excellent soldiers, not only in the 29th Infantry Division, but also in other Army units.[4]

In May 1943, the 29th Division received orders to move again, this time to the Cornwall region of England. Along with a new focus towards amphibious training, the move also meant that the 29th, in conjunction with British forces, was now responsible for the defense of that region. While the threat of German invasion had diminished, the assigned defensive mission reminded the American soldiers that they were in Britain for more than just training. To no one's surprise, Gerow directed that much of the 160-mile relocation was to be done on foot.

One immediate benefit of the new location was proximity to training areas large enough to allow regimental exercises and live firing for maneuvering units. Divisional artillery batteries were also able to practice fire support missions for the infantry units. An added emphasis on night training introduced another degree of realism that helped prepare the unit for the eventual campaign that every soldier knew was coming.

Soldiers of the 29th Ranger battalion practice an amphibious landing on a British beach in March 1943. By the time of the actual D-Day landings, this battalion had been disbanded and most of the rangers returned to their original units. *Courtesy National Archives.*

Major General Charles Hunter Gerhardt. Gerhardt commanded the 29th from July 1943 to the end of the war. Often criticized for his tactics and his high casualty rates, Gerhardt was nonetheless adept at training soldiers. Under his leadership and tutelage the 29th became a highly regarded division. *Courtesy National Guard Bureau.*

Another major change came to the soldiers of the 29th two months after the relocation. General Gerow was selected to be the commander of the U.S. Army V Corps. Taking his place as the new divisional commander of the 29th was the man who would lead them throughout the rest of the war, Major General Charles Hunter Gerhardt. For the first time since Major General Morton in 1917, the 29th would be led by a commander who was neither a National Guardsman nor, at least, a Virginian.[5] Upon taking command, Gerhardt's priority was to prepare his unit "to go ashore and stay ashore" in hostile territory. Gerhardt took to the mission with the same drive and enthusiasm he had evidenced throughout his military career, whether as a hard-charging cavalryman or the leader of the 89th Division's AEF championship football team. However, Gerhardt was also wise enough to perform an assessment of his new command prior to introducing his version of a training regimen. In fact, after taking command 22 July 1943, one of his very first acts was to declare a three-day training holiday, bringing some much needed rest to the division's foot-weary soldiers. Gerhardt also enthusiastically endorsed the use of the divisional symbol and the slogan "29 Let's Go." Under Gerhardt's guidance, the slogan was to be repeated at every opportunity and the number "29" was always to be pronounced "two nine."[6]

Gerhardt had spent most of the 1920s and 1930s developing a reputation as a cavalryman with an obvious enthusiasm for horses and mobility on the battlefield. By 1941, he was a "temporary" brigadier general commanding the 2nd Brigade, 1st Cavalry Division in the Louisiana maneuvers. Gerhardt's success in this large-scale exercise led to his assignment to the 51st Cavalry Brigade, which at the time was stationed on the Texas-Mexico border. After the Japanese attack on Pearl Harbor, he was reassigned to the 1st Cavalry Division until May 1942, when he was ordered to report to Camp White, Oregon, to take command of the newly-forming 91st Infantry Division.

While commanding the 91st, Gerhardt's leadership style continued to evolve. He quickly became known for his focus on marksmanship and small unit leadership. Gerhardt also insisted that officers be at least as proficient in the basic combat skills as the soldiers they led. Like Gerow, he also focused heavily on the individual fitness of the soldier. Gerhardt went so far as to announce to the 91st Division his philosophy: "The goal of an effective battle team is to move, shoot and obey."[7] The 91st Infantry Division would never know how this was to translate into actual combat experience, but the 29th, still road marching and training in England, would soon find out.

Just before Gerhardt's arrival, the 29th received orders directing them to begin amphibious landing training. At first, this training was hindered by a serious lack of landing craft and other amphibious equipment. Borrowing from the British and using barges as surrogate landing craft, the division began training in earnest. Their new location in Cornwell had moved them closer to the American and British amphibious training area on

HOW DIVISION SLOGAN STARTED

The slogan and battle-cry of the Division, "29 Let's Go" was first adopted while still in England. Gen. Gerhardt, now in the States on a 7th War Loan Drive mission, is a great believer in the use of mass commands in physical training. While inspecting a Bn. of the 115th Inf. one morning he overheard troops doing physical drill use "Let's Go" for cadence and also as a means of instilling spirit and pride in the outfit. The General added "29" to the yell and then and there the battle-cry was adopted and was the signal for the assault.

From D-Day to the Elbe as part of the First, Third and Ninth Armies the 29th Division has been an assault outfit.

It is now under the command of Brigadier General William H. Sands, Division Artillery Commander.

A clipping from the 29th Infantry Division's own newspaper "29 Let's Go," giving an explanation for the constant repetition of the slogan in spoken and written communications.

Woolacombe Beach, where the infantry units began to practice their new skills in beach landings. Soon they were introduced to the army's newest amphibious craft, a half-boat/half-truck officially known as the DUKW, but affectionately called the "Duck." The DUKW, designed in 1942, was meant for general utility duty as a truck that could operate on land, cross rivers, and even "swim" from larger landing craft to shore in support of amphibious landings. The DUKW's capabilities and weaknesses would become readily apparent during the Normandy landings. For the first time, the 29th was also exposed to the amphibious tanks that were to accompany them for beach assaults.[8]

With his initial assessment complete, it wasn't long before Gerhardt began putting his stamp on the division. He insisted that officers lead their men in every facet of the training program, to include the calisthenics that started off each training day. Unit commanders were often surprised to see Gerhardt wandering through their training areas and barracks, observing what was taking place. While the enlisted soldiers were getting a taste of Gerhardt's disciplinary style, the officers were even more exposed to his leadership. At one particularly painful session held soon after Gerhardt's arrival, he questioned the officers relentlessly on basic infantry tactics and weapons characteristics. While obviously well-intentioned and meant to deliver a clear message

A small group of 111th Field Artillery soldiers gather with their lieutenant for a group picture. *Courtesy 1/111th Field Artillery.*

A signalman from the 111th Field Artillery has set up his BD-71 Switchboard on the moors. The 29th's history described the moors as a "bleak wet wasteland" and this photograph confirms that description. *Courtesy 1/111th Field Artillery.*

indicating the type of knowledge the new commander expected his officers to have, the ultimate effect was more of an "inquisition" than a two-way exchange between professional soldiers.[9] Perhaps surprisingly, the one officer that did extremely well during his questioning was the long-time Virginia Guardsman and 54th Artillery Brigade Commander, William H. Sands. One of the after-effects of these impromptu interrogations between Gerhardt and his subordinates during these training sessions was that many junior officers took advantage of every opportunity to avoid him whenever possible. Nonetheless, some of the same officers that were avoiding Gerhardt would later acknowledge that there had been some method to his madness, and that the division was slowly taking shape as a combat-worthy outfit under his guidance. As for the enlisted men, they also figured it out quickly. They knew that if they kept their helmet chinstrap buckled at all times and could recite the basic tenets of marksmanship, they could escape relatively unscathed from a meeting with General Gerhardt.

Perhaps because of Gerhardt, or in spite of him, the Army soon added another important figure to the 29th Infantry Division. It was both fortunate, and a touch prophetic, when the amphibiously-experienced Brigadier General Norman D. Cota was named as the new assistant division commander. Not only was Cota an extraordinary officer with a wealth of insight into the complexities of landing an assault force on enemy territory, his first name and middle initial (Norman D.) sounded exactly like the location (Normandy) where the 29th was to attack. The officers of the 29th soon appreciated his appointment, since his common sense approach provided a much-needed balance to some of Gerhardt's more strident methods.

Although primarily focused on amphibious landings, the 29th did not neglect their other combat training: "Each infantry battalion was given an exercise…in assembly, approach, attack and defense, and troops were made to follow close behind the artillery fires which were supporting them."[10] The combination of Gerhardt and Cota soon proved to be an excellent leadership team. This was evidenced by the 29th's performance in an April exercise at Slapton Sands which showcased their ever improving skills. During this

A prized trophy from the championship football game between the 29th Infantry Division and their fellow Guardsmen of the 28th Infantry Division. Beating the Keystone Division soldiers 27 to 6 on 25 March 1944 must have been a great pleasure to General Gerhardt, the former West Point quarterback. *Courtesy 1/111th Field Artillery.*

Aerial view looking westward down Omaha Beach towards Pointe du Hoe. The critically important beach exit points, known as the Vierville, les Moulins, St Laurent, and Colleville Draws, are shown, as are the towns behind the beach. *Courtesy USAMHI.*

exercise, Cota's old unit, the 1st Infantry Division, worked closely with the 29th. The 1st Division, known more commonly as the "Big Red One," was an appropriate choice to team with the 29th. Plans were already underway to link the divisions together for the invasion of France. In early May, the forces now designated for the invasion were gathering in the southern part of England and moving into their marshalling areas. Although the actual date for the landing—soon to be known as D-Day—was still unknown, the soldiers of the 29th soon received official word that they had been selected for the initial assault on German-occupied France. Along with that notification, they soon found themselves sequestered in their staging areas to prevent any leakage of that information to the enemy. After the endless months of training at Fort Meade, Camp Blanding, and in Britain, the 29th Infantry Division was finally going into combat.

There would be one last minute delay caused by bad weather, which would postpone the attack for a day. When the ships carrying the 29th to France sailed again 5 June, there would be no turning back. Their destination was a beach ten miles east of the Cherbourg peninsula. This beach, code-named Omaha, was subdivided into smaller beaches and designated for attack by assault companies from both the 1st Division and the 29th. In the 29th's sector, the beaches and their assigned 116th Infantry Regiment first wave units were: Dog Green—Company "A"; Dog White—Company "G"; Dog Red—Company "F"; and Easy Green—Company "E"; while the 116th's left flank—a company from the 16th Infantry Regiment of the Big Red One—was to land on Easy Red Beach. Past the 1st Division's beaches to the east were the British and Canadian landing sites code-named Sword, Juno, and Gold. On the far right flank of the 116th, Company "C" of the 2nd Ranger Battalion was assigned to land on Charlie Beach to attack Pointe de la Percee.[11]

German soldiers and construction workers scramble to get away from a low-flying Allied 31st Photo-Reconnaissance Squadron aircraft. Taken 4 May 1944, this photo clearly shows some of the beach defenses awaiting the Allies on the Normandy coast. *Courtesy Charles G. Thomas.*

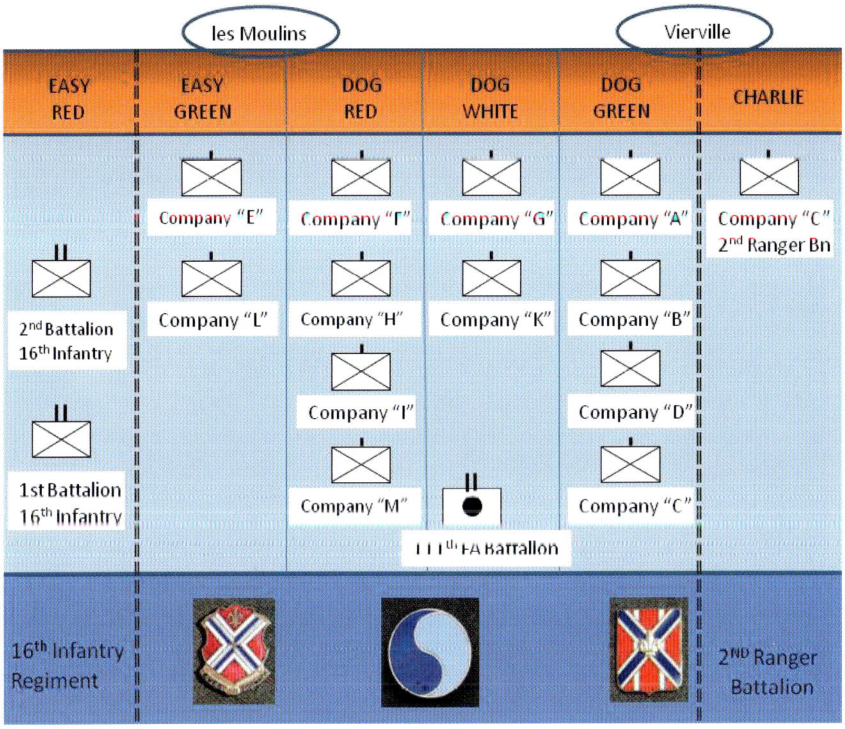

A graphic portrayal of how the 116th's landing on Omaha Beach was planned. Bad weather, bad luck, and German resistance would quickly destroy this concise operational plan.

Three miles past the Ranger's objective was Pointe du Hoe, a jut of land sticking out into the sea with a sheer cliff face and the suspected home of a large German coastal artillery battery. The "Pointe" would be assaulted by other Ranger Companies to ensure any artillery located there could not pound the Americans' invasion landing sites. To the west of the Pointe was the other American invasion beach, code-named Utah, and assigned to the 4th Infantry Division for assault. Leading that amphibious landing was a distant cousin of Norman Cota, Brigadier General Teddy Roosevelt, Jr.

The invasion plan was designed to ensure that before any of the landing craft touched French soil, British and American Airborne Divisions would be dropped behind the beaches to seal off the area, thus preventing entry of any German reinforcements to the landing sites. Interestingly enough, among the American paratroopers that would be part of the drop were several former 29th Infantry Division soldiers that transferred to the 101st

Chaplain Lewis Fulmer Koon, a Virginian in the 12th Infantry Regiment, 4th Infantry Division. Koon made it ashore safely on Utah Beach, but later recalled that it took three weeks for his portable altar kit to catch up to him, as it had been loaded on a jeep that had capsized during the 6 June landing. *Courtesy Penny Koon Santilli.*

Iconic view of Omaha Beach from one of the landing craft. The heavily-laden soldiers of the assault wave have exited the craft and now wade through waist-deep water towards the beachhead. What is clearly visible just inside the right side of the ramp is a waterproof cover on an M1 rifle being carried by a soldier. *Courtesy USAMHI.*

Airborne Infantry division, instead of returning to their original unit when the 29th Ranger Battalion was disbanded.[12]

The same bad weather that had caused the one-day delay on 5 June continued to torment the soldiers in the assault ships. Many, already nervous by the thought of impending battle, were seasick long before they even entered their smaller landing craft for the trip to shore. The giant convoys carrying the invasion force followed a strict traffic pattern to ensure that the landings would be both simultaneous in execution and a surprise to the German defenders. Travelling parallel to the Virginians of the 116th were ships of the 4th Infantry Division headed for Utah Beach. Among the soldiers on one of the 4th Infantry Division's Landing Craft Infantry (LCI) was a fellow Virginian, Captain (and Chaplain) Lewis F. Koon. On 3 June, Chaplain Koon, a Lutheran Minister, had been asked by one of his fellow officers to conduct a religious service for all of his soldiers—Protestant, Catholic, and Jewish alike.[13] He had done so willingly and without hesitation.

Koon's own words, written some fifteen years after the invasion, provide a clear and concise description of the general mood of the American soldiers during this short voyage to the French beaches. Underway from the British staging area: "our LCI emerged from the inlet in which it had waited since Saturday, we saw…literally hundreds of craft of all kinds sizes and descriptions similarly emerging as far up and down the coast as we could see. I spent the hours until dark — chatting casually and watching the huge armada fall into pattern, the LCIs each towing its barrage balloon, assembling in two long lines, neither end of which we could see." As it became too dark to see more, Chaplain Koon went below to the crowded compartments and attempted to sleep. As he lay in his bunk: "sleepless and tense in the silence, you could feel even in the darkness the wondering, the tension, the waiting, perhaps even the prayers of others, all around you, aboard your own craft and aboard the hundreds of others, steadily plowing with you thru the night toward a rendezvous, the nature of which none knew."[14]

Perhaps symbolic of the level of detail to which the Allies prepared for the Normandy landing; seen here is the front of the special vest designed for the troops of the first waves and capable of carrying a great amount of ammunition and equipment. This example was made by Tweedie Footwear in 1944. *Photo courtesy HPEnjames.*

The reverse side of the assault vest shown in the previous picture. When the four pouches on the front and the two much larger pouches on the back were filled with ammunition and equipment, one can easily understand the struggle the soldiers in the first waves endured getting ashore. Many troops abandoned the vests as quickly as possible to either avoid drowning, or to move more quickly under fire. *Photo courtesy HPEnjames.*

At approximately 2:30 in the morning, the *Thomas Jefferson*, carrying most of the 116th's assault companies, arrived off shore. By 3 a.m., the soldiers were climbing into the smaller landing craft and were lowered down the side of the ship. Each of the small landing craft could carry thirty fully-armed soldiers. In turn, each soldier was fully laden with their own weapon, ammunition, grenades, demolition charges, combat rations (known as K rations), raincoat, assault vest, small first aid kit, gas mask in a waterproof case, and even an inflatable lifebelt. Other soldiers with specialty missions, such as communications or demolition, were even more heavily laden.[15] When the descending landing craft reached the water, they cut loose from the larger ship and began to circle, waiting for the attacking force's entire first wave to assemble. As the small craft rolled and bobbed in the high seas, the men aboard became sicker and sicker. Finally, after what seemed an eternity, the landing craft headed for the beach. Adding to the seasick soldiers' discomfort, though perhaps somewhat encouraging, was the noise of the naval bombardment passing over their heads. Notable among the escorting ships, and providing some of that overhead fire, was the American battleship USS *Texas*. The *Texas* had escorted units of the 29th to France in 1918 during the First World War, and now the aged battleship was again helping to deliver soldiers of the Blue and Gray to combat.

Along with the bigger naval ships, smaller rocket-launching ships began to fire towards the enemy shore. Those men in the landing craft that could see to the shore thought that the rockets had been fired too soon. It seemed that the rockets were landing well short of the enemy positions on the beach. Ominously, many of the small landing craft began to take on water.[16]

Soldiers of the 29th marching to the assault ships. This undated picture clearly shows the amount of equipment they are carrying and how their rifles have been wrapped in waterproof covers. *Courtesy USAQM Museum.*

Looking apprehensively towards the shore and the carnage on Omaha Beach, these soldiers in a landing craft of one of the later waves will soon be joining the battle. *Courtesy USAMHI.*

Assault gas mask with waterproof carrier, standard M1941 field jacket, and M26 Inflatable life preserver combination worn by 29th Division soldiers during the Normandy landings. The unneeded mask, included in the attacking soldier's field equipment for fear that the Germans might use poison gas or other chemical weapons to defend the beach, may have served of some use to the heavily-laden soldiers through its buoyancy. What many soldiers failed to realize was that the life preserver was meant for wear under the arms and not around the waist. If inflated around the waist, the preserver tended to turn the top-heavy soldiers upside down in the water.

Soon, however, water leaking into the boats became the least of the soldiers' worries. Though the enemy shore had been quiet at first, as soon as the boats closed to within five hundred yards of the beach, the nearby splashes from German artillery and small arms let the attackers know that the aerial and naval bombardments had not driven the enemy away. Down the length of the attack the small boats began taking hits. Even near misses were causing casualties or making boats founder.

The dropping of the ramps caused an immediate increase in fire from the Germans defending the area above the beach. Rather than risking the deadly German machine gun fire sweeping the ramps, many soldiers chose to go over the sides of the landing craft, splashing heavily into the surf.[17] Among the attacking companies, Company "A" seemed to come ashore closest to their designated landing site. They would suffer heavily for their navigational accuracy. Some of the boats from Company "E" were so far off course that they landed on part of the beach designated for the Big Red One. Those lucky enough to reach the shore took shelter behind the sea wall. This provided some cover from German machine guns, but no protection from the enemy mortar shells that were landing steadily on the beach. Unarmed men, their rifles and equipment shed in order to stay afloat, took shelter as best they could. They huddled among the beach anti-boat obstacles and at the sea wall. To stay at water's edge was to die. One survivor would later declare that the D-Day landing on Omaha Beach was the only place he knew where the wounded were actually safer being dragged forward, towards the enemy. To be behind the sea wall or shingle was to be, at least temporarily, safe.

The "Field Jacket, Wool," most often referred to as an Ike Jacket, for a sergeant from the 116th Infantry Regiment. The six yellow bars on his left sleeve indicate that he served overseas more than three years. The bronze arrowhead on his WWII Victory ribbon indicates that he participated in the Normandy Landings.

An example of a 29th Infantry Division M1 helmet and liner with British-style netting in place.

Another view of the 116th Ike jacket. The nicely-embroidered Combat Infantryman's Badge (CIB) was most likely made in Germany while the 29th served there on occupation duty after the war.

The original guidon used by Battery "B" 111th Field Artillery, the morning of 6 June 1944. The slightly darker patches are embroidered repairs to holes made by German bullets that day. *Courtesy 1/111th Field Artillery.*

A closer view of some of the repairs made to the 111th's battle-damaged guidon. *Courtesy 1/111th Field Artillery.*

At 7 a.m., the second wave began its approach to the shore. It was a frightening replay of the first wave. One of the officers in the second wave later noted that by the time his landing craft was headed towards the shore, the nearest battleship was silent, having ceased fire in fear of hitting the men already on the beach. Similarly the air overhead, which should have been filled with fighter-bombers assisting the infantry, was empty except for heavy clouds. What visibility the second wave had of the beach was limited by the rainy mist and smoke from brush fires started by earlier naval gunfire.[18] Many boats were again landing far from their designated site. The soldiers of Company "B", landing near Company "A", received the same pounding, and were soon out of action as a viable force. The Rangers, on the far right of the 116th, were suffering heavily, also. As the water near the beach began to fill with the bodies of dead and dying soldiers, any thoughts of following the carefully planned movement to the beach exits disappeared. Survival became the only focus for the pinned down units. Joining the Stonewallers of the 116th on the beach were soldiers from some of the special engineer and beachhead support units that had run the same gauntlet and suffered the same casualties and confusion. By this time, the beach was littered with "bodies, weapons, boxes of demolitions, flame throwers, reels of telephone wire and personal equipment from socks to toilet articles."[19]

Though the German fire had continued in strength, its deadly coverage was not complete for the entire beach front. Some American units had managed to land with their cohesion intact and soon began to fight back. Company "C", almost 1,500 yards east of the Vierville draw, and Company "M", which mis-landed in the 1st Division's sector, had suffered fairly light casualties while retaining most of their equipment. Similarly, the 5th Ranger Battalion had reached the shore intact. In spite of these successes, Omaha Beach was a bloody mess and getting worse by the minute. The vast majority of the soldiers ashore were taking shelter behind the seawall and trying not to draw any attention from the German machine gunners.

Taken at a photography studio in London, Richard Inge poses for a formal portrait to send home to his family in Farmville, Virginia. *Courtesy Inge Family.*

General Cota landed on Dog White Beach at 7:30 a.m. He was accompanied by some of the staff assigned to the 29th's advance command post and Colonel Charles D. W. Canham. Colonel Canham was the commander of the 116th and also had with him some of his own regimental command staff. Quickly assessing the confusion, Cota took charge. Similar to Teddy Roosevelt, Jr. over on Utah Beach, who was also faced with the problem of mis-landed units (though nowhere near the violent reception), Cota began to organize the Blue and Gray. He sent Canham eastward to rally the soldiers on the left side of the 29th's zone, while he headed down the beach in the opposite direction. It was at this point that Canham's personality began to stamp itself on the surviving members of the 116th that he encountered. Already shot through the wrist and with his arm in a sling, Canham worked his way down the beach as he rallied his regiment. One soldier would later recall Canham's words as he exhorted the officers and NCOs to keep their men moving: "Get these men the hell off this goddamned beach and go kill some goddamned krauts."[20]

Though Cota had predicted earlier that just about anything that could go wrong would, he probably didn't expect everything to go so wrong so quickly. Over in the 1st Division's sector, the 741st Tank Battalion had lost twenty-seven of its thirty-two Sherman tanks before they even reached the shore. The 743rd Tank Battalion, supporting the 29th's landing, had fared somewhat better, because the landing craft carrying their tanks had pushed all the way onto the beach before discharging their armored cargo. However, these tanks were drawing German fire from every direction and were fighting just to stay alive themselves. The DUKWs assigned to bring the 111th Field Artillery ashore to support the 116th were too heavily overloaded. Eleven of the twelve howitzer-carrying amphibious vehicles sank before reaching the shore. One of the members of the lone surviving Duck, Bill Akers, would later recount that the Army does a lot of "crazy things, but the craziest was loading those guns onto ducks with no easy way to get them off."[21]

Meanwhile, Company "C" had managed to clear a path off the beach and was moving slowly inland. They were soon followed by the Rangers, and by 9 a.m., were atop the bluff looking down on the beach. While the Germans still held the main exits from the beach, these small groups of determined soldiers were making some headway. In fact, two small penetrations had been made in the enemy's defenses and approximately six hundred Americans were warily moving forward through mine fields behind the bluffs. By 11 a.m., soldiers of the 29th were in the small town of Vierville. Richard Inge, a veteran of Company "G", would later recount that he had no idea how he got from the beach to the bluffs, just that he did.[22]

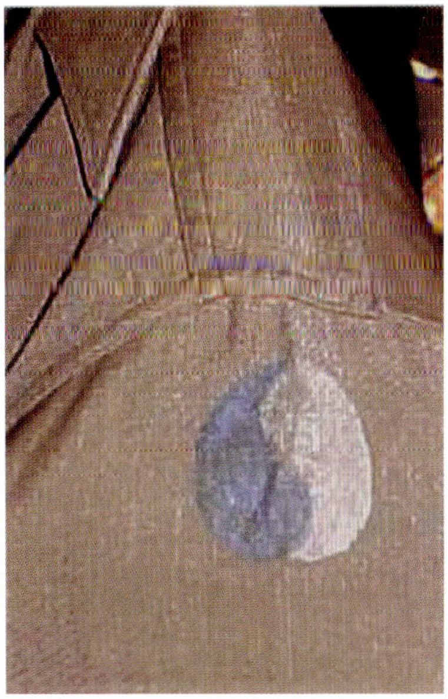

A seldom seen example of wool shirt with the 29th Division symbol painted directly on the sleeve. Richard Inge of Company "G", 116th Infantry Regiment, later recounted that many of the soldiers in his company had similar painted versions of the division patch on their wool shirts.

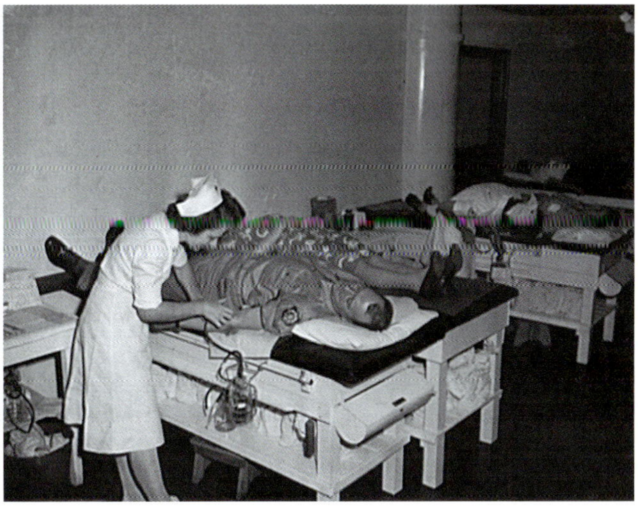

A clear sign of the patriotic feeling of the period. Almost immediately upon hearing of the D-Day invasion, Americans flocked to hospitals and Red Cross sites to donate blood. *Courtesy Library of Congress.*

This medal, presented to D-Day veterans by the Conseil Régional de Normandie, was awarded in honor of their participation in the liberation of France on the 50th anniversary of D-Day.

The distinctive unit insignia for the 115th Infantry Regiment. With a unit heritage that included service in the Civil War, Spanish-American War, and the First World War, units of the 115th would land on Omaha Beach shortly after 10 a.m.

A closer view of one of the 2004 awards presented by France to veterans of the Normandy landing on the 60th anniversary of the battle.

Another 116th Infantry Regiment, 29th Infantry Division Ike jacket, this time belonging to "Rock" Rothgeb. The two "D-Day 50th Anniversary" and "60th Anniversary" awards were added later.

From a larger picture of the officers and men of Company "H", 115th Infantry Regiment; a picture of Private First Class (later Sergeant) Wilber Fritz. Lightly wounded on D-Day, Fritz stayed with his unit and focused his effort to getting off the beach. *Courtesy Teena Gordon.*

An hour earlier, Colonel Eugene Slappey, Commander of the 115th Infantry Regiment, had received orders to move his unit ashore. Due to the ongoing heavy firing at the 115th's originally designated landing sites, it was decided to bring them to a sector where the German resistance was not as intense. Though the small arms fire was negligible where the 115th landed, there was still artillery and mortar fire slamming into the beach. Slightly wounded by some of this indirect fire, Wilber Fritz of Company "H" later told his family that his complete focus was on getting off that beach and moving to the relative security found inland beyond the bluffs.[23]

In fact, that security was illusory. The mine fields scattered throughout the area were deadly and German machine guns appeared to block the advancing Americans at every turn. In spite of this, the three rifle battalions of the 115th managed to move through the town of St. Laurent by that afternoon. With the infantrymen of the 115th were artillery forward observers from the 110th Field Artillery Battalion. Pre-invasion planning had called for them to direct artillery fire from the 111th Field Artillery Battalion in support of the 115th until the 110th's howitzers were ashore.[24] With eleven of the twelve howitzers belonging to the 111th now deep underwater off Omaha Beach, the forward observer teams of the 110th became infantrymen and moved inland with the 115th.

Helmet and souvenir wooden shoes brought home by a 29th Infantry Division veteran. The shoes have been marked to reflect the vet's participation in the D-Day landing. They also have been carefully marked with his name and that of his sweetheart.

Taken shortly after the beach was secured, this photograph shows the U.S. soldiers moving inland, either on foot or riding in halftracks and DUKWs as smoke obscures the distant ridges. Interestingly, the soldiers in the foreground are armed with the Springfield "03" bolt-action rifle. *Courtesy USAMHI.*

The full might of the Allied forces is clearly seen in this impressive shot as U.S. infantrymen march up the bluff and head inland while combat and logistics vehicles fill the land and sea behind them. *Courtesy USAMHI.*

Another view of the same helmet, but with the steel shell lifted to show the 29th Infantry Division marking on the helmet liner. *Courtesy Steve Klima.*

Front view of a steel helmet for an artillery forward observer in the 115th Infantry Regiment. Throughout the Second World War, the 110th Field Artillery Battalion was designated as the main source of artillery support for the 115th. *Courtesy Steve Klima.*

After clearing St. Laurent, the 115th set up defensive positions south of the town. On their left flank was the 1st Infantry Division's 16th Infantry Regiment and on their right was a patchwork unit comprised of the battered remnants of the 116th. A short time later, Captain Thomas Caldwell, a 110th liaison officer to the 115th, found four self-propelled 105mm cannons of the 58th Armored Field Artillery Battalion. Seeing they were without headquarters or communication, Caldwell and the 110th's commander, Lieutenant Colonel John Cooper, established control of the gun crews and guns and began to use them to provide fire support to the 115th.[25]

Another sign of the significance of D-Day; upon hearing of the attack, these New Yorkers have gone to church to pray for success of the operation and the safety of the Allied soldiers involved. *Courtesy Library of Congress.*

The distinctive unit insignia for the 175th Infantry Regiment. Held off-shore as part of the V Corps reserve, the 175th landed shortly after noon 7 June and immediately moved westward to capture the town of Isigny.

Back on the beaches, the tide was rising both literally and figuratively. Wounded men at the water's edge were in danger of drowning, but progress was being made in reducing the remaining isolated German strong points. Vast quantities of men and machines were piling up on the beaches, all seeking an exit that would get them away from the continuous enemy artillery fire. 29th Division engineers worked with non-divisional engineers to clear obstacles and cut more paths through the bluffs to relieve this congestion. Meanwhile, Cota continued his efforts to keep the soldiers moving inland. He had realized that the greatest danger to the landing now would be a German counterattack which could easily push the disorganized Americans back into the water. As more reliable communications were slowly being established, the all-important naval gunfire support became more accurate. Guided by landing force observers ashore who were able to pinpoint German targets, the Allied ships started to deliver powerful barrages on enemy positions. Likewise, observers for the field artillery units that had managed to get their guns ashore were starting to add their own contribution to the fight.

The unit insignia for the 110th Field Artillery Battalion. The three firing batteries of the 110th landed 7 June and almost immediately began to provide fire support with their 105mm howitzers for the 115th Infantry and the other infantry regiments of the 29th.

The unit insignia for the 224th Field Artillery reflects their Maryland background. They were formed when the 110th Field Artillery was reduced from a regiment to a battalion in 1942. The 224th maintained a habitual artillery support relationship with the 175th Infantry Regiment and therefore participated in their campaigns. *Courtesy TIOH.*

General Gerhardt himself came ashore in the afternoon with his staff. The 29th set up their first divisional headquarters in France using a quarry near the Vierville beach exit. Though still located within a hundred yards of the beach, the area was fairly well protected and secure. Meanwhile, Cota was still moving and coordinating with both the 1st Division and the V Corps headquarters. From Cota's updates to the 29th's headquarters, Gerhardt was able to get a clearer picture of the tactical situation, and what he saw and heard worried him. He was well aware of how tenuous a grip the Americans had on Omaha Beach. Among his first requests to V Corps was the immediate release of his third infantry regiment (the 175th) from floating reserve. Also, still on board ship were three of his field artillery battalions: the 110th, 224th, and 227th. Getting them ashore now became the highest priority. Ultimately, though their artillery support was desperately needed on the beachhead, these units would not come ashore until the next day due to beach congestion.

A view from Omaha beach looking towards the artificial port complex, code named Mulberry, constructed by the Allies to provide "over the shore" logistics support. The American Mulberry was only in operation for a few days before it was almost completely destroyed by a violent 19 June storm. *Courtesy Library of Congress.*

Taken some time after the assault landing, this picture gives an idea of the tremendous strength the Allies had by June 1944; a seemingly endless armada of ships lining up to off-load the men and machines needed to drive the Germans back to their own borders. *Courtesy USAMHI.*

The M1 steel helmet of a soldier from the 115th Infantry Regiment. Although the 115th did not suffer nearly the casualties that the 116th did on D-Day, by the end of June, they had suffered over 1,100 soldiers killed, wounded, or missing.

The reverse side of the 115th helmet showing clearly the white bar used to denote an NCO. This leadership marking would also be present on the removable helmet liners.

Casualties for the two assaulting American divisions at Omaha Beach are hard to quantify, and due to the scattering of the assault units, it is difficult to determine whether some soldiers died 6 June or the next day. Suffice it to say that between the 29th and 1st Infantry Divisions, there were some 2,500 killed and wounded soldiers on the beach that day. To place that number in human terms, consider the 116th Infantry Regiment's Company "A", which was recruited mostly from the area near the small Virginia town of Bedford. In the opening minutes of the landing, nineteen Bedford soldiers from Company "A" were killed. By the end of the war, of the thirty five original soldiers from Bedford, only thirteen returned home.[26] No other town in America paid so dear a price proportionally to gain a foothold in France. Just as in 1918, liberating French soil did not come cheaply for the soldiers of the 29th.

At the end of the day, the tally sheet was about even. The 29th and 1st Infantry Divisions were ashore, but their casualties were extremely high. Nowhere in the Omaha Beach sector were the Americans holding more than a mile of France. Fortunately, greater progress had been made on the other landing sites. The Allies had managed to carve out larger and more secure beachheads in those areas. In retrospect, that a previously untried division like the 29th had managed to overcome all of the bad weather, bad luck, and enemy opposition it faced was truly a tribute to its training and the incredible courage of the young sergeants and lieutenants. It was they, and a few fortunately placed senior leaders like Cota and Canham, who continued to fight against all odds. As night fell, the soldiers of the 29th took what rest they could and were thankful to have survived. Certainly, they thought, nothing in their future could be as deadly and dangerous as what they had faced that day on the beaches of Normandy. Little did they know that they would soon be introduced to a formidable, and equally deadly, terrain feature unique to that part of France—the hedgerow.

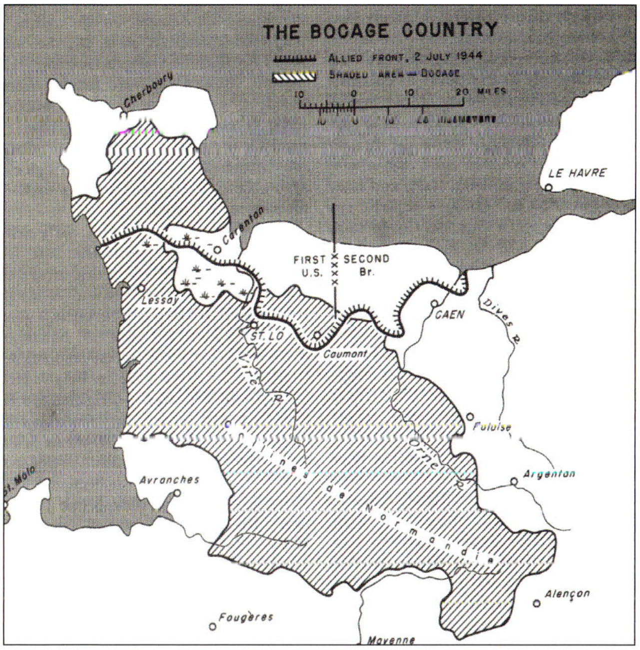

A map of the area of operations during the Normandy landings that clearly shows the extent of the Bocage terrain with which the invading forces had to contend after landing. Using the hedgerows in this area, smaller contingents of German forces were able to keep the Americans bottled up for weeks. *Courtesy U.S. Army.*

The morning of 7 June (known also as D+1) started early, when a German counterattack hit the 121st Engineers, located just to the southwest of Vierville. After that situation was stabilized, soldiers of the 3rd Battalion of the 116th were dispatched back to the beach area to reduce any German strong points that remained. Later, these troops joined with the 2nd Battalion and attempted to advance toward the town of Louvieres, only to be driven back to Vierville. How truly fragile the beachhead was these two days is evidenced by this action. In spite of a day's fighting, the 116th was actually defending pretty much the same area the night of 7 June as they had the night before.

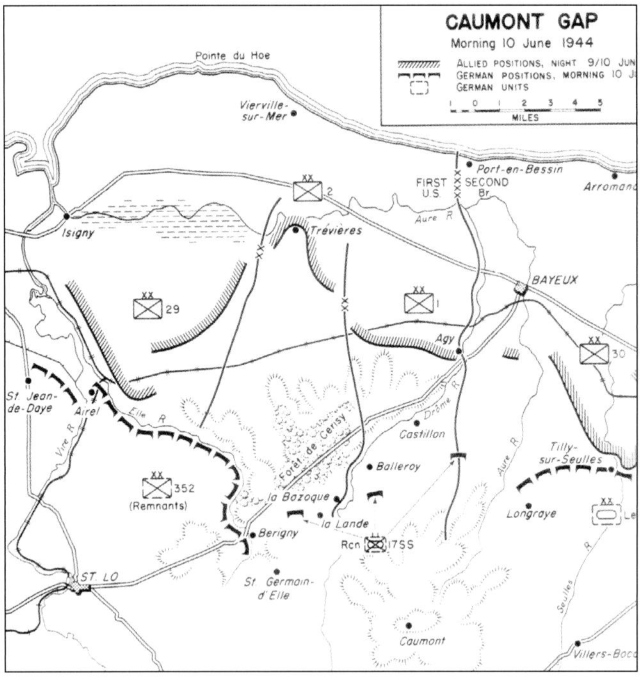

A clear indication of exactly how perilous the invasion was can be seen in this map of 10 June 1944. Although the Allied armies have been ashore four days, at only a few points have they advanced more than five miles from the beachhead. *Courtesy U.S. Army.*

Of all of the events of D+1, perhaps the most important was that a good portion of the 110th Field Artillery had landed safely and were now available to provide fire support. Since the beaches were still congested and under fire 7 June, the 110th's batteries were brought ashore in three different areas and were not reunited until the next day.[27] Meanwhile, in response to Gerhardt's request, the 175th Infantry Regiment was released from Corps reserve and landed during the afternoon of D+1. Even at this point in time, the process of landing was difficult. The 175th lost two of its landing craft to German mines. En route to the shore, they also encountered sporadic enemy machine gun fire. After landing and moving inland, the 175th received an order from Gerhardt to move westward and capture the town of Isigny. Isigny was significant for two reasons: it had a bridge that crossed the Aure River, and the town itself was on the direct route needed to link up with the American forces that had landed on Utah Beach.

Fighting in the hedgerows was tough and demanded a cautious approach while advancing. This picture clearly shows the height and thickness of these uniquely Norman hedges as American soldiers attempt to dislodge the Germans. The soldier in the center is using his M1 Garand with an M7 Grenade launcher to fire a rifle grenade. *Courtesy USAMHI.*

Reinforced by Sherman tanks of the 747th Tank Battalion, the 175th started their move to Isigny that evening. The next morning (D+2), they continued the march, but were slowed by an accidental strafing attack from Allied planes. The 175th encountered slight German resistance along the way, but continued to move to within striking distance of Isigny by late that evening. Inexplicably, they halted at the approach to the bridge over the Aure. Gerhardt himself came forward to see what was causing the holdup in the advance. The unit commander informed Gerhardt that the soldiers feared the bridge was mined or booby-trapped. Without hesitation, Gerhardt ordered the tanks to cross the bridge. Moving quickly, and with all guns blazing, the tanks rolled across the bridge and into Isigny. The infantrymen of the 175th followed closely behind, helping to liberate the town and capture the German defenders.

Earlier that same day, the 116th, again working with the Rangers, had continued westward on the coastal road until they met heavy resistance near the town of Grandcamp. Taking full advantage of their proximity to the ocean, the infantrymen paused and called for naval gunfire support. The HMS *Glasgow*, a British cruiser, obliged with an hour-long barrage. Moving up quickly after the bombardment ended, the 116th still had a tough fight on their hands before they were able to overcome all of the German resistance. During this action, a sergeant from Company "K" distinguished himself by single-handedly knocking out a German fortification. Using a combination of hand grenades and a bayonet, Tech Sergeant Frank Peregory killed eight enemy soldiers and captured three more. Still leading his prisoners, Peregory attacked and destroyed another German machine gun position along the way. Sadly, the brave sergeant wouldn't survive to receive the Medal of Honor he so deserved. He was killed a short while later and his award was made posthumously.[28] After the town was secured, the three infantry battalions of the 116th worked with the Rangers to clear up small pockets of resistance between Isigny and Grandcamp.

After cleaning up the area around Grandcamp, the 116th then became divisional reserve. In the meantime, the 115th and 175th regiments continued to press westward. The 175th passed through Isigny and continued their advance towards Carentan in an attempt to link up with either the paratroopers or the 4th Infantry Division soldiers from Utah Beach. Now moving south away from the beach, the 115th headed inland through a swampy marsh. After an initial attempt to cross this flood zone was unsuccessful, the 121st Engineers brought up their boats and helped the 3rd Battalion infantrymen get through. Moving on the 3rd's left flank, the remaining two battalions found their progress a little easier and they advanced farther, liberating a few small towns as they moved forward.

On the night of D+3, the infantrymen of the 2nd Battalion, 115th Infantry had been moving on foot for almost twenty hours. When they reached La Carretour at 1 a.m., they were finally given a chance to rest. Many of them just dropped to the ground and immediately began to sleep. A short while later, those men still awake could hear the sounds of vehicles approaching from the north, behind the 2nd Battalion. Before many of the sleeping soldiers could react, they were laced with machine gun fire from a retreating German column of assault guns and trucks. Though some of the Guardsmen were able to return fire and even managed to knock out a few enemy vehicles, it was a one-sided fight. Lieutenant Colonel William Warfield, commander of the 2nd Battalion, was killed in the fighting, and the remnants of the unit were soon scattered into small groups of soldiers looking to escape the German onslaught. Using the cover of darkness, many of these soldiers were able to evade the enemy and eventually linked up with other American units. The less fortunate were captured, including a naval gunfire control team that had been assigned to the battalion.[29]

During the night, Gerhardt had become concerned when communication was lost with the 2nd Battalion. With some other officers, he personally went in search of his missing troops and located some of the survivors near the attack site. Angered by the apparent lack of security precautions taken by the shattered battalion prior to their pounding by the Germans, Gerhardt directed the reorganization of the battalion and placed another officer in charge. Though still seething with anger, he had no time for a long tirade. The 175th was still in action over to the west and Gerhardt needed to go there and see what they were doing. A few days later, however, when the 115th was unable to cross the Elle River as ordered, Gerhardt decided the 115th was due for a change. He relieved the unit's commander, Colonel Eugene Slappey, and replaced him with the 29th's Chief of Staff, Colonel Godwin Ordway, Jr. Colonel Slappey was the first senior commander that Gerhardt would replace in France. For a variety of reasons, he would not be the last.

Two enlisted men's wool shirts from different manufacturers show the variations in material and slight differences in color. Although this shirt was intended for field use, it could also be worn with a tie and the four-pocket service coat or the Ike jacket.

On the afternoon of 12 June, two companies of the 175th were still on the outskirts of the village of Montmartin after having tried three times to take the town. As they prepared for another attempt, they heard gunfire nearby and sent a patrol to investigate. The patrol soon returned with soldiers from the 327th Glider Regiment, 101st Airborne Division. The 327th had also been attempting to take Montmartin and the nearby canal bridges. Together, the combined forces were finally able to capture the town and then quickly set up a joint defense. Unfortunately, the link between the two units was tenuous. The communication link between VII Corps (the 101st's higher headquarters) and V Corps (the 29th's higher headquarters) wasn't any better. Without knowledge that companies from both corps were now defending Montmartin, the 327th ordered their troops to withdraw back into the 101st's area. This left only a small contingent of Blue and Gray soldiers to hold Montmartin against a gathering enemy force.[30]

Concerned that the 175th's soldiers holding Montmartin might get overwhelmed, Gerhardt again took a hand by directly ordering Colonel Paul Goode, commander of the 175th, to reinforce them. Personally leading these reinforcements, Goode moved his troops forward through the dark night and directly into a sleeping German camp. Similar to the events at La Carretour a few nights earlier, the moving force got the better end of the deal. The American soldiers opened fire, inflicting heavy casualties on the surprised and sleepy enemy. At this point the similarity ended. The Germans recovered quickly, and soon other enemy forces surrounded the Americans. Trapped, and in an attempt to avoid surrendering to the Germans, Goode ordered his men to break into small groups and make their way back toward the American lines. Only thirty made it. The rest, including Goode, were captured or killed. The two-day total for the 175th during the fighting in the Montmartin area was fifty-three killed, fifty-seven wounded, and more than one hundred soldiers captured or missing.[31]

In relative safety, a large group of replacement soldiers have the opportunity to rearrange their combat loads and pick up some ammunition and K-rations prior to joining their new unit in the hedgerows. This would be the last time they would be safe in the open. Where they were going, a large concentration of soldiers such as this would quickly draw German artillery fire. *Courtesy USAMHI.*

A sign of the growing power of the Allied armies in Normandy. One of the many supply points located behind the front lines in Normandy. *Courtesy USAQM Museum.*

An officer's wool shirt displaying the 29th Infantry Division patch. The epaulets, designed for attaching rank, make it easily distinguishable from the enlisted version.

By 14 June, the entire 29th had settled into a fairly defensive posture. The infantry regiments, however, still maintained an active patrol rotation to detect any German buildup, and perhaps capture some prisoners. General Gerhardt also issued orders that the soldiers could get rid of the anti-gas impregnated uniforms that they had been wearing since D-Day. The specially treated uniforms may have been gas proof, but they had also proven to be even more air proof by not allowing any ventilation in the hot French summer. The combination of dirt, sweat, and gas proof wool uniforms had turned the soldiers into a foul smelling group. Gerhardt's order to switch to regular field uniforms as soon as they could was a most welcome one.[32] Of greater concern to Gerhardt was the fact that, in the week after the 6 June landing, the three infantry regiments had suffered almost 2,000 casualties and his troops were exhausted.[33] The few day's pause allowed them to catch their breath, but it was a very short-lived break.

On 16 June, the 29th and the 2nd Infantry Division received orders to attack towards the small city of St. Lô. With the link between the Omaha and Utah beachheads now fairly secure, St. Lô, a relatively small town of six thousand inhabitants, remained a critically strategic location due to its large network of roads.[34] Control of the St. Lô crossroads gave the Germans the ability to shift their defending forces quickly to wherever they were needed. If the Americans could gain control of this vital road hub, it would undoubtedly support their breakout from the beachheads. Unfortunately for the Americans, the terrain in this area of Normandy bestowed all of its advantages to the defenders. Known simply as the "Bocage," the countryside was "covered by the ubiquitous hedgerows. These solid earthen dikes ranged anywhere from four to nine feet high in height and several feet thick…with trees sprouting from their crests, obstructing [the] view into the next field."[35] The hedgerows divided the farmers' fields into workable plots with only limited passage between each section. As one artillery officer described the hedgerows, they were "five to eight feet thick at the bottom, four to six feet high and thickly overgrown with grass bushes and trees…[they] enclosed every field and apple orchard within miles, thus making ideal fortifications." As well as being a problem for the infantrymen, they confounded the artillery observers. Even while flying in their small spotter planes, these observers were "baffled by the continuous pattern of foliage which the Germans fully utilized to cover their movements."[36]

A National Guard 155mm howitzer fires towards a German target in Normandy in July 1944. With a well-trained nine-man crew, the 155mm could be fired three times a minute. Under magnification, it can be seen that the corporal in the center is holding the M1 Gunner's Quadrant used to set the proper elevation for the gun. *Courtesy USAQM Museum.*

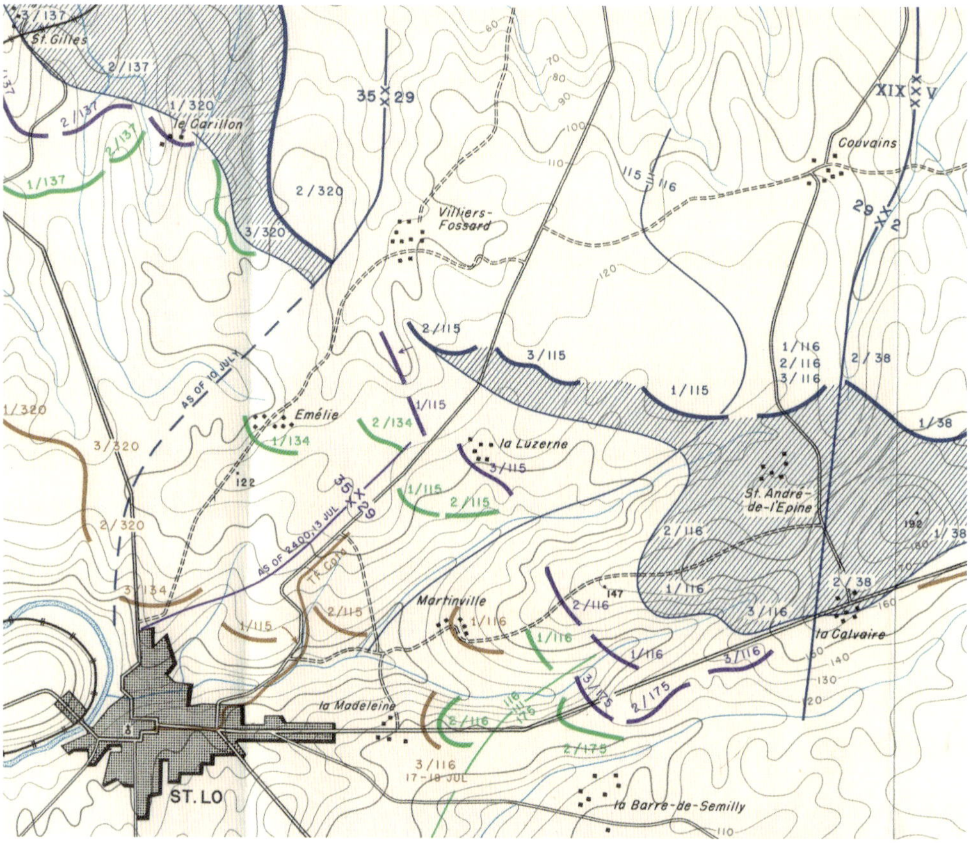

A map of the area around St. Lô during the period 11-18 July 1944. The strategic significance of Hill 192, on the far right of the map, is obvious, as its heights provided the Germans with clear observation of approaching American forces. The locations of the infantry battalions of the 116th and 115th Regiments are clearly marked, as is the approach route of Task Force Cota, which eventually broke into the city. Major Thomas Howie, the "Major of St. Lô," was killed by German mortar fire near La Madeleine 16 July 1944. *Courtesy U.S. Army.*

For a defending force, this area was a natural fortress. Small German units, equipped with a few machine guns and anti-tank weapons, could hold up a much larger American force with relative ease. The maze-like quality of the Bocage also made accurate close air support almost impossible; therefore, the U.S. Army's great airpower advantage over the German Army was nullified by the overhead cover.

Adding to the defender's advantage was Hill 192. Quite possibly one of the more natural defensive positions in the Bocage region, the Germans had prepared to defend it with strong points capable of providing interlocking fields of fire. To make matters worse, the elite German paratroopers defending this hill were able to observe any American movement towards St. Lô from the north, and immediately call in artillery fire on them. The 29th and 2nd Divisions gained some ground at first, but by the next day their progress slowed to a crawl. The combination of German firepower and French Bocage was proving to be deadly to the attackers. Among the first casualties was the newly appointed commander of the 175th Infantry Regiment, Colonel George. George had replaced the missing Colonel Goode only days before, and now, due to a serious wound caused by a German grenade, he needed to be replaced himself. Hill 192 would remain a constant problem for the U.S. forces attempting to capture St. Lô until mid-July when it finally fell to the 2nd Infantry Division.[37]

The roads and countryside in the Bocage were hotly contested by the German defenders. In this July 1944 photograph taken near St. Lô, two soldiers pause near the body of a dead German soldier, while ahead of them a stretcher team scrambles to get out of the line of fire. *Courtesy USAMHI.*

On 17 June, the 1st Battalion, 175th Infantry, made an evening attack that slipped through the enemy lines near the small village of le Mesnil-Rouxelin. With this local advance, they were the closest to St. Lô any unit had been to date. The next morning, the German reaction came with a heavy artillery barrage that raked the battalion and cut their telephone lines to the rear. German infantry followed behind the barrage and quickly put the 1st

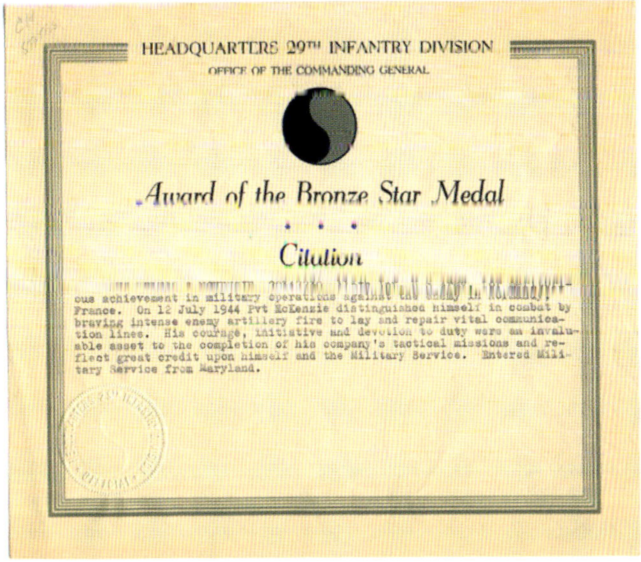

HEADQUARTERS 29TH INFANTRY DIVISION

OFFICE OF THE COMMANDING GENERAL

Award of the Bronze Star Medal

Citation

[illegible] ous achievement in military operations against the enemy in Normandy, France. On 12 July 1944 Pvt McKenzie distinguished himself in combat by braving intense enemy artillery fire to lay and repair vital communication lines. His courage, initiative and devotion to duty were an invaluable asset to the completion of his company's tactical missions and reflect great credit upon himself and the Military Service. Entered Military Service from Maryland.

Certificate with award citation for the Bronze Star presented to a Maryland National Guardsman in the 115th Infantry Regiment. Of interest here is the nicely embossed 29th Infantry Division seal in the lower left hand corner.

Battalion in danger of being overrun. Once the Americans were able to get one of their field radios back working, they began to receive accurate artillery fire support from the 105mm howitzers of the 224th Field Artillery Battalion. The combination of artillery fire and steadfast infantrymen held the line and the German attack failed.[38] The other infantry regiments of the 29th also joined in the fight, but progress was slow. By the 21st of June, the whole division had returned to a strictly defensive posture for "resting, refitting, and training and absorbing replacements."[39]

The rest and reorganization period for the 29th would last almost three weeks. While there was intermittent shelling and patrolling between the opposing forces, the lines remained comparatively quiet and stable. Gerhardt took advantage of this time to integrate replacements into his frontline units. He also had his troops work on improving squad level tactics needed for fighting in the hedgerows. Concurrently, he began a vigorous campaign to treat the many cases of battle fatigue that were greatly reducing the number of soldiers in his rifle platoons. As a result of this innovative program established at the 104th Medical Battalion Clearing Company, the 29th was able to keep many of the cases localized and did not have to evacuate them to higher level facilities. Now that they were better fed, somewhat rested, and receiving replacements to fill out their depleted ranks, the infantrymen of the 29th knew, sooner or later, this "static period" would end; they would have to go back into the hedgerows. St. Lô was still in German hands and somebody was going to have to take it away from them.

A new attempt was scheduled for the morning of 11 July. Just hours before the attack was scheduled to begin, the German artillery blasted the 115th with a heavy barrage, followed by an infantry attack. The 115th suffered heavy casualties driving off the Germans and were unable to begin their own attack on time. The 116th moved out as scheduled and made some initial progress. The 115th joined in the attack a while later and both regiments continued forward until the German defense solidified. Their defense of the hedgerows continued to torment the Americans. Any advances the Americans made were again measured in feet and yards. However, in spite of their successful defense of the area, the Germans too were feeling the strain of continuous combat. One German soldier would later recount that his "experience over the previous four days had convinced him that the war was lost... The Americans seemed to have endless supplies of everything, whether planes, guns or ammunition. The Germans, by contrast, did not even have enough food to eat."[40]

In hopes of breaking through the enemy defenses, Gerhardt scheduled another full scale effort to begin on 15 July. Though most of the attacking units struggled to make any headway, the 2nd Battalion of the 116th managed to advance almost to the town of la Madeleine, just a short distance from St. Lô. The unfortunate reward for this success was to be cut off from the rest of the division by German units moving in behind them. The 2nd Battalion was now isolated and running low on ammunition. Their only source of communications with the rest of the 29th was via the radio set operated by the 111th Field Artillery's liaison officer trapped with them.

Major Thomas Dry Howie: a graduate of The Citadel, a Virginia National Guardsman, and the Commander of 3rd Battalion, 116th Infantry Regiment. A courageous leader, Howie would become immortalized after his death as "the Major of St. Lô." *Courtesy The Citadel.*

Present-day picture of a small la Madeleine farm house. It was very close to this spot that Major Howie was killed by a German mortar barrage 17 July 1944. Martinville Ridge is clearly visible to the northeast in the center background.

Taken shortly after its capture by "Task Force Cota," this picture of St. Lô gives an indication of the damage to the town from the fighting there during the months of June and July 1944.

It would stay that way until 17 July, when the 3rd Battalion of the 116th, led by Major Thomas D. Howie, slipped through the German lines and linked up with the isolated unit. Since the rescued 2nd Battalion was in no shape to continue towards St. Lô as ordered, Howie received orders from Gerhardt to take his battalion into the city. As he was giving the operation order for the attack to his company commanders, a German mortar barrage swept the area and Howie was killed. The 116th's attack could not take place while German artillery and counterattacks kept the American soldiers busy just defending their own area. The soldiers of the 29th Reconnaissance Company also suffered under the heavy German mortar and artillery fire. While most of the company had dismounted from their vehicles to conduct a foot patrol, the area where they had left their vehicles came under extremely heavy fire. Corporal (Tech 5) "Rock" Rothgeb quickly began to move the vehicles out of the area to safety. As the artillery fire continued to fall, knocking over trees on top of some of the vehicles, Rothgeb persevered. Using an ax, he managed to remove the fallen trees, and was then able to save the rest of the vehicles and equipment. Rothgeb was later awarded a Bronze Star for this heroic action.[41]

The M1 helmet belonging to Tech-5 Ulric Rothgeb showing clearly the German "zeltbahn" camouflage material carefully fitted under the helmet net and neoprene band. Rothgeb would be awarded the Bronze Star for bravery near the town of St. Lô 17 July 1944.

In this picture, the camouflage material has been lifted to show the 29th's divisional symbol on the front of the helmet.

Similar to the previous shot, this time the camouflage material on the back of the helmet has been lifted to show the "leaders" mark for NCOs that has been painted onto the shell.

Rothgeb's helmet liner, showing the 29th's symbol on the front. Under Gerhardt's direction, the 29th's symbol was seemingly painted any place it could possibly fit.

Preserved by Rothgeb for many years after the war, these Military Payment Certificates were issued by the Army for use in France after the invasion.

Another picture of the devastation to St. Lô from bombings and artillery barrages during the battle. In the foreground and on the extreme right of the photograph can be seen stockpiles of supplies, indicating that American logisticians have already started to prepare for the next offensive phase of the campaign.

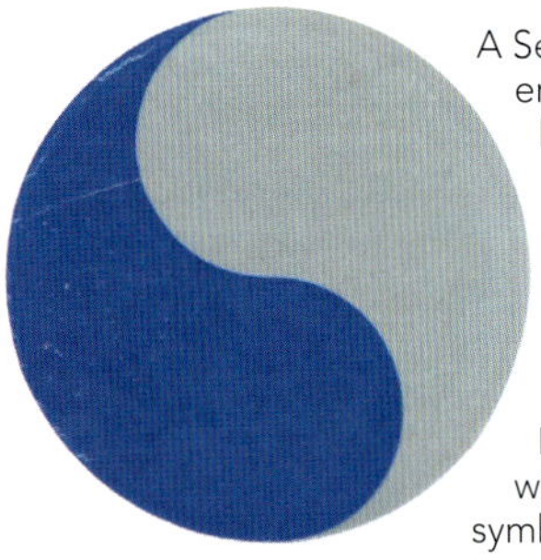

A Second World War era decal for the 29th Infantry Division. These decals would be used to mark helmet liners and anything else the soldiers of the Blue and Gray Division could mark with their famous symbol.

While the 116th and the Reconnaissance Company were being pounded by the German artillery, the other infantrymen of the 29th were keeping busy. The 175th made progress and advanced across the St. Lô—Bayeux road before running into heavy resistance. A staff sergeant of the 175th, Joseph A Farinholt would receive the second of his four Silver Stars during this action when he repeatedly crossed into the enemy's territory to recover some weapons and equipment that had been lost to the Germans. He would later receive his third and fourth Silver Stars for his actions near Aachen in October and Bourheim in November 1944.

On the morning of 18 July, the rest of the 115th moved in a flanking maneuver through the 116th's sector and closed to the outskirts of St. Lô. With his infantry regiments ringing part of the city, Gerhardt now unveiled a surprise; he had formed an ad hoc strike force consisting of the 29th Reconnaissance Company, some engineers, two cannon and anti-tank platoons, a platoon of Sherman tanks from the 747th Tank Battalion, and some other attached tank destroyers. The unit was named Task Force "C" in honor of Brigadier General Cota, the officer chosen by Gerhardt to lead it. Under German artillery fire, Task Force "C" moved quickly down the St. Lô—St. Clair road and burst into the city. Passing through the heavily rubbled streets, past the badly damaged buildings, the task force quickly captured what remained of the city. Though some house to house fighting was necessary, German resistance proved to be far less effective than the 29th had faced in the hedgerows and fields outside the town. Cota was wounded during the attack but continued to lead his troops. One of the first actions of his soldiers was the raising of the 29th's flag in the main square of the city. By that evening, the entire town was secure. Gerhardt sent a message to his Corps Commander, Major General Charles Corlett, informing him that "the 29th Division has secured the city of St. Lô after forty three days of continual combat from the beaches to St. Lô. 29 Let's Go."[42] Gerhardt also ordered that Howie's body be carried into the city, covered with an American flag, and placed on the shattered ruins of a church in the St. Lô square. This simple act of respect was captured by photographers and war correspondents and, although his name was not disclosed at the time due to wartime censorship, Major Howie became known as the "Major of St. Lô."

By 20 July 1944, most of the 29th Infantry Division had been pulled back from the front. The 29th's four field artillery battalions, however, remained in action to support the 35th Infantry Division which had taken over the 29th's sector of the front. The cannoneers would rejoin the division a week later. As the 29th moved completely out of combat and away from enemy fire for the first time in forty-five days, the cost of the battle for St. Lô became obvious. All told, the 29th had suffered higher casualties taking St. Lô than they had on Omaha Beach. Along with that realization, came an important lesson for the men of the Blue and Gray. As one infantry officer would later write "Any position that the German allows you to occupy without a fight is unlikely to be a bargain."[43] It was a lesson well worth remembering as the 29th prepared for its next campaign.

D-DAY TO ST. LO

29 LET'S GO

This Is To Certify That

PVT — MILNOR C MCKENZIE — 20342230

Grade — Name — A.S.N.

WAS A MEMBER OF THE

29TH INFANTRY DIVISION

ON D-DAY, 6 JUNE 1944, AND SERVED WITH IT CONTINUOUSLY UNTIL THE CAPTURE OF ST. LO ON 18 JULY 1944

C.H. GERHARDT,
MAJOR GENERAL, U.S. ARMY,
COMMANDING

A seldom seen document; the certificate provided to some 29th Infantry Division veterans attesting to the fact that they had been with the division from D-Day to St. Lô. Note that this example appears to have been personally signed by General Gerhardt.

CHAPTER 8

From breakout in Normandy till the end of the War

The capture of St. Lô enabled the 29th to move off the line and begin a period of rest and recovery from their nearly constant combat of the previous month and a half. Set back more than three miles behind the front lines, the soldiers of the Blue and Gray were safe from all but the most accidental or randomly fired enemy artillery shell. Even the all too familiar sounds of German machine guns and American rifles were too far away to be distinct.[1] Unfortunately, if the soldiers of the division thought that they were going to be able pass the time in letter-writing and movie watching, they were in for a bitter disappointment. Along with the issue of new uniforms, came a full dose of calisthenics, weapons training, and practical exercises in the tactics of hedgerow fighting.

Members of the 29th Reconnaissance Squadron take advantage of a break in the fighting to replenish the ammunition supply for their M-8 "Greyhound." *Courtesy Virginia National Guard.*

Though St. Lô had been captured, there was still more fighting in Normandy for the 29th. This picture, taken just outside the town of Vire, gives another view of the complications of hedgerow fighting. Strangely enough, as the 29th reached the German border in the fall of 1944, some 29th Division soldiers would write that they preferred fighting in the Bocage to fighting in the wide open spaces of the German farmland near the Roer River. *Courtesy USAMHI.*

The 29th Infantry Division was back in action on 29 July after only nine days of rest. Operation Cobra had begun with a massive "carpet bombing" of the German defenses. Determined to exploit the breach torn in the defender's line by the Allied bombers, the American Army waited for the bombers departure and then moved forward. Following closely behind the 2nd Armored Division, the three infantry regiments of the 29th moved towards the Vire River and the town of the same name. Vire was similar to St. Lô in that it was also a hub for many of the roads in the region, thus making it an important objective for both sides. Unfortunately, it quickly became apparent that the cost of taking Vire might soon equal the bill for St. Lô. The 175th suffered a particularly bad day on 30 July when a German artillery barrage blasted their regimental headquarters. The 175th's "Operations" tent took a direct hit and twelve of the thirteen soldiers inside were killed. This was soon followed by an infantry and armored attack close to the command post which cost more American lives. A short while later, Colonel Ollie W. Reed, the 175th's third regimental commander since D-Day, was fatally wounded by German artillery while riding in a jeep near the Villebaudon crossroads.

Colonel Ollie W. Reed, shown here with the regimental flag of the 308th Infantry, commanded the 175th Infantry Regiment from 23 June until his death just five weeks later on 30 July 1944. His son, Lieutenant Ollie W. Reed II, would also be killed in action that same month while serving in Italy. *Courtesy Dennis Whitehead.*

Henry Glasgow, seen here during a break from training at Fort Meade, would survive the D-Day landing, but be killed later when the house in which he was sheltering from a German artillery barrage received a direct hit.

With the 1 August capture of Avranches by the American VIII Corps, a gap in the German lines had been created. Racing through this breach, General George Patton's Third Army broke into the open and pushed westward meeting very little resistance. In front of the 29th however, the Germans were conducting a very violent and skillful tactical retreat. Through clever use of mines, 'booby' traps, and occasional ambushes by tanks or assault guns, the Germans managed to force the 29th and the neighboring American units to advance slowly. In spite of their caution, the infantry battalions continued suffering casualties every day, but still the 29th kept attacking. After four hard days of fighting, on 5 August, the lead units of the division were within a mile of the town of Vire. Unbeknownst to the 29th, the Germans had decided to make a stand at the town. Located on high ground with the river behind it, Vire was going to be a challenge to any attacking force. The German forces on the far side of the river, on even higher ground, enjoyed the advantage of being able to observe any advance by the attackers. When the Stonewallers of the 116th managed to fight their way into the town on the evening of 6 August, the soldiers would soon appreciate the full advantage this held for the defenders. Soldiers of the 29th would later recount that the next day the Germans focused on Vire with their "mortars and artillery ...pounding it with one of the heaviest German shellings of the war."[2] By 8 August, the 115th and 116th were in defensive positions south of the town. They had also taken possession of most of the high ground preventing the eyes of the German artillery from being able to pinpoint targets in the 29th's area. In these first eight days of August, culminating in the capture of Vire, the 116th suffered more than a hundred killed and almost six hundred wounded. The other two infantry regiments in the division paid a similar price during this period.[3]

While the 29th was busy at Vire, a German armored counterattack on the 29th's right flank blasted a hole into the American lines near the city of Mortain. The 30th Infantry Division, originally comprised of Guardsmen from North and South Carolina, and two nearby U.S. armored divisions, took the brunt of the attack. After four days of heavy fighting, the German attack had worn itself out. While this counterattack had thrown a scare into the advancing Americans, it didn't succeed in plugging the hole in the front lines caused by the earlier capture of Avranches. Patton's Third Army continued their strong attack and poured out of the Cherbourg peninsula. They were soon liberating France at a pace undreamed of by the soldiers of the 29th who were accustomed to measuring their daily progress in yards. By 16 August, the 29th found itself completely off the front lines as the war moved southward and eastward away from them. Joining the 29th's infantry regiments in the now peaceful sector were the four divisional field artillery battalions. This was the cannoneers' first break in action since coming ashore on Omaha Beach, having remained in combat to support the 35th infantry Division after St. Lô.

Given the large-scale demands of the war for infantry units, it was not surprising that the 29th's rest period was again short-lived. By 22 August, the division was loaded onto trucks and headed westward into France's Brittany region. For some of the senior officers and NCOs of the 29th, it was the equivalent of entering a time warp. In 1918, much of the division had landed at the port of Brest before moving on to their first taste of the front lines in the Alsace region. Also during the First World War, Brittany had been the home and training area for the 29th's artillery regiments and the 104th Ammunition Train.

This time in Brittany, however, the targets of the 29th's guns would be shooting back. The quick movement of Patton's forces through the area had cut off a number of German units in and around the city and port complex of Brest. The 29th had been chosen to take back the city of Brest from the German force that had been isolated there. Early intelligence estimates, with their descriptions of a downhearted and defeated foe trapped in a city with no hope of rescue or reinforcement, were encouraging. The pessimists among the 29th's soldiers, however, weren't buying it. Bitter experience in the hedgerows had proven the Germans to be hard fighters and their resistance to be skillful and deadly, even in retreat.

General Gerhardt standing outside his command post, reviewing the day's situation report. Very little escaped Gerhardt's eye and few could deny his ability as a trainer of combat troops. *Courtesy National Archives.*

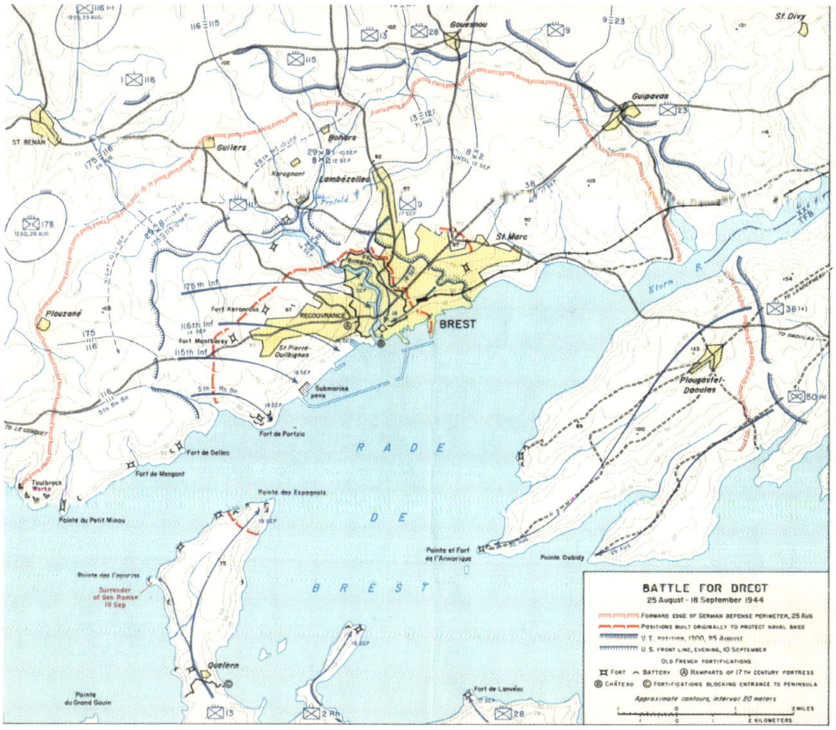

This map shows the fortifications of "Fortress Brest" and the movements of the three infantry regiments of the 29th Division in the campaign to capture the city. By the end of the 26-day battle, the 29th's infantry regiments suffered causalities of over 600 killed and 2,280 wounded. *Courtesy U.S. Army.*

This time, unfortunately, the pessimists were right. Among the enemy trapped in the city were some German paratroopers, similar to those who had proven to be such deadly foes in Normandy. Although initial estimates put the enemy strength in Brest at 20,000 soldiers and sailors, there were actually more than twice that number. Their morale was high, and they were well armed and well supplied. Furthermore, they were under the capable leadership of Major General Hermann Ramke, former defender of Monte Casino. The Germans were prepared to make the Americans pay dearly for Brest.

A helmet and M1923 Cartridge Belt belonging to a soldier in the Headquarters Company of the 115th Infantry Regiment. The iconic 29th Infantry Division symbol is barely visible on the front of the helmet. By the end of the war, six different commanders and five different executive officers had led the 115th in combat.

By the night of 24 August, the two attacking regiments (115th and 116th) were ready to make their move towards the city. Well-equipped German strong points quickly responded to the initial contacts, holding the Blue and Gray soldiers to minimal gains. In the following days, the attacking soldiers, now reinforced by the 175th Infantry Regiment, chipped away at the strong German defenses. It soon became obvious to both sides that a small knoll, known only as Hill 103, was the key to the German outer defenses. From its heights, either side's artillery observers could direct barrages onto their enemy's positions. The mission to attack and capture Hill 103 fell to the 175th.

After eight days of costly fighting Hill 103 was taken, but not before the Germans had put up a ferocious fight. At one point, in an attempt to dislodge the Americans holding the summit, the Germans even committed their elite paratroopers to attack the hill. During the attack by the paratroopers, the positions became intermingled and neither side seemed able to throw the other off the hill. On 3 September, with the 175th struggling to hold their part of the hill, soldiers of the 3rd Battalion, 115th Infantry made a swift flanking move to get behind the hill on the German side. This maneuver cut deep into the enemy's flank and threatened the Germans on the hill with encirclement. They hastily abandoned their positions and fell back into their next defensive line. The advantage in the fight had now shifted to the American side. As the new owners of Hill 103, the U.S. forward observers could see and report German targets for the divisional artillery units now set in place and supporting the attack on the city of Brest. The improved observation of the German positions also improved the accuracy of the aerial bombing of "Fortress Brest."

Over the course of the next few days, the 29th Division, with the U.S. 8th Infantry Division on their left flank, continued to gnaw away at the German strong points. Working with artillery support whenever possible and making unsupported attacks when necessary, the 115th continued to drive towards the outskirts of the city itself. By 9 September, the 115th had made the deepest penetration into "Fortress Brest," but it had come at a high price; from 24 August to 10 September, the regiment had suffered 115 dead and 382 wounded.[4] Casualties for the 116th and 175th were even higher, and there were still more lines of defense to be overcome. The small towns and hills of Brittany were proving to be as deadly as the Norman beaches and hedgerows.

Through it all, the 29th fought on. The German defenders continued to resist stubbornly as they were compressed into smaller and smaller arcs. The battle was quickly degenerating into small unit struggles for control of key houses, strong points, or terrain features. Each time the Germans were forced backward they gave up some territory, but the 29th and 8th Divisions paid dearly for these advances. With his unit stalled by one such strong point, Staff Sergeant Sherwood Hallman of the 175th took it upon himself to break the impasse. Ordering his men to provide him with covering fire, Hallman moved closer to an enemy position until he was able to jump over a hedge and land fighting in the midst of the German position. His Medal of Honor citation later stated: "Firing his carbine and hurling hand grenades, Sergeant Hallman, unassisted, killed or wounded four of the enemy, then ordered the remainder to surrender. Immediately twelve of the enemy surrendered... Seeing the surrender of this position, about seventy-five of the enemy in the vicinity surrendered, yielding a defensive organization which [Hallman's] battalion with heavy supporting fires had been unable to take." Sergeant Hallman was mortally wounded during the attack and he died the next day.[5]

By mid-September, the Germans had their backs to the sea. They had been pushed into a defensive sector nine kilometers long and only three kilometers deep. General Ramke continued to exhort his men to fight on. Despite their hopeless situation, the Germans had a seemingly endless supply of artillery shells and machine gun bullets. The deadly fire forced the American infantrymen to watch their every movement carefully. With no end to the battle in sight, the Americans were augmented with four Churchill flamethrower tanks from the British Army. Under the cover of a carefully laid smokescreen, the large armored flamethrowers went forward. The lead tank was lost almost immediately to an improvised mine and partially blocked the advance of the others. Fortunately, another tank managed to manouver around the damaged vehicle and pour its flames into the German positions. Troops from the 116th quickly moved to capture the now abandoned enemy strong point. In spite of this initial success, it was soon obvious to all that, although the flamethrower tanks were a powerful weapon, getting them into position to torch the German positions was extremely difficult. Debris from the shattered houses littered the narrow streets, hindering the tanks' movement. Even more troublesome were some of the thick walls of the inner city defenses, which would require more than just flame to breach them.

The infantrymen called for direct fire support, and it arrived in the form of tank destroyers. Smaller in size than the flamethrower tanks, the M-10 tank destroyers of the 644th Tank Destroyer Battalion were able to pick their way through the narrow streets. They then fired point blank at the enemy strongholds and pillboxes. At one fortification in particular (the Montbarey Redoubt), the American infantrymen added to the attack by attaching massive amounts of TNT to the outer walls and blasting the strongpoint. When they were finished, the American infantry were able to walk into the giant, newly-made entrance and easily take the dazed survivors prisoner.

The right sleeve of the same 3rd Infantry Division Ike jacket, showing the soldier's original service with the 29th Division. This combination of patches most likely reflects postwar service in the 3rd Division.

The Ike jacket of a 29th Infantry Division soldier who had also served in the 3rd Infantry Division, as indicated by the patch on the left sleeve.

By 17 September 1944, many of the defending German soldiers and sailors had had enough. Knowing that neither relief nor reinforcements were coming, they began to surrender. Unfortunately, others preferred to fight it out to the bitter end with the Americans. When the 115th finally penetrated to within a thousand meters of the waterfront submarine pen complex, they encountered a new defensive line. A series of "dome-shaped pillboxes" armed with machine guns guarded the cliffs over the giant, underground submarine facility.[6] These pillboxes proved to be a tough nut to crack. When the Americans brought up a large self-propelled artillery piece to provide direct fire on these steel and concrete bunkers, they were amazed to see the shells bounce off. The pillboxes also proved to be invulnerable to aerial attacks from fighter-bombers. The only success against these defenses had been made by a patrol of Rangers from the recently attached 5th Ranger Battalion. The Rangers managed to sneak up to one of these structures and were able to neutralize it by pouring gas into the ventilation holes and setting off dynamite charges.

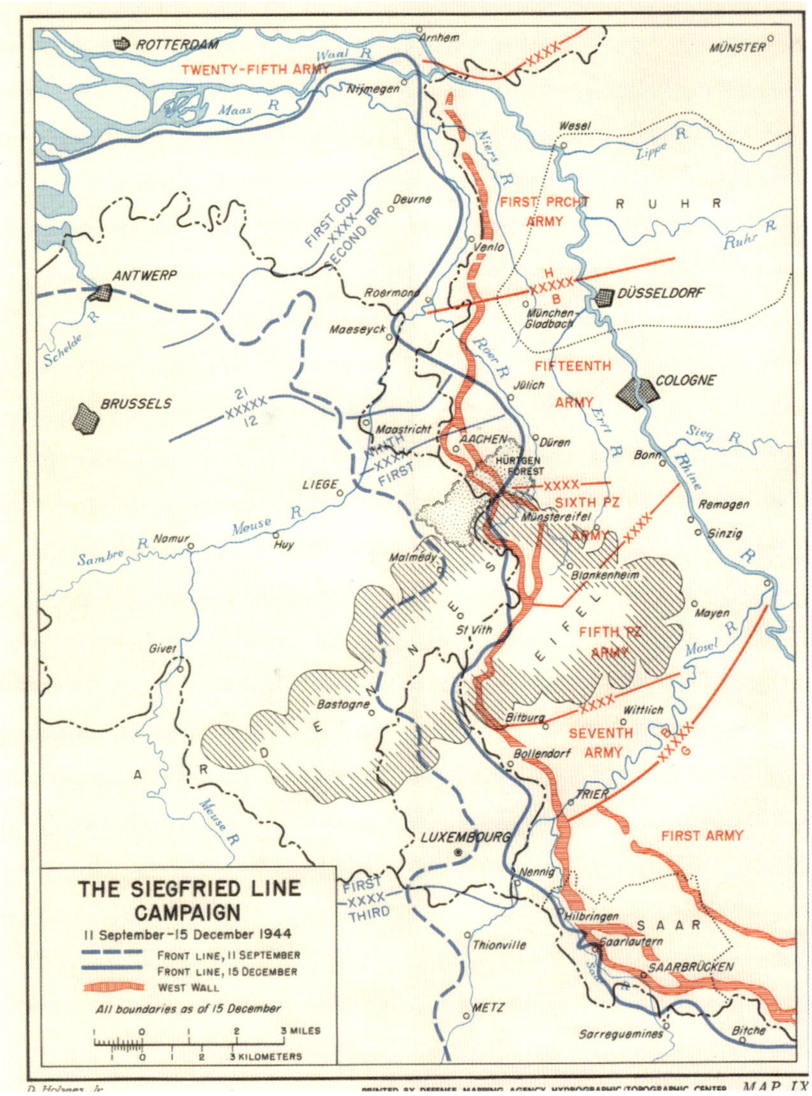

A map showing the 1944 campaign against the Siegfried Line. The 29th Infantry Division's plans to jump the Roer River were delayed twice: first by the German counterattack in the Ardennes in mid-December 1944 and later by the deliberate sabotaging of the Roer River Dam by the retreating German Army. *Courtesy U.S. Army.*

By 18 September, even the most determined German defenders had finally had enough and began to surrender. Throughout the 29th's sectors, the Guardsmen cautiously watched the approach of Germans with white flags. By 11 a.m., the fighting was over and the surviving Germans began to file out of their fortifications. General Ramke, the German commander, managed to escape across the bay to the Crozen Peninsula. He was captured there the next day by the 8th Infantry Division. Ironically enough, the American officer sent to take Ramke's surrender was Brigadier General Charles Canham, former commander of the 116th Infantry Regiment and now the assistant commander of the 8th Infantry Division. When the rank-conscious Ramke arrogantly demanded to see Canham's credentials before surrendering to him, Canham merely pointed to the American infantrymen standing nearby and said, "These are my credentials." Those four words soon became the motto for the 8th Infantry Division, and in the year 2000, would come to symbolize the entire Army through the slogan "Soldiers are our credentials."

With the surrender, the soldiers of the 29th took advantage of the opportunity to go on a souvenir hunt throughout the German fortifications.[7] They also managed to liberate some of the wines and liquors they found stored in the port facilities.[8] It was a well-earned celebration. The twenty-eight day campaign had cost the 29th's three infantry regiments more than six hundred dead and more than twenty-two hundred wounded. Across the board, the 29th was building a reputation as a tough unit capable of tackling the hard assignments, but that reputation had come with a steep price. By the end of the Brest campaign, there were very few of the original infantrymen left who had come ashore just three months earlier on D-Day.

On 18 September, the 29th was moved to a rest area on the nearby Couquet Peninsula after withdrawing from the inner city of Brest. The division was complete when the 116th Infantry and the 111th Field Artillery joined them the next day. Under relaxed conditions, the soldiers enjoyed several days of rest and recreation. Some even began to think about the prospects for leave and furloughs to visit Britain, but no such luck. Once again, infantry divisions and fighting soldiers were in high demand, and the 29th received orders to head eastward towards Germany.

A picture of Tech-5 Rock Rothgeb taken in November 1944. He is wearing the German camouflage material on his helmet, as shown in the previous chapter. Shortly after this picture was taken, Rothgeb would be wounded for the second time, effectively ending the war for him, as he was evacuated to the United States for recovery.

The move east commenced early on the morning of 24 September. The division was split into two groups. Some seven thousand of the soldiers would make the trip by train, while the rest would travel in long truck convoys. In some ways, the trip was almost a "victory lap" for the Blue and Gray Division, as the six-hundred-mile trek took them through a great deal of recently liberated France. Perhaps the most telling indication of how recently the Allies had landed was evident in the extremely warm welcome given to the soldiers en route by French citizens. During overnight stops and even during temporary halts, the soldiers managed to trade their rations for fresh fruit and bread.[9] As a 116th soldier later recounted, they "were greeted by the overjoyed French citizens who honored [them] with Calvados, wine and kisses."[10] Tempering the soldiers' enjoyment of the reception they were receiving was the certain knowledge that when the trucks and trains stopped for the last time, it would be on the German border. As vigorously as the Germans had defended Normandy and Brittany, there was little doubt they would fight even harder to defend their own soil.

By the end of September, the division was moving into defensive positions on the Dutch-German border. Their new mission was to relieve other U.S. Army units, thus allowing them to move south and join in the fighting taking place around the German city of Aachen. Aachen was the first major German city to be taken under direct attack by the Americans, and both sides were fighting for its control. Previously known as Aix-la-Chappelle, this city had served as the headquarters for the Belgian Army of Occupation after the First World War. The name change had come about because the Germans wanted to "Germanize" the names of some of their cities in the mid-1920s. In the same period, Coblenz became Koblenz and Cologne was changed to Köln. Whatever its name was, Aachen was turning into a very nasty fight. The city itself was part of the "West Wall" defenses—more often referred to as the "Siegfried Line"—and was reinforced to protect Germany's borders.

Only a few miles inside the German border, the soldiers of the 29th immediately noticed that they would be fighting a new style of warfare. Gone were the hedgerows and hills of Normandy and Brittany and the shattered streets of St. Lô and Brest. In their place was wide open terrain and farmers' fields which bordered the small German towns. In this environment, any structure or church steeple provided long distance visibility. Unfortunately, the advantage of this improved visibility usually resided with the defending Germans. As one officer of the 116th later wrote: "Overall, the scene was alien and foreboding…I actually missed the hedgerows and worried about attacking over ground that could be dominated for hundreds of yards by a section of machine guns."[11]

Along with being issued cold-weather uniforms and equipment, which included the long heavy woolen overcoats and sweaters that would be needed for fall and winter campaigning in northern Europe, the 29th received some badly needed personnel replacements. One of those replacements was John Henry "Jack" Smith, a former Army Specialized Training Program (ATSP) soldier from New Jersey. Smith, now assigned to the 29th, was processed through the divisional

Mascot of Company "G", 116th Infantry. Richard Inge sent this picture home and wrote that he found this puppy near the front line in France. The dog stayed with the unit for a short time, then disappeared. Inge wrote "He's been lost and found a dozen times, I guess." *Courtesy Inge Family.*

John Henry Smith, Sr., a replacement who joined the 175th Infantry Regiment after the campaign at Brest. Smith, seen here in an Air Corps uniform, would be assigned to Company "F" in time to participate in the late summer campaigns on the German border. *Courtesy Jack, Betsy, and Susan Smith.*

training camp, where he was issued a rifle and given a chance to "zero" it on a rifle range. After completing the reception training, he was assigned to Company "F" of the 175th Infantry Regiment and taken by truck to the front. His first impression was positive: "The weather was nice, sunny, and warm the day that I joined my company compared to the usual dark, cold days and nights....Men were sunbathing, cleaning up, reading or...listening to radios. It was a pretty a tranquil scene. The enemy, however, was less than one mile away. I learned later that whatever action took place usually happened at night."[12]

An extremely rare M1 helmet. The 29th Infantry Division symbol on the front of the helmet shell has been painted over with an orange square and a lion symbol has been added on the side by Dutch volunteers from the southern provinces of Brabant and Limburg, who joined the Allied forces in late 1944. Prior to the liberation of this area, these men belonged to the Dutch underground and were part of the *Knokploegen* (fighting teams) organized to resist the Germans. *Courtesy Paul Reijnders Collection.*

A small ditty bag that has been marked to show its owner's personal history of the war. This Company "B", 116th Infantry Regiment soldier may have joined the unit just after D-Day and served in the subsequent campaigns. Company "B" was originally raised in the area around Lynchburg, Virginia.

A closer view of the front of the Dutch volunteer's helmet showing how the blue and gray of the 29th is still visible under the orange square. *Courtesy Paul Reijnders Collection.*

One of the combat rations provided to a Dutch family by a 29th Division solder during the winter of 1944-1945. The Dutch family kept this box as a treasured souvenir of their American friend. *Courtesy Major General (ret) Ken Bowra.*

With the 115th and 175th Regiments holding a section of the front line and the 116th remaining in reserve, most activities were limited to patrolling the areas in front of the American lines. That changed within a few days, when the 29th received orders to move out on the offensive again. Major Randolph Millholland, now the commander of 3rd Battalion, 115th Infantry, was ordered to take Schierwaldenrath, a small town located north of the 115th's lines. Working with some M3 Stuart light tanks from the 747th Tank Battalion, Company "K" moved out to capture the town. Initially successful in reaching the target, things took a turn for the worse when German resistance stiffened. The light tanks of the 747th took a beating, and were soon forced to withdraw. It got progressively worse. By early evening, Company "K" was isolated in Schierwaldenrath and by 8 a.m. the next morning, there was no more radio contact with the company. All of the men who had been in the town were either killed or prisoners of war. Just as the soldiers of the 29th had feared, there was still a lot of fight left in the Germans.

The Ike jacket and garrison hat belonging to a medic, Technician 4th Grade Hilary M. Wachtel. *Courtesy Scott Stevens.*

On 6 October, Major General Charles Cotlett, XIX Corps Commander, issued new orders to the 29th Infantry Division. Under this latest guidance, they were ordered to: protect the left flank of XIX Corps, conduct probing actions in their sector against the Siegfried line, and be prepared to support the 2nd Armored Division in the event the tankers made a breakthrough near Aachen. In addition to these orders, the 116th was attached to the 2nd Armored. The 116th soon found itself working with the tanks and infantrymen of the 2nd Armored, while the other two regiments maintained their positions and conducted raids against the Germans to their front.

By mid-October, the 116th had been fighting in support of both the 2nd Armored and the 30th Infantry Divisions for more than a week. They worked together to close the gap in the lines near Aachen. One soldier from Company "A" would later write of the 116th's operations in Wurselen: "It was Friday, the thirteenth of October. A black Friday for us. The houses of Wurselen were old, built of solid stone and concrete close together…We had done some street fighting in the approaches to Brest, but nothing like what we were to face in Wurselen…house to house, or rather cellar to cellar…Our guys had to fire out cellar windows or sometimes blast a hole in the cellar wall to gain access to the next door cellar, advancing room by room below ground at all times. It did not go very well."[13] The 1st Infantry Division finally captured the smoking remains of Aachen on 21 October, thereby releasing the 116th to rejoin the rest of the 29th. Within a few days, most of the division was in a rest and training area in the vicinity of Eigelshoven, Holland. Following custom, the 29th immediately set up a tactical training center for the new men and some basic combat skills refresher courses for the rest.[14]

The other side of Tech-4 Wachtel's uniform, showing that he had served previously with an Advance Sector unit and later joined the 29th. *Courtesy Scott Stevens.*

November 1944 found the 29th holding a portion of the front line facing eastward into the German Rhineland. On their right flank was a division now well-known to the 29th, the National Guardsmen of 30th Infantry Division. On their left flank was one of the newer U.S. infantry divisions, the 104th. While inclement weather kept the 29th from going on the offensive, all of the soldiers knew that as soon as the weather improved, they would again attack. In the meantime, training continued and they tried to stay as dry and warm as possible. Meanwhile, orders from 29th Headquarters came filtering down to the infantry battalions. These orders directed that towns in Germany were not to be attacked frontally. Flanking movements would be used to move behind the town and seal it off from the enemy. Only when it was isolated would the infantry attempt to capture it. This guidance had come because Gerhardt wanted no repeat of St. Lô or Vire. As the infantrymen of the 29th digested the details of this new tactic, the steady autumn and early winter rains turned much of the 29th's sector into a muddy swamp.

Wooden unit marker for the 115th Infantry Regiment. The red four-leaf clover and green cactus symbols, tied to the heraldry of the 115th, have been rendered unrecognizable in this version.

With the onset of cold weather, the need for gasoline and diesel fuel increased. Even in a large and powerful force such as the American Army, there were some vehicles, like these tankers, that were too valuable to risk sending close to the front lines. This photograph, taken in late 1944, shows the operation required to down-load fuel from tankers into five-gallon "jerry" cans, which were easier to distribute near the front lines. An infantry division, like the 29th, maintained a huge fleet of motorized vehicles, all requiring fuel. *Courtesy USAQM Museum.*

The extremely heavy wool overcoat of a 29th Infantry Division soldier. Though awkward to run in, especially when wet or caked with mud, these overcoats served as a blanket or sleeping bag for many soldiers during the harsh 1944-1945 winter in northern Europe.

After days of waiting, word came down from headquarters that the attack was to take place 16 November. It would be prefaced by a smoke screen, then an artillery and aerial bombardment to soften up the enemy. This time, the 175th and 115th were leading the attack. As could be expected, the Germans contested the advance strongly and very little progress was made by the attacking force. By the second day of the campaign, the 29th discarded their new tactic of surrounding towns before attacking them. The close proximity of towns in this sector gave the German defenders a distinct advantage. They were able to provide interlocking fire support for each other against the Americans attacking over open fields. Attempts to follow the new flanking tactics ended dismally, as German machine guns punished the attacking GIs. Among the many wounded during the attack was the commander of Company "F", 175th Infantry Regiment. Jack Smith, the recent replacement, was one of the few unwounded soldiers left in the company. He was sent on a mission to locate a first aid team with the stretcher bearers needed to evacuate the wounded. Smith never made it. He was captured by a German patrol and marched to the little town of Neu Brandenburg. From there, he was sent to a prisoner of war camp until the end of the war.[15]

The next day, the 175th reverted to the old tactics of going head-on at an objective. Unfortunately, these direct attacks on the town were no more successful than the flanking moves, and casualties once again were heavy. The first two days of the operation had cost the 175th 41 dead, 141 wounded, and 3 missing.[16] The 115th's losses were comparable. Adding to the misery of the constant German gunfire was the never ending rain that soaked the attackers and made it difficult to evacuate the wounded. At this point, the tactics took another evolution; the objective would be pounded by mortar and artillery fire while a small force of tanks and infantrymen would advance. As the artillery barrage was lifted, the tanks would take over by raking the target using their machine guns and 75mm cannons. Under cover of this direct support fire, the riflemen would then close the gap and mop up the enemy. This carefully orchestrated "combined arms" approach soon became the favored method for attacking the Germans in their small towns.[17]

Using these tactics, the third day of the attack started with some promise. A platoon of Shermans from the 747th provided close support which allowed the 175th to capture part of the town of Siersdorf. However, the new attack method was still dangerous to the attackers and casualties began to mount again in both regiments. Even battalion commanders proved susceptible; Major Millholland, commanding the 3rd Battalion of the 115th, was seriously wounded, and a company commander was killed by a single German artillery shell. Soon, however, with an assist from the 115th, Siersdorf was captured and the division set its sights on the next town to be attacked.

A short while later, again with help from the tankers and their Shermans, the nearby town of Bettendorf was taken. Using the same assault techniques, the Germans were driven back during the course of the next few days. Now the Americans were able to use the church steeples and other high points for their observation posts to direct fire on the defenders.

While it appeared that the Americans on the Roer plain were finally gaining the upper hand, a particularly nasty battle broke out in the town of Bourheim. Several of the 175th's infantry companies were overrun while attempting to defend the recently captured town. On 23 November, the 175th took Bourheim again. With the added support of some tank destroyers, they prepared themselves for the inevitable German counterattack. When it came, it was memorable. In what some members of the 175th considered the heaviest shelling they endured during the war, German artillery pounded the center of the town. Following the barrage, German tanks and other armored vehicles attempted to force their way into Bourheim.

In the following three days (24 to 26 November), this pattern was repeated six times. Each time the Americans held the town. The night of 25 November, the Germans even added an aerial attack to precede another of their combined tank and infantry attacks. When an American request for their own air support was delayed, the 224th Field Artillery pitched in with their 105mm howitzers and did their best to break up the assault. But it was to no avail. A German tank forced its way into the town and began to kill or capture the exhausted Americans holding the town. Individual soldiers tried to stop the tank by using bazookas and satchel charges with little effect. The collapse of a building on top of the tank momentarily slowed it down, but it was soon pulled free by another German Panzer and then resumed the attack. Just as things were looking their worst for the 175th's soldiers, salvation finally appeared in the form of Army Air Force P-47 Thunderbolts. Arriving overhead at about 10:30 a.m., they attacked the German armor still outside the town and then began to strafe any German targets they could find. What remained of the German assault force withdrew from the town and headed back to their own lines still under attack by the P-47s. Bourheim would remain in American hands. With thirty-two dead, sixty-three captured, and over a hundred wounded, Bourheim had proven to be a costly victory for the 175th Infantry.[18]

The German town of Bourheim was captured by the 175th Infantry Regiment 23 November, after several days of hard fighting. Immediately the Germans tried to take it back, and over the following three days, their counterattacks battered the 175th's hard-pressed defenders. In this historically accurate painting by Larry Selmon, Technical Sergeant Joseph A. Farinholt is shown earning his fourth Silver Star by firing his 57mm antitank gun to blow the track off a German Tiger tank. Return fire from the now-disabled enemy tank wounded Farinholt and shattered his right leg. Bourheim remained in American hands. *Courtesy National Guard Bureau and Larry Selman.*

Perhaps luckier than most, the soldiers manning this machine gun post have a trench with a dry floor, plenty of rations, and a portable stove to heat their coffee and meals. With the constant heavy rain in November 1944 soaking the ground and creating mud, the soldiers' fighting positions quickly became reminiscent of the First World War. *Courtesy USAQM Museum.*

A close-up view of the dog tags (one brass and one stainless steel) belonging to a 29th Infantry Division soldier from Mokena, Illinois. The information on the tag includes next of kin, which indicates these are using the early format. Later versions omitted the next of kin and home of record information.

A typical example of what an infantryman in the 29th Division would be wearing in the Roer River campaign in late 1944. The heavy overcoat has been exchanged for the popular and extremely functional M1943 field jacket. Along with his canvas M1936 field bag, this soldier has two magazine pouches for his M1 carbine, a TL-122B model flashlight, and a British-made first aid kit. Under the helmet, the soldier has a knit wool cap.

The 116th was likewise occupied in a deadly battle for possession of the small town of Koslar, located less than a mile from the Roer River. In fighting both the German Army and the weather, the 29th's soldiers found themselves in combat reminiscent of the First World War: "Life was clammy and miserable during these last two weeks of the drive to the Roer. It rained nearly every day and the water that lay at the bottom of the trenches was more than ankle deep. Thick mud clung to shoes ...Trench foot spread through the wet battle line... any movement in daylight was impossible except through the narrow-walled trenches."[19] These same words could easily have described the battle environment the 29th had faced just twenty-six years earlier in the Meuse-Argonne campaign. Yet there was a difference. The battle was on German, not French soil, and there would be no Armistice to stop the fighting. Casualties had risen once again to the point that there were few members of the original National Guard contingent left in the 29th Division's rifle companies. Worse yet, some soldiers that had been wounded in Normandy and returned to their units had been wounded again. Even the St. Lô and Brest-era replacements had become battle hardened veterans by this time. One soldier who had joined the Division just before D-Day wrote: "I was learning to become extremely cautious. I would not trust anyone. If someone said it was clear up ahead, I didn't believe him....I came to distrust every report I heard."[20] With the capture of Koslar and the nearby town of Kirchberg, the 29th was now standing on the west bank of the Roer River. While the majority of the German soldiers had fallen back across the river, there still remained three strong German defensive positions on the western side of the Roer. These would have to be eliminated before the 29th could claim complete control of all land west of the Roer. The three strong points—a *Sportsplatz* (athletic stadium), a large swimming pool facility, and a collection of stone houses known as the "Hasenfeld Gut"—all lay close to the river. They were held by an enemy determined to contest each foot of their homeland.

An interesting picture clearly showing the wide variety of clothing worn by soldiers of the 29th Division in the autumn of 1944. Here they are seen wearing a mix of M1941 and M1943 field jackets, and even a Mackinaw coat. It is also interesting to note that, despite this mix of clothing, all of the men wearing helmets have the chinstrap buckled in accordance with General Gerhardt's instruction.

A 29th Infantry Division M1 helmet belonging to Everett C. Warren. Warren managed to mark the helmet as his by stamping his name on the sweatband of the helmet liner. *Courtesy Paul Reijnders Collection.*

A closer look at the extremely faded 29th Infantry Division symbol painted on the front of Warren's helmet. *Courtesy Paul Reijnders Collection.*

It fell to the 115th to take these German positions. Once again, the terrain favored the defenders. From the safety of high ground on the east side of the river, German artillery observers could direct their fire onto the attacking Americans. To further bolster their positions, at night, the Germans would send reinforcements and supplies across the river to their comrades holding off the attackers. On 1 December, the 115th attacked the three separate locations simultaneously. The attacking soldiers struggled to make progress after repeatedly encountering mine fields and artillery fire, as well as direct fire from the complexes themselves. Even with American artillery and air support adding to the 29th's firepower, the Germans managed to drive back the Blue and Gray infantrymen. The tankers of the 747th did their best to lend a hand by providing direct fire. They received heavy anti-tank fire in return and ended up leaving one of their Shermans burning in the field near the Hasenfeld Gut. The 116th added their weight to the American attack on 6 December, but even that met little success.

Another coordinated attack was made on all three sites 8 December. Under the cover of an artillery barrage and a massive smokescreen, the 115th was finally able to penetrate and capture the buildings of the Hasenfeld Gut. The other two strong points to the south—the swimming pool complex and *Sportsplatz*—also fell to the determined infantrymen. The morning of 9 December 1944 found the west bank of the Roer River cleared of Germans and declared secure. Leaving outposts forward on the Roer to keep an eye on the Germans, the majority of the 29th moved back from the river's bank to start a period of rest and, of course, more of the usual training. Knowing that the Roer would eventually have to be crossed, one of the main focuses of the training was in river crossing operations and tactics. Unbeknownst to the soldiers of the 29th, something dramatic was about to happen that would place all plans for the river crossing on hold.

A photograph of a forward fuel distribution point. From the snow on the ground, it is most likely this picture was taken in early December after the rains of November had turned into a more wintry mix. *Courtesy USAQM Museum.*

A well-worn M1941 field jacket belonging to a Company "F", 116th Infantry Regiment vet. Though quite comfortable and durable, the 1941 model had drawbacks. It offered little cold or wet weather protection below the waist and the pockets weren't deep enough to hold items securely while running. The lighter color also made it impractical for wearing on night patrols.

An M1943 Field Jacket with the M1943 Field Jacket Hood attached. When attached to the jacket, the hood would usually be worn under the helmet. These jackets made their first appearance in the autumn and winter of 1944-1945.

On 16 December, a counterattack by the Germans through the Ardennes Forest caught the Americans by surprise and the Battle of the Bulge was on! The next day, the 30th Infantry Division, on the 29th's right flank, was already moving to help seal off part of the collapsed American front. This left the 29th responsible for the 30th's sector, as well as their own. On the 20th, the 29th's northern flank neighbor, the 2nd Armored Division, also relinquished their sector to the 29th and moved south to shore up American forces in the growing Battle of the Bulge. As a result of the two divisions moving, the 29th's lines now stretched for twelve miles. They also took responsibility for a sector of the 104th Infantry Division's front. As precarious as this sounds, the situation on the ground was actually worse, primarily due to the heavy casualties suffered by the division during the preceding two months. Many of the killed and wounded were not replaced, as the Army divisions directly in the face of the German breakthrough received first priority.[21] If there was a bright side to the 29th's dilemma, it was that the Germans were also pushing everything they had into the Bulge fighting. This left little with which to attack the thinly-spread 29th. As a result, the front line soldiers of the infantry and artillery regiments were able to expend some time and effort in improving their winter living quarters in basements and dugouts throughout the division's area. While the fighting around Bastogne and on the sidewalls of the Bulge was increasing, the 29th experienced a comparatively peaceful and uneventful Christmas Day.

Gerhardt was a far too aggressive leader to let his division spend all of their time in winter quarters and writing letters home. The 29th constantly sent small patrols across the river to reconnoiter the enemy's positions in an attempt to glean some intelligence into their planning. At least sixty patrols from the 29th braved the cold weather and German outposts to cross the Roer and scout for information during this period while the Battle of the Bulge continued. In late January, the Roer was sufficiently frozen that one patrol was able to walk across the river and take on a German outpost in a small-scale fire fight before returning to their positions on the west bank. The 29th also conducted a series of raids, again reminiscent of First World War action, across the river to the area near the city of Julich. Similar to the division's raids in 1918 against the Germans in Alsace, the results were mixed and little was settled between the two sides. In one burst of exuberance, on 3 February 1945, the division marked its fourth year of active duty by conducting a mock attack against the German positions opposite the town of Kitchberg. Whether the false attack had an impact on the enemy is unknown. But, with the Battle of the Bulge now winding down to the south, the troops of the 29th knew that their quietest period of the war since landing in France was probably coming to an end. As a means of comparison, for the entire division, the casualties in January 1945 were less than three percent of the total suffered in either June or July 1944. Since all good things must end, the 29th knew that soon, probably very soon, they were going to have to cross the river and take Julich from the Germans.[22]

A Company "M", 116th Infantry Regiment soldier carrying a load of mortar rounds on a cargo pack board in Germany in 1945. *Courtesy Virginia National Guard.*

Taken from the divisional newspaper, this simple map shows the journey of the 29th from D-Day to their meeting with the Russians on the Elbe River.

Upriver from the 29th, the Germans had sabotaged one of the dams, which released an increased water flow to the Roer and other German rivers. As a result, the planned cross-river attack had to be postponed again until the water levels dropped. Due to the long delays, the soldiers of the 29th began to consider the city of Julich the ultimate symbol of the hated enemy—both feared and coveted. One of the key defensive points of the city was a fortification known as the "Citadel." With its thick stone walls, deep protected tunnels, and towering heights, the Citadel was a worthy target that the Americans pounded with everything they had every chance they got. What the attackers could not ascertain was whether or not, like Monte Casino in Italy, all of the rubble created by the bombs and artillery shells had actually made it more, rather than less, formidable. There was only one way to find out, and that meant crossing the river.

The morning of 23 February, they did. Using lightly armored amphibious vehicles known as "Alligators" and some assault boats, the 115th and 175th finally crossed the Roer River. Following close behind them, the 121st Engineers began construction of foot bridges, allowing additional infantrymen to quickly cross the river without the aid of boats. Working under fire, the engineers had the first bridge ready by 6 a.m. Shortly thereafter, the riflemen soon began their hurried dash across the river.

Running into heavy enemy fire, the 175th made slow progress. To the north, the 115th had an easier time of it. It soon was linked up with elements of the U.S. 102nd Infantry Division that had crossed the river on the 115th's left flank. By that evening, the 116th was also across the river and moving to assist in the attack on the Citadel. With the onset of darkness, most fighting ceased and the Americans consolidated their bridgehead. The 30th Infantry Division, now returned from their service in the Bulge, had also crossed the river to the south and was firmly in control of their sector on the 29th's right flank. Morning would bring the attack on the Citadel. There was a large contingent of newspaper correspondents and photographers waiting to document the attack. There was no way they could know that on that very same day, 23 February 1945, half a world away on the tiny volcanic island of Iwo Jima, their efforts would be overshadowed by a

A nicely-preserved M1 helmet liner and shell belonging to an unidentified member of the 29th Infantry Division. *Courtesy Paul Reijnders Collection.*

While many of the 29th Infantry Division symbols were carefully painted on helmets, others were more hastily applied, as shown in this example, where there is a significant gap between the blue and gray portions. *Courtesy Paul Reijnders Collection.*

Three members of the 29th Division pose for a picture with the sign welcoming the rest of the American Army to München-Gladbach. By the end of the war, almost every town captured or river crossed rated a sign similar to this one. *Courtesy Virginia Army National Guard.*

group of Marines photographed raising a flag on another enemy citadel called Mount Suribachi.

The attack on the Citadel was to be conducted by the 116th, while the 175th maneuvered in support to isolate the fortification. Blasted by the flame and 75mm cannon fire from the American flamethrower tanks of the 739th Tank Battalion, the gate to the citadel was breached and the 116th's infantrymen entered the ruins. It was anti-climatic; the Germans had fled, leaving behind only a few soldiers who quickly surrendered. With the fall of the Citadel, Julich was now indefensible, and the city was soon completely in American hands. The construction of vehicle bridges allowed the divisional artillery to quickly cross the river and they were soon available for fire support. Once past Julich, the 29th pivoted northward and drew a bead on their next objective, the city of München-Gladbach.

On 26 February, a German counterattack near the town of Ameln by two Tiger tanks and some assault guns gave some cause for alarm. However, it was quickly driven off by the 1st Battalion, 115th Infantry, with artillery support from the 110th Field Artillery. Moving quickly now, the 29th continued its northward trek. By the end of the month, they were outside their goal, the large industrial city of München-Gladbach. In a flanking maneuver, the 116th moved to cut off the city from reinforcements while the 175th moved directly into the center of town. The act of capturing the city had two immediate benefits for the victorious but tired riflemen of the 29th. The overnight accommodations in a large German city were certainly more luxurious than what they were accustomed to. More importantly, the advance of other U.S. units past the city had pushed the 29th out of the front lines and into a rear echelon reserve. For the first time, some of the Blue and Gray began to think that they might actually survive the war.[23]

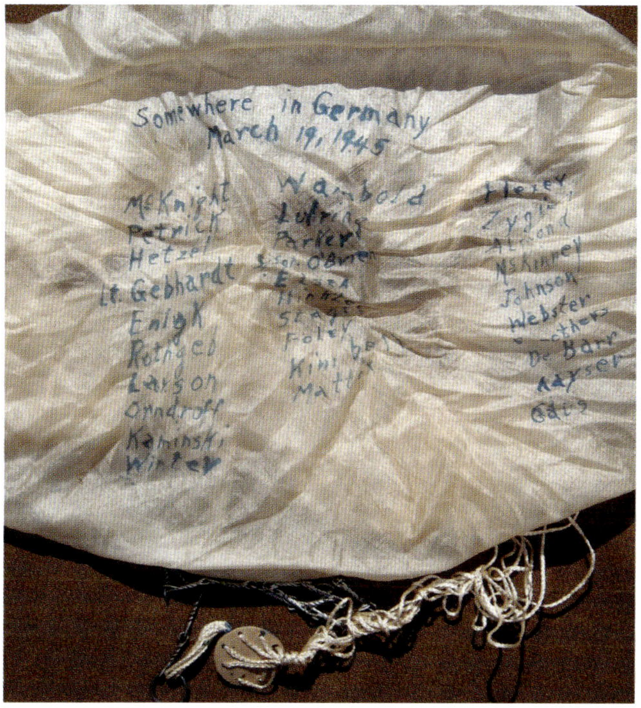

A unique souvenir, the parachute from a flare that has been marked with the names of soldiers in a unit, most likely the 29th Reconnaissance Company, dated 31 March 1945 "Somewhere in Germany."

A stern warning intended to scare away any GIs intent on hunting for souvenirs or loot. With the war winding down, the opportunities to gather up souvenirs to take home were increasing and many soldiers felt that anything found in Germany was fair game. *Courtesy USAQM Museum.*

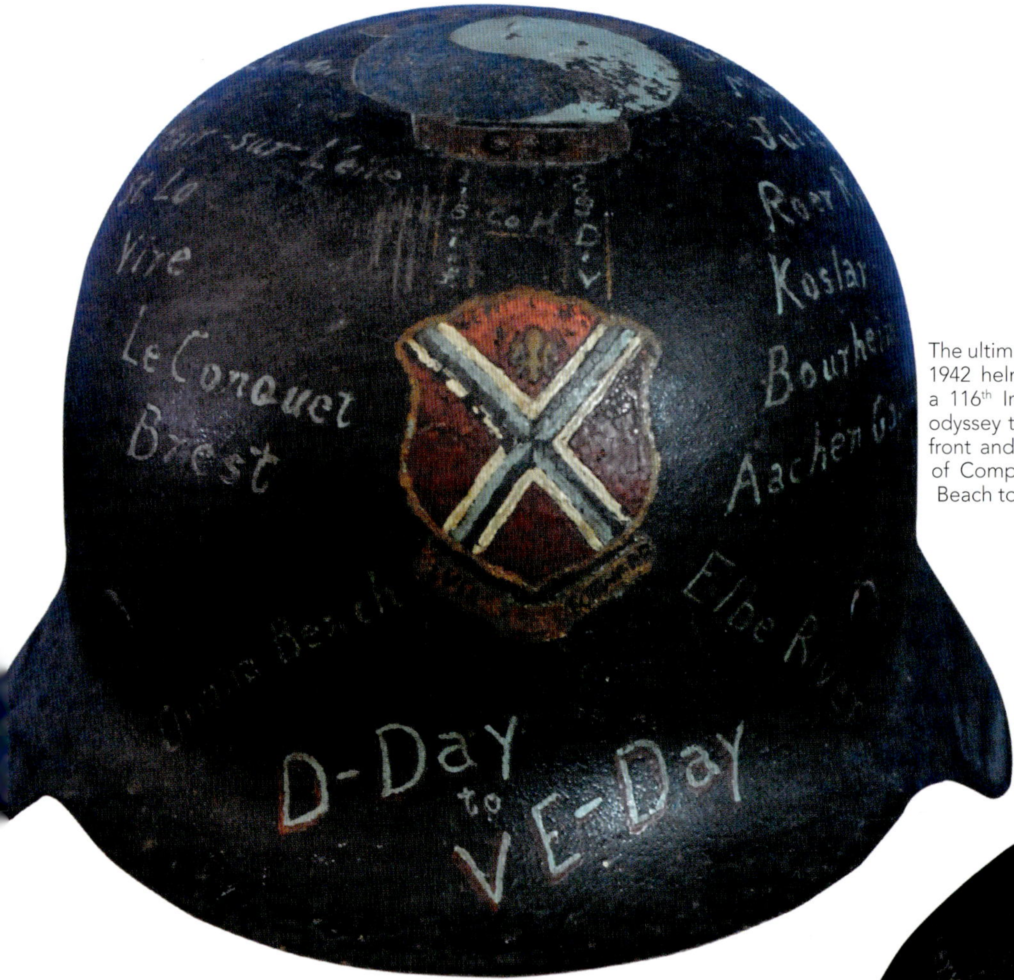

The ultimate in souvenirs. This German model 1942 helmet has been decorated to reflect a 116th Infantry Regiment soldier's personal odyssey through the Second World War. The front and top reflect that he was a member of Company "H" and served from Omaha Beach to the Elbe.

On the helmet's right side he has added the French towns he helped liberate. On the bottom left he has added a rudimentary German eagle and swastika.

Seen from the top are the Divisional symbol and slogan "29 Let's Go." Also visible on the helmet's left side is a list of German towns captured by the 29th during the last months of the war.

Despite such happy thoughts, the war was far from over for the 29th. The Allies had successfully jumped the Rhine River in two places: first using a railroad bridge captured near Remagen, and then two weeks later, in the large-scale cross-river attack known as "Operation Varsity." In spite of all this success, there continued to be a need for experienced infantry divisions. The 29th soon received word to mount up again, and by 31 March were rolling in large truck convoys across the Rhine River. The Stonewallers of the 116th were diverted after crossing the river and attached to the 75th Infantry Division as part of the force maneuvering to encircle the Ruhr, Germany's large industrial center.

On 4 April, the 116th was ordered to attack across the Dortmund-Ems Canal. This they quickly accomplished with little support. Although it was becoming obvious to all that the Germans were just about ready to throw in the towel, there was still enough danger in the air to keep the soldiers alert and watchful. Ironically, it was during this operation that Private First Class C. J. Galloway, the very last soldier of Company "A", 116th Infantry to be killed during the war, died after being hit by a short round from a 75th Infantry Division artillery unit.[24]

The 29th's divisional artillery was also temporarily detached and assigned to support the U.S. 79th Infantry Division near the town of Duisberg. With the encirclement of the Ruhr and the capture of Duisberg, both of these temporary assignments came to an end, releasing the artillery units and the 116th Infantry to return to their own division.

Once again a complete division, now the 29th's primary mission was developing and executing a plan for all of the displaced persons (soon referred to simply as DPs) who were roaming the area and clogging the roads. Most of the DPs were from countries overrun by the German armies early in the war and had been sent to Germany to work as forced or slave labor. In meeting the challenge of caring for these people, the division soon found itself administering 146 camps or facilities to service and feed the more than 72,000 DPs in their area of operations. Adding to the problem, many of the DPs were sick or extremely malnourished. While this was a major task for the staff of the 29th, their share of the mission was actually quite small compared to some other American units. A report issued shortly after the war estimated there were more than four and a half million DPs in the United States Army sector alone. This was only about half of the estimated ten million foreign laborers that had been brought to Germany.[25]

On 17 April, the 29th was again ordered to move out. This time, the operation was to sweep in a northeasterly direction with the goal of rounding up all of the German soldiers west of the Elbe River. The Elbe had been agreed to previously by the Allied High Command as the boundary between Eisenhower's Allied forces approaching from the west and the Russian Armies from the east. It would be the farthest advance of the American Army in Northern Germany. After meeting only token resistance on 21 April from enemy forces in two small German towns, the 29th continued its march to the Elbe. Within a week, the division found itself sitting on the west bank on the Elbe. Land mines within the sector remained one of the more dangerous aspects of the operation, along with an occasional skirmish from some die-hard German soldiers. For the most part, however, what little remained of the German Army was trying to get to the western bank of the Elbe so that they could surrender to the Americans instead of the Russians. On 2 and 3 May, the 29th accepted the surrender of over ten thousand German soldiers who had crossed the river to avoid captivity by the hated and feared Russian Army.

A nice souvenir leather folder, marked inside with the triangular logo of the Junkers airplane manufacturer, now has the 29th Division symbol painted on the outer cover.

Brigadier General William H. Sands, 29th Division Artillery commander, shakes hands with Russian Army General Chapurkin at their 3 May 1945 meeting near the Elbe River. It's interesting to note that Sands has gone to the effort of having his five overseas stripes sewn onto the left sleeve of his field jacket. *Courtesy National Archives.*

PARIS EDITION

EXTRA **THE STARS AND STRIPES** EXTRA

Daily Newspaper of U.S. Armed Forces in the European Theater of Operations

Vol. 1—No. 285 1 Fr. 1 Fr. Tuesday, May 8, 1945

VICTORY

Nazis Reveal Surrender To Western Allies, Russia

The unconditional surrender of Germany to the Western Allies and Soviet Russia was announced by the German high command yesterday morning.

The official announcements from the Allied governments are expected to come simultaneously from Washington, London and Moscow today.

The newspaper headline that the men of the Blue and Gray had waited a very long time to see. The war was over and they had survived, but before they could go home, some would spend an additional eight months on occupation duty in Germany.

Another nice souvenir brought home by a 29th Division soldier. He acquired a German labor unit hat and had a local tailor shop embroider the 29th Infantry Division patch onto the side. The significance of the Weimar souvenir pin is unknown.

On 3 May, a group of Russian soldiers crossed the river and were welcomed by the 29th. Later that evening, another group crossed and this time were led by a Russian major general. They were met by the Divisional Artillery Commander, Brigadier General William H. Sands, who presented them with gifts on behalf of General Gerhardt. While all of the visiting and exchanges were taking place, Gerhardt was busy at Ninth Army Headquarters. The 29th was about to get another mission.

When it became obvious to the Allies that they were going to win the war in Europe, they had established a postwar occupation plan known as "Operation Eclipse." When the phrase "Eclipse Conditions" was used in mid-April 1945, it provided authority to the American commanders to begin the process of governing and administering the areas of Germany under their control. One thing the American Army had learned during their occupation of the German Rhineland from 1918 to 1923 was the need to establish control of towns and cities quickly. They could then use the very structured German civilian government to manage the occupied area.[26] Under "Eclipse," the senior Army commanders were able to divert combat units not directly in action to support the civil affairs mission of governing occupied territory.[27] In fact, a November 1944 directive had provided clear guidance: "The conduct of military government operations is a command responsibility. Military Government will ultimately be based on the German regional system.... As the occupation progresses Military Districts will be established in the area occupied by your group of armies..."[28] The reason for such unusually clear guidance is obvious: for once, the American Army had read their own history and After Action Reports. In 1918, the United States Army was responsible for occupying over 2,500 square miles of Germany with over a million inhabitants. Upon arrival in their assigned occupation and administrative sectors, U.S. Army units attempted to impose a form of government based on the Army structure without realizing how well regimented the German local governments already were. Rather than take advantage of the highly organized German governmental structure already in place, the Americans tried to make the local government fit within the organizational framework of the combat units of the Third Army. This proved to be awkward and ineffective. As the U.S. troops gained a greater appreciation for German governmental procedures, the American method of administration began to mirror the German configuration, both for efficiency and convenience. With so many of the United States Army senior leaders having been veterans of the earlier occupation, they were determined to start off on the right foot this time.[29]

The 29th was now assigned to occupy and administer the area of Northern Germany, soon to become known as the "Bremen Enclave." Bordered on the north by the North Sea, the Enclave was a large sector that included two German ports, Bremerhaven and Bremen. Though the Bremen Enclave was located in an area initially under British Army control, with the bulk of the American forces operating further south, the two seaports had been designated as the logistics point of entry for American supplies. While in the course of moving northward to begin their duties in the Enclave, the 29th received word that Germany would surrender the next day. The war in Europe officially ended for the American forces with the signing of the surrender documents by the German representatives 7 May 1945. The next day, 8 May, has since become known to the United States as V-E (Victory in Europe) Day. The British Commonwealth countries, however, chose instead to celebrate 7 May as their V-E Day, while Russia celebrates 9 May as their V-E Day. For the soldiers of the 29th, it didn't matter; the war was over. While they still had a big job to do administering the Enclave, they had survived. Very quickly, like the Doughboys of 1918, their thoughts quickly turned to one question, "When do we go home?"

An unidentified soldier of the 29th division poses with his jeep somewhere in the "Bremen Enclave." Now wearing a clean uniform with creases in his trousers, the only indication of the hard campaigning this soldier has seen is shown by his rough-worn combat boots. *Courtesy Inge Family.*

Among the many duties performed by the 29th Infantry Division soldier during their period in the Bremen Enclave Military District was the enforcement of military law and movement control through the sector. Similar to these well-armed Army Constabulary soldiers seen searching a building for contraband or weapons, the 29th's soldiers were an effective police force. *Courtesy USAQM Museum.*

A unique souvenir displaying a number of patches, including the 29th Infantry Division. Obviously meant for some sort of display, the patch that seems out of place is the one closest to the tassel; the patch for the "Manhattan" project.

Tropical Worsted (TW) dress uniform coat belonging to a 29th Division officer. Introduced in 1942 for officers and warrant officers, this style coat, commonly referred to as "TWs," would stay in use until the mid-1960s.

VIERVILLE
ISIGNY
ST. LO
VIRE
LE CONQUET
BREST

SPECIAL EDITION — V-E DAY — SPECIAL EDITION

29 LET'S GO

BOURHEIM
KOSLAR
ROER RIVER
JULICH
MUNCHEN-GLADBACH
ELBE RIVER

VOL. 7 — BREMEN, GERMANY, SATURDAY, JUNE 30, 1945 — NO. 31

A WELCOME

To the Officers and Men Of the 69th

TODAY you are in the ranks of the 29th—an organization which was inducted in 1941, sailed overseas in 1942, spent 20 months in England, landed on D-Day, and had 238 days of actual combat.

We welcome you as veterans to veterans. We rejoice in the achievements and fame which you have won. We are delighted to have you with us to carry on our mission in the U.S. Enclave Military District as members of Task Force Bremen.

Hobby Schools Popular As Aid To Civilian Jobs

Three "hobby schools" now in full swing at the 3rd Bn. of the 175th Inf. are providing helpful instruction for advancement-minded GI's in the three categories of carpentry, typing and photography.

Enthusiasm is mounting in the program, and favorable comment is unanimous among those who have elected to attend school sessions.

The Carpentry school, held in two shops in Lilienthal and Worpswede, has the objective of presenting the fundamentals of carpentry for students. Instructors are Pfc. Ben F. Chandler, M Co., and Pfc. William L. Simms, I Co. Theory is being supplemented by practical work for the 50 students now attending.

Typing school for 85 men enrolled is held in four classrooms at Lilienthal for L Co.; at Frankenburg for K Co.; at Orasburg for M Co., and at Worpswede for Hq. Co.

Despite difficulties encountered in arranging necessary transportation, and particularly in having typewriters available, classes are proceeding with commendable success. The co-operation of Unit Personnel has been an important factor in the continued development of the typing schools.

Richard W. Obetts, M Co., is conducting the "touch typing" sessions, which are designed to familiarize the student with the first principles of the system.

Classes in basic photolgraphy, which have attracted an enrollment of 52 men, are held in Lilienthal in Co. L's recreation hall.

Photo Contest Ends At Midnight Tonight

Midnight tonight is the deadline for submitting photos to the Miss Blue and Gray Queen contest. The hundreds of entries we've received will make the judging a matter of several days. In the meantime we'll run some more of the cuties who've been gracing these pages the past few weeks.

Prizes to the winner will be announced shortly.

We wish to thank the men who contributed, and congratulate them upon their good fortune in having something so nice to come home to.

Baseball Circuit

Yesterday's Scores

115th Inf. 2, 116th Inf. 1

Attached Units 10, Divarty 5

Blue and Gray League Standings

	W	L	Per.
Attached Units	2	0	1.000

The newspaper produced by the 29th Infantry Division while on occupation duty in the Bremen Enclave. What other name could a paper for the Blue and Gray have but "29 Let's Go"? The issue seen here is a special one, intended to welcome the men of the 69th Infantry Division that have been reassigned to the 29th.

The answer to that question was the very same their Doughboy fathers and uncles received in 1919: "Not yet." After taking control of the Enclave from the British, the 29th administered the redeployment of Norwegian-based German forces to their homes. In a four-month period, they managed to process some 187,355 of these soldiers, moving them on to various locations in Germany, Austria, France, and Czechoslovakia.[30] Just like their Doughboy predecessors, the 29th Division staff decided the best way to keep the soldiers out of trouble was to keep them busy. Athletic competitions, parades, inspections, and opportunities to take tourist trips to Belgium, France, and Britain all filled the soldiers' weekly schedules. Nevertheless, soldiers of the Division rightly felt that they had done enough to beat the Germans and they should be among the first to head home. It didn't take too much effort for the soldiers to subvert their rallying cry of "29 Let's Go" to "29 Let's Go Home."

The hard to read, and even harder to photograph, interior of an M1 helmet shell reflecting a Marylander's record of the places he served during his time in the 29th.

With eight months of occupation duty, some soldiers used their artistic talent to decorate their helmets and personal equipment. Much like the Doughboys of 1918-1919, the soldiers of the Second World War were creative in embellishing their gear. This example is from Company "A", 116th Infantry.

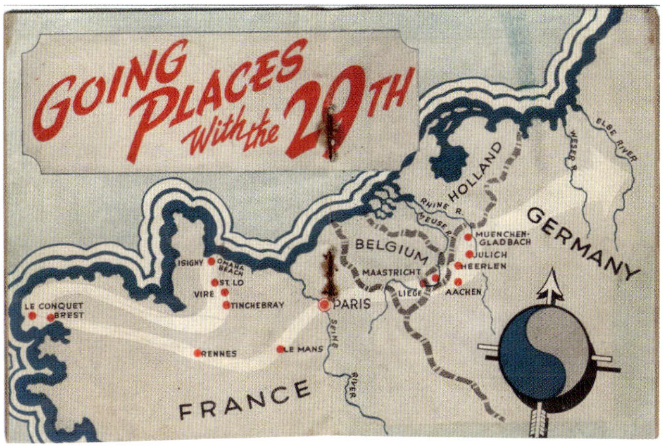

A small map from the "29 Let's Go!" pamphlet that shows the path of the division from landing on Omaha Beach to the end of the war at the Elbe River.

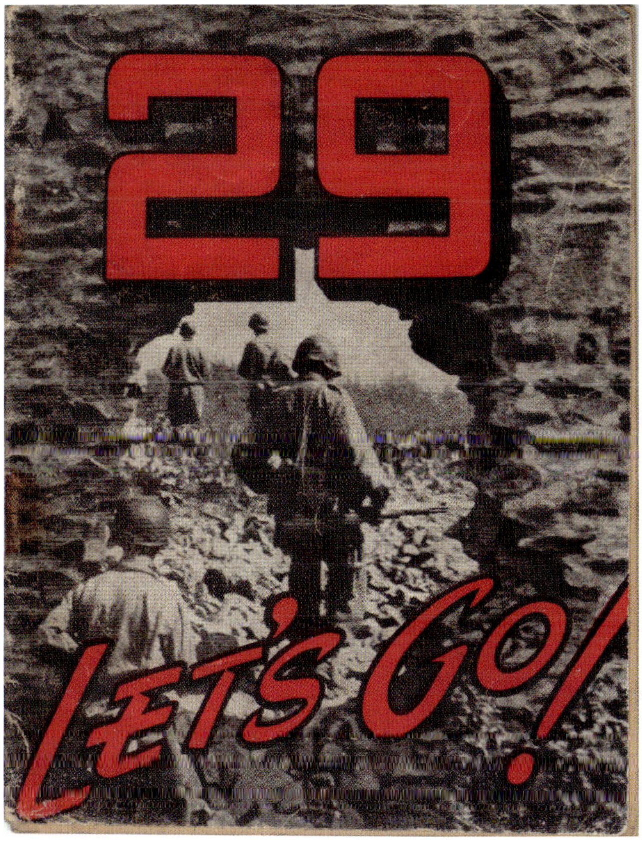

After the war ended, many of the divisions in the ETO produced small pocket-sized books as a souvenir for the soldiers to send home or keep for themselves. Seen here is the cover from the book produced for the 29th's soldiers.

When not actively performing their occupation duties, the soldiers took advantage of the opportunity to see some of the undamaged parts of Europe. In this photograph, soldiers wearing the patches of the 106th Infantry Division and the 8th Air Force enjoy the Dutch countryside with its picturesque windmills. *Courtesy USAQM Museum.*

That departure wouldn't happen until the division had spent almost eight months on occupation duty. When the orders came through, they instructed the 29th to prepare to depart in December 1945 in the following order: 116th Infantry, Divisional Artillery, 175th Infantry, Division Headquarters, and 115th Infantry.[31] The first transport ship appeared in the port of Bremerhaven 24 December and loaded the 116th. On Christmas morning, they were at sea. By 3 January, the entire division was aboard ship and homeward bound. After a quiet arrival in New York, the soldiers were moved to Camp Kilmer, New Jersey, and processed for discharge. On 17 January 1946, the last soldier had been processed, and the 29th Infantry Division now existed only on paper. That same day, the Department of the Army published orders stating that as of one minute before midnight on 17 January, the 29th Infantry Division was officially inactivated.

The 29th had been on active duty for more than 1,800 days. During that period, the 29th had suffered 19,814 killed, wounded, or captured. Their loyal comrades of the 747th Tank Battalion had suffered an additional 271 casualties.[32] The soldiers who had landed with the division in Normandy and remained with the outfit for all of its campaigns were eligible to attach four stars to their World War Two Victory Medal ribbon: Normandy, Northern France, Rhineland, and Central Europe. Those who had made the D-Day landing were also eligible to add the bronze arrowhead, which signified an assault landing on an enemy shore.

For most of the 29th, these honors were relatively unimportant. In later years, the medals and honors might gain greater significance, but for right now, with the war in the Pacific also over, the soldiers of the Blue and Gray looked forward to a long period of peace. Returning to their prewar jobs, starting a family, or getting an education were what mattered most of all. Hadn't the world seen enough of war to last at least a generation?

The Remagen Bridge was chosen as the symbol of the European Theater of Operations side of the Occupation Medal. For the Pacific and China-Burma-India theaters, the obverse side has the image of Mount Fujiyama to represent the occupation of Japan.

The soldiers of the 29th were never shy about marking things with their Blue and Gray symbol. In this case, a small metal version of their patch has been created to hang below their "Honorable Discharge" lapel pin. *Courtesy Allan Henderson.*

Another souvenir of service; this time it's a button to be worn by the vets or their family members at meetings and reunions. It is nice to see that, unlike the "Welcome Home" buttons created after the First World War (and shown in chapter four), this time the manufacturers got the 29th Division's colors in the correct order.

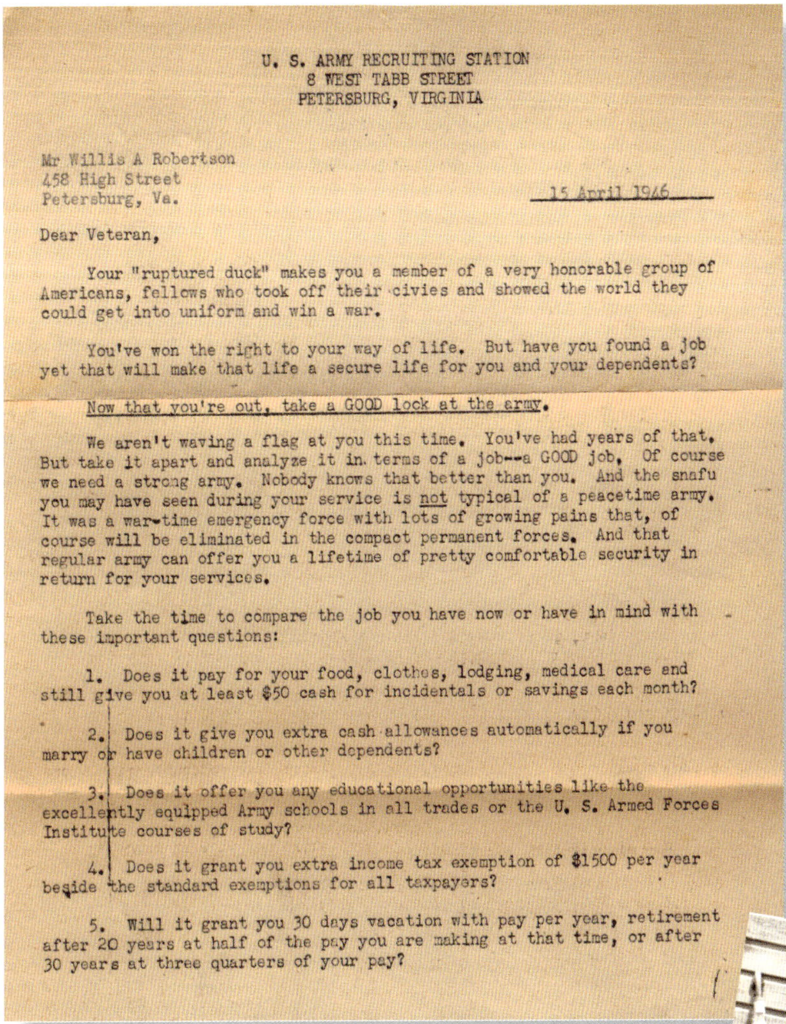

U. S. ARMY RECRUITING STATION
8 WEST TABB STREET
PETERSBURG, VIRGINIA

Mr Willis A Robertson
458 High Street
Petersburg, Va.

15 April 1946

Dear Veteran,

Your "ruptured duck" makes you a member of a very honorable group of Americans, fellows who took off their civies and showed the world they could get into uniform and win a war.

You've won the right to your way of life. But have you found a job yet that will make that life a secure life for you and your dependents?

Now that you're out, take a GOOD look at the army.

We aren't waving a flag at you this time. You've had years of that. But take it apart and analyze it in terms of a job--a GOOD job. Of course we need a strong army. Nobody knows that better than you. And the snafu you may have seen during your service is not typical of a peacetime army. It was a war-time emergency force with lots of growing pains that, of course will be eliminated in the compact permanent forces. And that regular army can offer you a lifetime of pretty comfortable security in return for your services.

Take the time to compare the job you have now or have in mind with these important questions:

1. Does it pay for your food, clothes, lodging, medical care and still give you at least $50 cash for incidentals or savings each month?

2. Does it give you extra cash allowances automatically if you marry or have children or other dependents?

3. Does it offer you any educational opportunities like the excellently equipped Army schools in all trades or the U. S. Armed Forces Institute courses of study?

4. Does it grant you extra income tax exemption of $1500 per year beside the standard exemptions for all taxpayers?

5. Will it grant you 30 days vacation with pay per year, retirement after 20 years at half of the pay you are making at that time, or after 30 years at three quarters of your pay?

Once they were home from the war, most soldiers wanted nothing more to do with being in the Army. Recruiters, however, recognized the value of enticing combat-experienced former soldiers into rejoining the active Army, Reserves, or the National Guard. In this letter, rather than appealing to their patriotism, the recruiters are pointing out the financial benefits of returning to military service.

Soon after the war ended, the National Guard divisions were returned to state control. Gradually, some of the vets of the war rejoined their old units and began to serve again. The 1st Sergeant and Company Commander of the Service Battery of the 111th Field Artillery proudly display their guidon and make sure the photographer can see the small "European Theater" banner attached. *Courtesy 1/111th Field Artillery.*

CHAPTER 9

Korean War and Cold War (1946 to 1963)

With the end of the Second World War, it appeared at first that the U.S. military would follow the same pattern as after previous wars and quickly fade away. Most of the Regular Army units had been reduced to a handful of combat veterans and many young draftees within a few short years after the war. Under the budget cutting ax wielded by Secretary of Defense Louis Johnson and President Harry S. Truman, himself a former National Guard field artillery officer and First World War combat veteran, the Armed Forces were crippled. As Clay Blair wrote in his history of the Korean War, "the army was not well trained or well manned. In 1948, owing to the shortage of funds, 'basic training' had been cut to a mere eight weeks."[1] Making matters worse, many of the draftees that did get inducted into the Army were reluctant soldiers at best and potentially trouble at worst. Equally troubling was the attitude of many of the volunteers for the Army who had actually joined to "see the world," instead of being prepared to defend it.[2] Conversely, National Guard units were filled with a preponderance of combat veterans.

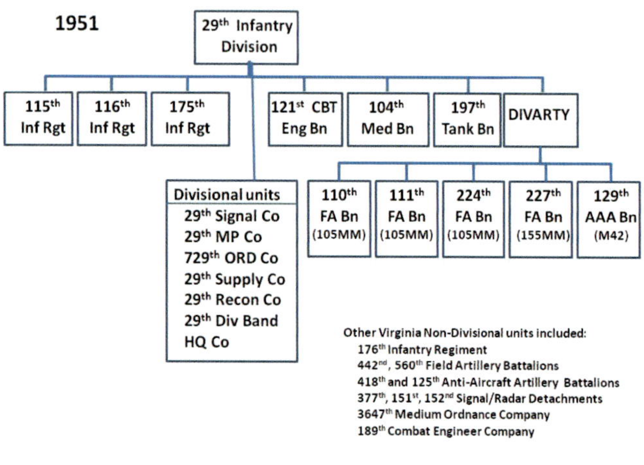

A basic diagram of the 29th Infantry Division as it appeared in 1951. Not counting the 197th Tank Battalion from West Virginia, there were over 8,000 Guardsmen from Maryland and Virginia in the 29th Division in April 1951.

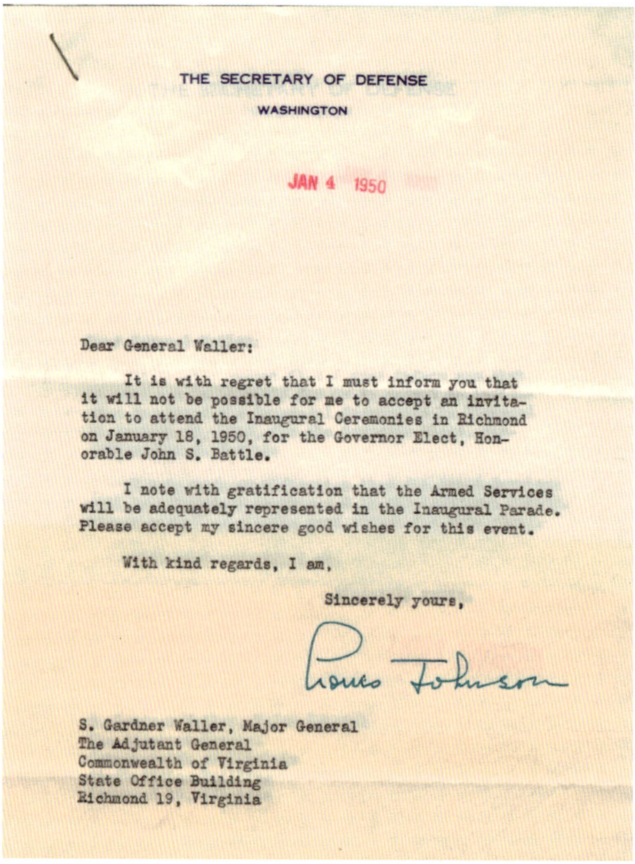

THE SECRETARY OF DEFENSE
WASHINGTON

JAN 4 1950

Dear General Waller:

It is with regret that I must inform you that it will not be possible for me to accept an invitation to attend the Inaugural Ceremonies in Richmond on January 18, 1950, for the Governor Elect, Honorable John S. Battle.

I note with gratification that the Armed Services will be adequately represented in the Inaugural Parade. Please accept my sincere good wishes for this event.

With kind regards, I am,

Sincerely yours,

Louis Johnson

S. Gardner Waller, Major General
The Adjutant General
Commonwealth of Virginia
State Office Building
Richmond 19, Virginia

A letter dated 4 January 1950 from Louis Johnson, Secretary of Defense, to the Adjutant General of Virginia. Within six months of this letter, Johnson and President Truman would see the negative results of their massive defense budget cuts as the American Army would be pushed to breaking point in Korea.

Unlike after the First World War, this "hollow" period would prove to be relatively short-lived but extremely dangerous. The increasingly aggressive behavior of the Communists, followed by their early successes in Korea, changed everything. Fear of a world dominated by Communist Russia soon colored all political and military decisions in the United States. The success of the military alliance against the Axis powers had left the Allies victorious, but only the Union of Soviet Socialist Republics (USSR) and the United States could truly be considered superpowers. Great Britain and France, though part of the victorious alliance, were greatly reduced in power and influence. These two European nations were also very much occupied with the growing independence movements within their African and Asian colonies.

The right side of the 115th Regiment helmet liner; since the regimental crest does not yet include the motto "Rally round the Flag," this liner can be dated to the late 1940s or early 1950s.

Steel outer shell for a 115th Infantry Regiment, 29th Division soldier's M1 helmet with a nicely applied divisional decal on the front. Note the size of the decal is larger than those used during the Second World War and so indicates postwar usage.

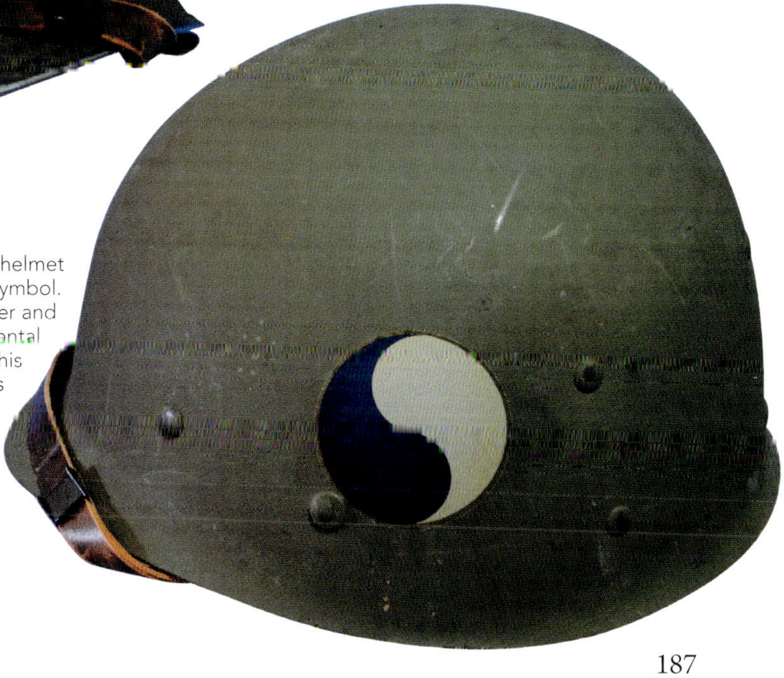

The other side of the 115th Infantry Regiment helmet liner showing the neatly-applied 29th Division symbol. The almost pristine condition of the helmet liner and these two decals (compared to the 116th regimental helmet liner shown later) would indicate that this helmet liner was not used in the field, but was perhaps either a presentation piece or used only for parades and ceremonies.

The United States and its non-soviet allies created the North Atlantic Treaty Organization (NATO) in 1949 as a means to limit the spread of communism throughout Europe. In turn, the USSR created the "Eastern Bloc" with the Eastern European countries it occupied, and in 1955, created the Warsaw Pact, which would become the military competition for NATO. During this period, the struggle between the East and West became known as the "Cold War." It earned that name primarily because, while there was no shortage of fighting and violence, the two major powers never faced each other in direct military combat, preferring instead to use their surrogates to pull the triggers. Nonetheless, there were several incidents during the postwar years that almost led to another world war, this time between the Eastern Bloc and the Western Allies. In the years that followed the Second World War, the most dangerous of these were the Berlin Blockade in 1948 and 1949, the Korean War from 1950 to 1953, and the crisis over the Suez Canal in 1956.

Adding to the increased awareness that the world was still a dangerous place, in 1949, Mao Ze-Dong's People's Liberation Army defeated Chiang Kai-shek's United States-backed Nationalist Army and drove the remnants to the island of Taiwan. The USSR wasted little time in creating an alliance with the Communist People's Republic of China. Faced with these events, the Truman administration began to look at seriously rebuilding the American military from the post-World War II drawdown. Once again, the Guard would play a critical role in that effort.

Official license plate for a Virginia National Guard vehicle.

This well-worn "Arm's Room" trunk, perhaps a veteran of the Second World War, stayed with the 116th for many years. The owner, Headquarters Company of the 2nd Battalion, 116th Infantry Regiment, was home-stationed in Lynchburg, Virginia.

Left side of the 116th Infantry Regiment helmet liner showing the 29th Division decal.

The right side of a helmet liner belonging to a 116th Infantry Regiment soldier. It's easy to see where a previous 116th decal had been applied, then removed.

To understand what that role would be, it is important to understand how the U.S. military was organized during this time. Earlier, on 9 March 1942, during the course of the Second World War, the United States War Department announced the plan for a complete reorganization of the Army. The new structure divided the Army into three commands: the Army Ground Forces, the Army Service Forces, and the Army Air Forces. While at the beginning of the war, the Army's aviation units were a small part of the overall organization, by the end of the fighting, the Army Air Forces had become a huge military force. These powerful aviation units had played a major combatant role and now consisted of quite a large number of air wings, groups, squadrons, and ground based support/maintenance organizations. As with the Army Ground Forces, the rapid demobilization of the Army aviation units after the Second World War reduced the overall size of the Army Air Forces. However, the force that remained was still an extremely potent and powerful tool for defending the country, as well as projecting American airpower around the world. In recognition of this, the National Security Act of 1947 created an independent service to be known as the Department of the Air Force. Under its first Chief of Staff, General Carl A. Spaatz, the Air Force joined the Army, Navy, and Marines as a separate service. Following that model, the aviation units belonging to the National Guard were soon converted and added to the Air National Guard, thereby also creating the nation's newest Reserve component.

Most likely taken in the 1960s, this photograph shows a well-painted sign for the 729th Maintenance Battalion Headquarters during an annual training period. The 729th's home station was in Cascade, Maryland, during the 1950s.

A representative photograph of a 1950s Virginia Guard unit in formation inside its armory.

The outer steel shell for a DIVARTY helmet with a 29th symbol painted on the front. This helmet shows the multiple repainting indicative of military equipment that was used from the 1940s until the 1980s. In this case, the gray side of the 29th symbol has either been painted in white or turned that way over time. *Courtesy Jason Mikles.*

Front of the DIVARTY helmet liner with a U.S. Army eagle decal applied. In the 1950s, the 29th's DIVARTY was headquartered in Pikesville, Maryland. *Courtesy Jason Mikles.*

Another example of unit-marked helmet liners; in this case, the liner is marked with the symbol for the 29th Infantry Division's Divisional Artillery (DIVARTY). *Courtesy Jason Mikles.*

While many of the prewar 29th Division units, such as the 116th Infantry and 111th Field Artillery, were revamped and reorganized in the Virginia National Guard after the war, some new units were also created and added to state rosters. These new units were designed to help defend the continental United States against the increased Soviet threat. Included among these were the anti-aircraft artillery (AAA) battalions belonging to the Maryland and Virginia National Guard. These units were organized to defend Washington, D.C., Baltimore, and the Hampton Roads region from enemy air attacks. Though initially armed with Second World War era anti-aircraft guns, units such as Maryland's 683rd Anti-Aircraft Artillery Battalion and Virginia's 129th and 418th Anti-Aircraft Battalions were soon equipped with Nike-Ajax surface-to-air missiles. At the same time, the structure of the state forces expanded beyond divisionally-based combat arms units to now include specialized non-divisional combat support and combat service support units, such as military police, transportation, engineers, signal, medical, and data processing detachments.

The left hand side of the DIVARTY liner with a 29th decal showing typical wear. *Courtesy Jason Mikles.*

Possibly of Second World War origin, but certainly used during annual training periods in the 1950s, this sign identifies the location of the divisional field laundry.

Another sign designed for use in the field, identifying the location of the Class "3" supply point. Supply Class Three is usually written in Roman numerals "III" and denotes petroleum, oil, and lubricants.

Designed as the distinctive unit insignia for a number of Maryland National Guard units, it was used by the 683rd Antiaircraft Artillery Battalion in the 1950s and the 70th Air Defense Artillery in the 1970s. The unit's primary function, the defense of Baltimore, is seen in the motto and the symbolic representation of Fort McHenry at the top of the shield. *Courtesy TIOH.*

All of the modernization and new organizations lay in the future, however, as the 1950s opened with an immediate threat. The Korean War began in June 1950, when North Korea invaded South Korea. While the South Korean Army and some American Army units attempted to hold back the invading forces, selected units of the Army Reserve and the entire Marine Corps Reserve were called up to active duty. At the same time, 138,600 Army National Guardsmen were also called to active duty because of the crisis in the Far East. Among the units being federalized were eight National Guard Infantry Divisions. Of these eight divisions, the 45th (Oklahoma National Guard) and the 40th (California National Guard) would actually deploy to Korea for combat operations. Four other National Guard Infantry Divisions: the 31st (from Alabama and Mississippi), 37th (Ohio), 44th (newly assigned to Illinois), and 47th (Minnesota and North Dakota) would all serve in the States. They would perform training missions to prepare other soldiers and units deploying to Korea. The final two Guard Divisions that were activated were the 28th (Pennsylvania) and the 43rd (from the New England region). These divisions were sent to Germany to release some Regular Army units for duty in Korea. At the time of this large-scale activation, the U.S. Congress had established twelve months as the maximum allowable time guard units could be brought on active duty without a formal "Declaration of War." A short while later, this period was extended to twenty-one months. As there was never a formal declaration of war for the Korean conflict, the guard units' active duty periods were carefully tracked both by the unit members and by their home state politicians to ensure compliance with the regulations.

A closer view of his 176th Infantry regiment patch. The 176th was home-stationed in the Richmond, Virginia, area during much of its existence.

The right sleeve of the major's uniform with his Second World War service patch for the 29th Infantry Division.

Ike jacket for an unidentified major in the 176th Infantry Regiment. A review of the ribbons indicates the owner served as an enlisted man during the Second World War, and since his right sleeve patch indicates service in the 29th Infantry Division, the spearhead on his European theater ribbon would represent participation in the Normandy landing.

In addition to these eight divisions, there were more than two hundred smaller units activated for federal service. Some of these units were designated for deployment to Korea, while others, including five from Virginia, were deployed to active duty posts in the States, releasing units there for action in Korea. The 149th Fighter Squadron of the Virginia Air National Guard was also mobilized, but remained in the States. No Virginia Guard unit fought in Korea, though many of the mobilized soldiers and airmen did serve as individual replacements to other Army units. In Maryland, an African-American unit (231st Transportation Truck Battalion) was activated and sent to Korea to provide much needed logistics support for the U.S. and United Nations soldiers fighting there. Some National Guard units from other states were sent to war and began arriving at the port of Pusan, South Korea, in January 1951. Within six months, there were a large number of non-divisional engineer and artillery units in the Korean theater of operations. By November, they were joined by the two National Guard Infantry Divisions: the 40th and the 45th.[3]

This envelope was addressed to Major General William Sands, 29th Infantry Division Commander, at a bank in Norfolk, Virginia. In private life Sands was a lawyer, having graduated from the University of Virginia School of Law in 1916.

Major General William H. Sands, formerly the 29th's senior artilleryman in the Second World War, took command of the entire 29th Infantry Division in 1946 and would continue in that role until 1954. By 1951, the 29th was essentially a Maryland and Virginia-based National Guard division. Although the West Virginia National Guard continued to provide the 197th Medium Tank Battalion to the 29th till 1959, the vast majority of the division called Maryland or Virginia their home. Maryland contributed two infantry regiments, a combat engineer battalion, two field artillery regiments, a medical battalion, and several other small divisional units. The Virginia National Guard provided an infantry regiment, two field artillery battalions, an anti-aircraft battalion, and a reconnaissance company, as well as several other non-divisional units, such as the 176th Infantry Regiment. The April 1951 strength reports for the National Guard showed Maryland with 4,244 men in uniform and Virginia with 4,359.[4]

A team from the 176th Infantry Regiment practices with their sixty millimeter mortar. Note the miss-match of uniform clothing, herringbone twill (HBT), and khaki, and the 176th Regiment decal on the helmet liner of the soldier setting the weapon. The difference in uniform parts is probably indicative of the Guard's inherent supply problems during peacetime.

An HBT shirt for a 29th Infantry Division Corporal. Due to their popularity and durability, the HBT uniforms were used as a field uniform from the mid-1940s until the 1960s.

Another photograph of the 176th Infantry Regiment in the field. Once again, there is an interesting mix of uniform types, as it appears two Army umpires or advisors, with white bands on their helmet liners, are discussing something with an officer from the 176th and a chaplain. The 176th was a separate regiment during this period; therefore, the officer on the far right does not have a 29th Infantry Division decal on his helmet liner.

The guidon for Battery "A," 111th Field Artillery, also from Norfolk, Virginia. During this period, the battery was equipped with 105mm Howitzers. *Courtesy 1/111th Field Artillery.*

The soldiers of Service Battery, 111th Field Artillery (commanded by Captain Roland E. Hopkins), pose for a unit photograph at Camp Pickett, Virginia, in July 1950. The Service Battery of the 111th was home-stationed in Norfolk, Virginia, and had a total authorized strength of sixty-three officers and men. *Courtesy 1/111th Field Artillery.*

Officer's privately purchased long sleeve khaki shirt displaying the 29th Infantry Division patch on the left sleeve.

The other sleeve of the officer's shirt showing the owner's previous service in the Eighth Air Force during the Second World War. During the 1950s, and even well into the 1970s, there were still many veterans of the Second World War in the National Guard.

With the end of active fighting in Korea and the signing of the truce in July 1953, many of the activated Guardsmen returned to their home states and civilian lives. Interestingly enough, the two National Guard combat divisions that served in Korea (40th and the 45th) were desegregated while serving overseas. Conversely, the stateside National Guard units were seemingly unaffected by the new presidential guidelines to desegregate the force.[5] In fact, it would not be until the mid- to late-1960s that African-Americans would begin to join the Maryland and Virginia National Guard in any appreciable numbers.

The remainder of the 1950s proved to be fairly quiet for the National Guard as they reverted to state duty. This meant an increase in training for natural disasters, as well as providing support to their state governments for civil disturbances and performing their annual training. In Virginia, an era came to an end with the passing of their State Adjutant General, S. Gardner Waller, in December 1955. Gardner had been a driving force in the Virginia Guard since before the First Word War and had served as Virginia's Adjutant General since 1931. The National Guard Depot in Richmond, Virginia, still bears his name. Waller was replaced by Sheppard Crump, another long-time Guardsman whose military career had included service in the 104th Ammo Train during the First World War.[6]

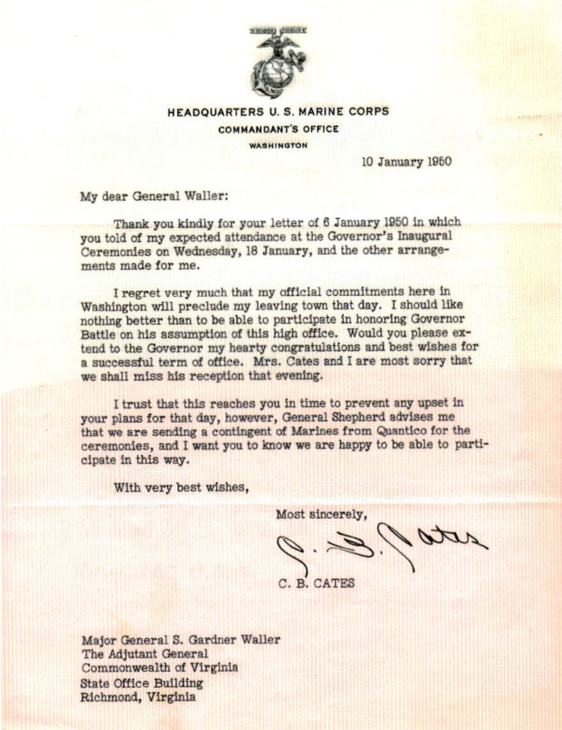

HEADQUARTERS U. S. MARINE CORPS
COMMANDANT'S OFFICE
WASHINGTON

10 January 1950

My dear General Waller:

Thank you kindly for your letter of 6 January 1950 in which you told of my expected attendance at the Governor's Inaugural Ceremonies on Wednesday, 18 January, and the other arrangements made for me.

I regret very much that my official commitments here in Washington will preclude my leaving town that day. I should like nothing better than to be able to participate in honoring Governor Battle on his assumption of this high office. Would you please extend to the Governor my hearty congratulations and best wishes for a successful term of office. Mrs. Cates and I are most sorry that we shall miss his reception that evening.

I trust that this reaches you in time to prevent any upset in your plans for that day, however, General Shepherd advises me that we are sending a contingent of Marines from Quantico for the ceremonies, and I want you to know we are happy to be able to participate in this way.

With very best wishes,

Most sincerely,

C. B. CATES

Major General S. Gardner Waller
The Adjutant General
Commonwealth of Virginia
State Office Building
Richmond, Virginia

A formal letter from the Commandant of the Marine Corps, General Clifton B. Cates, to Major General Waller, apologizing for his inability to attend the inauguration of the Governor of Virginia in January 1950 due to duty requirements. Cates, a Marine hero from Belleau Wood in the First World War, would serve as the Marine Corps Commandant from January 1948 to December 1951.

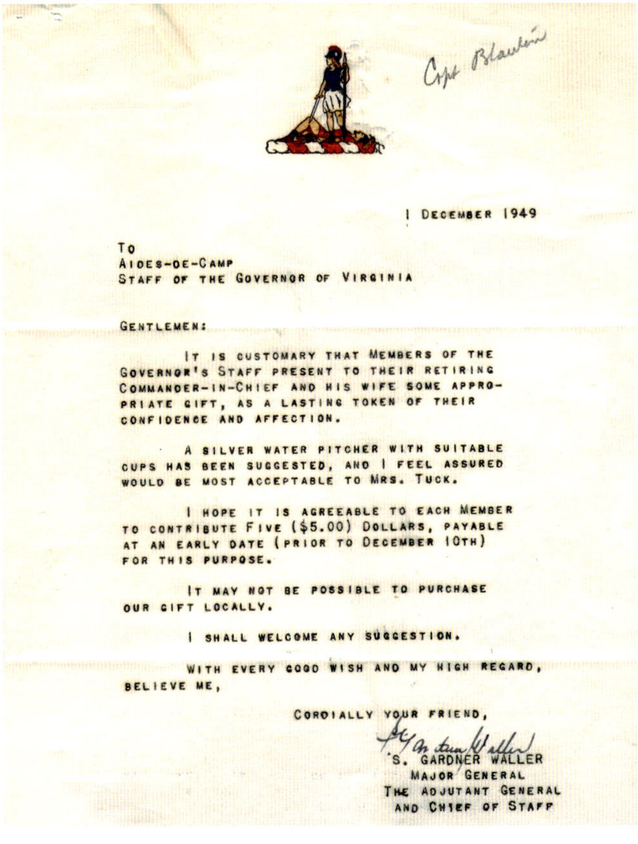

Capt Blanton

1 December 1949

To
Aides-de-Camp
Staff of the Governor of Virginia

Gentlemen:

It is customary that Members of the Governor's Staff present to their retiring Commander-in-Chief and his wife some appropriate gift, as a lasting token of their confidence and affection.

A silver water pitcher with suitable cups has been suggested, and I feel assured would be most acceptable to Mrs. Tuck.

I hope it is agreeable to each Member to contribute Five ($5.00) Dollars, payable at an early date (prior to December 10th) for this purpose.

It may not be possible to purchase our gift locally.

I shall welcome any suggestion.

With every good wish and my high regard, believe me,

Cordially your friend,

S. Gardner Waller
Major General
The Adjutant General
and Chief of Staff

Correspondence from Major General S. Gardner Waller, Virginia State Adjutant General, to the aides and staff of the Governor of Virginia, with a nicely embossed Virginia letterhead. Waller would serve as the Adjutant General of Virginia for twenty-five years.

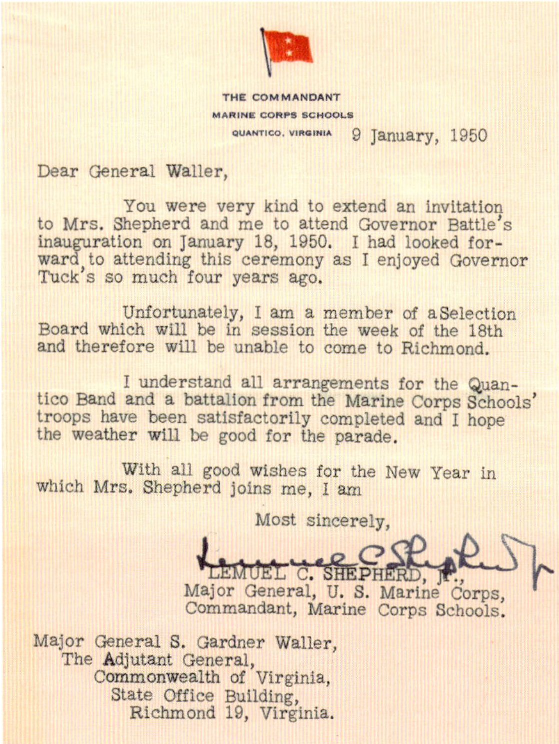

THE COMMANDANT
MARINE CORPS SCHOOLS
QUANTICO, VIRGINIA 9 January, 1950

Dear General Waller,

You were very kind to extend an invitation to Mrs. Shepherd and me to attend Governor Battle's inauguration on January 18, 1950. I had looked forward to attending this ceremony as I enjoyed Governor Tuck's so much four years ago.

Unfortunately, I am a member of a Selection Board which will be in session the week of the 18th and therefore will be unable to come to Richmond.

I understand all arrangements for the Quantico Band and a battalion from the Marine Corps Schools' troops have been satisfactorily completed and I hope the weather will be good for the parade.

With all good wishes for the New Year in which Mrs. Shepherd joins me, I am

Most sincerely,

LEMUEL C. SHEPHERD, Jr.,
Major General, U. S. Marine Corps,
Commandant, Marine Corps Schools.

Major General S. Gardner Waller,
The Adjutant General,
Commonwealth of Virginia,
State Office Building,
Richmond 19, Virginia.

This time, it's Major General Lemuel Shepherd's turn to apologize to Waller for not being able to attend the inauguration 18 January 1950. Like Cates, Shepherd was decorated for bravery in the First World War. He would later follow Cates as the Commandant of the Marine Corps from 1952 to 1956.

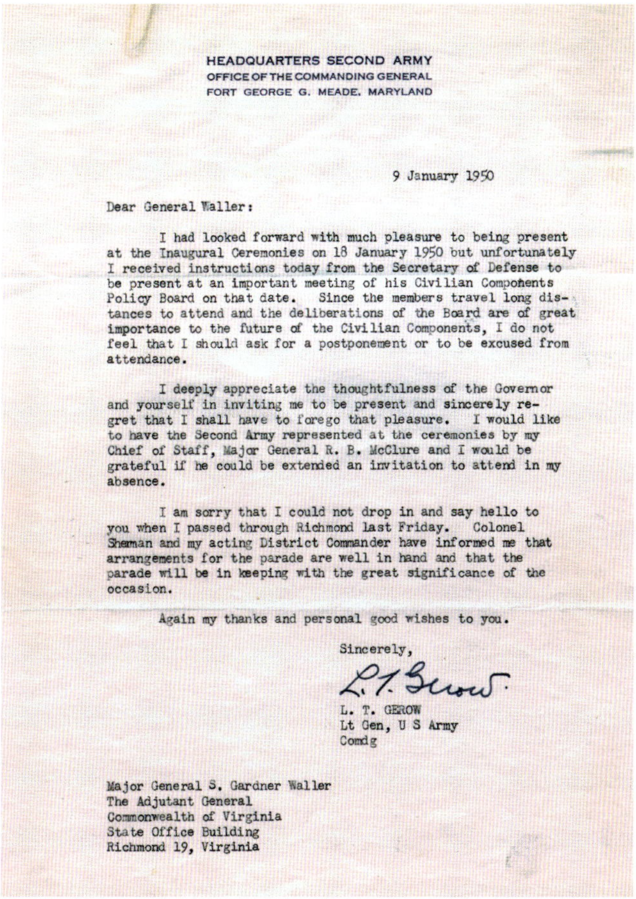

HEADQUARTERS SECOND ARMY
OFFICE OF THE COMMANDING GENERAL
FORT GEORGE G. MEADE, MARYLAND

9 January 1950

Dear General Waller:

I had looked forward with much pleasure to being present at the Inaugural Ceremonies on 18 January 1950 but unfortunately I received instructions today from the Secretary of Defense to be present at an important meeting of his Civilian Components Policy Board on that date. Since the members travel long distances to attend and the deliberations of the Board are of great importance to the future of the Civilian Components, I do not feel that I should ask for a postponement or to be excused from attendance.

I deeply appreciate the thoughtfulness of the Governor and yourself in inviting me to be present and sincerely regret that I shall have to forego that pleasure. I would like to have the Second Army represented at the ceremonies by my Chief of Staff, Major General R. B. McClure and I would be grateful if he could be extended an invitation to attend in my absence.

I am sorry that I could not drop in and say hello to you when I passed through Richmond last Friday. Colonel Sherman and my acting District Commander have informed me that arrangements for the parade are well in hand and that the parade will be in keeping with the great significance of the occasion.

Again my thanks and personal good wishes to you.

Sincerely,

L. T. Gerow

L. T. GEROW
Lt Gen, U S Army
Comdg

Major General S. Gardner Waller
The Adjutant General
Commonwealth of Virginia
State Office Building
Richmond 19, Virginia

Perhaps the most disappointing apology letter of all to the incoming Governor's military staff was from Army Lieutenant General Leonard T. Gerow. In addition to having served as the 29th Division Commander, Gerow was a Virginia native and long-time resident of the city of Petersburg.

A cigarette lighter for a member of the 115th Infantry Regiment.

A slightly different 29th DIVARTY helmet liner, this time with a lieutenant colonel's rank decal on the front.

The right side of the DIVARTY lieutenant colonel's helmet liner, this time with a flat finish to the paint. In the early 1950s, the DIVARTY Headquarters and six 105mm Howitzer batteries from the 110th and 224th Field Artillery Battalions were home-stationed in the Pikesville, Maryland, area.

As impressive as Waller's long tenure was, it was eclipsed by his fellow Adjutant General to the north, Milton Reckord from Maryland. Appointed Adjutant General of Maryland in 1920, after an exceptional combat performance as the commander of the 115th Infantry Regiment in the First World War, Reckord would serve until 1966, retiring at the age of eighty-six. Except for a short period during the Second World War while Reckord was serving in Europe as Eisenhower's Provost Marshal, he would serve for more than forty years as Maryland's Adjutant General.

The left side of the DIVARTY helmet liner showing the 29th Division symbol.

A vehicle marker, this time for the Service Company of the 115th Infantry Regiment. The Service Company for the regiment was based in Silver Springs, Maryland.

In 1959, the 29th, like all U.S. Army infantry divisions, was reorganized to prepare for meeting the threat of the nuclear battlefield. In order for units to be smaller targets and more flexible in maneuver, the concept of a triangular division was swept away. It was replaced with a new design that became known as the "pentomic" division. Divided now into five combined arms combat teams, the division had some organic tank battalions and some reconnaissance units added to their "Table of Organization and Equipment." Aviation units were also added at this time to provide organic helicopter support directly to the division. The pentomic experiment, however, quickly proved to be unsuccessful and had a very short lifespan. By 1963, the 29th had returned to the triangular format.[7]

A sign of the times, and also of the Civil War lineage of the 111th Field Artillery Battalion. In this ceremony, Lieutenant Colonel Warren A. Ott, Battalion Commander of the 111th, receives "Confederate Colors" from a representative of the local American Legion Post 35 of Norfolk, Virginia. *Courtesy 1/111th Field Artillery.*

Lieutenant Colonel Ott at his desk in the Norfolk Armory in October 1955. Ott was a veteran of the Second World War, though not with the 29th Infantry Division. *Courtesy 1/111th Field Artillery.*

The cover of the program put together by the 111th Field Artillery Battalion in honor of their 127th anniversary. It's interesting to note that the printer has misspelled their unit name by adding an extra "l" to battalion. *Courtesy 1/111th Field Artillery.*

At the end of the 1950s, the 29th Division, in its many different forms, had proven itself in peace and war for over forty years. While the Cold War continued in earnest, most Americans felt a degree of comfort while protected by the strength of America's nuclear forces. Accordingly, scant attention was paid to conventional forces. Similarly, interest in the National Guard had waned, and recruiters in all the states struggled to keep units up to strength. Few Americans suspected that in the next decade some unforeseen political and social events were going to transform America forever. Nor could anyone predict that before the 1960s were complete, the 29th would have undergone its biggest change in structure by disappearing altogether.

A selection of recruiting material used to interest young men in joining the guard. To get the word out to prospective recruits, the Guard used television, the newest form of media, as well as older forms: newspaper ads and comic books. The use of sports stars and military heroes was a common practice in these messages.

Built and equipped to provide air defense for the nation's capitol, this Nike-Ajax missile site was in Lorton, Virginia, and manned by the Virginia National Guardsmen of Battery "A," 1st Battalion, 280th Artillery Regiment. The site was shut down in 1974.

More recruiting material, this time preaching a message of safety while showcasing some of the Guard's newest equipment.

Though slightly damaged, this photograph provides an interesting look at the uniforms and social conventions of the Guard during this period. Seen here enjoying an after-church social and a cup of coffee at "Christ and St. Lukes" Episcopal Church are (from left) Chief Warrant Officer B. Williamson, Master Sergeant R. Shelton, Master Sergeant S. Anderson, and Chief Warrant Officer J. Luper. Williamson is wearing a 2nd Marine Division patch on the right shoulder of his uniform, indicating combat service with that unit. *Courtesy 1/111th Field Artillery.*

Another fascinating photograph and well worthy of careful study. This 176th Infantry display photo was most likely taken inside the Sandston, Virginia, armory. The walls have posters that speak to National Guard service at Valley Forge and on Corregidor, as well as a Virginia map marked with the location of all units in the state. Another sign reminds solders that drill for the 107th Anti-Aircraft Brigade is every Tuesday night. There is a reminder that Audie Murphy, America's most decorated soldier from the Second World War, was a National Guardsman. Under magnification, it's also clear that the heavyset soldier in the middle of the picture served in the 43rd Infantry Division during the war.

No subtle or hidden message here; join the National Guard and you get to drive a tank.

Detailed instructions and the rubber mimeograph stamps required to get the word out to the public about "National Muster Day" for the Guard in 1958.

In 1953, following Army regulations to improve the appearance of soldiers' hats, the "Ridgeway" hat with a stiff crown frame made its debut. Though popular in the peacetime Army, it was impractical for field use. It soon would be replaced by the baseball-cap styled "Cap, Field, Hot Weather" in the early 1960s.

As part of "Muster Day" activities, guard units were provided with a one-hour radio show featuring a salute to the National Guard by some of the biggest stars in Hollywood and the American music industry.

Four members of the 29th Infantry Division take time to pose for a picture in front of the 2nd Platoon barracks during annual training. The soldier on the far right is wearing the new style "dress green" uniform and hat that were issued to replace the previous "olive drab" uniforms. Hopefully, the soldier to his right didn't burn a hole in his friend's uniform with his carelessly held cigarette.

A September 1958 photograph of Earle Burdine, 115th Infantry Regiment, wearing the khaki uniform and posing in front of a late-model Sherman tank. This khaki uniform, though not as formal as the dress uniform, allowed the wearer to leave the base. This style uniform remained in service until the early 1980s. *Courtesy Burdine Family Collection.*

Another extremely interesting photograph, showing (from left to right) Colonel J.B. Moore III, Brigadier General Anthony Joseph Biddle, Jr., and Colonel Arnold Ellis, Commander of the 176th Infantry Regiment. At the time of the photo, Biddle was serving as the Adjutant General of Pennsylvania. Biddle, the son of a millionaire, had enjoyed an interesting life. He had been a former New York City night club owner and had been appointed Ambassador to Poland in 1937. He also served in the Army during both World Wars, including time on Eisenhower's staff, where he had been involved in the planning for the D-Day landings. Along with his notable military and political careers, Biddle was also known as the "best-dressed man in America."

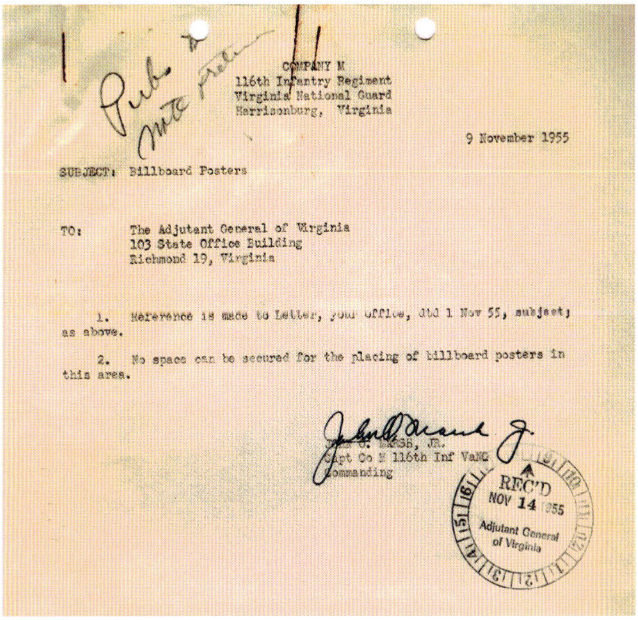

COMPANY M
116th Infantry Regiment
Virginia National Guard
Harrisonburg, Virginia

9 November 1955

SUBJECT: Billboard Posters

TO: The Adjutant General of Virginia
103 State Office Building
Richmond 19, Virginia

1. Reference is made to letter, your office, dtd 1 Nov 55, subject; as above.

2. No space can be secured for the placing of billboard posters in this area.

JOHN O. MARSH, JR.
Capt Co M 116th Inf VaNG
Commanding

REC'D
NOV 14 1955
Adjutant General of Virginia

A letter from the Commander of Company "M", 116th Infantry Regiment, to the Adjutant General's office, informing them that he was unable to post the "billboard posters" as they directed. Obviously this small failure did not affect his career; Captain John O. Marsh would later serve in the U.S. House of Representatives and also as Secretary of the Army from 1981 to 1989.

Now a member of the 176th Infantry Regiment, this officer had served previously in the 8th Air Force during the Second World War (patch on right sleeve and not visible in picture). The maker's tag on the inside lining reveals that this coat was especially tailored for the unidentified owner in London.

A closer view of the same coat, showing details of the 176th patch sewn on the left sleeve.

An officer's English-made long sleeve wool shirt displays the patch for the 176th Regimental Combat Team. The rank and branch insignia on the collar indicates that the owner was a 1st lieutenant in the artillery.

CHAPTER 10

Cold War and "Hot" War; Vietnam (1960-1970)

The decade started quietly enough. While small brush fire conflicts were taking place in a number of remote locations, the Americans and Russians had settled into a period of watchful and uneasy peace enforced by the realization that both sides had enough nuclear weapons to destroy the world. A large portion of the United States Regular Army was stationed in Europe to guard against further advances of Communist influence. It seemed that the Cold War would continue on its course uninterrupted.

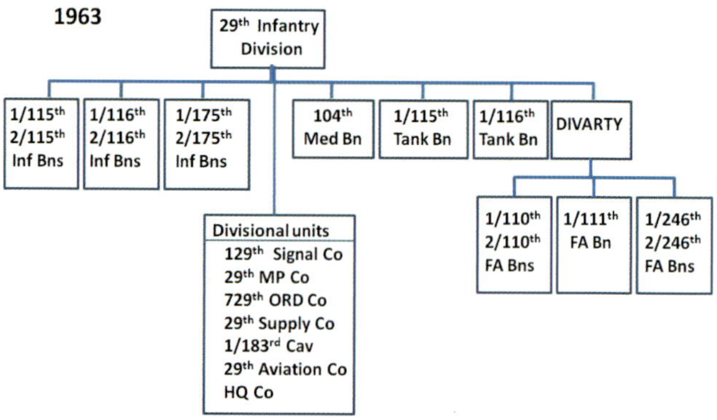

In 1963, the Army gave up on the "pentomic" experiment of the late 1950s and returned the active and reserve component divisions to the familiar "triangle" format. The 29th would maintain this structure until 1968.

Artillerymen of the 111th Field Artillery prepare to fire their 105mm Howitzer as part of a ceremonial salute. Besides the uniform with modified field gear and the neatly-blackened tires, the real clue that this is a ceremonial firing is that the gun's spades have not been dug into the ground. *Courtesy 1/111th Field Artillery.*

Under slightly different conditions, this time the 111th's artillerymen are firing as part of a tactical exercise or range firing. This picture draws praise from other artillerymen for the clever way the crew has made helmet covers from burlap and built a shelter to shade their propellant, thereby ensuring a stable and even temperature for the charges. This will greatly improve their accuracy. The one questionable point; the Number One gunner, ramming the charge, doesn't seem to have a pistol in his holster. *Courtesy 1/111th Field Artillery.*

With the election of a new President of the United States, John F. Kennedy, things were about to change. Kennedy was more inclined than his predecessor to take an active role in confronting the Communists. That confrontation started in the summer of 1961, when Kennedy decided to mobilize the National Guard in response to a Russian provocation in the occupied and divided city of Berlin. Constructing what came to be known as the "Berlin Wall," the Russians had managed to seal off the American, French, and British sectors from the rest of Berlin and Germany. By the fall of 1961, over 40,000 National Guardsmen had been brought on active duty and some 20 Air National Guard squadrons had deployed to Europe, mostly to Germany. Though many Army Guard units were activated during the Berlin Wall crisis, none actually deployed overseas. However, Kennedy's show of strength had its intended results, and though Berlin remained a walled and isolated city, the immediate crisis passed. Soon most Guardsmen had returned to their home stations.

Lieutenant Colonel H.R. Kogen, commander of the 1st Battalion, 111th Field Artillery. This photo, taken in 1963, is from the period when some battalions of the 111th were serving as Air Defense Artillery. That distinction is also reflected in Kogen's collar insignia. Also clearly visible, to his right, are Civil War battle streamers for Appomattox and Cold Harbor on the 111th Field Artillery flag. *Courtesy 1/111th Field Artillery.*

The guidon of Battery "C," 1st Battalion, 111th Field Artillery, one of Lieutenant Colonel Kogen's units. *Courtesy 1/111th Field Artillery.*

Officers and senior NCOs pose with the Battery "C" guidon as part of their unit photograph. Though the guidon and collar disks in these pictures of the 1st Battalion clearly show they are now "Air Defense Artillery," they still maintain the designation "Field Artillery." *Courtesy 1/111th Field Artillery.*

In the course of "after-action" reviews and studies, it became obvious to many of America's military and civilian leaders that if the National Guard were to remain a viable part of the national defense, it would require a great deal of reform. Aging equipment, manpower shortages, and a poorly defined doctrinal mission were high on the list of problems that clearly needed to be solved. Unfortunately, even with increased budgets and renewed senior leader interest, many of the Guard's problems would not be easily fixed. One significant change, however, was the movement of unit drill dates from weeknights to one weekend a month. There was also a requirement for a two-week annual training period that usually occurred in the summer. It was around this time that the popular, and sometimes pejorative, phrase "weekend warrior" entered the American lexicon as a synonym for National Guardsman. Ironically, during Operation Desert Storm in 1991, and again twelve years later during Operation Iraqi Freedom, many National Guard vehicles would be photographed in Southwest Asia while decorated with the same phrase, along with other more colorful and less repeatable phrases.

The more things change, the more they stay the same. Feeding the troops during field training is always a priority, and in this picture two cooks demonstrate how to prepare the field oven burners while nearby two unenthusiastic soldiers peel potatoes. *Courtesy 1/111th Field Artillery.*

Artillerymen of 2nd Battalion, 111th Field Artillery at Fort Campbell, Kentucky, during the Berlin Wall Crisis in 1961, waiting for chow. The wide variety of uniforms and helmet camouflage covers point out some of the supply problems that plagued National Guard units from the 1950s to the 1980s. On a positive note, it appears the enlisted men are being fed before the officers.

Officers collar brass for two mainstay Virginia units: the 116th Infantry and the 111th Field Artillery.

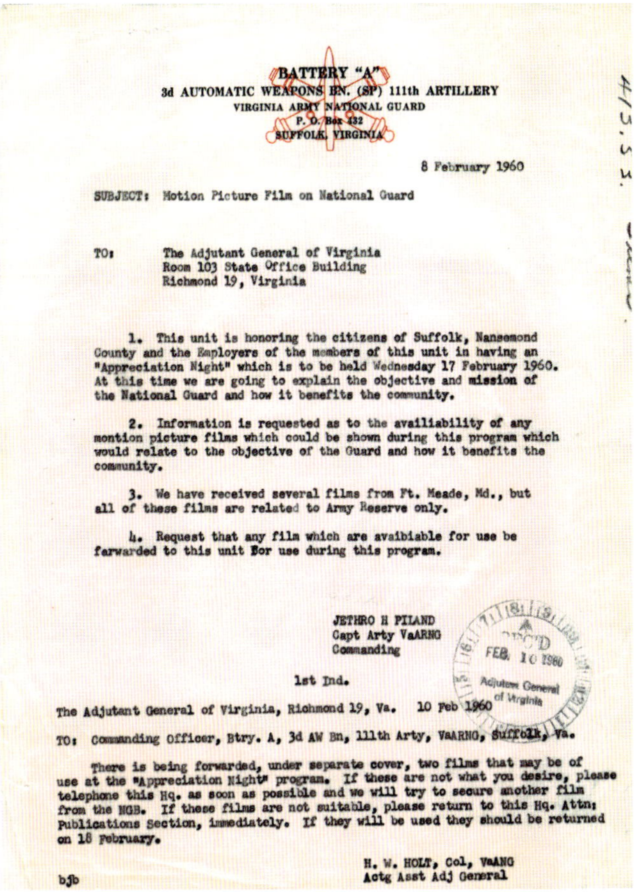

BATTERY "A"
3d AUTOMATIC WEAPONS BN. (SP) 111th ARTILLERY
VIRGINIA ARMY NATIONAL GUARD
P. O. Box 432
SUFFOLK, VIRGINIA

8 February 1960

SUBJECT: Motion Picture Film on National Guard

TO: The Adjutant General of Virginia
Room 103 State Office Building
Richmond 19, Virginia

1. This unit is honoring the citizens of Suffolk, Nansemond County and the Employers of the members of this unit in having an "Appreciation Night" which is to be held Wednesday 17 February 1960. At this time we are going to explain the objective and mission of the National Guard and how it benefits the community.

2. Information is requested as to the availiability of any montion picture films which could be shown during this program which would relate to the objective of the Guard and how it benefits the community.

3. We have received several films from Ft. Meade, Md., but all of these films are related to Army Reserve only.

4. Request that any film which are avaibiable for use be farwarded to this unit for use during this program.

JETHRO H PILAND
Capt Arty VaARNG
Commanding

RECD
FEB. 10 1960
Adjutant General of Virginia

1st Ind.

The Adjutant General of Virginia, Richmond 19, Va. 10 Feb 1960

TO: Commanding Officer, Btry. A, 3d AW Bn, 111th Arty, VaARNG, Suffolk, Va.

There is being forwarded, under separate cover, two films that may be of use at the "Appreciation Night" program. If these are not what you desire, please telephone this Hq. as soon as possible and we will try to secure another film from the NGB. If these films are not suitable, please return to this Hq. Attn: Publications Section, immediately. If they will be used they should be returned on 18 February.

H. W. HOLT, Col, VaANG
Actg Asst Adj General

bjb

Interesting letter written shortly after the 111th was converted to Air Defense Artillery and most likely equipped with M-42 Duster self propelled anti-aircraft guns. One of the critically important missions in any Guard unit is securing the support of the soldiers' full-time civilian employers. In this instance, the commander of Battery "A" is planning an "Employer Appreciation Night" and is seeking suitable motion pictures.

Members of the 115th Infantry help secure the outside of a medium-sized general purpose tent by wrapping chicken wire around its exterior. While working in this "admin" area, the soldiers have removed their heavy steel outer helmet shell and are wearing the liners with their clearly visible 29th Division patch on the left side.

In 1964, more changes took place. For the first time in many years, Guard units participated in a large-scale exercise with their active Army counterparts. At the same time, a number of National Guard divisions were inactivated and replaced with separate infantry brigades. In 1968, another round of these conversions would take place that would have a major effect on the 29th Infantry Division and its Virginia and Maryland soldiers.

Equipped with M1 Garand rifles and a M1918 A2 Browning Automatic Rifle (BAR), infantrymen from the 115th Infantry Regiment break through a tree line onto a country lane as they practice tactics. Note the Staff Sergeant stripes on the sleeve of the soldier closest to the camera; within a few years these bright stripes would give way first to subdued stripes and then eventually to small black stripes on the collar.

Now under observation by two evaluators, a rifle squad prepares to engage the enemy. During the 1960s, many of the soldiers brought in to evaluate and advise Guard units during training were from the Active Army.

The mid-1960s ushered in two events of much greater impact than any resizing of guard units and maneuvers with active duty units. These events would greatly affect all of America in general, and the National Guard in particular: the Vietnam War and civil disturbances in major cities and college campuses. Vietnam had begun as a civil war in a small Southeast Asian country and quickly became a test bed for President Kennedy's measured response in confronting Communism. At first, it was mainly a "special operations"/military advisory war, with little to no effect on the Guard. However, with the deployment of major Army and Marine ground forces in 1965, the war's impact on American society grew exponentially. Almost simultaneously, the combined outbreak of violence in inner cities and anti-war protests on college campuses began to share the headlines with the war overseas. President Lyndon Johnson deliberately decided not to activate the Guard and Army Reserve for combat duty in Vietnam, perhaps fearing that it would worsen the backlash to what was already becoming an extremely unpopular conflict. As a result, the war in Vietnam was fought almost completely by the active components of the American Armed Forces. Most of the manpower for these forces was provided by the draft. Although there were a few Guard units that served in combat, for most Guardsmen to go to Vietnam required them to volunteer for active duty and leave their Guard unit to serve on active duty. Perhaps as many as a thousand soldiers did just that during the course of the war.

Strangely enough, due to the complexities of the military draft legislation, service in a National Guard unit soon became a way for some to avoid service in Vietnam. By voluntarily enlisting in the Guard for six years, eligible young men were no longer subject to being drafted into the Regular Army. Many college-age men, and even some professional athletes, quickly enrolled into local National Guard units to be able to continue their studies or careers. Sadly, as the war continued, the National Guard began to be seen by many as a sanctuary for "draft dodgers" because of this phenomenon. This perception was a major blow to the Guard's reputation. When one of the authors enlisted in a National Guard infantry unit after leaving active duty in 1977, there were still a number of the six-year "draft dodgers" finishing out their enlistments. Ironically, many of these men had proven themselves to be excellent soldiers. While they seemed perhaps more irreverent than the other soldiers in the unit at times, they were tactically sound during field exercises and extremely proficient in executing complex training exercises, such as performing indirect fire missions, conducting vehicle maintenance, and in overall weapons qualification. By this time many had finished college, and it was not unusual to find a private first class (PFC) or specialist-4 (SPEC 4) in an 81mm Mortar Platoon with a master's degree.

Introduced in the 1960s, the 29th Infantry Division patch with a "merrowed" border. The border is the same shade of green as the new dress uniforms being issued to the soldiers as replacement for the olive drab uniform.

Collar disks for an infantryman of the 115th during the 1960s. Note the addition of the plastic "infantry blue" disks as backing.

A 1964-dated long-sleeved khaki shirt for a 29th Infantry Division soldier. By this time, the khaki shirt had been replaced by the green fatigues for field use and was strictly for dress or office work.

A rifle squad from the 115th, under the watchful eye of an evaluator, pauses during an exercise to look for signs of the enemy. Note that the soldier nearest the camera is still equipped with a metal canteen. By 1965, the Army was replacing these canteens with the new plastic model, more suitable for the jungles of Vietnam.

The motto "Rally Round the Flag" was added to the bottom of the shield of the distinctive unit insignia for the 115th Infantry in October 1968. The added phrase reflects the inspirational words of a 1st Maryland Infantry officer during a key moment in the battle of Front Royal, Virginia, in 1862.

Now seen from another angle, the medics continue work on the "wounded" soldier.

Two medics practice applying a field dressing and splint to a "wounded" Guardsman. From the looks of the empty first aid pouch on the wounded soldier, it appears the medics followed doctrine and used his dressing to apply to the wound.

Seen here is the Color Guard of the 115th Regiment parading with the National flag and the Army flag. The soldier on the far right is wearing a 2nd Army shoulder patch and is probably an observer or evaluator. During the 1950s and into the 1960s, the 2nd Army was the higher Headquarters for the National Guard units in the Mid-Atlantic States.

The 115th Infantry Regiment passes in review with all of their company guidons leading the formation. Here again, the use of the khaki uniform is present as part of a more ceremonial event.

A rifle squad of the 115th practices combined arms tactics by teaming with an M48 Patton tank. Throughout the 1960s and well into the 1980s, the M48 in its many variants proved itself to be a stable and reliable armored vehicle.

Other American men of the same age group counted on their college deferments to keep them out of the draft. As lower and middle class families watched their sons be drafted and sent to Vietnam, college campuses were becoming centers of anti-war protest. The increased use of "civil disobedience" as a tactic to further the cause of both civil rights and the anti-war movement had little direct impact on the Virginia Guard units, as they were lucky enough to avoid being activated by the Governor to enforce civil order. Along with their scheduled annual training, the Virginians were only activated for natural disaster duty. That said, their fellow 29th Infantry Division soldiers to the north experienced a completely different story.

Dressed in lightweight khaki uniforms and most likely participating in a ceremony, these artillerymen from the 110th Field Artillery prepare their Howitzer for firing at Camp Pickett, Virginia, in 1967. Note the use of "artillery red" scarves to denote their status as artillerymen.

A short sleeve khaki shirt for a staff sergeant of one of the 116th's infantry battalions. The blue neck scarf, shoulder lanyard, and collar disk backings are used to denote the wearer is an infantryman.

During the last forty years of the twentieth century, the Guard would spend much time training soldiers how to function while under Nuclear, Biological, or Chemical (NBC) attack. In this mid-1960s photograph, a Maryland National Guardsman has been equipped with a gas mask, helmet, and raincoat to help him withstand a simulated attack. By the end of the decade, many guardsmen would be very experienced in dispensing a chemical weapon (tear gas) in order to quell civil disturbances.

Religious services are conducted by unit chaplains for members of the 29th Infantry Division. Notable by their absence in this picture are African-Americans or female soldiers. During the next decade, with the abolishment of the draft, both groups would be heavily recruited by the National Guard to keep units at full strength.

In 1968, the Maryland Guard was called out to suppress protests and restore order in Baltimore after the assassination of the Reverend Martin Luther King, Jr. Dr. King's murder led almost immediately to wide-scale rioting and unrest across the country, with violence breaking out in more than a hundred American cities. Over a hundred thousand National Guardsmen were called to active duty for riot control operations as a result of these disturbances. Among the hardest hit areas in the country was the inner city section of Baltimore. Already a powder keg of racial tension and a growing anti-war movement, the city was rocked by Dr. King's murder and quickly burst into a frenzy of arson and looting. It soon became apparent that the local police could not contain the violence and Spiro Agnew, the Governor of Maryland, called out the National Guard. The Marylanders rapidly deployed to the troubled areas to enforce a curfew on all city residents. Other Maryland units deployed to control the access of people into and out of the city. Within four days, the worst of the rioting was over, but the extensive damage to public and private buildings would require much more time to be repaired. The Guard remained on the scene for several days, providing security for the area and support to local law enforcement officials. A few miles to the south, Washington, D.C., suffered a similar outbreak and the D.C. Guard was also required to patrol the streets there until order was restored.

Unfortunately, just two years later, much of the positive reputation the Guard had earned through its firm but fair enforcement of law and order during the 1968 riots was tarnished by an ugly incident at a college campus in Ohio. Believed to be caused by the anti-war movement's reaction to the invasion of Cambodia by U.S. forces in Vietnam, a particularly vicious and violent protest took place on the Kent State campus 2 May 1970. By the time the Ohio Governor authorized the Guard to restore order on campus, the protesters had burned down the ROTC building. The following day, more of the Ohio Guardsmen converged on the campus.

On 4 May 1970, using the Guard's presence on campus as a catalyst, more than two thousand students and activists gathered and began to throw rocks at the soldiers. Chanting anti-war slogans, the protesters soon added bottles and anything else they could find to the barrage. Reacting to the provocation, some of the soldiers began to move towards the students in an attempt to disperse them. Threatened by the approaching formation of gas mask-wearing soldiers, the protesters moved away and things appeared to be calming down when the soldiers suddenly opened fire on the crowd. Although less than half of the soldiers fired their weapons, and relatively few shots were fired, the damage was done. Four civilians were killed and nine wounded in the brief volley. To add to the tragedy, some of those wounded had nothing to do with the protest and had been merely walking on

A sign of the troubled 1960s; National Guardsmen patrol the streets of Washington, D.C. The Guardsman nearest the camera is equipped with an M79 Grenade Launcher. The M79 proved to be a versatile weapon, capable of shooting fragmentation rounds at a jungle enemy in Vietnam or tear gas rounds to disperse an angry crowd. *Courtesy Library of Congress.*

the campus grounds. No matter where an individual's sympathies fall regarding the issue of campus anti-war protest, there can be no doubt that this day in May 1970 was truly the low point for the National Guard's image in the twentieth century. Perhaps, ironically, the Second World War era veterans of the 29th Infantry Division began to enjoy a resurgence in interest and respect during this same period. This was probably due, in no small measure, to the acclaim that accompanied the 1962 release of "The Longest Day," a movie based on Cornelius Ryan's bestselling book by the same name, as well as a number of other movies casting Second World War service in a favorable light.[1]

As mentioned earlier, 1968 had proven to be a traumatic year for the soldiers of the 29th Infantry Division. The Army was reorganizing again, and this time it was the fate of the 29th to be inactivated. This left two infantry brigades: the 116th in Virginia, the 58th in Maryland, and a number of separate units. For command and control, most of these units were assigned to the 28th Infantry division, which was headquartered in Pennsylvania. For the next seventeen years, the two brigades and other state units in Virginia and Maryland would wear different shoulder patches, breaking long-standing unit relationships that stretched all the way back to Mexican border service in 1916. Vietnam, inner city riots, and college campus protests and violence had all taken a heavy toll on the American psyche during the final years of the 1960s and the first five months of 1970. For the old soldiers of the 29th Infantry Division, having to remove their "Blue and Gray" patch was just one more blow. With reputations, recruiting, and morale at their very lowest, many began to wonder how things could possibly get worse.

The 1950s had started with the violence of the Korean War, but ended rather quietly. Conversely, the 1960s had started peacefully enough, but ended with America in the middle of a vastly unpopular war, protests and riots in large cities and on campuses, and the 29th Division put out of business. As the 1970s began, everyone knew a new phase of American history was about to begin, but who knew what direction it would take? And more importantly for our story, would the 29th Infantry Division reappear?

During the 1960s, veterans associations and reunion groups would be very popular. One of the more active groups was the 29th Division Association. Seen here is the Association hat belonging to a twice-wounded veteran from Company "F", 116th Infantry, who joined the division just before the St. Lô campaign.

By 1965, with the twentieth anniversary of V-E Day, veterans' organizations continued to honor their past service with ceremonies and reunions. Shown here is a well-preserved example of a 29th Infantry Division Association flag.

Nicely embroidered 176th Infantry Regiment patch designed for use on a civilian blazer or suit coat. The 29th Infantry Division reunion badge for 24-25 June 1961 is interesting because, similar to the "Welcome Home" pins produced after the First World War, the colors on the divisional symbol have been reversed.

Equally popular at reunions and meetings were these high-quality banners showcasing the 29th Infantry Division patch.

CHAPTER 11

Cold War and Reorganization (1970 to 1990)

If the 1960s were a period of profound social change in America, the decade of the 1970s would prove to be a period of significant change for the National Guard in general, and in particular for the units of Maryland and Virginia. Among all the changes, there are two that will greatly influence our story: the increased emphasis on the National Guard to provide the Army with combat units, and the widespread emphasis on recruiting African-Americans and women into the ranks of the Guard.

The 29th Infantry Division had been inactivated in January 1968 and most of the units in Virginia were assigned to the 116th Infantry Brigade, while those in Maryland went to the 58th Infantry Brigade. This reorganization also resulted in both brigades being attached for command and control to the 28th Infantry Division, headquartered in Pennsylvania. Through the 1970s and much of the 1980s, the habitual relationships between the Guard units of the two bordering states were broken, as each now followed their own training and operational plans under guidance from Pennsylvania. Also, as a result of this reassignment, during the period from 1969 to the mid-1970s, the former divisional units in Maryland and Virginia replaced their Blue and Gray shoulder patch with the red "Keystone" patch of the 28th division on their uniforms.

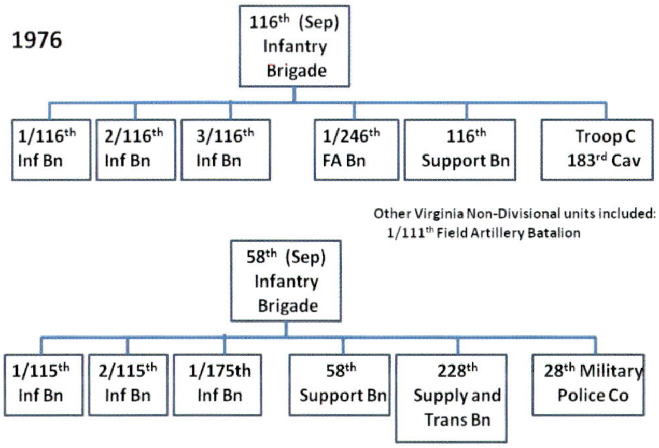

A diagram showing the two "Separate" Infantry Brigades formed in 1976 from the Virginia and Maryland brigades when they were detached from the 28th Infantry Division. NOTE: Prior to this time both brigades were attached to the 28th Infantry Division.

The distinctive unit insignia worn by some units of the 116th Infantry Brigade. The two *fleur-de-lis* represent service in both World Wars and the red arrow is symbolic of the landing on Omaha beach 6 June 1944. The motto "Rally on the Virginians" refers to the Civil War First Battle of Manassas, where the Virginia infantry helped General Jackson stand like a "Stonewall." *Courtesy TIOH.*

Considered by many Virginia Guardsmen to be their favorite unit patch. The 116th (Separate) Infantry Brigade is represented by the image of General Thomas Jonathan "Stonewall" Jackson sitting on his horse. Its inspiration is taken from the Jackson monument at the Manassas battlefield in Virginia.

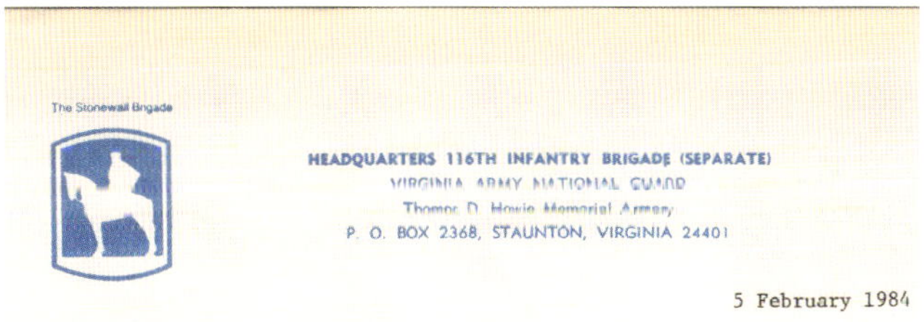

The Stonewall Brigade

HEADQUARTERS 116TH INFANTRY BRIGADE (SEPARATE)
VIRGINIA ARMY NATIONAL GUARD
Thomas D. Howie Memorial Armory
P. O. BOX 2368, STAUNTON, VIRGINIA 24401

5 February 1984

Letterhead for the Headquarters of the 116th Infantry Brigade, located in Stanton, Virginia. It reflects both the Civil War heritage of Stonewall Jackson with the Stonewall Brigade name and the Normandy campaign with the armory named after Major Thomas D. Howie, the "Major of St. Lô."

Subdued version of the 116th Infantry Brigade's patch

Major General John Castles, Adjutant General of Virginia from August 1982 to June 1994. Castles was a veteran of the Second World War and had a well-deserved reputation as a strict disciplinarian. *Courtesy Virginia Guardpost.*

In 1976, the two brigades were detached from the 28th Division and reorganized as "Separate" Infantry Brigades. A short while later, a new shoulder patch for the 116th Brigade was issued; the gray silhouette of a horse-mounted Stonewall Jackson on a blue background was in honor of the brigade's official nickname, "the Stonewall Brigade." Though the patch was soon given a less formal nickname ("Stoney on a pony"), most unit members had no real complaints about the new patch, except that the presence of the horse tended to give the false impression that the 116th was a cavalry unit.

The shoulder sleeve insignia for the 58th (Separate) Infantry Brigade. The 58th was comprised of Maryland National Guard units and the bayonet reflects the unit's lineage back to the Maryland Militia of the Revolutionary War.

The subdued version of the 58th Infantry Brigade patch designed for use on a soldier's field uniforms and tactical clothing.

The Distinctive Unit insignia, more commonly called a "unit crest," for the 58th Brigade. The lower *fleur-de-lis* reflects the unit's service in the First World War and the upper *fleur-de-lis* honors European service in the Second World War. The arrowhead centered in the upper *fleur-de-lis* recognizes the unit's participation in the Normandy landing.

To the north, the Marylanders were issued a patch that not only reflected their 29th Division heritage, but also their Maryland roots, with the red and white cross from the heraldic arms of Lord Baltimore. A bayonet was also added to the design to reflect the fact that the Maryland Militia had participated in a bayonet charge against the British at the Battle of Long Island in 1776.

The distinctive unit insignia for the 58th Support Battalion. Approved for use in 1979, this insignia represents the battalion assigned to provide logistics support to the 58th Infantry Brigade. *Courtesy TIOH.*

Although many northern states had begun integrating their units as early as 1947, many of the National Guard units in southern states remained closed to most non-white males and all females. While the Civil Rights Act of 1965 ensured African-American men were allowed to join all National Guard units, some local recruiters certainly did little to encourage them to do so. Restrictions on female soldiers were even more stringent prior to 1970, as reflected in the fact that the only women allowed in Guard units were nurses. It was not until the abolishment of the draft in 1973 that minorities and women were suddenly seen as an important and untapped recruiting pool. With the end of the draft, "strength management"—a polite euphemism for keeping a unit's strength up to the required level—became the focus for the Reserve Components through the end of the twentieth century. It remains a recurring theme for National Guard units and their commanders to this day.

A jeep-mounted TOW anti-tank launcher of the 58th Brigade gets ready to participate in a 4th of July parade in Maryland. The tactical markings on the rear bumper indicate that this unit is part of the 1st Battalion, 115th Infantry. Each four-man TOW section was equipped with two jeeps: one for the launcher and the other for carrying extra TOW rounds.

From the same 4th of July parade, several scout platoon jeeps with mounted M60 machine guns are lined up and being prepared to move. On the left hand side of the picture, behind the wrecker/recovery vehicle is one of the most unpopular vehicles in the Army, the M561 Gamma Goat. Ironically, the Goat has been selected as the vehicle to carry the National Guard recruiting banner with the slogan "Get Your Guard Up."

As the parade moves out, the wrecker has now been decorated with a recruiting banner and a pretty girl. With the end of the draft, maintaining unit strength through recruiting drives had become a major unit mission.

The end of the draft also meant the end to the easiest way of filling the ranks of the Active Army. Recognizing the potential for manpower shortfalls as a result of the draft ending, the U.S. military leaders reviewed their overall strategy. Under the guidance of President Richard Nixon, the Armed Forces established a new military doctrine that depended on using the National Guard and the Reserves to "round out" their active components in the event of a large-scale conflict. On 21 August 1970, Secretary of Defense Melvin Laird explained the new "Total Force Concept" at a press conference, stating that there would now be an increased dependence on the combat and combat-support units of the National Guard and Reserves. Under the tenet of the Total Force concept, the Army would now take a much greater role in "planning, programming, manning, equipping, and employing Guard and Reserve forces."[1]

While the Total Force Concept was of obvious benefit to the Guard, there were also two immediate benefits to the Active Army: it not only transferred a large number of logistics, combat arms, and specialized units (such as railroad operating or bridge building companies) into the Reserve Components, it also ensured that there would be local political support for the Army during any overseas military campaigns or deployments. The importance of obtaining "home town" support became crystal clear during the publicly-supported deployments of National Guard and Reserve units for Desert Shield/Desert Storm and the post 9/11 campaigns.

The only downside for the Army was that Guard and Reserve units would now have to be equipped with modern weapons and vehicles instead of the cast-off or worn out equipment routinely issued in the past. Though this effort would eat into the active component's budget, the large-scale military buildup during the Reagan administration would do much to ensure that all components received their fair share of new equipment. With the influx of new equipment and weapons, the Army also greatly increased the number of officers and senior NCOs available to support and evaluate Guard units. This became an integral part of the Army's program to link National Guard battalions and brigades to active duty units so they could train and, if necessary, deploy as one consolidated unit. Newer helicopters and fixed wing aircraft were issued to the Army National Guard to increase their organic aviation capabilities. In infantry units, some of the newer weapons, such as the Dragon and the TOW (short for Tube-launched, Optically sighted, Wire link guided missile system) anti-tank weapons systems, were fielded almost simultaneously to Active Army and National Guard units. Some Guard units were even selected to spend their two-week annual training in Germany with their active duty counterparts. By the late 1980s, entire National Guard Infantry Brigades were deploying to Europe to participate in the annual "Return of Forces to Germany" (REFORGER) exercises.

A member of 1st Battalion, 115th Infantry responds to a call for fire on the mortar range at Fort Pickett in 1982. Note that even the five-gallon plastic water can has been "Tac" marked to the 1st Battalion, 115th Infantry.

Under the watchful eye of an active duty advisor from the 82nd Airborne Division, two soldiers of a 4.2-inch mortar section apply firing data to the mortar in preparing for the mission. Note that the advisor is wearing the newly-issued Battle Dress Uniform (BDU), while the 115th soldiers are wearing basic OG107 utility shirts with their shirt tails out.

For the former 29th Infantry Division units now serving in the 58th and 116th Separate Infantry Brigades, foreign duty during this period was not yet in the cards. These brigades would continue to perform their one-weekend-a-month duties and then convoy to Fort Indiantown Gap, Fort Pickett, or Fort A.P. Hill for their two-week annual training. The most common image most citizens of the two Mid-Atlantic States had of their National Guard was of long convoys filling the interstate highways during summer months. Unfortunately, when passing these long lines of vehicles that tied up traffic, the occasional sight of a Guardsman sitting in a lawn chair while riding in the back of the trucks tended to inspire more animosity than pride in their state's soldiers.

Members of the mortar section prepare the round. The soldier with his back to the camera is wearing the new BDUs while his crewmates are still in the older uniforms. The subdued version 58th Separate Infantry Brigade patch is visible on the left sleeve of the soldier holding the mortar round.

All adjustments complete, the 4.2-inch mortar round is now being dropped into the tube.

Standard fatigue shirt worn by all ranks. During this period, the cotton sateen (OG-107) utility shirt would be replaced by a perma-pressed version, which in turn was replaced by the BDU. This example is for a Warrant Officer 1 (WO1) in the 116th Support Battalion.

The M65 model field jacket changed very little from the M1943 model introduced late in the Second World War. Many soldiers considered their four-pocket field jacket one of the most useful pieces of field gear the Army ever issued them. The most telling difference between this version and earlier models was the use of Velcro instead of buttons to secure the sleeve cuffs.

Typical license plates issued by the state of Virginia to National Guard members. These license plates were cheaper to purchase than standard Virginia plates; the lower the number, the higher the rank of the soldier. In this case, the four-digit plate was for an enlisted soldier and the three-digit plate belonged to a Warrant Officer.

Color and subdued versions of the patch worn by some non-116th Brigade affiliated Virginia National Guard units during this period. The patch is still in use today by soldiers of the State Area Readiness Command (STARC) and other Virginia units.

However, as the 1980s progressed, many of the more outrageous images faded away, and National Guard units began to take on a more serious and professional demeanor. Also helping to change the image of the Guard were a number of natural disasters, such as storms and floods, in which state units were quickly activated and deployed to provide comfort and support to the suffering citizens. With modern communication and engineering equipment, local Guard units became critical assets in states beset by hurricanes, tornadoes, or extreme winter storms. Among the first real tests of this period was the National Guard response to Hurricane Agnes in June 1972. Still considered possibly the greatest flood in the history of the eastern part of the United States, the storm ravaged cities and towns from New York all the way through Virginia. In Richmond, the James River overflowed its banks, flooded almost twenty percent of the city, and knocked out the city's water filtration plant. As a result, Fort A.P. Hill became the major source of drinkable water for the Richmond area as Virginia National Guardsmen patrolled the city streets. Also during this period, Guard units were called upon by their governors to serve in a wide range of duties that included the 1980 Winter Olympics, search and rescue teams, firefighting, and even prison guards.

Members of the Supply Platoon, Company "C", 116th Support Battalion, pose for a group picture at the Petersburg Armory. Since the soldiers are wearing the 116th Infantry Brigade patch, this picture can easily be dated to the 1980-85 period.

Soldiers of the 115th Infantry Regiment's Combat Support Company pose for a group picture. The success of National Guard recruiters in reaching out to minority soldiers is evident in this picture and is a reflection of the evolving racial makeup of the Guard.

Increased emphasis on developing senior leaders from the enlisted ranks led to NCO Academies and Officer Candidate School programs. Several soldiers in the previous picture are seen wearing this same version of the NCO Academy patch on their right breast pockets. *Courtesy Kevin Born.*

Even though women with prior active duty service had been allowed to join the National Guard as early as 1971, their numbers had remained small. By the 1980s, there were dramatic increases in military occupational specialties that were for the first time open to women. These job opportunities were documented in new Tables of Organization and Equipment for the various units and resulted in more and more women joining Guard units. Also during this time, great numbers of minority men joined their local units. By the early 1980s, almost a quarter of the entire National Guard's end-strength was African-American.

Members of the 58th Infantry Brigade Non-Commissioned Officer (NCO) Academy at Fort Indiantown Gap, Pennsylvania, pose for group photo after a field exercise in 1979. The red metal devices mounted on the end of their M16 rifles and M60 machine guns are Blank Firing Adapters (BFA) used during training.

These badges, designed for wear on the breast pocket of a soldier's dress uniform, reflected completion of Maryland's NCO and Advanced NCO Academies.

A picture of a group of Maryland National Guard NCOs on the steps of their barracks. Note the mixture of jungle fatigue and regular fatigue uniforms and several different styles of camouflage helmet covers, as well as a mix of nylon and canvas web gear.

The 1980s saw Guard units in several states actively participate in the war on drugs that was being waged by the Reagan administration. By mid-decade, at least fourteen states had designated some of their Guard units to assist the Federal Government in stopping the flow of illegal drugs into the country, as well as taking part in anti-drug missions in Latin America. Those governors who submitted plans for their National Guard members to support federal agencies in the war on drugs often received significant additional funding under the provisions of a National Defense Authorization Act.

Uniform for a quartermaster staff sergeant in the 116th Infantry Brigade. The distinctive unit insignia on the hat and shoulders indicate that the soldier was assigned to the 116th Support Battalion.

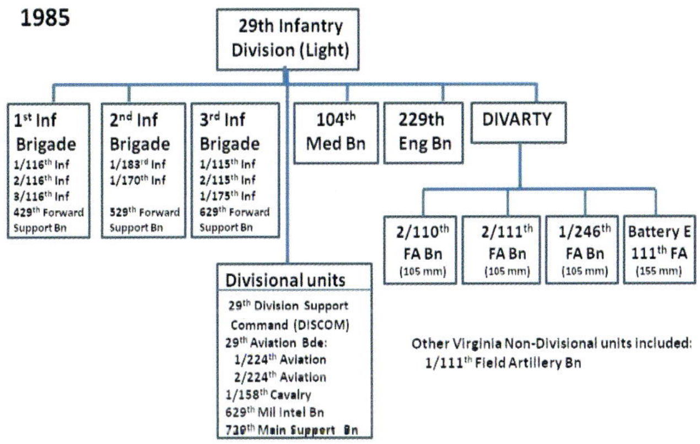

With the reactivation of the 29th Infantry Division as "Light Fighters," the Maryland and Virginia separate infantry brigades were reunited once again under a divisional structure.

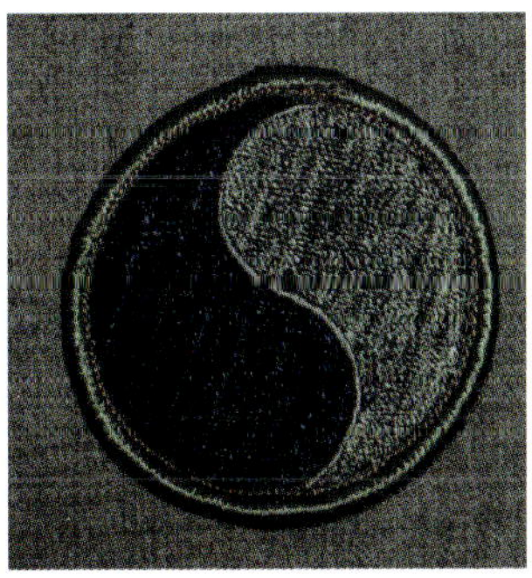

The subdued version of the 29th Infantry Division patch. Along with the reactivation of the 29th in the 1985-86 time period as a "Light" division, this patch became the standard shoulder patch for field uniforms.

The year 1985 was ushered in with a Department of the Army announcement that, as part of another restructuring, it had decided to bring back two inactive Army divisions: the 6th Infantry Division and the 10th "Mountain" Division. Keeping in line with the emerging doctrine for employing National Guard units for fighting conventional wars, the National Guard would also bring back two divisions: the 29th and the 35th Infantry Divisions. While the 35th, comprised of units from the Midwest, would be a mechanized infantry division, the 29th would become one of the new "Light" divisions. The new operational role for the 29th was meant to project a lean, yet powerful force for quick deployments to defeat "low intensity" enemy forces or prevent them from occupying a region. By not having the multitude of combat vehicles, support vehicles, and heavy equipment that comprised a regular infantry division, these lighter forces could be hurriedly flown to areas inaccessible to the heavier units. With an assigned strength of only 10,800 soldiers, new "Light" divisions would also be significantly smaller than other divisions and therefore require fewer aircraft for full deployment of the entire division. In fact, it was estimated that a light division would require less than a third of the aircraft required to move a regular infantry division.[2]

A recruiting technique: bumper stickers appealing to young men's interest in driving military vehicles. Different from the promise of driving a tank (as seen in chapter nine), the promise here is of driving the Army's replacement for the jeep, the High Mobility Multipurpose Wheeled Vehicle (HMMWV), commonly known as the "HUMVEE."

Another recruiting bumper sticker reflecting the new "Light Infantry" mission of the 29th Infantry Division.

Standard U.S. Army Helmet with BDU pattern camouflage of a soldier in the 116th Infantry Brigade. This pattern camouflage replaced the earlier lighter-colored Vietnam-era pattern. This style helmet remained in use until the "Army Ground Troops" Kevlar helmet became the standard in the late 1980s.

Once again, Maryland and Virginia were selected to provide the majority of the units that would make up the 29th Infantry Division. The 58th (Separate) Infantry Brigade of the Maryland National Guard and the 116th (Separate) Infantry Brigade from Virginia were the obvious choices, and soon other units were added or reorganized to provide the required personnel for the Division. Perhaps a telling sign of the emphasis the Army was placing on getting the 29th up to speed quickly was the stationing of the 29th Infantry Division Headquarters at Fort Belvoir, Virginia, an active duty Army post. Momentous as all this was for the National Guard in Virginia and Maryland, they were not alone. As a result of the Army's latest restructuring, there were twenty-seven new unit activations nationwide. There were more than two hundred other units converted into a new structure and designated to receive new equipment. These changes continued to convey the message to the National Guard that the Army was counting heavily on them should the need arise to fight another war. As part of their expanded role, the Army Reserve also received ten new units with missions to provide medical support, ammunition supply, chemical decontamination, or water production services.

Similar to the Maryland NCO Academy badge for the dress uniform seen earlier, this is the version issued by Virginia to those soldiers completing the course to wear on their dress uniforms.

These dress and subdued patches were designed for use by soldiers in Virginia's Officer Candidate School (OCS) program. *Courtesy Kevin Born.*

Virginia NCO Academy pocket patches designed for wear on the fatigue uniform. Shown here are two slightly different versions of the patch with their associated tabs indicating level of training completed.

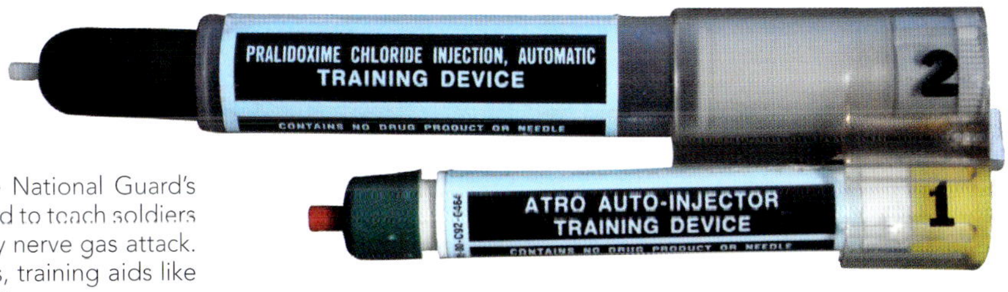

A subtle indication of the renewed interest in the National Guard's readiness by the Active Army; a training aid designed to teach soldiers how to self-inject atropine in the event of an enemy nerve gas attack. Until the larger defense budgets of the early 1980s, training aids like this were usually not available to National Guard units.

Along with regular military training, most National Guard combat arms units were required to practice riot control tactics during the training year. Here National Guard infantrymen dismount from their vehicles. Note that the bayonets on the M16s are fixed but with scabbards covering them, and that transparent face shields for the M1 helmets, flak jackets, and riot batons have been issued to the soldiers.

By the early 1980s, most opportunities to put the riot control training into action had passed. However, in September 1989, the 1st and 3rd Battalions of the 111th Field Artillery and the 229th Military Police Company were called out to restore calm after the "Greekfest" riots in Virginia Beach.

Another sign of the improved budgets for National Guard units was the sudden availability and issuing of the new Battlefield Dress Uniforms, commonly known as BDUs. Even soldiers' dress uniforms received concurrent upgrades. As the Army phased out khaki uniforms, Guard units in Virginia and Maryland were issued the new light green shirts for wear with the green dress coat as part of their clothing issue at about the same time as the Active Army. Other states, such as New York, that heretofore had not had sufficient funding to purchase dress uniforms for their soldiers, began issuing these uniforms to all ranks for the first time in many years.

The new increased budgets not only improved the equipment and uniforms of the soldiers, they also provided money for improved training opportunities for the 29th Infantry Division's new "Light Fighters." By 1987, the basic combat skills of some of the units had progressed to the point that they were invited to participate in an exercise with active duty units at Fort Hunter Liggett, near the Salinas Valley in California. The exercise, a classic test of "Light Fighter" capabilities, was designed to evaluate the ability of one unit to infiltrate an opposing unit's perimeter at night, then follow with an attack against another unit set up behind the line. The Army exercise coordinators were concerned about the training level and capabilities of the Guard unit, the 1st Battalion, 115th Infantry Regiment. They were hesitant to use the Guardsmen in either of the two more complicated roles: the infiltrating unit or the unit being infiltrated. They chose therefore to assign the Guardsmen to the simplest and most basic mission as the second echelon force behind the line that would be attacked after the infiltration had been completed.

The Commander's Handbook, designed by Major General Blum to be a single source of guidance and common sense for small unit commanders in the 29th Infantry Division.

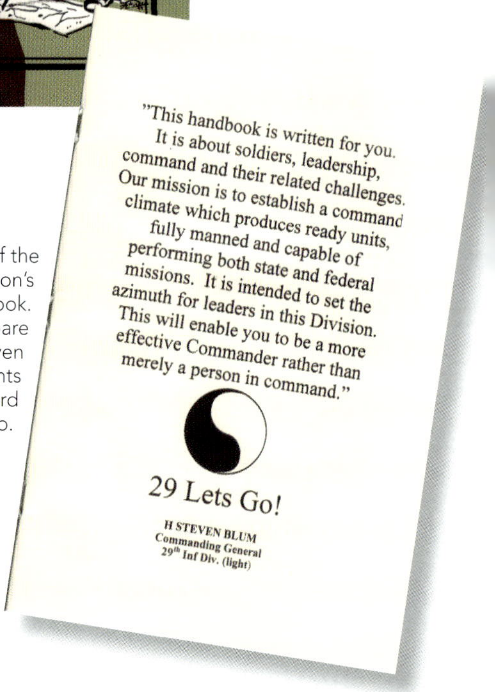

"This handbook is written for you. It is about soldiers, leadership, command and their related challenges. Our mission is to establish a command climate which produces ready units, fully manned and capable of performing both state and federal missions. It is intended to set the azimuth for leaders in this Division. This will enable you to be a more effective Commander rather than merely a person in command."

29 Lets Go!

H STEVEN BLUM
Commanding General
29th Inf Div. (light)

The inside cover of the 29th Infantry Division's Commanders Handbook. It is interesting to compare Major General H. Steven Blum's ideas and comments with the 29th Division card shown in chapter two.

Having previously run this same exercise with other units, the coordinators began to monitor the radio networks after darkness, expecting to hear reports of contact between the infiltrating units and the front line defenders. As the night progressed, the observers were impressed by the skills of the infiltrating unit, as they appeared to have successfully passed unnoticed through the enemy lines and were poised to attack the Guard unit's perimeter. However, they soon became concerned, as no reports of contact by any of the attacking forces were being passed on the radio. By daylight, there had been only sporadic fire and no indication of an actual attack on a fixed position. The "after action" review quickly revealed the reason. While the infiltrating force had successfully passed through the first line of defenders, they were unable to find and attack the Guardsmen's position. During the course of the previous day, the commander of the Guard battalion, Lieutenant Colonel Steven Blum, had secretly moved his forces out of their prepared positions and relocated them in a new defensive position. By using the unit's regularly scheduled chow trucks and trash trucks as transportation vehicles, he slipped his soldiers out of the attack zone, unnoticed by both the enemy and the exercise umpires. Blum left behind a skeleton force that, after dark, began to move around and place glowing chemical light markers in the abandoned fighting positions to give the impression they were still occupied. By the time the infiltration force was able to find the new positions, there was not sufficient time left to mount an attack. Blum's deception plan had worked perfectly, and the active Army observers were impressed by the skill with which his Guardsmen carried it out.[3]

As the 1980s came to a close, the 29th continued to gain a reputation for proficiency and hard, realistic training. In December 1989, the United States carried out operation "Just Cause" and deployed its military forces to Panama in order to protect the canal and re-establish democracy. The 29th was not deployed for this operation, since the active duty forces were sufficient to quickly depose the local dictator and defeat his forces. At the time, no one could know that this operation in Central America would be the last time the active components would take on a major combat operation without significant support from Army National Guard forces. Nor could anyone guess that the 1990s would usher in a totally new set of missions for Virginia and Maryland National Guard soldiers, or that the 29th Infantry Division's famous blue and gray patch would make a return to Europe.

The distinctive unit insignia for the 224th Aviation Regiment. Approved in 1987, the motto "Free Dominion" reflects the unit's locations: Maryland (The Free State) and Virginia (The Old Dominion). Courtesy U.S. Army

Introduced in the late 1980s, this flight suit patch was worn by flight crew members of 2/224th Aviation.

A Sound Protective Helmet-4 (SPH-4) model aviator's Helmet from the 224th Aviation Regiment. This style helmet was in use from the late 1960s through the early 1990s, when it was replaced by the "SPH-4s" model.

CHAPTER 12

Desert Storm, Sinai, and Bosnia (1990 to 2001)

The 80s bore witness to the "reincarnation" of the 29th as a Light Division and its rapid establishment as a solid outfit. The Guardsmen of Virginia and Maryland trained hard to achieve that image; the 29th was once again building a reputation as a "go to" unit and the "Light Fighters" enjoyed their status as a special organization.

By the start of the 1990s, the National Guard had grown to over 450,000 soldiers in units spread across the fifty states and associated territories. These units comprised approximately forty-six percent of the United States Army's combat arms strength and thirty-two percent of its combat support units. Recognizing the importance of logistics, the Guard also provided twenty-six percent of the Army's Combat Service Support soldiers.[1]

With the fall of the Berlin Wall in 1989, some began to question the need for the recent growth of the American military under the Reagan Administration. Before anyone in power could act on these doubts or begin to harvest a "peace dividend," the unexpected invasion of Kuwait by the Iraqi Army in August 1990 brought the necessity for a strong military back into focus.

For the 29th, the sudden emphasis on deploying a force to Saudi Arabia heightened the sense of preparing for a real "shooting war." However, as National Guard and Army Reserve units were mobilized and sent to Saudi Arabia, it became apparent that the war in Southwest Asia was going to be a war of open spaces and armored vehicles. Those units of the United States Army that were equipped with tanks and armored personnel carriers were at the top of the list for deployment, while the "Light" forces, both active and reserve component, were relegated to either supporting the deploying units or left to wait for other missions.

The years of training for Nuclear, Biological, and Chemical (NBC) attacks paid off for the American forces deploying to Saudi Arabia in 1990 and 1991. Though the Iraqis never resorted to such weapons, American soldiers were equipped and trained to operate under such attacks. *Courtesy COL Michelle Rose.*

The bright yellow sticker designed for high-priority shipments to U.S. Forces deployed to Saudi Arabia during Operation Desert Shield/ Desert Storm. Desert Express shipments did not follow the standard route through the supply chain. Each Corps deployed to Saudi Arabia was allowed three air shipment pallets per week using this faster delivery chain. Most of these shipments for deployed Virginia Guard units originated from the S. Gardner Waller Depot in Richmond.

Wearing the "chocolate chip" desert uniform, a female officer stands in the port of Ad Dammam in front of one of the large barges equipped with modular barracks units. Many Guardsmen from all states would use these facilities for billets while working in or transiting the port.

In Virginia and Maryland, National Guard units were activated and sent to Saudi Arabia to participate in Operation Desert Shield and Operation Desert Storm. For the most part, though, these were non-divisional units that provided the specific capabilities requested by the senior Army commanders in the Persian Gulf. From Maryland, two military police companies—the 200th (from Towson, Maryland) and the 290th (from Salisbury)—were activated and sent to Saudi Arabia to assist in the handling of Iraqi prisoners of war. Due to the wide open spaces of the desert and the subsequent long logistics distribution pipeline, there was a significant need for transportation units. Thus, the 1229th Transportation Battalion from Crisfield, Maryland, was called up and sent to the theater of operations. A short while later, they were joined by the Headquarters and Headquarters Detachment of the 29th Aviation from Edgewood, Maryland. In all, nine Maryland National Guard units would be activated for service during the war, but not all of them were actually deployed, as the war was brought to a violent but quick ending in February 1991.[2]

Virginia's list of units deploying to Saudi Arabia was longer, but again focused on the specific types requested by the commanders on the scene. Among those deployed were the 1032nd (from Big Stone Gap, Virginia) and 1033rd (from Gate City) Transportation Companies, the 986th Medical Detachment (Sandston), 229th Military Police Company (Chesapeake), 183rd Adjutant General Company (Sandston), and a History Detachment from Manassas. There were also two engineer units deployed: the Headquarters and Headquarters companies of the 176th Engineer Group (Richmond), and another Gate City unit, the 1030th Engineer Battalion. Others, such as Company "B" of the 2nd Battalion, 224th Aviation (Sandston), were activated but did not deploy to Southwest Asia.[3]

There were nearly 38,000 National Guard soldiers serving in the Southwest Asian theater of operations at war's end. Although the 29th Infantry Division was not called upon to deploy, they and the other combat arms units in the National Guard remained a key element of the American military strategy.

Just how important this expanded role was became evident in 1994, as the U.S. Army was struggling to meet all of the global deployment requirements placed on it by a number of high visibility, high priority missions. One of the mission areas that was proving to be a manning challenge was the Multinational Force & Observer (MFO) Sinai mission that the 82nd Airborne Division routinely supported by rotating its battalions in 12-month rotations. The Army approached the National Guard Bureau (NGB) in late 1993 with a proposal to raise a battalion within the structure of the 82nd to fulfill the U.S. Army's requirements for the MFO Sinai. The NGB turned to the 29th Infantry Division to join with the 82nd; the result was a renewed partnership between these two D-Day greats in the form of the 4th Infantry Battalion, 505th Parachute Infantry Regiment.[4]

An example of a "Chocolate Chip" desert camouflaged hat worn by a Virginia Guardsman during Desert Storm, which prominently displays the addition of a theater-made Desert Storm patch emblazoned with the U.S. and Saudi Arabian flags.

Working together for the first time since the Normandy campaign in France in the summer of 1944, the 29th Infantry Division and the 82nd Airborne Division together made up Task Force 4-505, the "Desert Panthers." The consolidated force deployed in 1993 to the Sinai as part of the United Nations peacekeeping force.

A closer view of the symbol of the Multi-National Force and Observers (MNF) used by the peacekeepers in the Sinai.

The executive officer of Task Force 4-505, Major Miles Altimus. Note he is wearing the newer model Desert Combat Uniform (DCU) with the BDU subdued version of individual and unit patches. The Desert panthers would serve in the Sinai from January to July 1995.

The 4th Infantry Battalion of the 505th Parachute Infantry Regiment, commonly known as the "Desert Panthers," traces its lineage to D Company, 505th Airborne Infantry Regiment. The administrative work to activate the unit began in March 1994, and by September, all of the soldiers had arrived. The 4th Battalion's activation ceremony took place in October 1994, and soldiers of the unit would spend the next three months preparing for their deployment in January 1995. By that time, the 29th provided approximately eighty percent of the battalion's strength and included key positions, such as the Battalion Executive Officer, half of the company command positions, and half of the first sergeant positions.

While this mission was restricted to volunteers from the 29th, the response from across the National Guard was overwhelming in terms of interest in deploying; this fact did not go unnoticed within the Pentagon, as well as Congress. As a result, when the next crisis broke out, there was little hesitation to involve the Guard.

In short order, ethnic rivalries in the Balkans, simmering since the death of Yugoslavia's dictator Josip Tito in 1980, began to boil over. Tito's passing set the wheels in motion that ultimately led Slovenia, Croatia, and Macedonia to declare their independence in 1991. This eventually led to the outbreak of war between Croatia and Bosnia. It was unfortunate for the citizens of the region that the dividing lines between the two sides were not clearly or easily defined. Therefore, many innocent families found themselves behind enemy lines by the simple accident of where they lived. Soon, marauding militias from all ethnic groups took advantage of the breakup of Yugoslavia to repay old insults or feuds. The conflict was made worse, as each side began to arm itself. There soon followed some of the most brutal killings, in the form of "ethnic cleansing," seen in Europe since the Nazi genocide of the 1940s. In many ways, the killings and brutality were encouraged by the ineffective and somewhat anemic response from the international community. While the United Nations attempted to stop the violence, a series of particularly brutal attacks occurred near Sarajevo in 1995 that prompted the North Atlantic Treaty Organization (NATO) to enter into the fray. NATO leaders began working with Bosnian and Croatian forces and attempted to conduct air operations against some of the more aggressive Serbian forces. In November 1995, the U.S. successfully brought the differing factions together in Dayton, Ohio, for a series of talks that resulted in a brokered peace deal that became known as the Dayton Peace Accord.

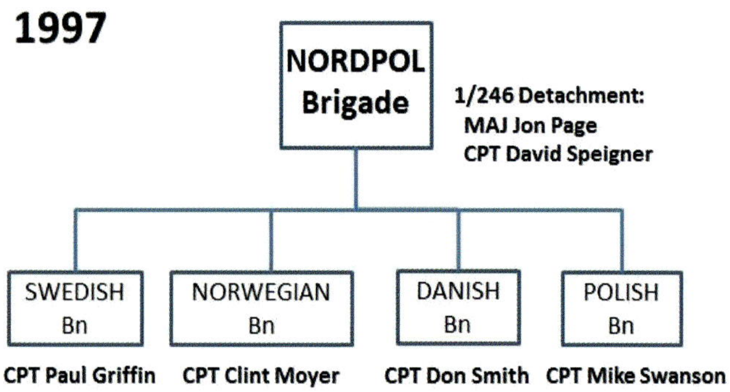

Soldiers of the 1st Battalion, 246th Field Artillery were attached to the Nordic and Polish (NordPol) Brigade headquarters and the subordinate battalions to provide fire support in case of renewed hostilities in Bosnia.

Closer view of Swanson's uniform showing clearly the subdued 29th Infantry Division patch. Prior to arriving in Bosnia, the soldiers received training at Fort Pickett and Fort Benning in the United States and at Grafenwoehr in Germany.

The protective body armor issued to 29th Infantry Division soldiers during their time in Bosnia. American soldiers serving in the Balkans wore their body armor constantly, so the U.S. Army set up a body armor cleaning and repair facility in nearby Hungary to support the force.

Battle Dress Uniform (BDU) belonging to Mike Swanson. At the time a captain and member of Detachment 1, 1st Battalion, 246th Field Artillery, Swanson served in the 29th Infantry Division's rotation to Bosnia March to November 1997.

While the U.S. had supported air operations throughout the previous few years, ground troops were now needed to help enforce the newly-minted Dayton Peace Accord. The European Community—the forerunner of the European Union—established a brigade led by the Norwegian Army and comprised four battalions from Norway, Sweden, Denmark, and Poland. While this formation was quite capable of conducting normal peace-keeping operations, they lacked the ability to coordinate with American artillery and aviation assets that were also deploying to the war-ravaged area. To remedy this, NATO turned to the Americans to provide artillery fire support teams. Among the many capabilities inherent in these teams, of paramount importance to NATO and the Nordic Brigade was the robust communications equipment the American artillery units were known to possess.

Once again, the United States Army leaders looked to the National Guard to provide the necessary forces for this mission. The operational name given to the mission was Operation Joint Guard. In the meantime, the overall name of the NATO forces in the Balkans changed their designation from "Implementation Force" (IFOR) to "Stabilization Force" (SFOR). This renaming was meant to reinforce the idea that, although the initial forces deployed into Bosnia had gone there to "implement" the Dayton Accord, the newer U.N. forces were now being sent to ensure the continued "stability" of the region.

The underlying reason for the 29th's service in the Balkans; a picture of the devastation left behind at the "Olympic Village" complex in Sarajevo by the factional fighting in former Yugoslavia. *Courtesy LTC Michael Swanson.*

A sign marking the "Zone of Separation" between the warring sides in Bosnia. During their tour of duty in Bosnia, the 246th's mission was to provide fire support coordination for the soldiers of the NordPol (Nordic and Polish) Brigade. *Courtesy LTC Michael Swanson.*

Plastic coated map showing the assigned sectors for the Polish Brigade which received support from the American soldiers of the 246th. Also shown here is a copy of the handbook designed to provide information about the people, cultures, social customs and laws of the area being monitored.

An American officer poses for a picture at Polish Checkpoint Z07 in Bosnia, March 1997. This checkpoint was located on the main supply route to the city of Tuzla, located in northeast Bosnia.

The 29th Infantry Division drew the honor of providing the fire support teams. In turn, the Commanding General and staff of the 29th tasked the 29th Division Artillery to provide the required forty-four soldiers from 1st Battalion, 246th Field Artillery headquartered in Danville, Virginia. The 129th Field Artillery Target Acquisition Detachment located in Sandston, Virginia, was also called up for Bosnia support during this period.

Subdued and non-subdued versions of the Stabilization Force (SFOR) patches common in the Bosnia and Herzegovina sectors patrolled by the peacekeeping forces in the 1990s. These patches, although not approved for official wear on U.S. uniforms, were nonetheless very popular with the American soldiers. Most SFOR soldiers from other countries wore them on their right sleeves.

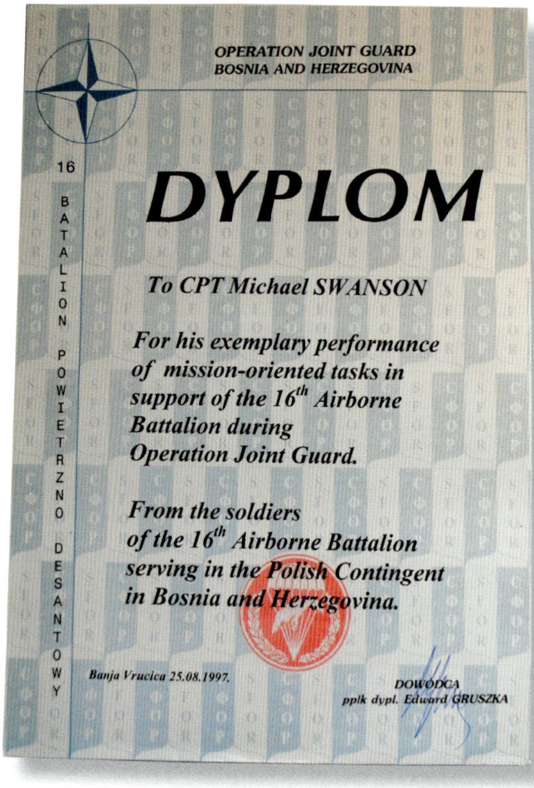

OPERATION JOINT GUARD
BOSNIA AND HERZEGOVINA

16 BATALION POWIETRZNODESANTOWY

DYPLOM

To CPT Michael SWANSON

For his exemplary performance of mission-oriented tasks in support of the 16th Airborne Battalion during Operation Joint Guard.

From the soldiers of the 16th Airborne Battalion serving in the Polish Contingent in Bosnia and Herzegovina.

Banja Vrucica 25.08.1997.

DOWÓDCA
ppłk dypl. Edward GRUSZKA

Certificate awarded to Swanson in recognition of his service in support of the 16th Polish Airborne Battalion during Operation "Joint Guard." Swanson would later recount that the paratroopers of this battalion were among the most professional soldiers with which he had served.

A collection of gifts and souvenirs received by an American soldier from his Polish paratrooper comrades while serving together in Bosnia. The Polish battalion proudly traced their linage to the 6th Polish Airborne Brigade that took part in Operation Market-Garden in Holland in 1944.

The 246th's doctrinal mission at the time was to provide direct support artillery for the Division's 1st Brigade, 116th Infantry Regiment; this would be set aside so that the artillerymen could deploy to Joint Guard. The soldiers of the 246th were notified of the mission in mid-November 1996 and were mobilized by Christmas. As the New Year arrived, the soldiers of the newly-formed detachment moved from Virginia to their mobilization station at Fort Dix, New Jersey, and were en route for Bosnia by the end of February 1997. Arriving in Europe, they made a short detour to the U.S. training area in Grafenwoehr, Germany, to receive more instruction prior to linking up with the Nordic and Polish (NORDPOL) Brigade. Their arrival marked the first overseas deployment, other than for training, of a unit from the 29th Infantry Division since the Second World War. Making the appearance of the 29th in Europe doubly ironic was the fact it had been the assassination of the Austrian Archduke Franz Ferdinand in June 1914 by Serbian Nationalists that led to the First World War, and ultimately the creation of the 29th Division. Now, soldiers of the 29th were deploying to the Balkans as part of a peacekeeping force intent on preventing further bloodshed in that same region.

Polish Airborne uniform, beret, and belt brought back from Bosnia by an American soldier.

Soldiers of the 29th Infantry Division receive medals in recognition of their NATO service from the Polish 16th Parachute Battalion Commander. The irony is obvious, only a few short years earlier, these same Polish troops would have been the sworn enemies of NATO forces.

Soldiers of the 29th stop for a drink of water and picture while participating in a Danish-sponsored road march training exercise in May 1997. *Courtesy LTC Michael Swanson.*

A pennant version of the NordPol flag used by the Danish battalion. The Danish Battalion and attached 246th artillerymen from the 29th Infantry Division were responsible for the large sector to the north of the Polish sector.

Soldiers from the 246th prepare to go on patrol with soldiers of the Polish 16th Airborne Battalion. The vehicle on the left is an American Humvee, while on the right is a Polish Tarpan Honker DZT 4012 truck. Both have been clearly marked with "SFOR" to ensure quick identification. *Courtesy LTC Michael Swanson.*

Formation consisting of soldiers from the Polish, American, and Danish Armies. These Danish soldiers were attached to the Polish battalion to provide additional communication support. *Courtesy LTC Michael Swanson.*

Poster of Bosnian Nationalist leader Radovan Karadzic after the warcrimes trials had been announced. The meaning to the Stabilization Force soldiers was clear; if you see him, leave him alone! The mood in the Serbian Zone of Separation and the town of Teslić went from friendly to cold and confrontational almost overnight after these posters appeared.

Uniform t-shirt for a Swedish soldier in the NordPol Brigade. The epaulet with three stars represents the rank of captain in the Swedish Army and was given to an American captain by his counterpart in the Swedish unit. *Courtesy COL Paul Griffin.*

The 246th Fire Support Elements were parceled out so that there was a team at the NORDPOL Brigade headquarters and with each of the Norwegian, Swedish, Danish, and Polish battalions. Throughout the deployment, the 246th provided critical support to the NORDPOL Brigade as they conducted peace-keeping operations. The 246th completed their rotation and returned home in August 1997.[5]

American Captain Paul Griffin, Detachment Commander for the Swedish battalion, is seen here with his Swedish counterpart and several of the documents used by the 29th's soldiers in Bosnia. These include: Operation Joint Guard redeployment guide, Logistics Support Area layout for the Swedish Battalion, and the operational order for "Thor's Hammer." *Courtesy COL Paul Griffin.*

A collection of official and unofficial unit patches worn by members of the Swedish Battalion. *Courtesy Colonel Paul Griffin.*

The city of Sarajevo. Taken in the summer of 1997, this picture shows a city again at peace after the violence of the Bosnian War, in which over 10,000 citizens of the city were killed. *Courtesy LTC Michael Swanson.*

The Sava River Bridge connecting Croatia and Bosnia. This picture, taken from a Blackhawk helicopter by a Virginia Guardsman in 1997, shows the area that would be under the control of Company "C", 116th Infantry.

The pace of mobilizations to Bosnia to support the Dayton Peace Accord accelerated. In June 1997, the 29th's 1st Infantry Brigade received notification that an infantry company was to be mobilized, also as part of Operation Joint Guard, for peacekeeping duties in Bosnia-Herzegovina. Company "C" from the 3rd Battalion, 116th Infantry, in Leesburg, Virginia, was selected this time. The infantrymen of Company "C" completed rigorous training during their initial annual training in the summer of 1997 at Fort A.P. Hill while under the watchful eye of the U.S. 1st Army advisory team. From there, the 147-man company deployed to Fort Polk, then eventually to Fort Benning for final evaluation and validation of their proficiency. They were also introduced to the special operational guidelines under which all U.S. forces would operate:

General Order Number 1
Applies to all U.S. Personnel. You will not:

- Possess or consume alcoholic beverages at any time or for any reason.
- Possess any weapon or military article that was captured during military operations.
- Touch any ordnance without legal authority.
- Possess or use privately owned firearms, ammunition, or explosives.
- Gamble in any form.
- Sell or exchange any currency other than at the official exchange rate.
- Sell, give, or transfer goods purchased at the PX to a person not authorized PX privileges.
- Allow someone else to use your SFOR ration card.
- Enter any mosque or other Islamic religious site.
- Remove, possess, or deface archeological artifacts or national treasures.
- Dine in local eating establishments not located on Multinational Division North base camp

Upon successful completion of the validation process, Company "C" was activated in September and deployed a month later, in October 1997. Their mission was to provide security for the critically important Sava River Bridge that connected Bosnia in the south to Croatia on the north side of the Sava. As one of the few remaining structures capable of handling vehicle traffic across the river, the bridge was of great significance if economic trade was to be reestablished in the region.

Ruins of houses near the American outpost on the Bosnian side of the river. On the right of the picture is one of the light sets used to illuminate the area.

An American patrol leaves the bridge area and walks toward Srpski Brod. The sign on the right points out the direction to Sarajevo, site of the assassination of the Austrian Archduke Franz Ferdinand that precipitated the First World War.

Part of "Troll Village" as seen from the Sava River Bridge. For the soldiers of the 116th, this would be their outpost for patrolling the town of Srpski Brod.

Armed with an M16 with M203 Grenade Launcher, Specialist-4 Brian G. Crawford of the 116th Infantry pauses during a patrol in Bosnia in 1997. During his second tour in Bosnia, Crawford would be on patrol in Tuzla when the 11 September 2001 attacks took place.

With typical American soldier humor, the Stonewallers quickly began to refer to their outpost and temporary living quarters under the bridge access ramps on the Bosnian side as the "Troll Village." This was because they felt a symbolic and literal kinship with the troll who lived under a bridge in the Norwegian fairy tale "Billy Goats Gruff." When not actively guarding the bridge complex itself, the solders would walk patrols through the shattered little town of Srpski (also spelled Srbski) Brod, on the Bosnian side of the river. The main support base for the Stonewallers of Troll Village was located some five miles away on the Croatian side of the river at Slovanski Brod. The soldiers returned to Virginia in April 1998 after their five-month tour was complete.[6]

Dress Green uniform and hat for Chief Warrant Officer belonging to the State Area Readiness Command of the Virginia Army National Guard.

A graphic portrayal of all the various National Guard units that made up the Virginia Army National Guard in the late 1990s and into the twenty-first century. Besides the patches previously identified are the patches for the 54th Field Artillery Brigade, Special Forces, and the 183rd Regimental Training Institute.

Dress green uniform coat for Staff Sergeant James Long, an Air Defense Artillery NCO assigned to the 111th Field Artillery.

A closer look at SSG Long's uniform, showing that his regimental affiliation (over the right breast pocket) is with the 111th Field Artillery, while his unit of assignment is the 29th Division.

Over the next few years, the 29th continued to sharpen its skills by participating in a number of exercises with active duty units. They also received a variety of state emergency missions, but among the most memorable was the deployment of Company "C" of the 429th Forward Support Battalion to the Central American country of Belize. The unit performed strictly humanitarian services for the local citizens and their efforts were greatly appreciated.[7]

The Commander and staff of the 1st Battalion, 111th Field Artillery take advantage of a break in the training scenario during their summer 2001 annual training at Fort Pickett to have dinner. Noteworthy is that they are using the battalion's 1940-dated mess set.

Another scene from the 2001 annual training of the 111th. The 1st Battalion Commander and his Executive Officer, on the left, pose in front of the battalion's recovery vehicle—an M88 Hercules. The Hercules is a mainstay of any U.S. Army unit equipped with large-tracked vehicles, such as a field artillery battalion's M109A5 self-propelled Howitzers.

During the summer of 2001, along with conducting regular annual training, the 29th began to prepare another contingent for a mission in Bosnia. This time, the 29th was to provide a headquarters element for the 10th Stabilization Force rotation. After performing the mission rehearsal exercise at Fort Polk, Louisiana, the designated soldiers returned home to prepare for the deployment. By the first week of September, the advance party for the 29th had already reached Tuzla, where they received "in-briefs" and conducted joint area familiarization patrols with the U.S. Army unit they were relieving. In the meantime, the rest of the unit was at Fort Dix, New Jersey, performing the last round of pre-deployment weapons checks and equipment issues.

One soldier later recalled that he and other members of his headquarters detachment were at the Central Issue Facility at Fort Dix when a soldier sitting in a nearby car mentioned that an airplane had flown into a building in nearby New York City. When the news became progressively worse, the soldiers began to wonder what effects the terrorist attacks would have on their deployment to Bosnia. As events would show, the National Guard across the country was quickly mobilized to provide enhanced security in airports and military installations. Ultimately, the soldiers of the 29th would deploy to Bosnia and join their advance party comrades to complete the SFOR 10 mission.[8]

Sergeant First Class John Cameron "Cam" Mills, a North Carolina National Guardsman attached to the 29th Infantry Division, poses for a picture near an uncleared mine field. Lesson Number 1 in Bosnia: "Stay on the roads!" *Courtesy MSG Jon Guttman*

Major General William Ingram, Adjutant General of North Carolina, welcomes home the North Carolina National Guard soldiers who served in Bosnia with the 29th at a ceremony in Raleigh 10 April 2002. *Courtesy of NCARNG, SSG Ed Eudy*

And what of that advance party already in the Balkans when the 9-11 attacks took place? One staff sergeant, a veteran of the 116th's Bosnia deployment in 1998, later recounted how he and other 29th soldiers were conducting their first joint recon with soldiers of the outgoing unit: "I had 20 rounds in my M16 and the officers had three rounds each in their [pistols], as the threat level was almost nil; we were in the Tuzla area and were driving a Toyota Land Cruiser. We were informed by the local Bosnians that ...attacks had occurred." The Americans were quickly hustled into a nearby bar with a television to see the replay of the airplanes crashing into the towers of the World Trade Center. The sergeant also clearly remembered the Bosnians' reaction to the attacks: "See, we told you about those Muslims, they are not to be trusted."[9]

Without warning, the United States was again at war. It is a fair assessment to say that the attacks on 9-11 truly closed out the twentieth century for the 29th Infantry Division. As a result of these attacks, the U.S. military started the new century with a now direct war on global terrorism that continues today with little end in sight. In the years since 11 September 2001, the soldiers of the 29th Infantry Division have taken their places in the front lines with the other famous units of the American military in fighting the long war.

As for the sergeant from the Blue and Gray who learned of his country's newest conflict while trying to maintain peace in a war-torn region of the Balkans, he would continue his patrol and complete his tour in Bosnia, but the irony is startling. As noted earlier, the underlying reason for the creation of the 29th Division during the First World War was an act of terrorism on a Sarajevo street just fifty miles from the Tuzla street where the Guardsmen learned of the terrorist attack. Almost a century later, the 29th was being called on again to "make the world safe for democracy." In the more than eighty years between 1917 and 2001, the 29th Infantry Division has served the country well and completed every mission assigned. In the years since 11 September 2001, that same dedication to duty and selfless sacrifice by the soldiers of the Blue and Gray has continued.

The more things change, the more they stay the same. In spite of all the modern technology, the most successful way to ensure security of an area is with ground troops. Here, a patrol from the 29th Infantry Division makes their rounds in Bosnia.

CHAPTER 13

Leaders of the 29th Division

No single book can ever hope to contain biographies of all of the many important leaders of a military unit as long-lasting and famous as the 29th Infantry Division. Recognizing that fact, however, we have attempted to bring together short summations of some of the more interesting and most influential soldiers of the 29th.

Major General Charles D. W. Canham, one of the unsung heroes of that bloody morning on Omaha Beach. Wounded and refusing to be evacuated, he worked with Norman Cota to get the 116th's infantrymen off the beach and up the bluffs. *Courtesy National Archives.*

Charles Draper William Canham (26 January 1901-21 August 1963)

Canham was born in Mississippi, but by 1910, his family had moved to Oregon. He enlisted in the Army in May 1919 and was promoted to sergeant within two years. Canham applied for entry into the United States Military Academy at West Point and received his commission upon graduation in 1926. While serving in the Philippines and China, he developed a well-earned reputation for intensity and discipline.

In 1942, he was assigned as Commander, 116th Infantry Regiment, replacing the National Guard officer commanding just prior to the unit's departure for Britain. As one NCO in the 116th later wrote: "Canham didn't look like a soldier, but he sure as hell was one. He was tall and thin, wore wire rimmed glasses, and had a pencil thin moustache."[1] Canham landed with the first assault waves on Omaha Beach. Although wounded in the wrist, he refused to be evacuated, choosing instead to work with Brigadier General Cota, encouraging the men to get off the beach and start fighting. Together these two leaders managed to inspire the Rangers and soldiers of the 116th to move inland and secure their sections of Omaha Beach.[2]

In the ensuing six weeks, Canham continued to lead the 116th as it fought through the hedgerows. The capture of St. Lô brought about two things: a respite from combat operations for the 29th and Canham was promoted to brigadier general. The promotion came at a price; Canham had to leave the 116th, and he was reassigned as the Assistant Division Commander of the 8th Infantry Division. During the siege of Brest, coincidentally conducted in conjunction with his former unit, Canham made the statement that would cement his place in American history, define his personality, and give the highest accolade to common American infantryman. When asked by the surrendering German commander of "Fortress Brest," Lieutenant General Hermann-Bernhard Ramke, for his "credentials" as a requirement for accepting Ramke's surrender, Canham pointed to a group of American soldiers and simply said "These are my credentials."[3]

This succinct four-word statement, praising the value of the American soldier, was reported in the American press and stands today (along with the description of Iwo Jima Marines: "Uncommon valor was a common virtue.") as the ultimate tribute to the American serviceman. After the war, Canham went on to command both the 82nd Airborne Division and the 3rd Infantry Division, and was subsequently selected to serve as the Commanding General of XI Corps. After forty-one years of service, Canham retired from the Army in 1960. He died just three years later and is buried in Arlington National Cemetery. At the time of his death, all three of his sons (Robert, Charles, and Thomas) were U.S. Army officers.

The 1917 West Point portrait of Norman D. Cota. Cota's previous amphibious landing experience with the 1st Infantry Division had prepared him to expect some chaos on the 6 June landing beaches, but what he encountered was worse than he could have ever imagined; his ability to motivate the soldiers of the 29th that day proved crucial in rallying the 116th and fighting their way off the beach. *Courtesy USMA West Point.*

Norman D. Cota (30 May 1893-4 October 1971)

Norman D. Cota was born in Chelsea, Massachusetts, and received the nickname "Dutch" early in life. He entered the United States Military Academy at West Point, arriving there in 1913. His class was graduated two months early due to the United States' entry into the First World War. While at West Point, Cota and Dwight D. Eisenhower both played on the football team and became friends.

Within eighteen months of graduation, Cota had reached the rank of Major. After the war, he was stationed at Langley Field, Virginia, and served as the Finance Officer for the post. In 1923, in the course of this duty, Cota and four other soldiers that had picked up the payroll shipment from a Hampton, Virginia, bank were robbed at gunpoint by two corporals. The corporals, both members of a Langley Field Air Service unit, surprised the payroll guards outside the bank and forced them to drive away in the large payroll vehicle. Running the car into a ditch, the robbers then forced Cota and the other guards into the woods and tied them to trees. After a massive search that included aircraft, the two payroll thieves were captured near Big Bethel, Virginia, a short while later.[4]

Cota subsequently served in Hawaii from 1924 to 1928, and later graduated from the United States Army Command and General Staff College (CGSC) at Fort Leavenworth, Kansas, in June 1931. From there, he served as an instructor at both the Infantry School and at the CGSC. At the outbreak of World War II, he was the G-2 Officer (Intelligence) and then G-3 Officer (Plans and Training) of the 1st Infantry Division. In June 1942, he was appointed the Chief of Staff of the 1st Infantry Division. In February 1943, he was promoted to brigadier general and transferred to Great Britain to prepare for the Normandy invasion. Soon thereafter, Cota was selected as the Assistant Division Commander for the 29th Infantry Division, where his pragmatic and common sense approach to issues acted as strong counterpoint to the Division Commander, Major General Charles H. Gerhardt.[5] During the D-Day planning phase, he was opposed to the daylight landings scheduled for initial assault waves and is quoted as saying that he did "not believe the daylight assault can succeed."[6]

In spite of the objections of Cota and other officers, the plans continued to call for daylight landings, with heavy naval and aerial bombardments preceding the attack. The afternoon of 5 June, Cota prepared the staff of the 29th Infantry Division for what was to come by saying: "You're going to find confusion. The landing craft aren't going in on schedule and people are going to be landed in the wrong place. Some won't be landed at all. The enemy will try, and have some success, in preventing our gaining a 'lodgement.' But we must improvise, carry on, not lose our heads."[7] He would soon see exactly how prophetic his words were. Cota landed on beach sector "Dog White" with the 116th Infantry Regiment in the second wave, less than an hour after the initial landing wave came ashore. As Cota's landing craft approached the beach, three soldiers were killed before they even got out of the boat. Once he stepped ashore, Cota became the highest ranking officer in the 29th's sectors of Omaha Beach on 6 June 1944. Coincidentally, personally leading the landing at Utah Beach was his distant cousin, Brigadier General Theodore "Teddy" Roosevelt, Jr. In yet another interesting coincidence, Cota's wife and Teddy Jr.'s wife were also cousins.

Cota soon became famous for his coolness under fire at Omaha Beach, as he praised, bullied, and inspired the American infantrymen into moving forward against the German positions. Two months later, Cota was given command of the 28th Infantry Division, a unit comprised primarily of Pennsylvania National Guardsmen.

As the commander of the 28th Infantry Division, and now Major General Norm Cota, he would lead them into the ill-advised Hurtgen Forest campaign. Once again, as in the D-Day planning, Cota did not agree with the operational plan he was given, but his complaints were ignored by the V Corps commander, Major General Leonard Gerow. Cota was just one of several senior American leaders whose reputation as a combat leader was tainted by the ultimately disastrous battles in the Hurtgen Forest. Cota retired from the Army shortly after the end of the Second World War. He died in Wichita, Kansas, 4 October 1971, and is buried in West Point Cemetery at the United States Military Academy.[8]

Sheppard Crump is seen here in his Richmond Light Infantry Blues uniform. Crump enlisted in the Blues in 1903, serving with them on the Mexican Border and later in France as a member of the 104th Ammunition Train. He was selected to be the Adjutant General of Virginia in 1956, a position he held until his death in 1960.

Sheppard Crump (24 May 1882-6 January 1960)

A native Virginian, Sheppard Crump was born and raised in Henrico County, near Richmond. He began his fifty-five year military career in 1903, when he enlisted in the Richmond Light Infantry Blues. He served in the Mexican Campaign with the Blues, then in France as a member of the 104th Ammo Train in the 29th Division.[9] After the war Crump remained in the Virginia Guard, and by 1922 was a lieutenant colonel, serving as the Executive Officer of the 183rd Infantry Regiment. In 1941, he was appointed as Virginia's Assistant Adjutant General. Crump was later appointed Adjutant General in 1956 by Governor Stanley when the serving Adjutant General, S. Gardner Waller, died. Like his predecessor, Crump died in office. He is buried in Hollywood Cemetery in Richmond.

John Abram Cutchins (9 November 1881-24 September 1976)

Cutchins was born in Richmond, Virginia, and attended prep schools before entering the University of Virginia in 1899. He graduated with master of arts and bachelor of law degrees in 1905 and began his law practice in the family-owned firm of Cutchins and Cutchins. He joined the Richmond Light Infantry Blues in 1904 and was promoted to captain by the time the unit deployed to the Mexican border in October 1916 as part of the 1st Provisional Cavalry Regiment. When the Virginia Guard was federalized and became part of the 29th Division of the American Expeditionary Force, Cutchins was named Assistant Chief of Staff to the Division Commander, Major General Morton. Cutchins was later transferred to the staff of General John J. Pershing and was the American representative on the international commission on financial and administrative questions about the Allied occupation of Germany. Cutchins renewed his law practice in Richmond after the war and also served as the Director of Public Safety from 1935 to 1940. He wrote *An Amateur Diplomat in the World War*, *A Famous Command: The Richmond Light Infantry Blues*, and *History of the Twenty-Ninth Division 1917-1919*. Cutchins is buried in Hollywood Cemetery in Richmond.

Charles Gerhardt's 1917 West Point portrait. Early in his career, Gerhardt cultivated the image of a "dashing cavalryman" and was generally recognized as one of the best horsemen in the Army. *Courtesy USMA West Point.*

Charles Hunter Gerhardt (6 June 1895-9 October 1976)

Charles Gerhardt was born into an Army family, his father

eventually achieving the rank of brigadier general. A gifted athlete, Gerhardt attended West Point, where his greatest accomplishment was leading the football team to an upset victory in 1916 over the Notre Dame team led by George Gipp; it would be Notre Dame's only loss that year. After graduation, Gerhardt was sent to a cavalry unit and later deployed to France as part of the 89th Division. Serving in the American Army of Occupation in the German Rhineland, Gerhardt would spend most of his time working out and playing quarterback for the 89th Division's AEF championship football team. Gerhardt continued his Army career after the war. The 1920s were marked by a period in which he seemed unable to let go of his need to be a "dashing cavalryman," and his annual evaluations reflected this to some degree.[10] However, he slowly began to exhibit more maturity, and in 1932, due to his skilled horsemanship, Gerhardt was selected to be a judge for the equestrian events at the Olympic Games held in Los Angeles, California. With the advent of World War II, he first served as the commander of the 91st Infantry Division, but was subsequently transferred to the 29th Infantry Division, where he would make his greatest impact in American military history. By now, Gerhardt had developed his personal mantra, which stated "The goal of an effective battle team is to march, shoot and obey."[11]

Interestingly, Gerhardt apparently developed many of the same personality and leadership traits as Major General Morton, the 29th's World War I commander. Like Morton, Gerhardt was a stickler for appearance and discipline. Unbuckled chinstraps on helmets drove him to distraction, yet he was recognized by many as an excellent trainer and administrator. However, under Gerhardt's command, the 29th was noted for extremely high casualty rates in the campaigns that followed the Normandy landings. Whether this high rate was due to Gerhardt's flawed tactics, or to the fact that the 29th was often in the middle of the heaviest fighting, remains open to individual analysis and opinion. Regardless, it was a common saying in the ETO that

Charles Gerhardt is seen here, behind and to the right of the center, striking a football pose with his teammates from the 89th Division's AEF champion football team. Gerhardt had also played on the West Point football team that beat Notre Dame in 1916.

Gerhardt commanded three divisions: one in the field, one in the hospital, and one in the cemetery. Despite heavy losses, Gerhardt maintained his self-confident personality throughout the tough days of the Normandy campaign and those that followed. Perhaps the most telling analysis of Gerhardt's command style came from MacDonald's *The Siegfried Line Campaign*: "No detail—from distribution of cigarettes to an unauthorized type of jacket worn by a company commander—was beyond General Gerhardt's province."[12] In an after action report, Gerhardt wrote "No reports of disaster should be allowed. THEY ARE NEVER TRUE."[13] Gerhardt was also, perhaps surprisingly, extremely interested in ensuring that "combat fatigue" casualties be treated effectively and without stigma. When his staff discovered that the fatigue rate was highest among the replacements the 29th received during and after the fighting at St. Lô, it was also noted that a majority of these soldiers had received very little infantry training. Acting on this information, Gerhardt re-established a divisional training center for basic combat skills. This concept of continuous training would remain with the 29th for the duration of the war.[14]

Following the Second World War, Gerhardt was reduced in rank to colonel and served as the United States Defense Attaché in Brazil. He was subsequently reinstated to brigadier general and was eventually able to retire at his highest rank, major general. Gerhardt is buried in Arlington National Cemetery.

Brigadier General Leonard Gerow is using a pencil as a pointer on a world map to accentuate a point with other officers of the War Plans Division in November 1941. The officer on the far left is Gerow's brother, Colonel Lee S. Gerow. Standing with his face partially obscured is Lieutenant Colonel Matthew Ridgeway. *Courtesy USAMI II.*

Leonard Townsend Gerow
(13 July 1888–12 October 1972)

Leonard T. Gerow was born in Petersburg, Virginia, and attended the Virginia Military Institute (VMI), where he was elected class president three of the four years he was there.

A unique presentation plaque made for Lieutenant General Leonard Gerow, showing all of the major units that served under his command in V Corps from 6 June 1944 to 16 January 1945. Apparently, the patch for the 90th Infantry Division came loose at some point and was remounted upside down.

He graduated as recipient of the "Honor Appointment" and was commissioned a 2nd lieutenant in the Army 29 September 1911.

Gerow served in a series of assignments as a company-grade officer in the Infantry and also served in the Mexican Campaign. During the First World War, he served on the Signal Corps staff in France and was responsible for procuring the radio equipment needed by the AEF. After the war, Gerow had a variety of assignments, as well as attending the Army's senior leader training courses. He served in China during the 1930s. Gerow was promoted to major general 14 February 1942 and was selected to be the Commanding General of the 29th Infantry Division. During Gerow's tenure as the 29th Division's commander in Britain, the unit seemed to suffer increasingly poor morale. This was due to a combination of factors: the drab surroundings and food, the lack of a clearly defined mission, and Gerow's "seven day training week," with its emphasis on long distance hikes as the means to maintaining fitness and discipline.[15] He continued to command the 29th until 17 July 1943, when he relinquished that position to Charles Gerhardt and was appointed V Corps Commander that same day. In this role, Gerow played a major part in the planning of the D-Day invasion. He was the first corps commander to go ashore on D-Day, and led the V Corps throughout the early days of the Normandy campaign, as well as during the breakout from the beachhead.

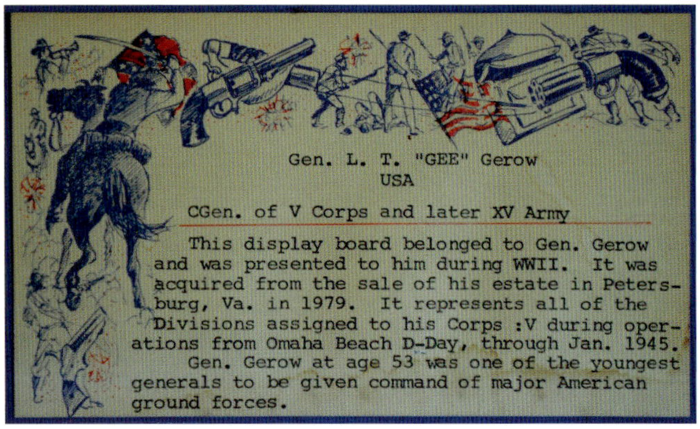
Gen. L. T. "GEE" Gerow
USA
CGen. of V Corps and later XV Army
This display board belonged to Gen. Gerow and was presented to him during WWII. It was acquired from the sale of his estate in Petersburg, Va. in 1979. It represents all of the Divisions assigned to his Corps :V during operations from Omaha Beach D-Day, through Jan. 1945. Gen. Gerow at age 53 was one of the youngest generals to be given command of major American ground forces.

The information card that is currently on the back of General Gerow's Presentation Board.

In a February 1945 memo, Gerow's old classmate, Dwight D. Eisenhower, listed the senior American commanders in order of merit based on his impression of their service during the war. Gerow was eighth on the list out of thirty-two officers. Gerow assumed command of the U.S. Fifteenth Army 15 January 1945. After the war, and now a lieutenant general, Gerow was appointed Commandant of the Army's Command and General Staff School. He retired in July 1950 and was appointed to the rank of general on July 19, 1954, by Special Act of Congress. Gerow died in 1972 and is buried in Arlington cemetery. As a side note, General Gerow's younger brother, Lee S. Gerow, graduated from VMI in 1913, served in the First World War and the subsequent occupation of Germany, and would reach the rank of brigadier general.

A portrait of Thomas D. Howie as a cadet at The Citadel. An excellent trainer and combat leader, Howie would unfortunately achieve his greatest fame in death when he became known as the "Major of St. Lô." *Courtesy of The Citadel.*

Thomas Dry Howie (12 April 1908-17 July 1944)

Thomas D. Howie was born in Abbeville, South Carolina. He attended The Citadel and graduated in 1929. From there, he taught English at the Staunton Military Academy, Staunton, Virginia, and joined the Virginia National Guard. Howie's unit, the 116th Infantry Regiment, was federalized and entered active duty in 1941, deploying to Britain in 1942, where it spent most of the next two years in training for the assault on the European continent. In the fall of 1943, Howie was appointed commander of the 2nd Battalion of the 116th. It was not a job he would hold for long, as he soon found himself on the losing side of an argument with Major General Gerhardt and was relieved of his command. Shortly thereafter, Gerhardt reconsidered and appointed Howie to be the Regimental Operations Officer, a key leadership role in any combat unit.[16] It was in this role that Howie participated in the 6 June 1944 landing on Omaha Beach. Five weeks later, on 13 July, Major Howie was assigned to command the 3rd Battalion of the 116th. He led his unit in a desperate attempt to rescue the beleaguered 2nd Battalion of the 116th near the town of la Madeleine. After breaking through the German lines and reaching the 2nd Battalion, he assessed the situation and decided that what remained of the 2nd Battalion was too battered to be of much assistance to his battalion in taking the town of St. Lô. As a result, Howie decided that his battalion would conduct the attack alone. Howie phoned General Gerhardt and, after providing an update, said "See you in St. Lô." Shortly thereafter, as he was giving his company commanders their instructions for the attack on St. Lô, his headquarters came under heavy fire from a German mortar barrage and Howie was killed. Two days later, with St. Lô captured by Task Force "C," Howie's body was brought forward into the city in a field ambulance in accordance with Gerhardt's orders. When the vehicle reached St. Croix Cathedral, the soldiers removed the flag-draped body and placed it on a bier of rubble. A newspaper photographer was present and took a pictures of Howie's American flag-covered body set among the ruins of the church. It soon became well known as a symbol of self sacrifice and devotion to duty. Due to wartime censorship requirements Howie's name and unit could not be disclosed, so the picture and Thomas Howie simply became known as "The Major of St. Lô."[17]

He is buried at the Normandy American Cemetery. In 1956, the town of St. Lô built a monument to Howie. There is a plaque on a wall of the now-rebuilt church to show where his body was placed amidst the rubble. National Guard armories in both South Carolina and Virginia are named in his honor.

Manus MacCloskey's 1898 West Point portrait. Originally assigned to the Coastal Artillery Corps, MacCloskey would become an experienced field artillery officer while serving in Cuba and later in China during the Boxer Rebellion. Thanks to his careful tutelage during the Mexican Border Campaign, the Virginia field artillery batteries would become recognized for their proficiency. *Courtesy USMA West Point.*

Manus MacCloskey (24 April 1874-11 May 1963)

Manus MacCloskey was born in Pittsburgh, Pennsylvania, and attended the U.S. Military Academy at West Point. Upon graduation in 1898, he joined the Coast Artillery Corps. His first few years of service were in a number of military campaigns: Cuba during the Spanish-American War, the Philippines during the insurrection, and even in China for service in the China Relief Expedition during the Boxer Rebellion. Of greatest importance for this story, MacCloskey was the commander of the Provisional Artillery Regiment in which the Virginia National guard artillery had been assigned during the Mexican Border Campaign in 1916. Under his firm and professional guidance, the Virginia artillery batteries soon became recognized as highly proficient units.[18]

During the First World War, MacCloskey commanded the 12th Field Artillery Regiment of the 2nd Division in battles near Verdun, at Chateau-Thierry, Belleau Wood, and Soissons. By 1919, he was commanding the 2nd Field Artillery Brigade in the Third Army as part of the Army of Occupation in Germany.

After returning from occupation duty, McCloskey attended both the General Staff College and the Army War College. Thereafter, he commanded Fort Myer, Fort Sheridan, and Fort Bragg. He retired from the Army in 1938 and started a new career as the administrator of the Cook County Hospital in Chicago. His son, Monro MacCloskey, would also serve in the Army and later retire from the U.S. Air Force as a brigadier general. He is buried beside his father in Arlington National Cemetery.

Randolph Millholland, seen here seated with his hands crossed in his lap with the soldiers of his command, Company "G", 115th Infantry Regiment. Millholland would later command the 29th Ranger Battalion. He would be seriously wounded while commanding the 2nd Battalion of the 115th in November 1944.

Randolph Millholland (21 September 1906–21 April 1983)

Randolph Millholland was born in Maryland and was the son of Randolph and Jean Millholland. Some records indicate that his grandfather had served in the Union Army during the Civil War and had been a prisoner in Andersonville Prison. Randolph joined the National Guard during the 1930s and was working as an accountant in civilian life when the 29th Infantry Division was federalized in February 1941. By this time, he had risen to the rank of captain and was commanding Company "G", 115th Infantry Regiment. Though pictures of the time show him as a relatively tall and slender soldier, they do not give any indication of the powerful drive to succeed that Millholland possessed. When the 29th deployed to Britain in late 1942, Millholland was with the 115th Regiment, but was soon sent to the British General Headquarters Battle School in Durham, England.[19] In December, he returned and was placed in command of the 29th Ranger Battalion that was being formed. Millholland would serve as the only commander the 29th Rangers would have, as the unit was disbanded in October 1943, with the assigned soldiers returning to their original units. On detached duty during the period, Millholland was not with the 29th on D-Day or during the St. Lô campaign. When he returned, he pitched into the fighting as if to make up for lost time. By August, he was commanding the 3rd Battalion of the 115th just in time to lead them in the fighting to liberate the French port city of Brest from the German defenders. During one particular fight, Millholland picked up an M1 Garand rifle and began firing at German soldiers he saw in the open. This aggressive style of leadership met with the approval of his troops. One was quoted as saying that Millholland will "be a damn good battalion commander—if he lives long enough."[20]

It was an apt prophecy. Millholland lasted only until the middle of November; he was seriously wounded in the leg by an artillery shell during the battle to capture the German town of Siersdorf. Millholland would later return as a lieutenant colonel to command the 3rd Battalion of the 115th and was still in command on V-E day.[21]

In the postwar years, Millholland would rise to the rank of brigadier general and eventually command the unit in which he had served so bravely, the 115th Infantry. Perhaps the finest tribute to Millholland was given by one of his Rangers, Jack Womer. Though Womer chose not to return to the 29th when the Rangers were disbanded, deciding instead to become a paratrooper in the 101st Airborne Division, he still maintained a strong regard for Millholland. He later wrote: "Millholland was a good man. I liked him [and] I told him that I would soldier under him any day of the week. He looked straight into my eyes and shook my hand."[22]

Charles Morton's 1883 West point portrait. Morton would bring over thirty years experience in the Army as an infantry officer to Camp McClellan when he assumed command of the 29th Division. *Courtesy USMA West Point.*

Infantry Regiment and serving in the Philippines during the Spanish-American War. Morton served as an instructor with the Massachusetts National Guard in 1912. He commanded the 5th Infantry Regiment from 1913 to 1916, then served as Commanding General of the 10th Division, securing the Texas/Mexico border during the Mexican Expedition. With the advent of the First World War, Morton was assigned as Commander of the 29th Division. He assumed command and conducted their training at Camp McClellan, deploying with them to France in 1918. Morton led his 29th Division through the Meuse-Argonne campaign, where the 57th and 58th Infantry Brigades performed extremely well in fighting on the eastern side of the Meuse River.[23]

Upon returning to the States at the end of the war, Morton was selected to command the Department of Hawaii from 1919-1921. He died at age seventy-two from a tetanus infection he incurred while lighting firecrackers during a Fourth of July celebration in San Francisco. His will specified that most of his estate be given to the Army Relief Society and to the U.S. Military Academy. During the Second World War, a United States Navy transport ship was named in his honor; the USS *General C. G. Morton* (AP-138). The *Morton* also served during the Korean War, under Army command, and earned three battle stars.

Early pictures of Charles G. Morton as a young man and as a West Point Cadet. Selected to serve as the very first commander of the 29th Division, Morton would put his stamp on every aspect of the newly-created division to ensure it was a disciplined outfit. *Courtesy National Park Service.*

A picture of Colonel John M. Palmer during his service as commander of the 58th Infantry Brigade. Palmer had served in Cuba, China, and the Philippines prior to the First World War and was highly esteemed for both his combat leadership and his operational planning skills. *Courtesy National Guard Educational Foundation.*

Charles Gould Morton (15 January 1861-8 July 1933)
Charles G. Morton was born in Cumberland, Maine. He was the son of Brigadier General Charles Morton. He entered the U.S. Military Academy in 1879 and graduated in 1883. Over the next twenty years, he spent most of his time with the 6th

John McAuley Palmer (23 April 1870-26 October 1955)
Born in Carlinville, Illinois, John McAuley Palmer was named for his grandfather, General John McAuley Palmer, a Civil War officer in the Union Army who also served later as the Governor of Illinois. He was appointed a lieutenant

Palmer as a brigadier general. Working for General George Marshall after the Second World War, Palmer devised the concept of a three-part U.S. Army: Regular, National Guard, and Army Reserve. *Courtesy U.S. Army.*

During the interwar period, Palmer wrote a number of well-received books and articles about the Army. He was recalled to active duty by Army Chief of Staff George C. Marshall just before the attack on Pearl Harbor and served throughout the war as an advisor on military policy to the War Department General Staff. He returned to private life after the end of the Second World War and passed away 26 October 1955. Due to the depth and breadth of his military knowledge, Palmer was considered by his contemporaries to be a visionary, as well as an eloquent spokesman for the "citizen soldier" and the Army. He was elected into the Fort Leavenworth Hall of Fame in 1982 with three other extremely influential and well-known generals: General George S. Patton, Jr.,; General Lucian Truscott, Jr.,; and Major General Edwin V. Sumner. Palmer was also elected into the Army's Force Development Hall of Fame in 2005.

in 1892 and served with the 15th Infantry at Fort Sheridan, Illinois. Palmer had a wide variety of assignments, including service as an aide to General Edwin Sumner in the Cuban campaign during the Spanish-American War. He followed that up with an assignment that took him to China during the Boxer Rebellion. He was later appointed a district governor in the Lanao District on Mindanao, Philippines, from 1906 to 1908. Returning to the States, Palmer was assigned to the War Department in Washington, D.C. In 1910, he was again assigned to an Army regiment in China. After another staff position in the Philippines, he returned to the General Staff in Washington, D.C. With the impending American involvement in the First World War, Palmer played a key role in developing the plans for an American Expeditionary Force (AEF). His expertise in this endeavor soon brought him to the attention of General John J. Pershing. Pershing selected Palmer to accompany him to France and assigned him as the Assistant Chief of Staff for Operations. His first mission was to develop a school system for training the soldiers of the AEF upon their arrival in France. Palmer was later selected to command the 58th Infantry Brigade of the 29th Division in the Meuse-Argonne campaign. The excellent performance in combat of his two infantry regiments (the 115th and 116th) added even more luster to his already solid reputation.[24]

After the Armistice, the War Department requested Palmer be returned to the States to initiate the process of redesigning the Army for the future. After much study, discussion, and argument, Palmer's ideas became codified in the National Defense Act of 1920; a legislative act establishing America's "Total Army" concept, in which national defense depended on the joint efforts of the Regular Army, the National Guard, and the Army Reserve.[25] Palmer was promoted to the permanent rank of brigadier general in the Regular Army in 1922. He commanded the 19th Infantry Brigade in Panama until his retirement in 1926.

William C. Rafferty's 1880 West Point portrait. Among his early assignments was command of the coastal artillery battery on Alcatraz Island in San Francisco Bay. Rafferty would later marry the daughter of Civil War Union Cavalry General Judson Kilpatrick. *Courtesy USMA West Point.*

William Carroll Rafferty (11 April 1859-22 May 1941)
William C. Rafferty was born in Indiana and attended the United States Military Academy from 1876 to 1880.

He was appointed a 2nd lieutenant in the 1st U.S. Artillery 12 June 1880, and served as the Commander of Alcatraz prison. Rising through the ranks, he also commanded Fort Myer, Virginia, and Fort Hamilton, New York. In 1917, Rafferty was assigned to the 29th Division as Commander, 54th Field Artillery Brigade.

Though early in his career he had served as a regular artilleryman, the vast majority of his career had been spent in coastal artillery units. As a result, his knowledge of contemporary field artillery operations, especially for mounted units, was "nil."[26] This soon became apparent to all the members of the 54th Field Artillery Brigade at Camp McClellan, when Rafferty would insist that all of the more than thirty animals of a firing battery could be fed, watered, and cared for by a single soldier. While at McClellan, the artillery units suffered the additional burden of having most of their senior officers sent to schools or training at Fort Oglethorpe. Concurrently, many of the senior enlisted men were transferred to other units in the 29th to fill personnel shortages. Rafferty did nothing to improve this situation. In one instance, he ordered artillery batteries to move from their camps to other unprepared sites in the midst of extremely foul weather. Halfway through the move the order was rescinded, but by then, some batteries were already at the new locations and suffering from the cold in obsolete tents. Reduced to sheltering around the Sibley stoves in their tents, the artillerymen spent most of December and January trying to find firewood to stay warm.

Brigadier General William Rafferty. Originally a coastal artillery officer, Rafferty was the first commander of the 54th Field Artillery Brigade during its training at Camp McClellan. He was relieved just before the 29th deployed to France in 1918. *Courtesy National Guard Educational Foundation.*

When the inevitable fire broke out and burned down an officer's mess, Rafferty reacted by conducting numerous fire drills: "sometimes 2 or 3 times each night."[27] While the 111th seemed to be the particular target of Rafferty's ire, the other regiments also drew some unwanted attention. After several arbitrary relocations at Camp McClellan, one gunner in the 110th Field Artillery reported "We ain't a battery, we're a building association."[28]

By February 1918, the 111th was under-strength by four hundred men and had not trained as artillerymen in months. During this period Rafferty appeared to revel in ruining the careers of officers assigned to the 111th, as noted in their unit history: "Being incompetent, he fancied that he was acquiring merit with his superiors by forcing officers to quit the regiment and the service."[29] His methods were particularly cruel, as almost daily he would demand that the 111th Regimental Commander send him the most inefficient officer in the unit. When the chosen officer appeared, Rafferty would grill him on obscure information, such as the longitude and latitude of certain cities, or ask the officer to name the last five kings of Babylon. When the officer failed to answer correctly, he would be sent back to his unit and the 111th Regimental Commander would be informed that the officer would need to appear before an "Efficiency Board" to determine his suitability to remain in the unit. At times, more than forty percent of the officers in the 111th were awaiting judgment from the "Efficiency Boards."

Sadly, Rafferty himself was probably the most incompetent officer in the 54th Brigade. This was best evidenced by his inability to understand that, to an artilleryman, the term "Fire Discipline" was integral to the orderly and disciplined control of a field artillery battery in combat operations. When told by an outsider that the "fire discipline" in the 54th Brigade was poor, he responded by establishing a series of fire drills complete with buckets and ladders.

Just prior to the 29th Division leaving Camp McClellan, Rafferty was finally relieved of his command, and on 31 May 1918, was reduced to the rank of colonel. Replacing Rafferty was Lucius Holbrook, who would lead the brigade through France and the redeployment home. Perhaps the nicest thing that could be said about Rafferty's tenure as commander of the brigade was that it was "tragic." An true indication of just how poorly Rafferty understood the quality of the soldiers under his command is the fact that, of the more than three hundred enlisted men "harvested" from the 111th Regiment for transfer to officer candidate school, only three would fail to receive commissions.

As a postscript, Rafferty would make the news one last time in June 1921 when the house he inherited from his father in law, Civil War General Judson Kilpatrick, was destroyed in a fire. The damage was estimated to be in excess of $10,000 and included many of the souvenirs Rafferty had collected during his military service.[30] Rafferty is buried in Arlington National Cemetery.

A portrait of Milton A. Reckord. Reckord joined the National Guard in Maryland in 1901 and served continuously until his retirement sixty-five years later. While serving in two World Wars, Reckord proved to be both an excellent combat leader and an extremely capable administrator. The Milton Reckord Trophy is presented annually to a National Guard battalion for excellence in Training, Readiness, Marksmanship, and other unit functions. *Courtesy National Guard Educational Foundation.*

Milton Atchison Reckord (28 December 1879-8 September 1975)

Milton A. Reckord was born in Harford County, Maryland. After high school, he worked at his father's milling plant and enlisted in Company "D", 1st Maryland Infantry, Maryland National Guard February 15, 1901. Displaying a strong natural aptitude for the Army and military service, Reckord would eventually command this same company when he was commissioned as a captain just three years later. In 1916, Reckord would command the 2nd Battalion, 1st Maryland Infantry, stationed on the Mexican border from 28 June to 4 November. When the 29th Infantry Division was created in 1917, Reckord was selected to command the 115th Infantry Regiment. Perhaps the most telling evidence of Reckord's abilities as a military leader was that he was the only one of the original regimental commanders in the 29th Division *not* to be relieved by Major General Morton during the war.[31]

In 1920, Reckord was appointed Adjutant General for the state of Maryland by Governor Albert C. Ritchie. Reckord would serve in this position for almost forty-five years. In June 1920, Secretary of War Baker asked him to serve on the high-level committee that created amendments to the National Defense Act of 1916. These changes elevated the National Guard from its existence as a purely state force to becoming a reserve component of the Army. In 1934, while still Maryland's Adjutant General, he assumed command of the 29th Infantry Division. When the 29th Infantry Division was mobilized for Federal service in February 1941, Reckord went with it. At this point his age played against him, as it was believed that a sixty-three year old officer would not be able to handle the stress of leading an infantry division into combat. Reckord was replaced by Major General Leonard Gerow as 29th Infantry Division Commander in January 1942.

Reckord later deployed to the European Theater of Operations to serve as the Theater Provost Marshal until June 1945. With the end of the war in Europe, Reckord returned to his post as the Adjutant General of Maryland and continued to serve until his retirement in 1966 at age eighty-six. In addition to his military service, Reckord belonged to many organizations and clubs, including the Adjutants General Association, the 29th Division Association, the Veterans of Foreign Wars, and the National Rifle Association (NRA), for which he served as Executive Vice-President for many years. He died 8 September 1975 at ninety-five years of age.[32]

Ollie W. Reed poses for a formal portrait in his reserve officer training uniform. Reed served as an enlisted man on the Mexican border during the Punitive Campaign against Pancho Villa. In November 1919, he would be assigned to the American Forces in Germany and serve as a quartermaster officer at the Army supply depot at Bendorf, Germany. *Courtesy Dennis Whitehead.*

Ollie William Reed (18 July 1896-30 July 1944)

O.W. Reed was born in Norton, Kansas, and attended Kansas State University prior to enlisting in Company

"I", 1st Kansas Infantry. When the Kansas National Guard deployed to the Mexican Border, Reed went with them and was stationed at Eagle Pass, Texas, from July to November 1916. During this period, Reed rose through the ranks to sergeant, was selected to attend Reserve Officers Training Camp at Camp Funston, and was subsequently appointed a Regular Army 2nd lieutenant in October 1917. Reed would spend the First World War stationed in Utah, Iowa, and Massachusetts, but would later be assigned to the Army of Occupation in Germany in November 1919. While there, he served with the 50th Infantry Regiment and as a quartermaster officer at the Rhine River supply depot at Bendorf.[33] Reed was assigned to the 31st Infantry Regiment in the Philippines from 1939 to November 1941, when he would be evacuated back to the States due to severe malaria.

Reed's oldest son, Ollie William Reed II, would graduate from the U.S. Military Academy at West Point in 1942 and be appointed a 2nd lieutenant in the 363rd Infantry regiment, 91st Infantry Division. Prior to his deployment overseas to Italy, Ollie, more commonly called "Buddy," and his wife would celebrate the birth of a son, Ollie William III.

Colonel Reed arrived in Normandy 23 June 1944, and took command of the 175th Infantry Regiment as the 29th prepared for its next attempt to take St. Lô. Shortly thereafter, his son, Lieutenant Ollie Reed, would land in Italy and be killed in action 6 July 1944, after only two days in combat. Colonel Reed would outlive his son by only a few weeks. On 30 July, the jeep he was riding in was caught in a German artillery barrage near the Villebaudon crossroads.[34] Reed Sr. would die of the wounds he received. News of the deaths of both men reached their home in Manhattan, Kansas, the same day in August 1944. The two men are buried side by side in the Normandy American Cemetery.

Captain Ollie Reed posing with his family in the 1920s. His oldest son, Ollie W. Reed II (second from left), would follow his father into the Army and later be killed in action in Italy in July 1944. *Courtesy Dennis Whitehead.*

Richard H. Ryan poses for a formal portrait. This picture can be dated to the period around 1921, because Ryan is still wearing the upright collar on his uniform; these would be phased out shortly thereafter in favor of uniforms with lapels. *Courtesy LTC (ret) James Ryan.*

Richard Hillsdon Ryan (26 August 1896-4 January 1987)
Richard H. Ryan was born in the small town of Allisonia, in Pulaski County, Virginia, to a Canadian father and American mother. An outstanding athlete, Ryan was drawn to the military at an early age and served as a corporal along the Mexican Border with the Virginia Field Artillery. During the First World War, he served as an Officer Candidate School instructor at Camp Gordon, Georgia, and Camp Polk, Louisiana.

Ryan returned to Virginia at the end of the war and began to work in the newspaper business. By the mid-1920s, he had worked his way up to being a manager at the *Petersburg Progress-Index*. He maintained his Army skills as a member of the Virginia National Guard and was soon appointed commander of Company "G" of the 183rd Infantry Regiment,

Now assigned to the Army Air Force, Ryan poses for a portrait. During his long career, Ryan had the fortune to work directly for General Henry H. "Hap" Arnold and General Douglas MacArthur. *Courtesy LTC (ret) James Ryan.*

nicknamed the "Petersburg Greys." Remaining in the Guard throughout the interwar period, Ryan was noted for his athletic skills and his rifle marksmanship. Among his athletic skills was his ability to run extremely fast. He often showcased this skill by running down possums and snakes, catching them with his bare hands. With the federalizing of the 29th Infantry Division, Ryan led his unit to Camp Meade and began the process of training them for deployment to Europe. Ironically, in spite of his athletic accomplishments, the medical staff determined that Ryan had flat feet and was therefore ineligible to serve in the infantry. He was transferred to the Army Air Corps and was involved in moving the first Army units into the newly-built Pentagon building in Washington, D.C., where he worked for General Henry H. "Hap" Arnold.

At the end of the Second World War, Ryan was assigned to Japan, where he served as MacArthur's Chief of Information in Tokyo. He later transferred to the United States Air Force and also served as the editor of the *Pacific Stars and Stripes*. Colonel Ryan retired from military service in 1959.[35]

In 1939, Richard Ryan was selected by the YMCA in Petersburg, Virginia, as the "Greatest Athlete from Petersburg." The truest indication of Ryan's skills is evidenced by the second place finisher: Eric Tipton, a major league baseball player and a member of the College Football Hall of Fame.

Front cover of the retirement program for Major General Sands held in Norfolk, Virginia, in 1954. Attending the ceremony and tribute were an impressive number of military and civic leaders. *Courtesy 1/111th Field Artillery.*

William Hamilton Sands (13 May 1892-4 July 1978)

William H. Sands was born in Richmond, Virginia, and attended the University of Virginia, graduating in 1916 with a law degree. With the entry of the United States into the First World War becoming inevitable, Sands joined the Army and was appointed a 2nd lieutenant in the field artillery 15 August 1917. Assigned to the 80th Division (known alternately as the "Blue Ridge" Division and "Robert E. Lee's Last Division" because of its southern roots), Sands deployed with them to France and served in the St. Mihiel and Meuse-Argonne Campaigns.

Colonel William H. Sands, commander of the 111th Field Artillery Regiment, in a unit staff picture taken during annual training at Tobyhanna, Pennsylvania, July 1924. Note the two overseas chevrons on his left sleeve, indicative of his service with the 80th Division Artillery in the First World War.

He joined the Virginia National Guard in 1922, and was appointed as a captain in the Norfolk Light Artillery Blues. During the Interwar period, Sands first commanded the Blues and later the entire 111th Field Artillery Regiment. In 1939, he was promoted to brigadier general and took command of the 54th Field Artillery Brigade. In 1942—when the 29th was reorganized—after mobilization, Sands was appointed commander of the 29th's Divisional Artillery, which now consisted of four field artillery battalions: the 110th, 111th, 224th, and 227th. He deployed with them to Britain in 1942.

When Major General Gerhardt assumed command of the 29th Infantry Division in 1943, Sands was one of the very few officers in the organization who managed to impress the incoming commander. Gerhardt's badgering style and relentless questioning did not bother Sands and he was able to answer Gerhardt's questions about weapon capabilities and soldier skills without too much difficulty. Sands remained in command of the 29th Infantry Division artillery throughout the war and represented Gerhardt during the first meeting with the Russian Army at the Elbe River.

Sands remained with the 29th after the war and was appointed to command the entire division 2 July 1946. He remained in command until 30 May 1954, when he retired from military service. His retirement ceremony drew attendance and observations from a veritable pantheon of 29th Infantry Division and National Guard leaders: Lieutenant General Leonard Gerow (former Commander of the 29th); Major General Edgar Ericson (Chief of the National Guard Bureau); Major General Milton Reckord (Adjutant General of Maryland and former Commander of the 29th); Major General Samuel Gardner Waller (Adjutant General of Virginia); and Brigadier General Charles Fox (Adjutant General of West Virginia). There is no record of Gerhardt attending the ceremony. Sands died in 1978 and is buried in Arlington National Cemetery.

Jo Lane Stern began his military career as a thirteen year-old telegraph operator in the Confederate Army of Northern Virginia during the Civil War. He would later serve two separate times as Virginia's Adjutant General and played a key role in reorganizing the Virginia National Guard after the First World War. *Courtesy Virginia National Guard Historical Collection.*

Jo Lane Stern (23 December 1848-3 May 1932)

Jo Lane Stern was unique in being one of the very few Civil War veterans to also serve in the American Army during the First World War. Stern joined the Confederate Army in 1861 when he was thirteen years old and remained on duty until Lee's surrender in 1865. Stern was present at the Battle of Yellow Tavern and was later reported to have been one of the very few men allowed to ride Robert E. Lee's horse, Traveller. After the war, he joined the 1st Virginia Infantry and served until he was selected in 1882 to be the State Inspector General. He remained in that position for forty years and retired in 1922. During this period, he also served as the State Adjutant General for a short period in 1898, then again from 1918 until 1922. In his position as Adjutant General, Stern was responsible for helping to re-establish the Virginia National Guard structure after the 29th Division returned from France in 1919. At the time of his retirement, the end-strength of the Virginia guard was over 2,000 soldiers. A contemporary history reported that "General Stern has done more for the militia of Virginia than any other man in the service."[36]

Samuel Gardner Waller, one of the key figures in the history of the Virginia National Guard and the 29th Division during the twentieth century. Waller served as a company and battalion commander in the First World War and would later serve as Virginia's Adjutant General for twenty-five years. *Courtesy Virginia National Guard Historical Collection.*

Samuel Gardner Waller (26 March 1882-2 December 1955)

Samuel G. Waller was born into a prestigious family in Front Royal, Virginia. He graduated from the University of Virginia Law School in 1903, the same year he received a commission in Company "D", 2nd Virginia Infantry. He was elected to be the Mayor of Front Royal from 1906 to 1914. In 1916, he served on the Mexican Border as Commanding Officer of Company "D." When the 29th Division deployed to France, Waller served in a variety of positions, and by the end of the war he was commanding the 2nd Battalion of the 116th Infantry Regiment. He continued to rise through the ranks and was promoted to brigadier general in 1921 to serve as Commander of the 91st Infantry Brigade (1st and 116th Virginia Infantry Regiments). Appointed as the Virginia State Adjutant General in July 1931, Waller would serve in that role until his death in 1955. His twenty-five year service as Adjutant General was marked by several important events: the Bonus March, World War II, and the Cold War era.[37] He also presided over the addition of the Air National Guard in Virginia to the state's military force.

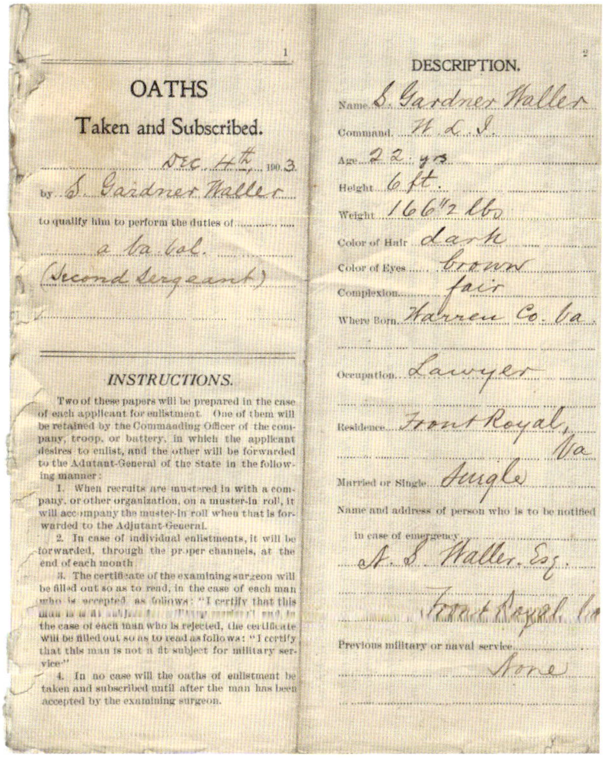

1

OATHS

Taken and Subscribed.

Dec. 4th 1903.

by S. Gardner Waller

to qualify him to perform the duties of

a Va. Vol.

(Second Sergeant)

INSTRUCTIONS.

Two of these papers will be prepared in the case of each applicant for enlistment. One of them will be retained by the Commanding Officer of the company, troop, or battery, in which the applicant desires to enlist, and the other will be forwarded to the Adjutant-General of the State in the following manner:

1. When recruits are mustered in with a company, or other organization, on a muster-in roll, it will accompany the muster-in roll when that is forwarded to the Adjutant-General.

2. In case of individual enlistments, it will be forwarded, through the proper channels, at the end of each month

3. The certificate of the examining surgeon will be filled out so as to read, in the case of each man who is accepted, as follows: "I certify that this man is a fit subject [illegible] the case of each man who is rejected, the certificate will be filled out so as to read as follows: "I certify that this man is not a fit subject for military service."

4. In no case will the oaths of enlistment be taken and subscribed until after the man has been accepted by the examining surgeon.

2

DESCRIPTION.

Name S. Gardner Waller

Command. H. L. I.

Age 22 yrs.

Height 6 ft.

Weight 166½ lbs

Color of Hair dark

Color of Eyes brown

Complexion fair

Where Born Warren Co. Va.

Occupation Lawyer

Residence Front Royal, Va

Married or Single Single

Name and address of person who is to be notified in case of emergency

A. S. Waller, Esq.

Front Royal, Va

Previous military or naval service

None

Waller's 1903 application to join the Virginia State Guard. Thanks in part to his law degree from the University of Virginia, Waller would soon be placed in command of an infantry company, as well as win the election to become the mayor of Front Royal, Virginia.

CHAPTER 14

"Two Shooting Nine Looting Let's Go!"— Vignettes and the Unofficial History of the 29th

In the course of studying and writing history, it quickly becomes apparent that unlike a book, history is not linear. It doesn't begin on page one and end at the back cover. It bends, twists, turns, and repeats itself. The historian or writer is seldom blessed with complete versions of any event and often must tie together threads from various sources to make a tapestry. Because there are gaps in the historical record, momentous events occur, often randomly at times, and are then forgotten if no one records them. Most readers of military history have a fairly clear picture in their minds about the sacrifice and valor exhibited by the soldiers of the 29th on D-Day. Nevertheless, the history of the 29th Infantry Division is much more than just the Normandy landings. The 29th's history is rich in characters and events that came before 6 June 1944, and is equally rich into the present day. What follows in this chapter are some of those events, episodes, or incidents that don't fit neatly into a chronological progression of the 29th Infantry Division's history from 1917 to 2001. In fact, most of what follows might best fit into the category of stories that would be swapped while sitting around the table at an NCO club and drinking a beer. Truly, the devil is in the details.

Necessity is the Mother of Invention: Maryland Field Artillery (May 1916-August 1917)

National Guard units that were called to duty for service on the Mexican border took advantage of every opportunity to train at their home station prior to departing. One battery of the 3rd Maryland Artillery used Fort McHenry, located outside Baltimore, as their training site after they had received all of their cannons and equipment, except for the horses. Subsequently offered a chance to take part in a patriotic parade through downtown Baltimore in May 1916, the artillerymen quickly agreed. Not having the horses needed to pull their caissons and cannons, they promptly borrowed all the animals they needed from a local gas company.[1]

Shortly after returning to Maryland from service along the border, the artillery units were again called to active duty. The Pikesville Armory became the training and mobilization site for the 1st Maryland Field Artillery Battalion. Again, however, there was a shortage of equipment. This time, there were not enough tents for the soldiers to sleep in during the night. The fortunate men who lived nearby were given permission to sleep at home in their own beds, provided they reported in by 8 a.m. every morning. As a result, each morning there would be a line of cars pulling into the Armory's grounds, as the more affluent soldiers would drive themselves to duty. Very quickly, the 1st Maryland was given the nickname "the Limousine Battery."[2]

The 29th's Long-Running Revue: "Snap It Up" (1917-1919)

Returning to Camp McClellan, Alabama, after his visit to France in the fall of 1917, General Morton directed that the division assemble an entertainment troupe. Using his aide, Captain Murray Cobb, as the talent scout, Morton had the selected soldiers present a vaudeville-type show in February 1918. Performances in the U.S. were well received, both at Camp McClellan by the soldiers and in nearby Anniston by the local citizens. Plans were made to continue the show after the division's arrival in France. Unfortunately, the plan went astray when all three of the artillery regiments and the 104th Ammo Train were sent away from the rest of the division to artillery training bases in Brittany. While the artillerymen were undergoing their specialized training, the rest of the division was occupying front line sectors in the Alsace region, then participating in the Meuse-Argonne campaign.

On a positive note, since the preponderance of talent appeared to have been in the 112th Field Artillery Regiment, the Doughboys in that unit had time to improve and polish the original production. When they were through practicing and rehearsing, they had a new and very entertaining show entitled "Snap It Up." Shortly after the war ended and the division was reassembled, members of the troupe gave a highly-praised performance of their show in Paris. They were quickly recognized as the premier "soldier show" in the AEF and soon were performing throughout the First Army region. They even put on a command performance before General Pershing at the AEF Headquarters in Chaumont. Their final performance in Europe was at the port of embarkation shortly before they left for home.

Deactivation of the division did not mean the end of the highly-acclaimed show. In true theater tradition, the members of the troupe reassembled in Newark and performed "Snap It Up" for a week-long stand. The troupe also performed in Baltimore, Washington, D.C., and a number of other locations, making their final curtain call in Atlantic City, New Jersey.

By then, the soldiers had had enough of show business, and though they were offered the chance to continue performing by some theatrical promoters, they disbanded the troupe and went home.[3]

Maryland Artillery? (June 1918)

When the 110th Field Artillery Regiment finally departed Camp McClellan for deployment to France, they first went to Camp Mills, New York. There, they were issued the field gear, equipment, and steel helmets the regiment would use in France. Shortly thereafter, the 110th moved by train to Baltimore and were loaded onto the S.S. *Keemun* for the Atlantic crossing. It was noted at the time of sailing, that of the 1,499 officers and enlisted men in the Maryland-based regiment, only 40 percent were actually from Maryland.[4] Similarly, the 112th Machine Gun Battalion, originally raised from Maryland and Virginia units, had soldiers from thirty-three states, the District of Columbia, and two other countries: Canada and Russia. Occupations represented among the 112th's machine gunners were everything from farmers and clerks to street car conductor and "ball player."[5]

Elsie Janis, known as the "Sweetheart of the AEF," was a well-known singer and entertainer before the First World War. Her willingness to travel to the front lines to entertain the American soldiers in France made her a favorite of the Doughboys.

Elsie Janis and the 29th Division's Liaison Officer (June 1918)

If Elsie Janis's name is unfamiliar to most readers, it is quite understandable. Much of her career was before radios were commonly available and her last film role was in 1940. Yet, to the Doughboys of the American Expeditionary Force, she was as iconic as Betty Grable was to the GIs of the Second World War and as Raquel Welch was to American soldiers and Marines of the Vietnam War in the 1960s and 1970s. As a comedian, singer, songwriter, and actress, Elsie was extremely well-known before the American Army deployed to France. Starting at a young age in vaudeville, she quickly became a big star on both the stage and in the emerging motion picture business.

With the death of her English actor and soldier fiancée, Elsie, already an ardent fundraiser for the British war effort, redoubled her efforts when the American soldiers began arriving in France. After meeting with Elsie, General Pershing presented her with a camouflaged vehicle, a military driver, and a pass permitting her to travel anywhere in the American sector she chose. Travelling throughout the war zone with her mother, Elsie would make her way into the front lines and perform for the Doughboys in the trenches. Often coming within range of German artillery shells and machine gun fire while giving her performances, she soon became known as the "Sweetheart of the AEF." Working for free, and always willing to perform before the muddy troops, she was apt to show up anywhere there were American soldiers.[6]

The 29th's own Captain John Cutchins would have an interesting encounter with Elsie and her mother in Paris in June 1918. Temporarily assigned to the AEF Headquarters Staff, Cutchins was detailed to act as a liaison officer to Otto Kahn, an American industrialist, banker, and patron of the arts who was visiting France after a trip to Switzerland. One evening, Cutchins and Kahn were invited to a dinner party and accepted. Upon hearing that Elsie Janis and her mother were also invited to the dinner, Kahn suddenly appeared less than enthusiastic about dining with the star. When Cutchins asked him if there was problem with Elsie, Kahn explained that the problem was not with Elsie, but with her mother. He also requested "for heaven's sake, do not let her mother sit by him."[7] As Cutchins was to find out, among Kahn's many jobs, he was the President of the Metropolitan Opera House in New York City and Ms. Janis's mother was the ultimate ambitious stage mother.

Making the seating arrangements to meet Mr. Kahn's request, Cutchins ensured that he sat between the mother and the target of her interest; Mr. Kahn. Though the meal started well, Elsie's mother was soon leaning across Cutchins while trying to engage Kahn in an unending conversation in order to secure future employment for Elsie at the Metropolitan Opera. By the end of the meal, the mother had practically crawled over the Virginia National Guard captain in her pursuit of Kahn. Also, much to the embarrassment of the other Americans present, Elsie's mother took the opportunity to stridently lecture some English dinner guests about America's "Glorious Fourth of July." Cutchins later wrote that the mother had proven to be "a first class nuisance."

That evening, however, Cutchins went for the first time to see one of Elsie's shows for the soldiers. After watching her sing and dance for the wildly enthusiastic Doughboys, he wrote simply that she "was as popular as she was lovely."[8]

After the war, Elsie continued in her multi-faceted career and always enjoyed talking to veterans in the audience that had seen her perform in France. She also became involved in screenwriting for the movies and wrote several books. She died in 1956 and is buried in the Forrest Lawn Memorial Park Cemetery in

Glendale, California, and has a star on the Hollywood Walk of Fame. Somewhat ironically, John Cutchins, her onetime dinner companion and enthusiastic fan, is buried in Richmond, Virginia, in Hollywood cemetery.

Pershing and the Salute (August 1918)

In the fall of 1917, when General Morton returned to Camp McClellan from his visit to the front lines in France, he brought back more than just an appreciation for the ongoing combat there. He had observed a British Army method for saluting senior officers that was used when the saluting soldier's hands were busy, such as when carrying a heavy load or driving a vehicle. In cases such as this, the soldier would snap his head to the side, thereby rendering a salute. Morton liked the idea and quickly established it as a standard procedure for saluting in the 29th Division.

When General Pershing conducted a unit inspection of the 29th Division in the Alsace in August 1918, he was very pleased with all that he found, except for the British-style salute. He reminded Morton that the United States Army was governed by United States Army regulations, which should be sufficient. The hands-full, head-snapping salute was immediately discontinued in the 29th Division.[9]

Welcome Home? (18 May 1919)

Not every homecoming from France was marked by celebration and a spirit of victory. Several infantrymen from Company "E" of the 114th Infantry Regiment refused to attend a luncheon being held in their honor in Asbury Park, New Jersey. The reason for their refusal was simple; they were angry that the city had not arranged automobile transportation to the event for them from Camp Dix, where they were undergoing demobilization processing. They also refused to participate in a combination May Day and soldiers' parade being held the same day for the same reason.[10]

In a strange land: the statue of Brigadier General Harry Hill Bandholtz stands near the United States Embassy in Budapest, Hungary. The monument was built by a grateful Hungarian nation to honor and thank General Bandholtz for saving the treasures of the Hungarian National Museum in 1919. *Courtesy Attila Nemeth and the U.S. Embassy, Budapest.*

A 29th Division Officer Lays Down the Law (October 1919)

Brigadier General Harry Hill Bandholtz was a graduate of the Military Academy and had served in the Spanish-

A closer view of the plaque on the statue, providing Bandholtz's modest comment on the incident: "I simply carried out the instructions of my government as I understood them as an officer and gentleman of the United State Army." *Courtesy Attila Nemeth and the U.S. Embassy, Budapest.*

American War and in the Philippines before being appointed to command the 29th Division's 58th Infantry Brigade. He led the brigade until September 1918, when he was named the U.S. Army Provost Marshal General. In this role, he was responsible for reorganizing the AEF's military police and even established a school to train them in France. After the end of the war, Bandholtz continued to serve in the AEF, then was appointed to the Inter-Allied Military Mission to Hungary in August 1919. In this role, he was responsible for supervising the withdrawal of the Romanian and Serbian armies from Hungary. As the senior Allied officer on this commission, Bandholtz made his biggest contribution in October 1919. Armed only with his riding crop, Bandholtz confronted a band of Romanian soldiers that were intent on ransacking the Hungarian National Museum in Budapest. Clearly intimidated by the American officer blocking their path, the Romanians beat a hasty retreat and Hungary's treasure was safe.

General Bandholtz would later be responsible for planning the ceremony for the entombment of the "Unknown Soldier" in Arlington National Cemetery in November 1921. Along with his many other accomplishments, Bandholtz is also considered to be the "Father of the Military Police Corps." Bandholtz died 7 May 1925 and is buried in his hometown, Constantine, Michigan.

There is a full-sized bronze statue of Bandholtz, commissioned in 1936 by a grateful Hungarian government, located near the U.S. Embassy in Budapest. The statue, which had been removed during the Communist era in 1949, was restored in 1993 to its original spot.

Are You Sure You Spelled Brottovich right? (21 June 1921)

As part of the ongoing selective service process, and to support local Draft Boards, the War Department would provide lists of draft evaders or "slackers" from their localities. One such list was provided in June 1921 to the board in Passaic, New Jersey, and included the name Joseph Brottovich. Unfortunately for the War Department, the local Draft Board, and most of all Joe Brottovich, the list was in error. Not only had Brottovich served honorably as a mechanic in Company "I" of the 114th Infantry Regiment, he had been gassed twice and wounded three times in the Argonne. Also making the list of "slackers" from Passaic was a Doughboy who had served in the 28th Division, a sailor who had made four voyages across the Atlantic on a troop transport, and a man who had served in the Canadian Army and was still recovering from influenza he had contracted in France during the war. There is no record of how accurate the next list was.[11]

Perhaps waiting for the aerial inspection of the National Guard camp in Virginia Beach by the 29th Division Commander, Major General Anton Stephen. These five Virginia soldiers show a wide variety of emotions while standing outside the Company "H" cookhouse.

Taken around the same time as the previous picture, these Virginia National Guardsmen seem to be enjoying at least this part of their annual training; the opportunity to meet some of the local girls on the Virginia Beach boardwalk.

The 29th Division Commander Conducts an Aerial Inspection (1 August 1930)

Major General Anton Stephen, the second commander of the 29th Division, used an innovative technique to perform an inspection of his Virginia-based 91st Infantry Brigade, Taking off in an Army aircraft from Bolling Field, Washington, D.C., and piloted by a First World War ace, the division commander flew over Camp Pollard (located near Virginia Beach) as the troops were falling into formation for reveille. Stephen, commander of the 29th from April 1920 to April 1924, made the visit in response to an invitation from Brigadier General Samuel Gardner Waller, the senior ranking Virginia National Guardsman at the camp and commander of the Virginia Brigade. After the aerial inspection of the troops, Stephen's plane flew to Langley Field on the peninsula and landed there.

The assembled thirty-three hundred Virginia soldiers were the single largest gathering of the state's National Guard since the First World War. Usually only about two thousand soldiers were involved in the brigade's annual training period. However, with advance notice of Stephen's flyover inspection, and expecting a more conventional land visit by the Governor of Virginia a few days later, the Virginia Guard wanted to make the best impression possible. The unit commanders in the brigade cleaned out all of the usual admin "stay behind" detachments from the armories and ensured every soldier was present. One commander went as far as having the Sheriff of Rockingham County round up delinquents and drive them to training.[12]

Playbill for "Snap It Up Again," the Second World War version of the soldier show produced by the 29th Infantry Division soldiers. Ultimately, the show would only be presented twice, as the 29th was scheduled to take part in the large-scale Carolina Maneuvers. *Courtesy Womor Family.*

"Snap It Up" - Part Two (August-September 1941)

In August 1941, the staff at 29th Division Headquarters decided to dust off the concept of having a "soldier show" in an attempt to keep the soldiers busy and entertained. The overall intent was to encourage patriotism and showcase the talents of the soldiers in the division. Copying the title from the First World War production, "Snap it Up Again" went into rehearsal. Though interest was lukewarm at first among the potential performers, when the word was passed that the show might go on tour, many more soldiers began to audition for the musical revue. Among the acts was a thirty-six man drill team from the 175th Infantry Regiment known as the "Dandy Fifth," in acknowledgement of the regiment's 5th Maryland Infantry heritage. The first performance of "Snap It Up Again" was to a packed house in Baltimore at the Maryland Theater. The show went off without a hitch and was well received. The second scheduled performance was to be at the Mosque (today know as the Landmark Theater) in Richmond, Virginia, the very next day. Unfortunately, the trucks scheduled to move the soldiers, props, and the stage equipment showed up late. By the time the troupe arrived in Richmond, it was almost midnight. The audience for the show was waiting patiently, so the soldiers immediately went to work setting up the stage. By 3 a.m., everything was ready and the show went on. This was to be the show's last performance. Shortly after the Richmond presentation, the 29th started moving its units into place for an even bigger event: the large-scale Carolina Maneuvers. Any theatrical ambitions the performers may have harbored were set aside. There was still a war to be fought.[13]

Jack Womer poses for a studio portrait and displays the 29th Ranger arc sewn above his 29th Infantry Division patch. After the Rangers were disbanded, Womer would transfer to the 506th Parachute Infantry Regiment and jump with them into Normandy. *Courtesy Womer Family.*

A British Commando provides marksmanship instruction to American soldiers from the 29th Infantry division undergoing Ranger training in Scotland. *Courtesy USMHI.*

29th Division Rangers (December 1942-October 1943)

The 1st Ranger Battalion was the first American Army Ranger battalion established during the Second World War. It was formed primarily from men of the 34th Infantry Division—a National Guard division drawn from the Midwest—and the 1st Armored Division. The 1st Ranger Battalion was stationed in Europe until the fall of 1942, when it deployed to North Africa. September 30, 1942, the European Theater of Operations (ETO) Headquarters issued a directive for the formation of another Ranger battalion in Britain to replace the 1st Ranger Battalion. The directive ordered that the new Ranger unit be formed from the 29th Infantry Division and exist as a provisional Ranger battalion. Once formed, the 29th Provisional Ranger Battalion would be the only American ground force available for highly specialized covert combat operations in the ETO for the foreseeable future. Since raiding the German-occupied "Atlantic Wall" coastline was the extent of ground attacks taking place against the enemy on the continent at this time, the idea of having a raiding force drawn from the newly-arrived 29th Infantry Division,and some other non-divisional soldiers already in Britain made good sense. A similar experiment in the China-Burma-India Theater on a larger scale led to the establishment of the 5307th Composite Unit (provisional), which later became known as Merrill's Marauders.

Major Randolph Millholland, a Maryland National Guardsman and former commander of Company "G", 115th Infantry, was selected as the first commander of the 29th Ranger Battalion. When the call went out in late November 1942, there was no shortage of volunteers within the 29th Infantry Division. The reasons for wanting to become Rangers were varied: some were looking for a chance to do something more challenging and others were enticed by the rumor that Rangers had better food than regular soldiers.[14] No matter the reason, they all believed that the training they would endure would be strenuous and exacting. They were right. After several weeks of initial training in the 29th's area, those who were still with the program were moved to Scotland in late January 1943, for training at the British Commando Depot located in Glen Spean, Scotland. The actual training site was built around a Scottish castle and had a wide variety of terrain, from rolling plains and pastures to the highest mountain in Britain. While undergoing training and combat exercises, the men of the 29th were under direct command of the British Special Services Brigade. This meant that the American officers were required to perform the same combat training as the enlisted men and take orders from the enlisted British instructors. To accompany the physically demanding combat training, the prospective Rangers were also immersed in classroom training. The classroom work was focused on sharing the instructors' real-life combat experiences and designed to sharpen the Rangers' decision-making process when under the stress of actual combat operations. By the end of the five-week training period, the soldiers who had completed the course had met the rigorous requirements, doing everything from making speed marches, overcoming obstacle courses, reading German maps, climbing sheer cliffs, and perhaps, most importantly, thinking both strategically and tactically at all times. Only half of the initial volunteers remained to the end. Those that did were awarded the red "29th Ranger" tab to go over their 29th Division patch.[15]

29th Division Rangers practice their raiding skills in August 1943. *Courtesy National Archives.*

The 29th Ranger Battalion was originally organized as a Headquarters Company with two line companies: "A" and "B." In March 1943, another group of 29th soldiers reported for Ranger training and the battalion was expanded with two additional companies "C" and "D," with the Headquarters merging with the heavy weapons company.[16] The battalion, now well established, participated in a series of maneuvers with the British Army and the 29th Division. Performing well, the Rangers were praised by the exercise evaluators for their skills and endurance.

Of greater importance, some of these Rangers were also allowed to join their British Commando counterparts on some small-scale raids across the channel. A number of these took place in Norway, as the British would send in commando teams to observe shipping or raid remote outposts.[17] In early September 1943, on another, larger-scale raid, British Commandos accompanied by eighteen Rangers attacked a German radar station on the island of Ile de Ouessant, located off the Brittany coast. Working with a British force, the Americans helped destroy the facility and left behind a webbed pistol belt and an American helmet marked "Maj. R. Millholland U.S. Ranger" for the Germans to find.[18]

In spite of their reputation and successes, the Rangers' days as a separate battalion were numbered. An order was sent down from higher headquarters to disband the 29th Ranger Battalion. While General Gerow was disappointed at the order, he did as directed. The unit was officially disbanded in October 1943. While most of the Rangers returned to their previous 29th Division units, some had enjoyed being part of an elite unit, and when the opportunity arose, transferred to the 101st Airborne Division.[19] Those that returned to the 29th were highly regarded for their leadership, knowledge, and specialized skills. By the end of the war in 1945, many infantry divisions would develop their own small "Ranger" style units for conducting patrols and reconnaissance, but none of them were ever as formal, well trained, or tactically proficient as the 29th Ranger Battalion.

A soldier from the Army Service Command demonstrates the newly-designed assault vest. Though well intended, the vest would prove to be a major hindrance to many of the 116th Infantry Regiment soldiers making the assault on Omaha Beach. *Courtesy USAQM Museum.*

The Assault Vest in the D-Day Invasion (June 1944)

Faced with the incredibly difficult and dangerous task of invading the German-occupied European mainland, the Allies put their best minds together for ideas on special equipment for use in the landings. Some of the innovations were very successful, such as the wide variety of British mine-clearing, trench crossing, and bunker busting tanks known as the "Funnies."[20] Some were only marginally successful, such as the American amphibious tanks. Other innovations and ideas just didn't work at all. Among the latter category were the assault vests that were issued to the American soldiers taking part in the early waves of the attack. Based on a British "Battle Jerkin" used by their commandos, the vest, with its extra pockets and pouches, seemed like the perfect piece of equipment for troops coming ashore under hostile fire. Accordingly, the U.S. Army issued contracts for the vests to be made and shipped them to the appropriate units for use in the upcoming invasion.

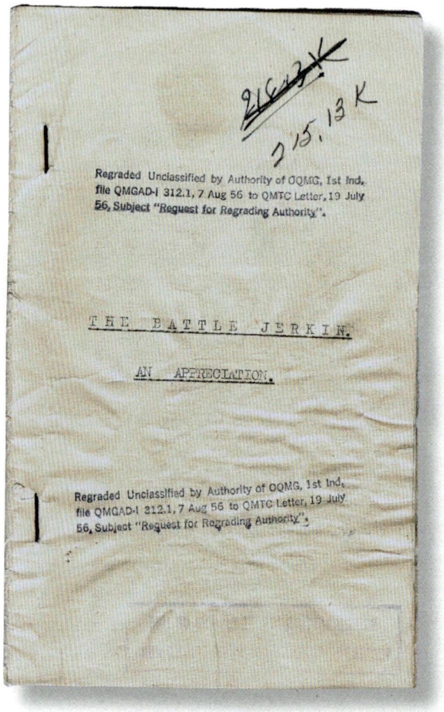

Regraded Unclassified by Authority of OQMG, 1st Ind, file QMGAD-I 312.1, 7 Aug 56 to QMTC Letter, 19 July 56, Subject "Request for Regrading Authority".

THE BATTLE JERKIN.

AN APPRECIATION.

Regraded Unclassified by Authority of OQMG, 1st Ind, file QMGAD-I 312.1, 7 Aug 56 to QMTC Letter, 19 July 56, Subject "Request for Regrading Authority".

Some requirements for the assault vest were derived from this unique document, the British study on the uses and effectiveness of the "battle jerkin" in combat operations. *Courtesy USAQM Museum.*

The assault vest shown from the back. *Courtesy USAQM Museum.*

A closer view of the large pocket located on the upper back of the vest, as well as the metal grommets and retaining strap designed to securely fasten shovels, picks, or other important equipment to the back of the vest. *Courtesy USAQM Museum.*

The assault vest, clearly showing the sturdy construction and a variety of pockets for carrying essential gear into combat. *Courtesy USAQM Museum.*

Unfortunately, by the time the landing craft ramps dropped off Omaha Beach 6 June 1944, the cold, wet, and overloaded soldiers of the 116th were already under German artillery and machine gun fire. The soldiers almost immediately found the vests to be a hindrance in getting ashore, as the large pockets quickly filled with water and sand. Those soldiers that were dropped off in water over their heads scrambled to rid themselves of as much weight and equipment as they could. The vests were among the first things to be dumped. Sergeant Bob Slaughter of Company "D" of the 116th Infantry managed to make it ashore with his vest, but noted that "Almost everyone dumped their heavy assault jackets and weapons, as getting to dry land became the prime objective."[21] John J. Barnes of Company "A" later wrote that his platoon leader saved him from drowning by cutting off his assault vest with a bayonet, freeing him to swim to shore.[22]

A Stonewaller Shows a Sense of Humor (7 June 1944)

With the heavy casualty rate suffered by the 116th on D-Day, a good portion of the following day was spent trying to gather up scattered equipment and organize the soldiers. Captain Charles Cawthon, adjutant of the 2nd Battalion, 116th Infantry, was one of those officers trying to patch back together the survivors of the unit into a fighting force. As he was walking through Vierville, he was offered a ride in a halftrack headed in the same direction. When he climbed aboard, he was surprised to find that Colonel Canham and some of the regimental staff were already in the vehicle. Cawthon noted that Canham, the 116th's Commander, still had the same dirty bandage and sling that he had worn the previous day when he was exhorting the men to get off the beach and go kill some Germans. Perhaps sensing Cawthon's discomfort at being suddenly in the presence of his regimental commander, and having a little fun, Colonel Canham surprised the captain by asking how his soldiers' haircuts were. Writing of the episode many years later, Cawthon could see the humor in the question but could not remember what his response to Canham had been.[23]

The Maryland Horse Artillery Rides Again (July-August 1944)

In late July 1944, the 110th Field Artillery Battalion was occupying a position near le Mesnil Herman, in Normandy. The area had previously been home to German artillery units and when the Germans retreated, several of the horses they used as prime movers for their artillery pieces had been abandoned. Some of the older soldiers in the 110th had served with the unit while it was horse-drawn, and therefore had a working knowledge of the care and feeding for such animals. They began to care for the horses and quickly nursed them back to full health.

Having the horses soon proved to be a valuable addition. The artillerymen began a courier service, riding the horses between the firing batteries and staff sections. It was quickly noticed that the horses raised less dust than motorized vehicles, therefore drawing less enemy fire. They were also capable of rapid cross country movement in any weather. Equally important to the artillerymen, they seemed much less likely to set off mines than motorized forms of transportation.

Since no one told the artillerymen they couldn't have the horses, they felt it better not to ask permission and perhaps get an answer they didn't like. The issue, however, came to a head one day as General Gerhardt was visiting the battalion's command post to present an award. While he was in the act of pinning the award on the recipient's chest, a messenger from one of the batteries came galloping into the battalion area. He reined his horse to a quick stop and dismounted while saluting the assembled officers. Gerhardt stared at him for a moment, then asked him about the horse and how it handled. After getting a positive response from the rider, the general swung himself up into the saddle and rode off at a gallop. When he returned, he also commented on how well the horse handled. Gerhardt then drove away in his vehicle without further comment. With this tacit approval, the 110th kept their horses until it was time to make the long motor march to participate in the siege of Brest. The horses were given to local French farmers as a parting gift from the last "horse artillery" unit in the Army.[24]

Gerhardt Recruits for the 29th Division (October 1944)

In October 1944, a soldier, dissatisfied with serving in a rear echelon unit, wrote a letter to the *Stars and Stripes*. His complaint? He had joined the army to fight and thought he had trained for months assaulting beaches and climbing English hills, but he had ended up performing guard duty for the Navy. He further stated: "I joined the Army to fight and I trained to fight. I'm not looking for glory... [but] I'd like a chance to prove my worth." General Gerhardt wasted no time in writing his own letter to the paper that said: "The 29th Infantry Division can use that soldier and any like him who desire combat." He also requested the soldier's name and unit so he could help him join the 29th. Soon other soldiers began to write to the paper with the same request, and Gerhardt quickly wrote back, authorizing them to request a transfer to his division. Within a short period of time almost a thousand letters had been sent to the paper. At this point, the *Stars and Stripes* published a request that no more letters be sent on this topic. By then, the rear-echelon volunteers had started to appear in the 29th's reception center. At first, Gerhardt made it a point to meet with every soldier to personally welcome them to his division. He also reportedly told them "You're a damn fool, but you got guts." In time, there were so many volunteers he couldn't meet with them all as they were processed and sent to the combat battalions of the 29th. The 29th received almost three hundred soldiers from the surge of volunteering and later added some five hundred more that had passed similar requests through other channels.

Strangely enough, the soldier whose letter started the entire episode was never able to complete his transfer to the

29th. Though Gerhardt personally dispatched one of his staff to locate and help the anxious volunteer, they never were able to navigate the rear-echelon maze in time to find him and bring him to the 29th.

The history of the 29th records that almost without exception these "volunteers" turned out to be excellent soldiers. Sadly, none of the combat-weary soldiers of the 29th recorded their opinions about other soldiers that voluntarily gave up safe rear-echelon jobs to join them in the rain, mud, and violence of the front line. Chances are they were just too amazed to write down their thoughts.[25]

Mickey Rooney Visits the 29th (February 1945)

Delays in crossing the Roer River had pushed the assault date back to late February. It had been initially delayed in December 1944 as a result of the massive German offensive in the Ardennes. The second delay was caused by the Germans sabotaging the Roer River dams and releasing enough water to flow over the river banks and create an impenetrable swamp. Taking advantage of the second delay, units of the 115th Infantry Regiment were rotated back into the division training area near the German town of Durboslar. While there, they practiced clearing mine fields, loading boats, and river crossing techniques. They also took advantage of the nightly movies shown in a local theater.

Adding to their entertainment was the surprise appearance on 15 February of a muddy jeep that made its way into Durboslar. Among the occupants was Mickey Rooney, a well-known motion picture actor who had obviously travelled a long way to entertain them. Although the front line soldiers of the 115th were "hostile to the diminutive Hollywood star at the beginning, [they] quickly warmed to his personality and obvious effort to be just another GI doing the job he was assigned."[26] The two performances by Rooney and his troupe included songs and skits that the weary infantrymen enjoyed immensely. By the time Rooney had to leave to drive to his next performance, he had posed for pictures and given autographs to every soldier that wanted one. The show had been a welcome break from the training, but with Rooney's departure, the 115th had to get back to work. The date for the cross-river assault had now been set. Based on previous experience, crossing water under German fire could be a deadly enterprise, and the 115th was going to be in the first wave to cross the river 23 February.

Necessity is the Mother of Invention - Again (1945)

As the 29th was preparing for their attack across the Roer River, the two small Piper Cub observation planes that belonged to the 110th Field Artillery were getting a workout. Since the Normandy campaign, it had been standard operating procedure in the 110th to fly infantry officers and forward observers over the areas they would be attacking. These flights allowed the attacking officers an unusual opportunity to see and visualize the terrain better than a simple map study. The long delays in the cross-Roer attack meant that more than forty infantry officers and a number of forward observers were given the opportunity to fly over their avenues of approach and get a clear picture of their objectives.

Lieutenant Colonel John Cooper commanded the 110th Field Artillery Battalion throughout the Second World War. He would later command the 29th Infantry Division DIVARTY as a brigadier general, as shown in this 1950s photograph. *Courtesy 1/111th Field Artillery.*

While the aerial assets of the 110th were busy assisting the infantrymen in their preparations, Captain Charles H Kinsey, Company Commander of the Service Battery, and his First Sergeant were equally busy on the ground. An African-American truck platoon from the 3695th Quartermaster Truck Battalion had been attached to the 110th in order to carry extra artillery ammunition across the river to keep the batteries supplied during the first few days of the offensive. When the fifteen trucks appeared in Captain Kinsey's area, he noted the overall poor condition of their vehicles and set his sergeants and mechanics to bring the vehicles and soldiers up to standard. While the vehicles were being fixed, the 110th's NCOs taught classes in military subjects to the drivers and also gave them rudimentary training in artillery operations.

The efforts expended on behalf of the truckers and their trucks paid off after the 29th crossed the river. After four straight days of continuous firing and moving the guns of the batteries, the cannoneers of the 110th were exhausted. The truck drivers pitched in and took turns replacing the gun crews so they could rest. One group of truckers even went forward to assist the artillery observers attached to the infantry companies. When the 110th's Battalion Commander, Lieutenant Colonel John P. Cooper, received orders to return the truck platoon to their own battalion, he did so reluctantly. As a small token of his appreciation, he sent a letter of commendation to their battalion commander to ensure he was made aware of their fine performance as adopted artillerymen.[27]

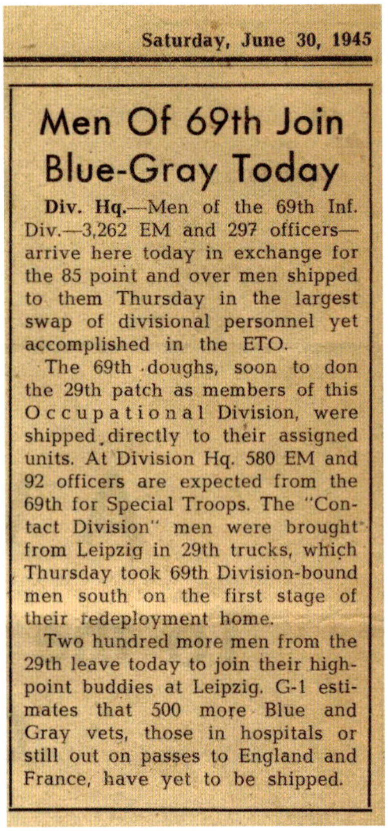

Saturday, June 30, 1945

Men Of 69th Join Blue-Gray Today

Div. Hq.—Men of the 69th Inf. Div.—3,262 EM and 297 officers—arrive here today in exchange for the 85 point and over men shipped to them Thursday in the largest swap of divisional personnel yet accomplished in the ETO.

The 69th doughs, soon to don the 29th patch as members of this Occupational Division, were shipped directly to their assigned units. At Division Hq. 580 EM and 92 officers are expected from the 69th for Special Troops. The "Contact Division" men were brought from Leipzig in 29th trucks, which Thursday took 69th Division-bound men south on the first stage of their redeployment home.

Two hundred more men from the 29th leave today to join their high-point buddies at Leipzig. G-1 estimates that 500 more Blue and Gray vets, those in hospitals or still out on passes to England and France, have yet to be shipped.

A clipping from the *29 Let's Go!* newspaper dated 30 June 1945, detailing the large-scale transfer of soldiers between the 29th and the 69th Infantry Divisions.

The Postwar Soldier Exchange (June 1945)

After the war had ended, the most important number in a soldier's life was no longer his service number, his rifle number, or even his unit's number; it was his points total for going home. A soldier earned points based on his length of service, his campaign or battle credits, and whether or not he was married. The sum of these points provided his "Adjusted Service Rating." If his rating was equal to, or greater than, the declared redeployment point total, he was assured of an earlier rotation back to the States. Those soldiers whose totals did not equal the required amount would have to stay with their unit until the "high point" men had rotated home and the "new" required point total was announced. Having been on active duty for almost five years and with significant battle credits, the original members of the 29th obviously had earned many points. Therefore, they looked forward with some anticipation that they would be returning home soon. The Army, however, had to maintain viable combat units in Europe in order to complete their occupation missions. So, with the need to keep some units active while still sending home the high-point total soldiers, the Army began to trade soldiers back and forth.

A closer view of the 29th and 69th Infantry Division medic's uniform, showing the details of the Combat Medic's Badge and enlisted medical brass collar disk. *Courtesy Major General (ret) Ken Bowra.*

A 29th Infantry Division Technician Third Grade (T-3) medic's Ike jacket. The fact that this jacket has a 69th Infantry Division patch on the right sleeve would indicate that the uniform belonged to one of the many 69th Division soldiers that would join the 29th after the end of the war. Large-scale transfers took place as part of the "point total" program for determining priority for returning to the States. *Courtesy Major General (ret) Ken Bowra.*

After some of the initial, extremely "high point total" soldiers had left, the next wave of returning Blue and Gray soldiers (some 297 officers and 3,202 enlisted men) were transferred to the 69th Infantry Division for their trip home in June 1945. A similar number of 69th "low point total" men were transferred into the 29th to replace them. Two more similar swaps took place with the 69th in the months of July and August, and when completed, there were very few men in the division that had actually served with the 29th in combat.[28]

The Colorful Career of a 110th Field Artillery Soldier

When Colonel Thomas J. Shyrock, Jr. passed away in Rockville, Maryland, 24 February 1953, it was noted that an important figure in the 110th's history had died. Shyrock had served on the Mexican border and also in the First World War as a 1st lieutenant in the field artillery. After the war, he became involved in reorganizing the 110th during its return to state service. He also served as the 2nd Battalion Commander and later the Regimental Executive Officer. By the start of the Second World War, Lieutenant Colonel Shyrock was serving as the Executive Officer of the 54th Field Artillery Brigade. When the 29th was reorganized, he was serving as the senior anti-tank officer. Under the new structure, the anti-tank sections were dispersed to other units and organizations, and Shyrock went with them. Now assigned to another division, Shyrock participated in the fighting in Tunisia, French Morocco, Algeria, and Italy. Leading from the front as usual, Shyrock was the first artilleryman ashore during the Salerno landings and later participated in the battles near Monte Casino. He would also add campaigns in France and Germany to his impressive record, as well as a period of time as the Chief of Staff to the Military Governor of Rome. His son, Captain Thomas J. Shyrock III, of the 877th Bomber Squadron, was killed in action while serving in the Pacific Theater. Shyrock is buried in Arlington National Cemetery. The historian of the 110th would later write "Though duty called him far afield, his heart remained with the old regiment."[29]

A Former Stonewaller Gets His Priorities Straight (19 February 1954)

With the Korean War winding down to a stalemate, some Hollywood actors and American sports celebrities appeared in the "Land of the Morning Calm" to entertain the troops. Among the favorite visiting stars was Marilyn Monroe. Recently married to Joe DiMaggio, a New York Yankee baseball great, the blonde starlet made her way to Korea and put on several performances for the front line troops of the 25th and 3rd Infantry Divisions. Though not particularly known for her singing skills, the troops of the 25th "Tropical Lightning" Division didn't seem to mind as she performed in a bare shouldered gown while the snow fell.

When it was the turn of the 3rd Infantry and some of their attached British and Greek soldiers to attend a performance by Marilyn, they were equally enthused. The Division Commander of the 3rd, Major General Charles D.W. Canham, former commander of the 116th Infantry Regiment at Omaha Beach, saw it differently. Immediately after he personally welcomed Marilyn to the 3rd Infantry Division, he left, returning to his office to fix some problems he had uncovered in the unit's scheduled training program.[30]

A D-Day Vet Sets the Record Straight (1980s)

One of the basic strengths of a National Guard unit is the almost family-like bond of many of the members. In many cases, they *are* family: brothers, cousins, fathers, and sons all serve together in the same unit. It also means that veterans of the unit from previous wars or prior service are often invited to visit and share the benefit of their historical knowledge with the current members. For soldiers of the Virginia and Maryland National Guard during the 1980s, this meant that many Second World War veterans were able to pass on some of the lesser known "behind the scenes" details on their experiences in the 29th Infantry Division.

One well-known former Sergeant and 116th Infantry Regiment veteran always enjoyed talking about Major General Gerhardt, the Commander of the 29th. Gerhardt, being an enthusiastic proponent of the "Two Nine Let's Go!" slogan, insisted that the troops use it on every possible occasion and training event. Eventually, the constant use of the phrase began to wear on some of the enlisted men, who modified the phrase. Whenever possible that they could do it undetected, they would yell instead: "Two shooting Nine looting Let's Go!" According to the former NCO, it would just about drive Gerhardt crazy.

Basic Tenets of Artillery. Lesson One: The Importance of "Sight to Crest" (1980)

In early 1980, the Richmond Howitzers, also commonly known as the 2/111th Field Artillery, were conducting live fire training at Fort Pickett, Virginia. The forward observer (FO) teams took up their position on an Observation Post (OP) that was directly between one of the firing batteries and the impact area. In spite of the location of the OP in relation to the firing battery, all missions went well until the FOs called in a fire mission for "troops in the open." For troops in the open missions, it was standard practice to fire air burst using Time or Variable Time (VT) fuses, which cause the artillery rounds to detonate at a predetermined height above the ground to increase effects on the targeted "troops." However, when these VT rounds were fired, the fuses sensed the tall line of pine trees directly to the left of the OP and began exploding over the OP, raining shrapnel and tree branches everywhere. Luckily, everyone in the OP managed to scurry under the jeeps that were close by and no one was injured.

Later, after review of the situation, it was determined that when the battery pulled into their firing position they had miscalculated the "sight to crest." This miscalculation, undiscovered in the earlier fire missions, became evident during the "troops in the open" mission, because the VT fuses armed shortly after leaving the tubes. As the ultimate result, when the VT fuses sensed the tall row of pine trees, they detonated, giving the OP personnel a very realistic experience in being on the receiving end of artillery fire.

Basic Tenets of Artillery. Lesson Two: The Importance of the "Observer Target Line" (1980)

During the same training period, shortly after the previous "Sight to Crest" incident, the FO team captain decided it might be a good idea to change the OP location. He therefore shifted the team to an OP that was on the opposite side of the impact area. When calling in the first mission from the new location, after the first round impacted, the team needed to adjust fire to move the round onto the target. The first set of corrections was given to the Fire Direction Center (FDC), but when the next round was fired, the round fell further away from the target, rather than closer. Another adjustment was called into the FDC by the FO team. This time, the round fell even further away from the target. The FO, somewhat puzzled, thought a bit more and figured it was time for a "bold correction." He called in his final adjustment and ended it with "Fire for Effect," which signaled for the actual fire mission to be executed.

Fortunately, one of the soldiers in the FDC was suspicious of the unusual adjustments. He called back to the FO and requested his "Observer Target Line" information; critically important information for adjusting fire. The information he received back was a shock to him and quickly the FDC announced "End of Mission" over the radio net.

The problem was simple; the FO team had failed to notify the FDC that they had changed location, so the FDC had been using the previous OT-Line to calculate the corrections. After plotting the FO's current location, the FDC determined that if they had simply followed the last adjustment they were given and fired for effect, the same OP team would have had more practice in sheltering under their jeeps.

The 29th DIVARTY Attacks Fort Pickett (1980s)

Shooting large field pieces always entails an element of risk. Artillery rounds are, by their very nature, dangerous. However, with care, knowledge, and proper procedure, firing on an artillery range is usually a fairly safe proposition. Fort Pickett, Virginia, being blessed with some of the larger and better artillery ranges on the east coast of the United States, has always been a favored location for artillery units to shoot cannons. During annual training one summer, a unit of the 29th DIVARTY accidentally missed their range target and dropped their rounds into the parking lot of a small post exchange. Fortunately, the only damage was to several civilian vehicles parked there and to the parking lot itself. The parking lot was quickly repaved and restitution made to the owners of the vehicles. Though little remains in the historical record to provide details of the day the 29th DIVARTY attacked the Fort Pickett Post Exchange, artillerymen from that period still enjoy recounting the story. Not surprisingly, they all insist that it had been someone else's battery that fired the errant rounds.

The 29th Division Commander Helps His Artillerymen Understand the "Big Picture" (1990s)

The 29th Division's annual training in June one year saw units spread between the oppressively hot and humid Fort A.P. Hill and the even more oppressively hot and humid Fort Pickett, Virginia. As part of the overall evaluation process, the 29th Division Commander visited Battery "C" of the 1st Battalion, 246th Field Artillery during their third straight day of live-fire operations at Fort Pickett. Immediately upon arrival, the general began quizzing the battery commander and his senior staff with a series of questions: "How many MILs (degrees) does an artillery piece traverse per rotation?" "How about elevation?" "How do you know if your soldiers are moving fast enough?" Perhaps discouraged by not receiving much in the way of answers from the sweaty, tired artillerymen, he finally decided to give them a nugget of advice: "You have to make sure your soldiers have pep!" With that said, the general departed, leaving the battery officers and senior NCOs puzzled and asking each other: "Where exactly would you find 'pep' in the Army Training and Evaluation Program (ARTEP) manual?"

Fort Pickett has always been known for its field artillery ranges. In this picture, Batteries "A" and "B" of 1st Battalion, 111th Field Artillery prepare their M109A5 155mm guns for turn-in to the Maintenance and Training Equipment Site (MATES) facility at the end of annual training. A particularly hot day has resulted in the water "buffalo" being a popular spot to congregate!

I Hear You Knocking, but You Can't Come in... (Bosnia 1997)

One of the missions that the 246th Field Artillery soldiers, working with the 16th Polish Airborne Battalion, participated in during their time in Bosnia was the search for and inspection of weapons storage sites near the Bosnian city of Teslić. While some Bosnian police stations were allowed to store a designated number of weapons, the American and Polish soldiers would keep track of the serial numbers. They were never pleased to find that, while the total number of weapons stayed the same, the serial numbers were almost always different; a strong indication that there were a lot more weapons in the area than were allowed and, even worse, someone was taking them out and using them. Given such blatant disregard for the rules by the Bosnians, the American artillerymen and Polish paratroopers' supply of patience with the local Bosnian militia was eroding quickly.

After several such episodes, a patrol went out to look at a site where several Bosnian tanks and armored vehicles were known to be stored near a large wooden barn. When the patrol arrived at the site, they could see deep track groves in the ground that could only have been made by movement of heavy armored vehicles—another violation of the peace treaty. It was readily apparent to the patrol that they needed to look inside the barn. However, it became equally apparent that the Bosnians were not going to open the large wooden entrance door. As the officer in charge of the patrol argued with the Bosnians, everyone was suddenly surprised by a crashing sound and turned to watch as the big wooden door was smashed inward. Tired of arguments and fruitless negotiations with the Bosnians, a Polish soldier had driven his BMP (a former Warsaw Pact tracked infantry fighting vehicle) up to the barn and smashed the door inward. The patrol could now easily inspect the contents of the barn, and thanks to the Poles, another weapons storage site was added to the watch list.

The 246th Returns from Bosnia…Almost (1997)

After completing their tour of peacekeeping duties in the Balkans, the officers and men of Detachment 1, 1st Battalion, 246th Field Artillery looked forward, like the Doughboys of 1918 and the GIs of 1945, to the trip home to family and friends. After a seemingly endless journey that took them from Bosnia through Germany, they finally made it to Fort Benning, Georgia, to complete their "out-processing." After all the administrative details were complete and paperwork dispatched, the troops were ready for the final leg of the trip that would carry them home to the Danville, Virginia, Regional Airport and the large celebration planned by their families for them at 4 p.m. Unfortunately, while all of Danville was prepared to give them their well-deserved "Heroes' Welcome," the West Virginia Air National Guard C-130 cargo plane had different plans and broke down on the runway.

The Fort Benning Transportation Movement Office went in to scramble mode and devised a new plan that included putting the soldiers on a bus, driving them to the Atlanta airport, and placing them on commercial flights. Eventually, the soldiers made it home, but many hours after their expected arrival. It was a much quieter Danville than everyone had anticipated.

Task Force Wrench, Fort Polk, Louisiana (June 2001)

In order to prepare the 29th Infantry Division for another rotation to Bosnia, a number of senior NCOs, warrant officers, and officers deployed from Virginia to Fort Polk. The soldiers that would be going to Bosnia had been gathered at Fort Polk for a Mission Rehearsal Exercise (MRE) to prepare them for their eventual mission. Fort Polk had built a replica Bosnian village complete with radio station, checkpoints, and a "Bosnian" population. All this was designed to train the troops in various scenarios that they might encounter in the Balkans.

The senior leaders coming from Virginia were experts in Army supply and maintenance procedures, and were sent to ensure that the vehicles and equipment being taken to Bosnia were in the best possible condition. They were also to ensure that the soldiers had all of their required uniforms and field gear and that it also was in top shape.

Unfortunately, except for the Bosnian village, there was very little about Fort Polk or Louisiana in June 2001 that would remind anyone of Bosnia. After the first few sweltering, muggy days, the region was visited by Tropical Storm Allison, which proceeded to dump nearly forty inches of rain throughout the state and even managed to flood nearby Houston, Texas. The rains were so strong and so persistent that one night's entertainment for several of the sergeants and warrant officers was watching the snakes climb trees at Fort Polk to get out of the rising water. After listening to the sergeants complain about nearly everything associated with Louisiana, Fort Polk, and the weather, one of the warrant officers attempted to put a positive spin on the conversation. He ventured an opinion that, although the current conditions were indeed pretty humble, at least they had all had a chance to eat some pretty good Cajun food. The oldest sergeant in the group looked at him with pity and said, "Chief, there's a lot of good restaurants between Richmond and the Louisiana state line. If I live long enough to get back to Virginia, I'm gonna nail my boots to the armory floor and I'm never gonna leave again."

The terrorist attacks of 11 September 2001 were less than ninety days later.

The 29th Comes Full Circle (November 2001)

The soldiers of the 29th deployed to Bosnia in the fall of 2001 were surprised and honored to be visited by the noted author Stephen Ambrose, his wife Moira, and ten veterans of the 29th from the Second World War. Among the visiting vets was Joseph A. "Lightning" Farinholt, former member of the 175th Infantry Regiment and recipient of four Silver Stars in a five-month period. Also making the trip were several Stonewallers from the 116th that had landed on Omaha Beach on D-Day. These included John Robert "Bob" Slaughter and Dr. Harold S. Baumgarten. Perhaps making the visit by the Blue and Gray vets all the more poignant to everyone involved was the knowledge that the United States was once again at war. Although the older vets seemed to enjoy the trip—for some their first visit to Europe since 1945—it was the soldiers of the 29th serving in Bosnia that received the most benefit from the visit. As one sergeant would later recall: "They told us that they were proud of us and what we were doing in Bosnia. They even thanked us for our service. Can you believe that?"

CHAPTER 15

Lineage and Units of the 29th

Anyone who studies U.S. Army history or delved the intricacies of unit lineages and heraldry will appreciate the difficulty research entails. In this chapter, we attempt to provide as complete a picture as possible of some of the major units of the 29th Infantry Division. At times, it will seem that some units appear and disappear almost randomly and their lineage is passed on to new units. Nevertheless, what follows is an attempt to provide a synopsis of the units and relevant information about some of the soldiers who served in them.

113th Infantry Regiment

The 113th was originally formed with soldiers from the 1st, 2nd, and 4th New Jersey Infantry Regiments. The regiment served with the 29th Division during the First World War as part of the 57th Infantry Brigade and is credited with campaign streamers for Alsace, Lorraine, and Meuse-Argonne. Following the war, the 113th returned to state control and never again served in the 29th Division. During the Second World War, the 113th served in the 44th Infantry Division and received credit for the Northern France, Rhineland, Ardennes-Alsace (the Alsace for the second war), and Central Europe campaigns. After the war, it was converted to armored infantry for a brief period, then back to regular infantry in 1961. The tree displayed in the middle of its crest represents service in the Argonne in the First World War with the motto "FIDELIS ET FORTIS," which means "Faithful and Brave."[1]

The coat of arms for the 113th Infantry Regiment. The 113th was originally formed from the 1st, 2nd, and 4th New Jersey Infantry Regiments and would serve in the 57th Infantry Brigade of the 29th Division in the First World War. *Courtesy TIOH.*

114th Infantry Regiment.

The 114th was originally formed from the 3rd and 5th New Jersey Infantry and the 1st Delaware Infantry. The 114th served during the First World War with its sister regiment, the 113th, in the 57th Infantry Brigade of the 29th Division, and is credited with participation in the Alsace and Meuse-Argonne campaigns. After returning to state control, the regiment never again served in the 29th Division. The 114th served as part of the 44th Infantry Division during the Second World War, receiving credit for the Northern France, Rhineland, Ardennes-Alsace (also in the Alsace for the second time), and Central Europe campaigns. The regimental crest contains a miniature 29th Division symbol to acknowledge its service in the First World War with the 29th Division. It also has a small four-leaf clover to represent service in the Spanish-American War. The motto "IN OMNIA PARATUS" was taken from the original 3rd New Jersey's motto, which means "Prepared in All Things."[2]

The distinctive unit insignia for the 114th Infantry Regiment. Comprised originally of infantry units from New Jersey and Delaware, the 114th would also serve in the 57th Infantry Brigade of the 29th Division.

A well-worn collar disk and a unit crest for the 115th Infantry Regiment. Raised originally from Maryland infantry units, the 115th has been a permanent fixture in the 29th since the First World War.

The inside of an M1 helmet shell with a nicely painted 115th unit insignia. Note the 115th's motto "Rally Round the Flag," which was added to the unit crest in 1968.

115th Infantry Regiment.

The 115th was originally formed from the 1st, 4th, and 5th Maryland Infantry Regiments. The 115th served in the 58th Infantry Brigade of the 29th Division during the First World

War. The 115th was credited with participation in the Alsace and Meuse-Argonne campaigns and was commanded by Milton Reckord, later Maryland Adjutant General and commander of the 29th Infantry Division. Between the wars, the regiment reverted to state control and was designated the 1st Maryland Infantry Regiment. Redesignated the 115th in January 1941, the unit would remain with the 29th after the division was triangularized. The 115th received credit for four campaigns in the Second World War: Normandy (with assault arrowhead), Northern France, Rhineland, and Central Europe. After the war, the 115th would remain with the division until 1968, when the 29th was inactivated. The 115th was attached to the 28th Infantry Division until 1975, when it was assigned to the 58th (Separate) Infantry Brigade. In 1988, the 115th rejoined the newly-created 29th (Light) Infantry Division. The motto "Rally Round the Flag" was added to the unit crest in 1968. The crest also contains an image of a red four-leaf clover for the Spanish-American War, a cactus for the Mexico Border campaign, and three alerions representing service in the Meuse-Argonne. In 1950, the First Battalion was awarded the French *Croix de Guerre* embroidered with the name "St. Lô."[3]

The unit crest for the 116th Infantry Regiment. Originally comprised of National Guardsmen from Virginia, the 116th traces its lineage back to the "Stonewall Brigade" of the Army of Northern Virginia in the Civil War. Like the 115th, the 116th has been with the 29th Infantry Division throughout its long history and remains so today.

116th Infantry Regiment.

The 116th was originally formed from the 1st, 2nd, and 4th Virginia Infantry Regiments. Between them, these regiments shared campaign streamers for thirteen Revolutionary War, one War of 1812, and eighteen Civil War battles or campaigns. During the First World War, it served in the 58th Infantry Brigade of the 29th Division. The regiment was credited with participation in the Alsace and Meuse-Argonne campaigns and received its motto "Ever Forward" for service there. Following the war, it retained the 116th numeric designator and would continue to be a key part of the 29th Infantry Division from that time until the division was deactivated in 1968. During the Second World War, the 116th received credit for four campaigns: Normandy (with assault arrowhead), Northern France, Rhineland, and Central Europe. In 1968, the regiment was assigned to be part of the 28th Infantry Division. It remained with the 28th until 1975, when it became part of the 116th (Separate) Infantry Brigade, at which time it also re-established use of the nickname "the Stonewall Brigade." It rejoined the 29th Infantry Division in the mid-1980s, when the 29th was reactivated to become a "Light" division. In 1950, the regiment was awarded the French *Croix de Guerre* with palm, embroidered with the words "Beaches of Normandy" to reflect its role in the initial assault waves of the D-Day invasion.[4]

The medal awarded to soldiers of the 175th in recognition of their attaining perfect attendance at units drill. In an era before "weekend drills" became the standard, this was much more difficult to achieve than it might seem. Guardsmen of this period were expected to attend drill one night a week, every week.

Four versions of the 175th Infantry Regiment unit crest showing slight differences in details. The 175th traces its history to the 5th Maryland Infantry, which explains the "5" in the center of the crest.

175 Infantry Regiment

The 175th originally served in the 29th Division as the 112th Field Artillery Regiment, part of the 115th Infantry Regiment, and several machine gun companies. Its lineage is credited with nine Revolutionary War, two War of 1812, and seven Civil War Campaigns, in addition to the Alsace and Meuse-Argonne campaigns from the First World War. Between the wars, it was redesignated the 5th Maryland Infantry, also known as the "Dandy Fifth," and maintains that unit crest to this day. It was renumbered as the 175th Infantry Regiment in 1941 and received credit for four campaigns during the

Second World War: Normandy (with assault arrowhead), Northern France, Rhineland, and Central Europe. The 175th remained with the 29th until the division was inactivated in 1968 and was reassigned to the 29th Infantry Division in 1985 when the division was re-established as a "Light" division. The unit retains the motto "DECUS ET PRAESIDIUM," which means "An Honor and a Guard."[5]

The unit crest for the 176th Infantry Regiment. The 176th can trace its lineage back to the 1650s militias of Tidewater, Virginia, and also to the 1st Virginia Infantry and the Richmond Light Infantry Blues. Although the unit itself was reorganized and renumbered several times, it would retain this distinctive unit insignia.

The award presented to members of the 176th Infantry Regiment for serving faithfully for fifteen years. Note it retains the numbering of "1st Virginia" on the medal to reflect its heritage.

176th Infantry Regiment

The 176th was originally comprised of some units of the 116th Infantry Regiment and the 104th Ammunition Train. As such, it received credit for the two First World War campaigns, as well as nine Revolutionary War campaigns: Virginia 1775, Long island, Trenton, New York 1776, Princeton, Brandywine, Germantown, Monmouth, and South Carolina 1780. The 176th is also credited with participation in the War of 1812, the Mexican War, and ten Confederate Army service campaigns of the Civil War. A major component of this regiment was the Richmond Light Infantry Blues, an elite unit that reorganized themselves into cavalry in order to serve in the Mexican Border campaign in 1916 and 1917. The regiment was reorganized after the First World War as the 1st Virginia Infantry. When the 29th Division was "triangularized" in 1942, the 176th drew the unfortunate role of being detached from the 29th, first to serve as the defense force for Washington, D.C., then deploying to Fort Benning as a separate infantry regiment. After the Second World War, the 176th was re-established as a separate regiment of the Virginia Army National Guard with headquarters in the Richmond area. In 1968, the 176th was converted to Combat Engineers and redesignated the 276th Engineers while retaining the crest of the 176th. The *fleur de lis* is reflective of the unit's service in the First World War. Numbered among the 176th's famous commanders throughout its history are George Washington, John Marshall, and Patrick Henry, with the latter being the inspiration for the unit's motto: "Liberty or Death."[6]

183rd Infantry/Cavalry Regiment

The crest of the 183rd Infantry regiment, a unit that also draws its lineage from some of Virginia's most famous military units. The 183rd has served the state and the country in many forms, including a period of time as an armor unit and later as a cavalry unit. *Courtesy TIOH.*

The 183rd also draws its long and, at times, somewhat confusing heritage from the Richmond Light Infantry Blues. The "Blues" served in the 104th Ammunition Train in France as part of the 29th Division. Between the wars, they served alternately as the 1st Virginia Infantry, the 183rd Infantry Regiment, and then again as the 1st Virginia. Throughout this period, those companies of the regiment that were from Petersburg, Virginia, were also known as the "Petersburg Greys." The 183rd was once again rolled into the 176th Infantry Regiment at the beginning of the Second World War. After the war, it continued as such until 1959, when it was split out from the 176th to become the 183rd Armor Regiment as part of the "pentomic" experiment. In 1963, they were redesignated the 183rd Cavalry and retained the "Blues" as their nickname. The unit crest is primarily blue and gray, reflecting the long association with the 29th Infantry Division, and the American dogwood flower (*Cornus florida*) represents Virginia, the unit's home state. It also borrows the Virginia motto for its own: "Death to Tyrants."[7]

Artillery Units

The unit crest and collar disk for the 110th Field Artillery Regiment. One of the original units of the 29th Division during the First World War, the 110th would be restructured as a field artillery battalion in 1942 and its 2nd Battalion would become the 224th Field Artillery Battalion. *Courtesy Allan Henderson.*

110th Field Artillery Regiment

The 110th was originally formed with the artillery batteries from Maryland and the District of Columbia, as well as the

Another perfect attendance award, this time from the 110th Field Artillery Regiment for the year 1937.

District of Columbia cavalry units. Just as all the other 29th Division field artillery regiments, the 110th spent the First World War in Brittany undergoing training and suffering from the Spanish Flu. Between the wars, the 110th was equipped with French 75s and was a horse-drawn regiment until 1934. When the 29th was "triangularized" in 1942, the 110th was downsized to a battalion, issued 105mm M2A1 howitzers, and was designated as the direct support artillery for the 115th Infantry Regiment. In this role, it participated in all of the 29th's campaigns in the Second World War and was considered one of the premier artillery units in the European theater. In a year of combat, the 110th fired 124,165 artillery shells, set up 49 separate firing positions, and covered 1,100 miles while fighting the Germans. Its aerial observers, flying Piper Cub observation planes, earned 35 Air Medals. As well as supporting the infantry regiments of the 29th, the 110th also provided artillery support at various times to the 35th, 79th, and 102nd Infantry Divisions. The 110th remained with the division after the war, but was converted in 1963 to 155mm howitzers and given a divisional support mission. During the 1960s, the 110th was twice activated to restore order during civil disturbances. In 1985, the 110th rejoined the newly reactivated 29th Infantry Division as a 105mm howitzer battalion.[8]

111th Field Artillery Regiment

The unit crest for the 111th Field Artillery Regiment. One of the founding units of the 29th in 1917, the 111th was raised from the artillerymen of the 1st Virginia Field Artillery.

The 111th was originally comprised of soldiers from the 1st Virginia Artillery and was part of the 54th Artillery Brigade in the 29th Division. Like its sister artillery regiments, the 111th spent the First World War in training at Camp McClellan and in the Brittany region of France, never seeing front line duty. Between the wars, it remained a key part of the 29th Division and was reduced to battalion size in 1942, when the division was reorganized to fit the Army's new "triangle" configuration for infantry divisions. The 111th was assigned as the direct support field artillery battalion for the 116th Infantry Regiment and was part of the initial assault waves 6 June 1944. High waves and overloading of their assault craft caused

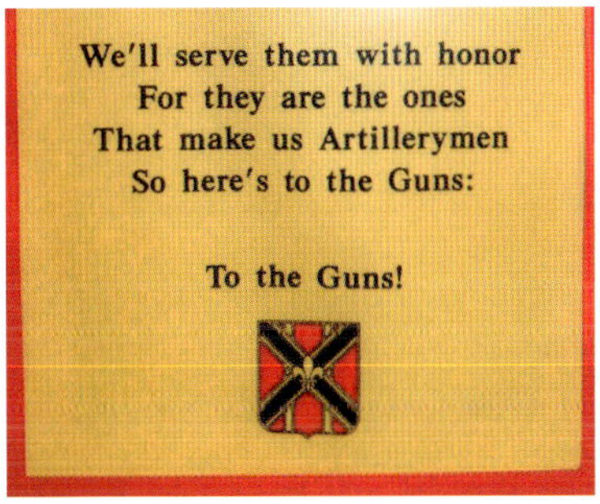

A portion of the toast, known to all artillerymen of the 111th, in honor of the centerpiece of their unit's existence, "the Guns." *Courtesy 1/111th Field Artillery.*

the 111th to lose eleven of their twelve howitzers before they reached Omaha Beach. Assessing the situation, their battalion commander, Lieutenant Colonel Thornton Mullins, declared "To hell with our artillery mission. We're infantrymen now." He was killed by a German sniper bullet a short while later. The 111th participated in all of the 29th Infantry Division's campaigns. The 111th remained with the 29th and would later be reorganized to create two units: the 111th and 691st Anti-Aircraft Artillery Automatic Weapons Battalion (later redesignated the 129th AAA AW Battalion). By the 1950s, the 111th would change form again, and some units would be equipped with anti-aircraft guns, while others remained traditional field artillery. The 111th was activated for service during the Berlin Wall Crisis in 1961 and deployed to Fort Campbell, Kentucky, for further training. The battalion returned to Virginia in 1962 when the tensions lessened. In 1968, when the 29th was deactivated, the 111th would continue to serve in the Virginia National Guard as a non-divisional unit. Battery "E" would later be assigned to the 29th "Light" Infantry Division in 1985 and be outfitted with 155mm howitzers. The 111th's motto is "NUNQUAM NON PARATUS" (meaning "Never Unprepared"), but its unit distinct identification insignia (unit crest), in conformance with most other United States Army field artillery crests, does not display any wording.[9]

The 112th Heavy Field Artillery Regiment was formed in 1917 from New Jersey artillery and cavalry soldiers. Its only period of service with the 29th Division would be during the First World War.

112th Field Artillery Regiment

The 112th Field Artillery Regiment was originally comprised of soldiers from the 1st New Jersey Field Artillery Regiment and troops "B" and "D" of the New Jersey Cavalry. The 112th returned to the New Jersey National Guard after the First World War and was assigned to the 44th Infantry Division. In 1943, it was split into the 695th and 696th Field Artillery Battalions and later converted to armored field artillery battalions. In 1959, these and other artillery units would again be rolled up into the 112th Field Artillery Regiment to serve with the 50th Armored Division. They would be detached from the 50th in 1993 and assigned to the 42nd Infantry Division.

They are credited with campaign streamers for the Second World War that include Normandy, Northern France, Rhineland, Ardennes-Alsace, and Central Europe. Battery "D" (also known as the Camden Light Artillery) has Civil War Union service streamers for Bull Run, Virginia 1863, Wilderness, Spotsylvania, Cold Harbor, Petersburg, Shenandoah, and Appomattox. Along with the cactus for Mexican Border service and the *Fleur de Lis* for service in France, the unit crest has two Gatling guns to represent earlier service periods as Gatling gun units. The unit crest also contains the motto "A OUTRANCE," meaning "To the Utmost."[10]

The 224th Field Artillery Battalion was created when the 29th was converted to the new "triangle" configuration in 1942. Its linkage and lineage to the 110th is obvious from the use of the 110th's crest in the middle of the 224th insignia.

224th Field Artillery Battalion

The 224th Field Artillery Battalion was formed in 1942, when the 110th Field Artillery Regiment was downsized to a battalion. During the Second World War, the 224th and its 105mm Howitzer batteries were assigned to provide direct support to the 175th Infantry Regiment, also a Maryland National Guard unit. In this role, the 224th shares all the campaign streamers of the 175th during this period. The unit insignia for the 224th reflects the direct link to the 110th by displaying their crest in the center. The 224th's motto is "QUERCUS CRESCIT," meaning "the Oak Grows," another reflection on the 110th lineage, since their motto is "As the Oak."[11]

227th Field Artillery Battalion

Owning perhaps one of the most convoluted lineages of any unit in the 29th Infantry Division is the 227th Field Artillery Battalion. The 227th was created originally out of the 2nd Battalion of the 111th Field Artillery Regiment when the 29th Infantry Division was triangularized. The 1st Battalion of the 111th was renamed the 111th Field Artillery Battalion. Upon conversion, the 227th was assigned the medium field artillery mission and equipped with 155mm howitzers. The 227th provided general support to the infantry units of the division and its 155mm shell, when fully charged, could reach almost 13,000 yards. The 227th participated in all of the 29th's campaigns in the Second World War. After the war, part of the battalion was split off to create the 442nd Field Artillery Battalion, which became a non-divisional artillery unit stationed in the Richmond area. In this role, the 442nd was designated as the artillery component of the 176th Regimental Combat Team. The remaining part, still named the 227th, was stationed in the Covington and Clifton Forge area of Virginia. As such, it remained a part of the 29th Division throughout the 1950s, until it was consolidated with the 246th Field Artillery in 1959.[12]

Drawing its lineage from a number of units, including the 246th Coast Artillery Regiment, the 246th Field Artillery Battalion has also served in a number of variations. The rainbow in the center of the crest reflects service with the 42nd "Rainbow" Division in the First World War. *Courtesy TIOH.*

Image of the unit insignia used by the 246th when they were still performing the coastal artillery mission. *Courtesy National Guard Educational Foundation.*

246th Field Artillery Regiment

The 246th traces their lineage back to the Virginia National Guard coast artillery units and to service in the 42nd "Rainbow" Division during the First World War. This service is represented on the unit crest with a rainbow. It also shares a tie to Company "C" of the 116th Infantry Regiment. Historically, the units in the part of the state from which the regiment was formed are known as the "Danville Grays." During the Second World War, the 246th served as a coastal defense unit until deactivation. The unit was reactivated in 1948, this time as the 560th Field Artillery Battalion. The 560th was federalized in 1951 during the Korean War, but remained in the States. The unit was reorganized several times after returning to state control and finally equipped with 105mm howitzers. It was then designated the 1st Battalion, 246th Field Artillery Regiment and assigned to the 29th Infantry Division in 1963. A second Battalion of the 246th was designated as the 2nd Rocket Howitzer Battalion, 246th Field Artillery, and later issued the M31 "Honest John" rocket systems. The Honest John was the first U.S. Army surface-to-surface missile capable of delivering either conventional or nuclear warheads. The unit motto "Prepared to Defend" was added to the unit crest in 1968.[13]

Other Units

The unit insignia for the 104th Medical Battalion. Originally serving in the 29th during the First World War as the 104th Sanitary Train, the 104th has maintained its lineage, in various forms, throughout the history of the 29th. *Courtesy TIOH.*

104th Medical Battalion

The 104th was originally formed during the First World War as the 104th Sanitary Train and contained all of the regimental and higher level hospitals and ambulance companies for the 29th Division. These units served with their assigned regiments during the war and earned the same campaign credit. Between the wars, the unit was redesignated the 104th Medical Regiment and had soldiers from Maryland, Virginia, and the District of Columbia. The 104th was converted to a battalion when the 29th was triangularized in 1942. The 104th was extremely busy due to the high casualty rates during the war, but also because of General Gerhardt's interest in solving the problem of "combat fatigue" by treating the affected soldiers quickly and in an area close to their units. Following the war, the 104th remained part of the division until it was deactivated in 1968. At this point, the unit was redesignated the 136th Combat Evacuation Hospital, and a short while later, the 136th Combat Support Hospital. During the period 1975 to 1985, when there were two separate infantry brigades; the 104th served as the Medical Company in the 116th Support Battalion. When the 29th was reactivated, the 104th returned to its role as the divisional medical battalion. The unit's motto is "PRO DEO, PATRIA, ET VICINO," meaning "For God, My Country, and My Neighbor." Just as many other 29th Division units, the unit crest displays a cactus, representing Mexican Border Service, and a castle, which represents the unit's First World War service near Verdun.[14]

A unit crest with a long history of providing direct support to the infantry units associated with the 116th (Separate) Infantry Brigade and later the 29th (Light) Infantry Division. The crest was first used by the 116th Support Battalion and then, starting in 1992, by the 429th Support Battalion. *Courtesy TIOH.*

116th/429th Support Battalion

The 116th Support Battalion was formed to provide administrative, logistical (supply, transportation, maintenance), and medical support to the 116th (Separate) Infantry Brigade during the late 1970s and early 1980s. After the 29th was re-established in 1985, the support mission was spread across several support battalions to provide such support to the three infantry brigades of the division. In 1992, the unit crest used by the 116th Support Battalion was redesignated for the 429th Support Battalion, as was the Motto: "Support is Survival." The spear in the center of the crest represents the triumph over tyranny, a common theme in Virginia heraldry. The blue and gray colors represent the linkage to the 29th Infantry Division.[15]

The unit crest for the 729th Support Battalion. The 729th has served in various forms (Quartermaster and Ordnance) since the 29th was formed in 1917. *Courtesy TIOH.*

729th Support Battalion

Originally formed from Company "D" of the 104th Quartermaster Regiment, the 729th was activated as part of the 29th Infantry Division in 1942 as a light maintenance company. It participated in all of the 29th's Second World War campaigns and shares the same streamers, including the assault arrowhead for the Normandy landing. The 729th was expanded in 1951 to battalion size and renamed the 729th Ordnance Battalion. It remained with the 29th until 1968, when the division was inactivated. In 1985, it was redesignated the 729th Maintenance Support Battalion, and a short while later, the 729th Support Battalion. The unit motto is "Maintain for Freedom," and the crest has the symbol of a fort in the center representing Fort Frederick, the fort that protected Maryland's frontier settlers during the French and Indian War.[16]

The unit emblem for the 224th Aviation Regiment. Comprised of units from both Maryland and Virginia, the 224th's motto reflects both states: Maryland (The Free State) and Virginia (The Old Dominion). *Courtesy TIOH.*

224th Aviation Regiment

The 29th Infantry Division has a long history of association with aviation units that started after the First World War, when the 104th Observation Squadron was added to the division. Throughout the Second World War, the aerial observers attached to the field artillery units were critically important in breaking up enemy attacks on several occasions. In 1963, an aviation battalion was authorized, resulting in the 29th Aviation Battalion being added to the division. Never fully staffed, the 29th Aviation consisted of a headquarters detachment, a general support helicopter company, and an aviation maintenance platoon that was detached from the 729th Maintenance Battalion. The unit changed designation several times between the years 1968-1978. It was part of the 28th Infantry Division on two occasions and later served with the 116th (Separate) Infantry Brigade. When the 29th was reactivated in 1985, the organic aviation unit was designated the 29th Aviation Regiment, with an aviation battalion in Virginia and another in Maryland. These were later consolidated into a single battalion with the Headquarters in Sandston, Virginia. The 29th Combat Aviation Brigade, headquartered in Maryland, was created from the $1/224^{th}$.

Some units of the 224th were activated for service during Desert Shield/Desert Storm, and though the units themselves did not deploy to Saudi Arabia, some of the unit members did. Some soldiers of the 224th were already deployed to Bosnia when the 11 September 2001 attacks took place, and others soon joined them to complete the SFOR rotation. The motto reflects this joint ownership of the unit, with the words "Free Dominion" drawing on Maryland's nickname as "The Free State" and Virginia's nickname as "The Old Dominion."[17]

The unit crest for the 229th Engineers. The crest was officially approved for use in 1986, as the 229th became part of the 29th Infantry Division again. *Courtesy TIOH.*

The unit crest for the 276th Engineers. The 276th follows the lineage of the 1st Virginia and 176th Infantry Regiments. Through this linkage, the 276th maintains a historical lineage with the Richmond Light Infantry Blues.

229th Engineer Battalion

The 229th Engineers draw their lineage from the 29th Divisional engineer units. Their unit crest reflects both this lineage and their historical lineage to Confederate service in the Civil War. While the castle tower represents the Engineer Corps, the *fleur de lis* is in honor of service in France during both World Wars. The 229th has historically been located in the Fredericksburg area of Virginia and their motto is "Sappers Lead."[18]

276th Engineer Battalion

The 276th Engineers receive their lineage in part from the 1st Virginia Infantry Regiment and 176th Infantry Regiment. The unit crest was initially approved in 1929 for the 1st Regiment, amended in 1941 to reflect the 176th, then further amended in 1968 to reflect the 276th Engineers. Through the 1st Virginia heritage it reflects service in the French and Indian War with the use of an arrow centered on a red cross, the cross then reflecting Revolutionary War service. The gray cross on the blue background is symbolic of Civil War infantry service and the *fleur de lis* signifies service in Franc in the First World War. The unit's motto "Liberty or Death" commemorates the words of Patrick Henry, a former commander of the unit.[19]

CHAPTER 16

The 21st Century and Global War on Terrorism

The twenty-first century was more than a year old when terrorists attacked the United States on 11 September 2001. For the purpose of our story, we have chosen to consider that date and malicious attack to be the herald of the new century. Had it not occurred, there is a good chance that the 29th Infantry Division would have continued as before, supporting rotations to Bosnia, Kosovo, and other hotspots or disaster areas where the president and Department of the Army would deploy them. For certain, the genie came out of the bottle during Operations Desert Shield / Desert Storm and the National Guard became a key component of the national military strategy. All that, however, is supposition. The attacks did take place, and in the ensuing years, the units of the 29th Infantry Division, as well as many non-divisional units of the Virginia and Maryland National Guard, have served in Kuwait, Iraq, and Afghanistan. The images that follow are just a very small sampling of pictures to recognize the courage and multi-faceted fortitude of the soldiers of the 29th since 9-11.

Their story remains to be told.

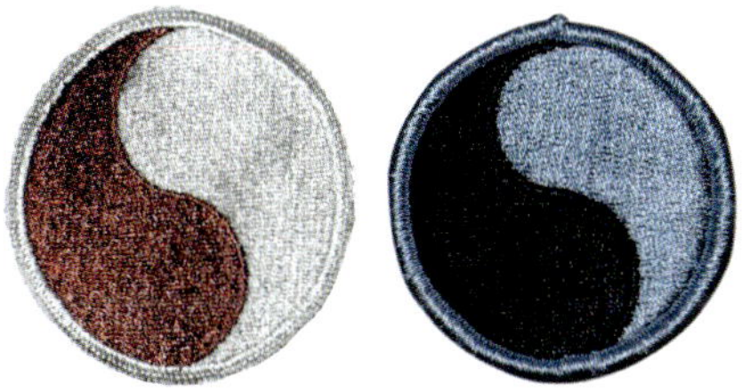

With the addition of the Desert Combat Uniform (DCU), and later the Army Combat Uniform (ACU), the 29th Infantry Division patch took another evolution. Shown on the left is the DCU version and on the right is the newest version, with Velcro backing for use on the ACUs.

The ACU worn by a lieutenant colonel assigned to the 116th Infantry Brigade Combat Team in 2007 and 2008 in Baghdad, during Operation Iraqi Freedom (OIF). *Courtesy LTC Michael Swanson*

A Desert Camouflage Uniform (DCU) blouse worn by a 29th Infantry Division soldier during Operation Iraqi Freedom. The DCU was a very short-lived uniform and was replaced by the Army Combat Uniform (ACU) in the 2004-2005 timeframe for most soldiers.

Command Sergeant Major Carl Holcomb pauses to overlook the city of Baghdad during Operation Iraqi Freedom.

Members of the elite Italian Army *Alpini* Mountain unit receive an award from an American officer in recognition of their service together in Afghanistan. Note the ISAF (International Security Assistance Force) patches present on the Italian and American Uniforms. *Courtesy COL Michelle Rose.*

A 29th Infantry Division captain takes a break and poses for a picture during Operation Enduring Freedom (OEF) in Afghanistan. Of note here, in addition to the body armor and equipment, is the small patch with the Afghanistan and United States flags on the captain's left shoulder.

Same as it ever was; soldiers awaiting deployment to a combat zone have to learn patience. Here, members of the 529th Combat Sustainment Support Battalion pass time while awaiting the transportation that will take them from Fort Hood to Afghanistan. Note that most of these soldiers already have a patch on their right sleeve, indicating previous service in a combat zone. *Courtesy COL Michelle Rose.*

Two Virginia Guardsmen instruct their Afghani counterparts in a table top exercise as part of their duties in an Embedded Training Team (ETT). *Courtesy MAJ Michael Booker VaARNG Brigade Embedded Training Team.*

A closer view at a section of the previous picture showing two very familiar patches: the 1st Infantry Division and the 29th Infantry Division. Landing side by side on Omaha Beach 6 June 1944, these two divisions became forever linked in American military history. Now, two modern-day veterans of those units are getting ready for another deployment. *Courtesy COL Michelle Rose.*

Another shot of an American officer in Afghanistan, this time with full equipment, preparing for a movement "outside the wire" as part of a combat logistics convoy.

The other side of the coin; an American officer hands a backpack and other school supplies to a young Afghan girl at a school in the village of Shindand, Afghanistan.

Reminiscent of the picture in chapter five of the 111th Field Artillery's symbol created out of local materials at Fort Indiantown Gap, this large protective concrete barrier in Afghanistan has been decorated by American soldiers. Among the unit patches portrayed is the Virginia Army National Guard patch, in this case representing the 529th Combat Sustainment Support Battalion of the 43rd Sustainment Brigade. *Courtesy COL Michelle Rose.*

CHAPTER 17

Lest We Forget...

The 29th Infantry Division, in its many forms, has left a mark on American military history. It may seem flippant to think that the 29th has been fighting "bad guys" and defending the United States since 1916. Yet, it's a very accurate statement. Even before there officially was a 29th Division, the units that would eventually form it were serving together to protect the United States' southern border from raids by Pancho Villa and his followers. In the meantime, the First World War was raging across Europe, mainly because of a series of events that started in the Balkans with an assassination in Sarajevo. While the United States tried to remain neutral, it reached the point where President Wilson could no longer stay out of the fighting. America quickly began to train for war and the 29th Division was born. A short while later, they were facing soldiers of the Imperial German and the Imperial Austro-Hungarian Armies. Moving into the maelstrom of the Meuse-Argonne campaign, the Doughboys of the 29th found that liberating French soil came at a high price, but they persevered. By the time the war was over, so were Imperial Germany and the Austro-Hungarian Empire.

The headstone in the Baltimore National Cemetery for Sergeant Howard E. Madsen, member of the 115th Infantry Regiment and recipient of the Distinguished Service Cross for bravery during the Meuse-Argonne Campaign in 1918. *Courtesy John Simmons.*

Brigadier General Harry H. Bandholtz's monument in Budapest. The statue was removed by the Communist regime in 1949 and remained out of sight until 1985, when it was placed on the U.S. Embassy grounds. It was later returned to its original site in front of the U.S. Embassy in 1989. *Courtesy CW3 Clay Deckert.*

General Bandholtz's headstone in the cemetery in his hometown of Constantine, Michigan.

Some twenty-three years later, another group of 29th Division soldiers found themselves at war, once again with German soldiers, and once again in France. Serving as part of the great cross-channel attack 6 June 1944, the Blue and Gray clawed their way ashore while suffering heavy casualties. This new generation of the 29th soon learned what their fathers already knew; freeing French soil came with a steep price tag. By the closing days of the war, the 29th was deep in the heart of Nazi Germany, providing care to thousands of displaced persons and linking up with the Russian Army on the Elbe River.

The final resting place of Major General Sheppard Crump in Hollywood Cemetery, Richmond, Virginia. Crump had served in the First World War and succeeded Gardner Waller as the Adjutant General of Virginia in 1955.

Approximately fifty yards from Crump's resting place is the grave of his contemporary, John Abrams Cutchins. Cutchins, like Crump, had a long military career and was associated with the 29th Division for many years.

Another marker for Crump near his family monument. Coincidentally, also buried in Hollywood cemetery are Jefferson Davis, George Pickett, Jeb Stuart, and two U.S. Presidents: John Tyler and James Monroe.

A Sherman tank recovered off the coast of Normandy and placed on display in the Pont-en-Bessin Underwater Wreck Museum.

A view from Margraten Cemetery in the Netherlands, capturing the shadows from the headstones in formation. *Courtesy Major General (ret) Ken Bowra.*

With the end of the Second World War, the 29th returned home and quietly protected their share of the American homeland while continuing to serve the citizens of their states during natural disasters and civil disturbances. The reemergence of the National Guard in the mid-1980s as a key part of the nation's military strategy was once again led by the 29th as it was re-configured into one of the premier "Light" divisions.

A U.S. Army M-3 Stuart light tank recovered from the water off the invasion beaches on display in Pont-en-Bessin, France.

Flag of the 111th Field Artillery with the "Beaches of Normandy" battle streamer.

Mr. Pete Myer, a member of Company "F", 116th Infantry, landed in first wave on Dog Red 6 June 1944. He made it to the shore and managed to fire his rifle approximately 18 times before he was seriously wounded by German artillery. He lay on the beach almost two days before a fellow soldier used a group of German prisoners to carry him to an aid station for evacuation to England, where he spent six months in a hospital.

Mr. William "Bill" Akers (standing) and Mr. Allen Moorefield at a Veterans Appreciation Dinner. Akers served in Battery "B," 111th Field Artillery, and was a member of the only 105mm Howitzer team of the 111th to get their gun ashore on D-Day. He was later severely wounded near Aachen and spent three years in a hospital. Moorefield served as a cook in Company "F", 116th Infantry, and recalls landing late on D-Day due to beach congestion.

The headstone for Colonel Ollie W. Reed, commander of the 175th Infantry Regiment. Reed was killed in action near the Villebaudon crossroads in Normandy 30 July 1944.

Standing next to his father's marker in the Normandy American Cemetery is the headstone for Lieutenant Ollie W. Reed II, killed in action in Italy 6 July 1944.

Operation Desert Shield/Desert Storm in 1990-91 ended before the division was called upon to add its famous Blue and Gray symbol to the other legendary Army and Marine divisions in the Saudi Arabian desert. Yet, still the 29th trained and prepared itself for any and all national, state, or local missions. Ironically, when the whistle blew for the 29th to mount up for another overseas mission, it was in the Balkans—the same place where the First World War had started. This time, the units of the 29th drew a different kind of mission. Instead of assaulting beaches or firing massive artillery barrages, the soldiers of the 29th returned to Europe, for the third time in the twentieth century, to protect innocent citizens from being slaughtered by raiding bands of militia; ruthless marauders who were not so very different than Villa's border raiders of 1916. Working with soldiers from other nations, the soldiers of the 29th carried out their difficult mission while serving in cities, towns, and countries they would not have been able to locate on a map just a few years earlier.

Sadly, it was while the 29th was in the process of sending more soldiers to Bosnia—in fact the advance parties were already there—when America was attacked 11 September 2001. While the global war on terror lies beyond the scope of this work, it is important to recognize the bravery and sacrifices of the soldiers of the 29th Infantry Division and the other Maryland and Virginia National Guard units that have served in Kuwait, Iraq, and Afghanistan. They have carried the legacy of selfless service into the deserts and mountains of Southwest Asia and continue today.

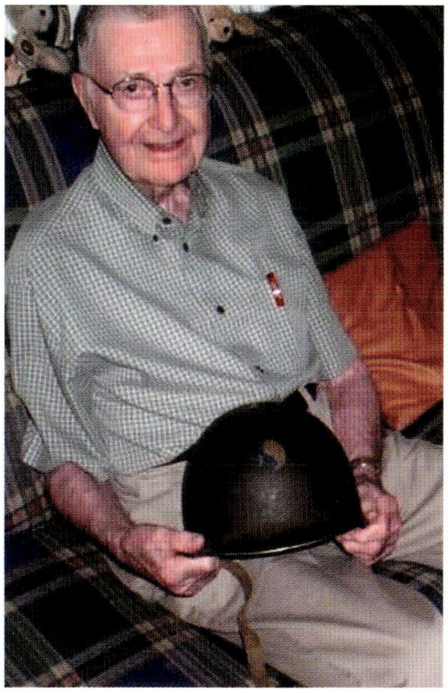

George Davis, a D-Day vet and forward observer in the 115th Infantry Regiment, poses with his 29th Infantry Division helmet. He landed near St. Laurent around 10 a.m. on the morning of 6 June 1944. Courtesy Steve *Klima.*

The Margraten Cemetery headstone for Anthony J. Woronecki, a soldier of the 115th Infantry Regiment. *Courtesy Major General (ret) Ken Bowra.*

A quiet stretch of Maryland highway, just south of Gettysburg, Pennsylvania, is dedicated in honor of the 115th Infantry Regiment.

Mr. Richard D. Inge (left) and Mr. John M. Harris, both of Company "G", 116th Infantry, pose for a picture. One of Inqe's earliest actions after reaching the beach on D-Day was to throw away the dynamite charges he was carrying in his assault vest because he was convinced they would blow up and take him with them.

This chapter has presented representative pictures and images of monuments, tributes, statues, and resting places of some of the soldiers of the 29th who served in this great division. There are also a few pictures of some of the soldiers of the 29th whose words and deeds have been documented in this work. Though we can never thank them enough for what they accomplished, this book has been our honest attempt. "Greet Them Ever With Grateful Hearts." Two Nine Let's Go!

Headstone for Hilary Wachtel, a 29th Infantry Division veteran buried in the Pioneer Rest/Calvary Cemetery in Two Rivers, Wisconsin. *Courtesy Scot Stevens.*

Resting place of Private Merlin W. Way. Way was killed in action during the fighting to clean out the last three German outposts on the west side of the Roer River in December 1944. *Courtesy Major General (ret) Ken Bowra.*

Program for the July 15, 2006, reunion of Company M, 11th Infantry Regiment.

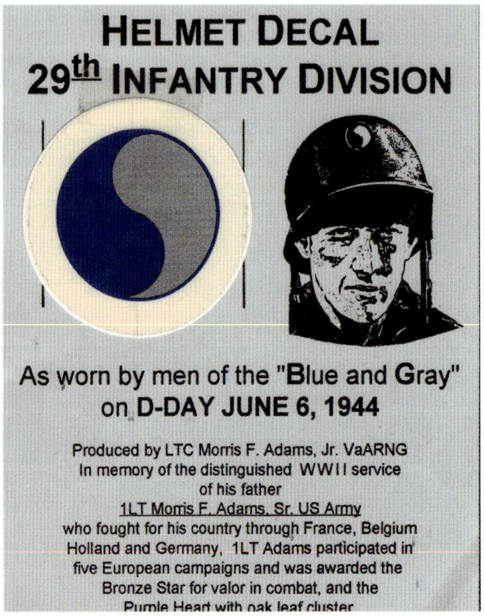

A tribute created for Morris F. Adams, Sr., a 29th Infantry Division veteran, by his son Morris F. Adams, Jr. *Courtesy BG (VA-ret) Morris F. Adams.*

Headstone for 1st Lieutenant Verne V. Morse, 116th Infantry Regiment, at the Margraten American Military Cemetery in the Netherlands. *Courtesy Major General (ret) Ken Bowra.*

Memento of a close call; this helmet was brought back to the States after the war by a 29th veteran and kept as a souvenir. The shrapnel that struck the helmet tore through the netting and ripped open a hole in the steel shell, but only scratched the inner liner.

The Grosvenor Square, London, statue of General Dwight D. Eisenhower, Supreme Commander of the Allied Forces in Europe and later the 34th President of the United States. It was his decision to land the troops in Normandy 6 June 1944. *Courtesy Adam Cogley.*

The resting place for James C. Thomas, who was killed in action the same day that the 29th captured the Citadel in Julich, Germany. *Courtesy Major General (ret) Ken Bowra.*

Carved into the base of Ike's statue in London are the first words from his 6 June 1944 Order of the Day. *Courtesy Adam Cogley.*

A stunningly detailed photograph of a sculpture from the National D-Day Memorial in Bedford, Virginia, that portrays the struggle of a 29th Infantry Division soldier to reach the shore while helping a wounded comrade. *Courtesy Library of Congress.*

A modest marker on State Highway Route 29, near Warrenton, Virginia, informs all passersby that this highway is dedicated to the soldiers of the 29th. The American flag and the yellow ribbon serve as a daily reminder that there are still U.S. troops serving overseas in harm's way.

APPENDIX A

29th Division Medal of Honor Recipients

Regan, Patrick J. Rank: Second Lieutenant
Unit: Company "H", 115th Infantry, 29th Division
Born: Middleboro, Massachusetts
Action: Bois-de-Consenvoye, France, 8 October 1918
Citation:
While leading his platoon against a strong enemy machine gun nest which had held up the advance of 2 companies, 2d Lt. Regan divided his men into 3 groups, sending 1 group to either flank, and he himself attacking with an automatic rifle team from the front. Two of the team were killed outright, while 2d Lt. Regan and the third man were seriously wounded, the latter unable to advance. Although severely wounded, 2d Lt. Regan dashed with empty pistol into the machine gun nest, capturing 30 Austrian gunners and 4 machine guns. This gallant deed permitted the companies to advance, avoiding a terrific enemy fire. Despite his wounds, he continued to lead his platoon forward until ordered to the rear by his commanding officer.

Costin, Henry Gilbert Rank: Private
Unit: Company "H", 115th Infantry, 29th Division
Born: Baltimore, Maryland
Action: Near Bois-de-Consenvoye, France, 8 October 1918
Citation:
When the advance of his platoon had been held up by machine gun fire and a request was made for an automatic rifle team to charge the nest, Pvt. Costin was the first to volunteer. Advancing with his team, under terrific fire of enemy artillery, machine guns, and trench mortars, he continued after all his comrades had become casualties and he himself had been seriously wounded. He operated his rifle until he collapsed. His act resulted in the capture of about 100 prisoners and several machine guns. He succumbed from the effects of his wounds shortly after the accomplishment of his heroic deed.

Gregory, Earl Davis Rank: Sergeant
Unit: Headquarters Company, 116th Infantry, 29th Division
Born: Chase City, Virginia
Action: At Bois-de-Consenvoye, north of Verdun, France, 8 October 1918
Citation:
With the remark "I will get them," Sgt. Gregory seized a rifle and a trench-mortar shell, which he used as a hand grenade, left his detachment of the trench-mortar platoon, and advancing ahead of the infantry, captured a machine gun and 3 of the enemy. Advancing still farther from the machine gun nest, he captured a 7.5-centimeter mountain howitzer and, entering a dugout in the immediate vicinity, single-handedly captured 19 of the enemy.

Peregory, Frank D. Rank: Technical Sergeant
Unit: Company "K", 116th Infantry, 29th Infantry Division
Born: Esmont, Virginia
Action: Grandcamp, France, 8 June 1944
Citation:
On 8 June 1944, the 3d Battalion of the 116th Infantry was advancing on the strongly held German defenses at Grandcamp, France, when the leading elements were suddenly halted by decimating machine gun fire from a firmly entrenched enemy force on the high ground overlooking the town. After numerous attempts to neutralize the enemy position by supporting artillery and tank fire had proved ineffective, T/Sgt. Peregory, on his own initiative, advanced up the hill under withering fire, and worked his way to the crest where he discovered an entrenchment leading to the main enemy fortifications 200 yards away. Without hesitating, he leaped into the trench and moved toward the emplacement. Encountering a squad of enemy riflemen, he fearlessly attacked them with hand grenades and bayonet, killed 8 and forced 3 to surrender. Continuing along the trench, he single-handedly forced the surrender of 32 more riflemen, captured the machine gunners, and opened the way for the leading elements of the battalion to advance and secure its objective. The extraordinary gallantry and aggressiveness displayed by T/Sgt. Peregory are exemplary of the highest tradition of the armed forces.

Hallman, Sherwood H. Rank: Staff Sergeant
Unit: Company "F", 175th Infantry, 29th Infantry Division
Born: Spring City, Pennsylvania
Action: Brest, Brittany, France, 13 September 1944
Citation:
For conspicuous gallantry and intrepidity at risk of his life above and beyond the call of duty. On 13 September 1944, in Brittany, France, the 2d Battalion in its attack on the fortified city of Brest was held up by a strongly defended enemy position which had prevented its advance despite repeated attacks extending over a 3-day period. Finally, Company F advanced to within several hundred yards of the enemy position but was again halted by intense fire. Realizing that the position must be neutralized without delay, S/Sgt.

Hallman ordered his squad to cover his movements with fire while he advanced alone to a point from which he could make the assault. Without hesitating, S/Sgt. Hallman leaped over a hedgerow into a sunken road, the central point of the German defenses which was known to contain an enemy machine gun position and at least 30 enemy riflemen. Firing his carbine and hurling grenades, S/Sgt. Hallman, unassisted, killed or wounded 4 of the enemy, then ordered the remainder to surrender. Immediately, 12 of the enemy surrendered and the position was shortly secured by the remainder of his company. Seeing the surrender of this position, about 75 of the enemy in the vicinity surrendered, yielding a defensive organization which the battalion with heavy supporting fires had been unable to take. This single heroic act on the part of S/Sgt. Hallman resulted in the immediate advance of the entire battalion for a distance of 2,000 yards to a position from which Fort Keranroux was captured later the same day. S/Sgt. Hallman's fighting determination and intrepidity in battle exemplify the highest tradition of the U.S. Armed Forces.

(Note: the information for "Appendix A: Medal of Honor Recipients," is provided courtesy of the National Guard Educational Foundation and the Congressional Medal of Honor Society.)

APPENDIX B

Commanders of the 29th Infantry Division

Charles G. Morton	25 Aug 1917	to	20 Apr 1919
Anton Stephen	26 Apr 1920	to	13 Apr 1934
Milton A. Reckord	14 Apr 1934	to	28 Dec 1941
Leonard T. Gerow	29 Dec 1941	to	22 Jul 1943
Charles H. Gerhardt	23 Jul 1943	to	19 Jan 1946
William H. Sands	2 Jul 1946	to	30 May 1954
Henry C. Evans	1 Jun 1954	to	30 Sep 1957
William C. Purnel	1 Oct 1957	to	19 Nov 1962
William J. Witte	20 Nov 1962	to	15 Sep 1964
Archibald A. Sproul	16 Sep 1964	to	15 Jan 1968
James A. Baber	2 Feb 1985	to	6 Dec 1987
Boyd M. Cook	7 Dec 1987	to	3 Dec 1989
Thomas T. Thompson	4 Dec 1989	to	5 Dec 1992
Joseph H. Langley	6 Dec 1992	to	31 Jul 1996
Carroll E. Childers	1 Aug 1996	to	1 Jul 1999
H. Steven Blum	1 Aug 1999	to	31 Jul 2002
Daniel E. Long	1 Aug 2002	to	31 Aug 2004
Arthur H. Wyman	1 Sep 2004	to	9 Sep 2007
Grant L. Hayden	10 Sep 2007	to	4 Jan 2010
Frank E. Batts	5 Jan 2010	to	6 Oct 2012
Charles W. Whittington	7 Oct 2012	to	Present

Endnotes

Foreword

1. Hylton, Renee, *Citizen Soldiers: An Illustrated History of the Army National Guard*. National Guard Bureau, Historical Services Division, Office of Public Affairs: Washington D.C., 1994. pp. 7-16.

Chapter One Notes

1. Harris, Stephen L., *Duffy's War*. Dulles, VA: Potomac Books, 2006. pp. 19-29.
2. Musicant, Ivan, *The Banana Wars*. New York, NY: MacMillan Publishing Company, 1990. pp. 157-284.
3. Mason, Herbert Malloy, Jr., *The Great Pursuit*. New York, NY: Random House, 1970. pp 76-99; Miller, Roger G., *Wings and Wheels* in Air Power History, Air Force Historical Foundation, Winter 1995. pp. 18-20.
4. Miller, Roger G., *Wings and Wheels* in Air Power History, Air Force Historical Foundation, Winter 1995. p. 15.
5. Stubbs, Mary Lee and Stanley Russell Connor, U.S. Department of the Army, *Army Lineage Series Armor-Cavalry Part I: Regular Army and Army Reserve*, Office Of The Chief Of Military History, United States Army, Washington, D.C., 1969. p. 35.
6. Mead, Gary, *The Doughboys; America And the First World War*. Woodstock, NY: Overlook Press, 2000. pp. 117-118.
7. Seal, Henry F. Jr., *History of the 111th Field Artillery Regiment 29th Infantry Division 1917-1919*, Richmond, VA: Private publishing by the Virginia Army National Guard, 1953 p. 44.
8. Cutchins, John A., *A Famous Command: The Richmond Light Infantry Blues*. Richmond, VA: Garrett and Massie Publishers, 1934. pp. 223-233.
9. Mason, Herbert Malloy, Jr., *The Great Pursuit*. New York, NY: Random House, 1970. pp. 183-212.
10. Ibid, pp 185-187.
11. Mead, Gary, *The Doughboys; America And the First World War*. Woodstock, NY: Overlook Press, 2000. p. 65.
12. Reynolds, Chaplain F.C. and Chaplain William F. McLaughlin, *115th Infantry U.S.A. in the World War*, Baltimore, MD: The Read-Taylor Company, 1920 p. 17.
13. *ibid*, p. 17

Chapter Two Notes

1. American Legion. Source Records of the Great War Volume VII. Edited by Charles H. Horne. Indianapolis IN: The American Legion, 1931. p. 9.
2. Wilson, John B., *Armies, Corps, Divisions and Separate Brigades. Army Lineage Series*, Center of Military History, United States Army, Washington D.C. 1993. pp. 52-73.
3. Stallings, Laurence T., *The Doughboys; The Story of the AEF 1917-1918*. New York, NY: Harper and Row, 1963. p. 33.
4. U.S. Department of the Army, *American Military History Vol I.* Richard W. Stewart, Chief Editor, Army Historical Series. Washington D.C., 2005. p. 15.
5. Harris, Stephen L., *Duffy's War*. Dulles, VA: Potomac Books, 2006. pp. 52-53.
6. Ibid, pp. 55-68.
7. Cutchins, John A., *History of the Twenty-Ninth Division "Blue and Gray" 1917-1919*, Philadelphia, PA: McCalla and Company, 1921 pp. 12-15.
8. American Legion. Source Records of the Great War Volume VII. Edited by Charles H. Horne. Indianapolis IN: The American Legion, 1931. p. 30.
9. Cutchins, John A., *History of the Twenty-Ninth Division "Blue and Gray" 1917-1919*, Philadelphia, PA: McCalla and Company, 1921 p. 16.
10. Ibid, p. 29.
11. Harris, Stephen L., *Duffy's War*. Dulles, VA: Potomac Books, 2006. pp. 121-122.
12. Cutchins, John A., *History of the Twenty-Ninth Division "Blue and Gray" 1917-1919*, Philadelphia, PA: McCalla and Company, 1921 p. 28.
13. Ibid, p. 40.
14. Reynolds, Chaplain F.C. and Chaplain William F. McLaughlin, *115th Infantry U.S.A. in the World War*, Baltimore, MD: The Read-Taylor Company, 1920 p. 23.
15. Cutchins, John A., *History of the Twenty-Ninth Division "Blue and Gray" 1917-1919*, Philadelphia, PA: McCalla and Company, 1921 p. 43.
16. Coffman, F. Wilmer, *Rockingham County in the World War*. Bridgewater, VA: Old Dominion Label Co, 1931. pp. 1-11.

Chapter Three Notes

1. Cutchins, John A., *History of the Twenty-Ninth Division "Blue and Gray" 1917-1919*, Philadelphia, PA: McCalla and Company, 1921. pp. 72-73.
2. Cutchins, John A., *History of the Twenty-Ninth Division "Blue and Gray" 1917-1919*, Philadelphia, PA: McCalla and Company, 1921 p. 67.; Reynolds, Chaplain F.C. and Chaplain William F. McLaughlin, *115th Infantry U.S.A. in the World War*, Baltimore, MD: The Read-Taylor Company, 1920. pp. 63-67.
3. Seal, Henry F. Jr., *History of the 116th U.S. Infantry regiment 29th Infantry Division 1917-1919*, Richmond, VA: Private publishing by the Virginia Army National Guard, 1953. p. 17.
4. Reynolds, Chaplain F.C. and Chaplain William F. McLaughlin, *115th Infantry U.S.A. in the World War*, Baltimore, MD: The Read-Taylor Company, 1920 p. 70. Of significant interest; this was the last successful voyage of the *Covington* as she was sunk by a German submarine on her return voyage to the United States.
5. Cutchins, John A., *History of the Twenty-Ninth Division "Blue and Gray" 1917-1919*, Philadelphia, PA: McCalla and Company, 1921 p. 73.
6. U.S. Department of the Army, Historical Division, *United States Army in the World War 1917-1919, Reports of the Commander-In-Chief, A.E.F, Staff Sections and Services, Volume 12*. Washington D.C., 1948 p. 173.

7. Koehn, Robert, Collection of Letters 1918-1919. Private collection.
8. U.S. Department of the Army, *Medical Department of the United States Army in the World War, Volume II Administration American Expeditionary Forces*. Colonel Joseph H. Ford M.C, Government Printing Office, 1927.pp. 462-468.
9. Farwell, Byron, *Over There; The United States in the Great War 1917-1918*. New York, NY: W.W. Norton and Company, 1999. p. 233.
10. Cutchins, John A., *History of the Twenty-Ninth Division "Blue and Gray" 1917-1919*, Philadelphia, PA: McCalla and Company, 1921 pp. 239-244.
11. U.S. Department of the Army, Historical Division, *United States Army in the World War 1917-1919, Volume 9. Military Operations of the American Expeditionary Forces*. Washington D.C., 1948. p. 81.
12. Cutchins, John A., *An Amateur Diplomat in the World War*. Richmond, VA: The Commanders Committee, The American Legion, 1938. p. 58.
13. U.S. Department of the Army, Historical Division, *United States Army in the World War 1917-1919, Reports of the Commander-In-Chief, A.E.F, Staff Sections and Services, Volume 12*. Washington D.C., 1948. p. 291.
14.Cutchins, John A., *History of the Twenty-Ninth Division "Blue and Gray" 1917-1919*, Philadelphia, PA: McCalla and Company, 1921. p. 85.
15. Ibid, p. 76.
16. Ibid, p. 94.
17. Cutchins, John A., *History of the Twenty-Ninth Division "Blue and Gray" 1917-1919*, Philadelphia, PA: McCalla and Company, 1921 pp. 101-103. and Reynolds, Chaplain F.C. and Chaplain William F. McLaughlin, *115th Infantry U.S.A. in the World War*, Baltimore, MD: The Read-Taylor Company, 1920. pp. 93-95.
18. Cutchins, John A., *An Amateur Diplomat in the World War*. Richmond, VA: The Commanders Committee, The American Legion, 1938. p. 68.
19. Ibid, p. 72.
20. Marshall, George C., *Education of a General 1880-1939*. New York: The Viking Press, 1963. pp. 173-74.
21. Cutchins, John A., *History of the Twenty-Ninth Division "Blue and Gray" 1917-1919*, Philadelphia, PA: McCalla and Company, 1921. pp. 108-113.
22. Ibid, p. 120.
23. Ibid, p. 124.
24. U.S. Department of the Army, Center of Military History, *American Armies and Battlefields in Europe*. Washington D.C.: Government Printing Office, 1995. p. 515.
25. Commanding General 88th Division. *The 88th Division in the World War of 1914-1918*, New York, NY: Wynkoop Hallenbeck Crawford, 1919. p. 41.
26. MacDonald, Charles B., American Military History; *Army Historical Series*. Office of the Chief of Military History, United States Army, Washington D.C. 1989. p. 400.
27. U.S. Department of the Army, Historical Division, *United States Army in the World War 1917-1919, Reports of the Commander-In-Chief, A.E.F, Staff Sections and Services, Volume 12*. Washington D.C., 1948 p. 15.
28. Pershing, General John J. U.S.A. Commander in-Chief, American Expeditionary Forces, *Report cabled to the Secretary of War, November 30, 1918*. Corrected January 10, 1919.
29. U.S. Department of the Army, Historical Division, *United States Army in the World War 1917-1919, American Occupation of Germany*. Washington D.C.: GPO 1948. p. 418.
30. Cutchins, John A., *An Amateur Diplomat in the World War*. Richmond, VA: The Commanders Committee, The American Legion, 1938. p. 79.
31. Seal, Henry F., Jr., *History of the 116th U.S. Infantry regiment 29th Infantry Division 1917-1919*, Richmond, VA: Private publishing by the Virginia Army National Guard, 1953. p. 100.
32. Reynolds, Chaplain F.C. and Chaplain William F. McLaughlin, *115th Infantry U.S.A. in the World War*, Baltimore, MD: The Read-Taylor Company, 1920 p. 129. And Cutchins, John A., *History of the Twenty-Ninth Division "Blue and Gray" 1917-1919*, Philadelphia, PA: McCalla and Company, 1921. p. 153.
33. Cutchins, John A., *An Amateur Diplomat in the World War*. Richmond, VA: The Commanders Committee, The American Legion, 1938. p. 113.
34. U.S. Department of the Army, Center of Military History, *American Armies and Battlefields in Europe*. Washington D.C.: Government Printing Office, 1995. p. 212.
35. Cutchins, John A., *History of the Twenty-Ninth Division "Blue and Gray" 1917-1919*, Philadelphia, PA: McCalla and Company, 1921. p. 161.
36. Faulkner, Richard S., "The Disappearing Doughboys; The American Expeditionary Forces' Straggler Crisis in the Meuse-Argonne" in *Army History* Spring 2012. pp. 13-17.
37. Cutchins, John A., *An Amateur Diplomat in the World War*. Richmond, VA: The Commanders Committee, The American Legion, 1938. p. 92.
38. U.S. Department of the Army, Historical Division, *United States Army in the World War 1917-1919, American Occupation of Germany*. Washington D.C.: GPO 1948. p. 410.
39. Cutchins, John A., *An Amateur Diplomat in the World War*. Richmond, VA: The Commanders Committee, The American Legion, 1938. p. 97.
40. Stallings, Laurence T., *The Doughboys; The Story of the AEF 1917-1918*. New York, NY: Harper and Row, 1963. p. 225.
41. Cutchins, John A., *An Amateur Diplomat in the World War*. Richmond, VA: The Commanders Committee, The American Legion, 1938. pp. 85-86.
42. U.S. Department of the Army, Quartermaster Corps School, *Operations of the Quartermaster Corps U.S. Army during the World War*, Monograph No 9, Notes on Army, Corps and Division Quartermaster Activities in the American Expeditionary Forces—France. Schuykill Arsenal, Philadelphia Pennsylvania, undated. pp 90-105.
43. Cutchins, John A., *History of the Twenty-Ninth Division "Blue and Gray" 1917-1919*, Philadelphia, PA: McCalla and Company, 1921 p. 181.
44. Seal, Henry F., Jr., *History of the 116th U.S. Infantry regiment 29th Infantry Division 1917 1919*, Richmond, VA: Private publishing by the Virginia Army National Guard, 1953. p. 25.
45. Cutchins, John A., *History of the Twenty-Ninth Division "Blue and Gray" 1917-1919*, Philadelphia, PA: McCalla and Company, 1921. p. 104.
46. Ibid, p. 200.
47. Coffman, F. Wilmer, *Rockingham County in the World War*. Bridgewater, VA: Old Dominion Label Co, 1931. pp 8-21.
48. Seal, Henry F. Jr., *History of the 116th U.S. Infantry regiment 29th Infantry Division 1917-1919*. Richmond, VA: Private publishing by the Virginia Army National Guard, 1953. p. 121.
49. Cutchins, John A., *History of the Twenty-Ninth Division "Blue and Gray" 1917-1919*, Philadelphia, PA: McCalla and Company, 1921. p. 205.
50. Cutchins, John A., *An Amateur Diplomat in the World War*. Richmond, VA: The Commanders Committee, The American Legion, 1938. p. 108.
51. Ibid, p. 111.

52. Ibid, p. 111.
53. Pershing, General John J. U.S.A. Commander in-Chief, American Expeditionary Forces, *Report cabled to the Secretary of War, November 30, 1918.* Corrected January 10, 1919.
54. U.S. Department of the Army, Historical Division, *United States Army in the World War 1917-1919, Reports of the Commander-In-Chief, A.E.F, Staff Sections and Services, Volume 12.* Washington D.C., 1948. p. 51.
55. U.S. Department of the Army, Historical Division, *United States Army in the World War 1917-1919, American Occupation of Germany.* Washington D.C.: GPO 1948. p. 432.
56. Stallings, Laurence T., *The Doughboys; The Story of the AEF 1917-1918.* New York, NY: Harper and Row, 1963. p. 374.
57. U.S. Department of the Army, Historical Division, *United States Army in the World War 1917-1919, American Occupation of Germany.* Washington D.C.: GPO 1948. p. 475.
58. Stallings, Laurence T., *The Doughboys; The Story of the AEF 1917-1918.* New York, NY: Harper and Row, 1963. p. 374.

Chapter Four Notes

1. Cutchins, John A., *History of the Twenty-Ninth Division "Blue and Gray" 1917-1919*, Philadelphia, PA: McCalla and Company, 1921. p. 242.
2. Ibid, p. 119.
3. Ibid, p. 247.
4. Ibid, p. 248.
5. Cutchins, John A., *History of the Twenty-Ninth Division "Blue and Gray" 1917-1919*, Philadelphia, PA: McCalla and Company, 1921. pp. 251-252; Barnes, Alexander F., *In a Strange Land; The American Occupation of Germany 1918-1923.* Atglen, PA: Schiffer, 2011. p. 286.
6. Cutchins, John A., *History of the Twenty-Ninth Division "Blue and Gray" 1917-1919*, Philadelphia, PA: McCalla and Company, 1921. p. 249.
7. Reynolds, Chaplain F.C. and Chaplain William F. McLaughlin, *115th Infantry U.S.A. in the World War*, Baltimore, MD: The Read-Taylor Company, 1920. p. 171-173.
8. Cutchins, John A., *History of the Twenty-Ninth Division "Blue and Gray" 1917-1919*, Philadelphia, PA: McCalla and Company, 1921. pp. 260-261; Barnes, Alexander F., *In a Strange Land; The American Occupation of Germany 1918-1923.* Atglen, PA: Schiffer, 2011. p. 127.
9. Reynolds, Chaplain F.C. and Chaplain William F. McLaughlin, *115th Infantry U.S.A. in the World War*, Baltimore, MD: The Read-Taylor Company, 1920 pp. 180-183.
10. Cutchins, John A., *History of the Twenty-Ninth Division "Blue and Gray" 1917-1919*, Philadelphia, PA: McCalla and Company, 1921. p. 265.
11. Marshall, George C., *Education of a General 1880-1939.* New York: The Viking Press, 1963. pp. 194-195.
12. Reynolds, Chaplain F.C. and Chaplain William F. McLaughlin, *115th Infantry U.S.A. in the World War*, Baltimore, MD: The Read-Taylor Company, 1920. p. 195.

Chapter Five Notes

1. MacDonald, Charles B., *American Military History; Army Historical Series.* Office of the Chief of Military History, United States Army, Washington D.C. 1989. p. 60.
2. Barnes, Alexander F., *In a Strange Land; The American Occupation of Germany 1918-1923.* Atglen, PA: Schiffer, 2011. pp. 200-201.
3. Francillon, Rene J., *The United States Air National Guard*, London: Aerospace Publishing Ltd, 1993. p. 22 and Ball, Ron. Executive Editor, *The Maryland Air National Guard: A Commemorative History, 1921-2000.* Dallas, TX: Taylor Publishing Co, 2000. p. 25.
4. Cutchins, John A., *A Famous Command: The Richmond Light Infantry Blues.* Richmond, VA: Garrett and Massie Publishers, 1934. p. 284.
5. *The Nashua New Hampshire Telegraph*, November 1930.
6. Schultz, Steven Patrick, "*'Carry Me Back To Old Virginny': Virginia and the Bonus March of 1932*" MA Thesis-History Department, University of Richmond, 2008. pp. 1-3.
7. Ibid, p. 37.
8. Ibid, p. 79.
9. Ibid, p. 84.
10. Stubbs, Mary Lee and Stanley Russell Connor, U.S. Department of the Army, *Army Lineage Series Armor-Cavalry Part I: Regular Army and Army Reserve*, Office Of The Chief Of Military History, United States Army, Washington, D.C., 1969. p. 50.

Chapter Six Notes

1. Cooper, John P., Jr., *The History of the 110th Field Artillery with Sketches of Related Units.* Baltimore, MD: War Records Division, Maryland Historical Society, 1953. p.43.
2. Greenfield, Kent Roberts, Robert R. Palmer, and Bell I. Wiley, *United States Army in World War II, The Army Ground Forces: The Organization of Combat Ground Troops.* WASHINGTON, D.C.: Center Of Military History, United States Army, (First printed in 1947) 1987. p. 191.
3. MacDonald, Charles B., *American Military History; Army Historical Series.* Office of the Chief of Military History, United States Army, Washington D.C. 1989. p. 68.
4. Cawthon, Charles R., *Other Clay. A Remembrance of the World War II Infantry.* Niwot, CO: University Press of Columbia, 1990. p. 4.
5. McGeorge, Stephen Chute, *Joining Battle: Mobilization, Training and Leadership of the 29th U.S. Infantry Division February, 1941—September, 1944.* Master's Thesis, Department of History and Faculty of the Graduate School, University of Kansas, 1994. pp. 20-22.
6. Stafford Soldiers And The Virginia Reserve Militia (VRM) website.
7. Cole, Merle T., *The Special Military Police at Morgantown Bridge, 1942-1943* in *Military Affairs*, Volume 52, No 1. Published by the Department of History, Kansas State University for the American Military Institute, January 1988. pp. 18-22.
8. McGeorge, Stephen Chute, *Joining Battle: Mobilization, Training and Leadership of the 29th U.S. Infantry Division February, 1941—September, 1944.* Master's Thesis, Department of History and Faculty of the Graduate School, University of Kansas, 1994. p. 27.
9. Ibid, p. 28.
10. Cooper, John P., Jr., *The History of the 110th Field Artillery with Sketches of Related Units.* Baltimore, MD: War Records Division, Maryland Historical Society, 1953. p. 50.
11. Ibid, pp. 42-43, 85.
12. McGeorge, Stephen Chute, *Joining Battle: Mobilization, Training and Leadership of the 29th U.S. Infantry Division February, 1941—September, 1944.* Master's Thesis, Department of History and Faculty of the Graduate School, University of Kansas, 1994. pp. 36-49.
13. Ewing, Joseph H., *29 Let's Go.* Washington D.C.: Infantry Journal Press, 1947. p. 13.

Chapter Seven Notes

1. Inge, Richard D., Oral history and Interview in Farmville, Virginia, 2006.
2. McGeorge, Stephen Chute, *Joining Battle: Mobilization, Training and Leadership of the 29th U.S. Infantry Division February, 1941—September, 1944.* Master's Thesis, Department of History and Faculty of the Graduate School, University of Kansas, 1994. p.62.

3. Fritz, Wilber M., Personal reminiscences of service in the 29th Infantry Division provided by his daughter Teena Gordon (Fritz recollection)

4. For more details on the 29th Ranger Battalion, see "Fighting With the Filthy Thirteen, The World War II Story of Jack Womer, Ranger and Paratrooper (Jack Womer, Stephen C. DeVito)", Jack Womer is truly an American hero and his service in both the 29th Infantry Division and 101st Airborne Division makes him uniquely qualified to comment on both organizations.

5. Gerow was born in Petersburg, Virginia, and attended the Virginia Military Institute. When he replaced Reckord as 29th Division Commander, both of these factors made him a more acceptable choice to the National Guard hierarchy, which still had some animosity about Pershing's replacement of Guard officers with regular Army officers in the First World War.

6. Cooper, John P., Jr., The History of the 110th Field Artillery with Sketches of Related Units. Baltimore, MD: War Records Division, Maryland Historical Society, 1953. p. 73.

7. McGeorge, Stephen Chute, *Joining Battle: Mobilization, Training and Leadership of the 29th U.S. Infantry Division February, 1941—September, 1944*. Master's Thesis, Department of History and Faculty of the Graduate School, University of Kansas, 1994.p.92.

8. Ewing, Joseph H., *29 Let's Go*. Washington D.C.: Infantry Journal Press, 1947. p. 22.

9. McGeorge, Stephen Chute, *Joining Battle: Mobilization, Training and Leadership of the 29th U.S. Infantry Division February, 1941—September, 1944*. Master's Thesis, Department of History and Faculty of the Graduate School, University of Kansas, 1994.p. 111.

10. Ewing, Joseph H., *29 Let's Go*. Washington D.C.: Infantry Journal Press, 1947. p. 23.

11. Ibid.,p. 34.

12. Womer, Jack and Steven DeVito, *Fighting with the Filthy Thirteen*. Havertown, PA: Casemate Publishers, 2012. And Killblane, Richard and Jake McNiece, *The Filthy Thirteen*. Havertown, PA: Casemate Publishers, 2003.

13. Ryan, Cornelius, *The Longest Day*. New York, NY: Crest (Fourth Printing), 1962. p. 82.

14. Koon, Lewis, Personal Reminiscences of D-Day. Provided by Penny Koon Santilli. (Koon oral history)

15. Ewing, Joseph H., *29 Let's Go*. Washington D.C.: Infantry Journal Press, 1947. P. 37; Ryan, Cornelius, *The Longest Day*. New York, NY: Crest (Fourth Printing), 1962. p. 157.

16. Ewing, Joseph H., *29 Let's Go*. Washington D.C.: Infantry Journal Press, 1947. p. 39.

17. Ibid, p. 40.

18. Cawthon, Charles R., *Other Clay. A Remembrance of the World War II Infantry*. Niwot, CO: University Press of Columbia, 1990 pp. 51-58.

19. Ibid, p. 55.

20. Slaughter, John Robert, *Omaha Beach & Beyond: The Long March of Sgt. Bob Slaughter*. Minneapolis, MN: Zenith Press, 2009. p. 113.

21. Akers, William "Bill", Personal reminiscences of Battery "B" and the D-Day landing during April 2006 Veteran's Appreciation dinner in South Boston, Virginia.

22. Inge, Richard. Oral history and Interview in Farmville, Virginia, 2006.

23. Fritz, Wilber M., Personal reminiscences of service in the 29th Infantry Division provided by his daughter Teena Gordon.

24. Cooper, John P., Jr., The History of the 110th Field Artillery with Sketches of Related Units. Baltimore, MD: War Records Division, Maryland Historical Society, 1953. pp.91-92.

25. Ibid, pp.93-94.

26. Haines, Don, "Bedford's Valiant Boys." In *WWII History Magazine*. Published by Sovereign Media in May 2012. p. 78.

27. Cooper, John P., Jr., The History of the 110th Field Artillery with Sketches of Related Units. Baltimore, MD: War Records Division, Maryland Historical Society, 1953. pp.97-98.

28. Ewing, Joseph H., *29 Let's Go*. Washington D.C.: Infantry Journal Press, 1947. p. 65.

29. Ewing, Joseph H., *29 Let's Go*. Washington D.C.: Infantry Journal Press, 1947. pp. 68-70; Cooper, John P. Jr. The History of the 110th Field Artillery with Sketches of Related Units. Baltimore, MD: War Records Division, Maryland Historical Society, 1953. p.104.

30. Ewing, Joseph H., *29 Let's Go*. Washington D.C.: Infantry Journal Press, 1947. p. 80.

31. Ewing, Joseph H., *29 Let's Go*. Washington D.C.: Infantry Journal Press, 1947. P. 81; McGeorge, Stephen Chute, *Joining Battle: Mobilization, Training and Leadership of the 29th U.S. Infantry Division February, 1941—September, 1944*. Master's Thesis, Department of History and Faculty of the Graduate School, University of Kansas, 1994. p.173.

32. Cooper, John P., Jr., The History of the 110th Field Artillery with Sketches of Related Units. Baltimore, MD: War Records Division, Maryland Historical Society, 1953. p. 111.

33. Ewing, Joseph H., *29 Let's Go*. Washington D.C.: Infantry Journal Press, 1947. pp. 304-307.

34. Binkoski, Joseph and Arthur Plaut, *The 115th Infantry Regiment in World War II*. Nashville, TN: The Battery Press, Reprinted 1988. pp. 66-67.

35. Barkley, Cleve C., "Key to the Normandy Breakout." In *WWII History Magazine*. Published by Sovereign Media in March 2012. p. 40.

36. Cooper, John P., Jr., The History of the 110th Field Artillery with Sketches of Related Units. Baltimore, MD: War Records Division, Maryland Historical Society, 1953. p. 115.

37. War Department, *ST-LO (7 July - 19 July 1944)*. CMH Pub 100-13, American Forces in Action Series, Historical Division, Center of Military History, United States Army, Washington, D.C. Facsimile Reprint, 1984, 1994, Original 1 August 1946. pp. 51-70.

38. Ewing, Joseph H., *29 Let's Go*. Washington D.C.: Infantry Journal Press, 1947. pp. 85-87.

39. McGeorge, Stephen Chute, *Joining Battle: Mobilization, Training and Leadership of the 29th U.S. Infantry Division February, 1941—September, 1944*. Master's Thesis, Department of History and Faculty of the Graduate School, University of Kansas, 1994. p. 175.

40. Milton, Giles, *The Boy Who Went to War*. New York, NY: Thomas Dunne Books, St. Martin's Press, 2011.

41. Ulric Rothgeb's Bronze Star citation was provided by his sister-in-law, Gladys B. Rothgeb, on 19 February 2003.

42. Ewing, Joseph H., *29 Let's Go*. Washington D.C.: Infantry Journal Press, 1947. P. 102.

43. Cawthon, Charles R., *Other Clay. A Remembrance of the World War II Infantry*. Niwot, CO: University Press of Columbia, 1990. p. 84.

Chapter Eight Notes

1. Ewing, Joseph H., *29 Let's Go*. Washington D.C.: Infantry Journal Press, 1947. p. 105.

2. Ibid, p. 116.

3. Ibid, p. 306.

4. Ibid, p. 306.

5. Ibid, p. 136.

6. Ibid, p. 143.

7. Cawthon, Charles R., *Other Clay. A Remembrance of the World War II Infantry*. Niwot, CO: University Press of Columbia, 1990. pp. 145-146.

8. Barnes, John J., *Fragments of My Life with Company A, 116th Infantry Regiment*. Holland Patent, NY: Steffen Publishing Company, 2000. p. 92.
9. Ewing, Joseph H., *29 Let's Go*. Washington D.C.: Infantry Journal Press, 1947. p. 149.
10. Barnes, John J., *Fragments of My Life with Company A, 116th Infantry Regiment*. Holland Patent, NY: Steffen Publishing Company, 2000. p. 93.
11. Cawthon, Charles R., *Other Clay. A Remembrance of the World War II Infantry*. Niwot, CO: University Press of Columbia, 1990. p. 151.
12. Smith, John Henry, Sr,, Personal memoirs and oral history of service in the 175th Infantry Regiment provided by his children: Jack, Betsy, and Susan Smith.
13. Barnes, John J., *Fragments of My Life with Company A, 116th Infantry Regiment*. Holland Patent, NY: Steffen Publishing Company, 2000. pp. 98-99.
14. McGeorge, Stephen Chute, *Joining Battle: Mobilization, Training and Leadership of the 29th U.S. Infantry Division February, 1941—September, 1944*. Master's Thesis, Department of History and Faculty of the Graduate School, University of Kansas, 1994. p. 18; Ewing, Joseph H., *29 Let's Go*. Washington D.C.: Infantry Journal Press, 1947. pg 167.
15. Smith, John Henry, Sr, Personal memoirs and oral history of service in the 175th Infantry Regiment provided by his children, Jack, Betsy, and Susan Smith
16. Ewing, Joseph H., *29 Let's Go*. Washington D.C.: Infantry Journal Press, 1947. p. 305.
17. MacDonald, Charles B., *The Siegfried Line Campaign*. U.S. Department of the Army, Center of Military History, Washington D.C.: Government Printing Office, 1984. p. 536.
18. Ewing, Joseph H., *29 Let's Go*. Washington D.C.: Infantry Journal Press, 1947. pp. 188-189 and 305.
19. Ibid, p. 190.
20. Barnes, John J., *Fragments of My Life with Company A, 116th Infantry Regiment*. Holland Patent, NY: Steffen Publishing Company, 2000. p. 111.
21. Ewing, Joseph H., *29 Let's Go*. Washington D.C.: Infantry Journal Press, 1947. pp. 200-201.
22. Barnes, John J., *Fragments of My Life with Company A, 116th Infantry Regiment*. Holland Patent, NY: Steffen Publishing Company, 2000. p. 117.
23. Ibid, pp. 126-128.
24. Ibid, p. 128.
25. Potter, Harold E, *Civil Affairs: Occupation Forces in Europe Series, 1945-46*. (Regraded: Unclassified HQ European Command 11 May 1948) Frankfort-Am-Main, Germany: Office of the Chief Historian, European Command. 1947. p. 29.
26. Barnes, Alexander F., *In a Strange Land; The American Occupation of Germany 1918-1923*. Atglen, PA: Schiffer, 2011. pp. 82-83.
27. Potter, Harold E, *Civil Affairs: Occupation Forces in Europe Series, 1945-46*. (Regraded: Unclassified HQ European Command 11 May 1948) Frankfort-Am-Main, Germany: Office of the Chief Historian, European Command. 1947. pp. 34-35.
28. Ibid, p. 64.
29. Barnes, Alexander F., *In a Strange Land; The American Occupation of Germany 1918-1923*. Atglen, PA: Schiffer, 2011. pp. 169-180, 282-301.
30. Ewing, Joseph H., *29 Let's Go*. Washington D.C.: Infantry Journal Press, 1947. p. 273.
31. Ibid, pp. 272-274.
32. Ibid, p. 304.

Chapter Nine Notes

1. Blair, Clay, *The Forgotten War, America in Korea 1950-1953*. New York, NY: Time Books, 1987. p. 28.
2. Ibid, pp.28-29.
3. Ibid, p. 770.
4. National Guard Units and Strength. Second Army Area. Headquarters Second Army, Fort George G. Meade, April 1951.
5. Blair, Clay, The Forgotten War, America in Korea 1950-1953. New York, NY: Time Books, 1987. pp. 867-868.
6. Cutchins, John A., *History of the Twenty-Ninth Division "Blue and Gray" 1917-1919*, Philadelphia, PA: McCalla and Company, 1921. p. 338.
7. Balkoski, Joseph M., "Hardened in Two World Wars, 29th Infantry Division Faces Bright Future as "Light" Force. Published in the *The Freestate Guardian*. June, 1991.

Chapter Ten Notes

1. Ryan, Cornelius, *The Longest Day*. New York, NY: Crest (Fourth Printing), 1962.

Chapter Eleven Notes

1. The Globalsecurity.org homepage: arng-history-cold-war.htm.
2. The U.S. Army Center of Military History homepage: Department of the Army Historical Summary: FY 1985. *Structuring the Force*. p. 60.
3. Killblane, Richard E., *Manchu Two*. Undated/Unpublished manuscript.

Chapter Twelve Notes

1. Melnyk, Les', Mobilizing for the Storm; The Army National Guard in Operations Desert Shield and Desert Storm. National Guard Bureau Office of Public Affairs, Historical Services Division, 2001. p. 2.
2. Ibid, p. 48.
3. Ibid, p. 53.
4. "Desert Panthers" 4-505 PIR. MFO South Camp, Sinai, Egypt. January-July 1985. Benesh Publishing.
5. Swanson, Michael H., LTC (VaARNG). Personal reminiscences of service with the 29th Infantry Division in Bosnia in 1997. 2012.
6. Calvert, Brian R, "Virginia Infantrymen Return from "Troll Duty" in Bosnia." In *National Guard Magazine*. Published by the National Guard Association of the United States in July 1998, Volume 52, Number 7.
7. Shuey, Theodore G., Jr., *Ever Forward*. Staunton, VA: Lot's Wife Publishing, 2008. pp. 249-269.
8. Mills, John "Cam" Cameron, Personal reminiscences of service with the 29th Infantry Division in Bosnia 2001-2002. 2012
9. Crawford, Brian G, Personal reminiscences of service in the 29th Infantry Division and his two rotations in Bosnia. 2012

Chapter Thirteen Notes

1. Slaughter, John Robert, *Omaha Beach & Beyond: The Long March of Sgt. Bob Slaughter*. Minneapolis, MN: Zenith Press, 2009. p. 113.
2. Ibid, pp. 112-114.
3. Blumenson, Martin, *Breakout And Pursuit*. Center of Military History, United States Army, Washington D.C. 1961. p. 650-652; *Stars & Stripes. "These are My Credentials":The Story of the 8th Infantry Division*. G.I. Stories Series published in Paris, France, 1944-1945 p. 1.
4. *Palm Beach Post* 31 January 1923.
5. McGeorge, Stephen Chute, *Joining Battle: Mobilization, Training and Leadership of the 29th U.S. Infantry Division February, 1941—September, 1944*. Master's Thesis, Department of History and Faculty of the Graduate School, University of Kansas, 1994. pp. 3-5.
6. McGeorge, Major Stephen C., *"Seeing the Battlefield: Brigadier General Norman D. Cota's "Bastard Brigade"* at Omaha Beach". combatleadership.com, U.S. Army.

7. McGeorge, Stephen Chute, *Joining Battle: Mobilization, Training and Leadership of the 29th U.S. Infantry Division February, 1941—September, 1944.* Master's Thesis, Department of History and Faculty of the Graduate School, University of Kansas, 1994. pp. 99-112; Irving, David, *The War Between the Generals.* Focal Point Publications. 2010. p. 148.
8. Miller, Robert A, *Division Commander: A Biography of Major General Norman D. Cota.* Spartanburg, SC: Reprint Company Publishers, 1989. pp. 12-14, 25, 160-161.
9. Cutchins, John A., *History of the Twenty-Ninth Division "Blue and Gray" 1917-1919,* Philadelphia, PA: McCalla and Company, 1921. p. 338.
10. McGeorge, Stephen Chute, *Joining Battle: Mobilization, Training and Leadership of the 29th U.S. Infantry Division February, 1941—September, 1944.* Master's Thesis, Department of History and Faculty of the Graduate School, University of Kansas, 1994. pp 84-86.
11. Ibid, p.92.
12. MacDonald, Charles B., *The Siegfried Line Campaign.* U.S. Department of the Army, Center of Military History, Washington D.C.: Government Printing Office, 1984. p. 537.
13. McGeorge, Stephen Chute, *Joining Battle: Mobilization, Training and Leadership of the 29th U.S. Infantry Division February, 1941—September, 1944.* Master's Thesis, Department of History and Faculty of the Graduate School, University of Kansas, 1994. p. 169; the 29th Infantry Division after action Report
14. McGeorge, Stephen Chute, *Joining Battle: Mobilization, Training and Leadership of the 29th U.S. Infantry Division February, 1941—September, 1944.* Master's Thesis, Department of History and Faculty of the Graduate School, University of Kansas, 1994. pp. 175-186.
15. Ibid, p. 62.
16. Cawthon, Charles R., *Other Clay. A Remembrance of the World War II Infantry.* Niwot, CO: University Press of Columbia, 1990. p. 35.
17. Ewing, Joseph H., *29 Let's Go.* Washington D.C.: Infantry Journal Press, 1947. pp. 96-104.
18. Seal, Henry F. Jr., *History of the 111th Field Artillery Regiment 29th Infantry Division 1917-1919.* Richmond, VA: Private publishing by the Virginia Army National Guard, 1953. p. 44.
19. Ewing, Joseph H., *29 Let's Go.* Washington D.C.: Infantry Journal Press, 1947. p. 18.
20. Binkoski, Joseph and Arthur Plaut, *The 115th Infantry Regiment in World War II.* Nashville, TN: The Battery Press, Reprinted 1988. p. 130.
21. Ewing, Joseph H., *29 Let's Go.* Washington D.C.: Infantry Journal Press, 1947. p. 309.
22. Womer, Jack and Steven DeVito, *Fighting with the Filthy Thirteen.* Havertown, PA: Casemate Publishers, 2012. pp. 107-108.
23. Cutchins, John A., *An Amateur Diplomat in the World War.* Richmond, VA: The Commanders Committee, The American Legion, 1938. pp. 83-103.
24. Cutchins, John A., *History of the Twenty-Ninth Division "Blue and Gray" 1917-1919.* Philadelphia, PA: McCalla and Company, 1921. pp. 144-160.
25. Marshall, George C., *Memoirs of my Service in the World War 1917-1918.* Boston: Houghton Mifflin Company, 1976. p. 204
26. Seal, Henry F., Jr., *History of the 111th Field Artillery Regiment 29th Infantry Division 1917-1919.* Richmond, VA: Private publishing by the Virginia Army National Guard, 1953. p. 53.
27. Ibid, p.53.
28. Cutchins, John A., *History of the Twenty-Ninth Division "Blue and Gray" 1917-1919,* Philadelphia, PA: McCalla and Company, 1921. p. 21.
29. Seal, Henry F. Jr., *History of the 111th Field Artillery Regiment 29th Infantry Division 1917-1919,* Richmond, VA: Private publishing by the Virginia Army National Guard, 1953. p. 54.
30. *New York Times,* 3 June 1921.
31. Cutchins, John A., *History of the Twenty-Ninth Division "Blue and Gray" 1917-1919,* Philadelphia, PA: McCalla and Company, 1921. p. 111.
32. University of Maryland Homepage.
33. Adams, James G., *Review of the American Forces in Germany.* Coblenz, Germany: Adams, 1921. p.172.
34. Ewing, Joseph H., *29 Let's Go.* Washington D.C.: Infantry Journal Press, 1947. p. 110. While there is still some discussion whether Colonel Reed was killed by small arms fire or artillery shells, the ultimate result was the same; a fine officer and even better father, was killed in the service of his country. At time of this publication, a video documentary and book were being produced by Dennis Whitehead entitled "Love and Sacrifice: A Story from the Heart of America." It will cover the lives and tragic sacrifices of the two officers and the lasting effects on their wives and families. "Upon such sacrifices, my Cordelia, The gods themselves throw incense." King Lear Act V, scene iii.
35. Ryan biographical information provided by his son, LTC (ret) James Ryan.
36. Wingfield, Marshall, *A History of Caroline County.* Baltimore, MD: Regional Publishing Company, 1969 reprint. p. 221.
37. Schultz, Steven Patrick, "*'Carry Me Back To Old Virginny': Virginia and the Bonus March of 1932*". MA Thesis-History Department, University of Richmond, 2008. p. 37.

Chapter Fourteen Notes

1. Cooper, John P., Jr., *The History of the 110th Field Artillery with Sketches of Related Units.* Baltimore, MD: War Records Division, Maryland Historical Society, 1953. p. 17.
2. Ibid, p. 20.
3. Cutchins, John A., *History of the Twenty-Ninth Division "Blue and Gray" 1917-1919.* Philadelphia, PA: McCalla and Company, 1921. pp. 253-254.
4. Cooper, John P., Jr., *The History of the 110th Field Artillery with Sketches of Related Units.* Baltimore, MD: War Records Division, Maryland Historical Society, 1953. p 25.
5. Cutchins, John A., *History of the Twenty-Ninth Division "Blue and Gray" 1917-1919.* Philadelphia, PA: McCalla and Company, 1921. pp. 313-315.
6. Farwell, Byron, *Over There; The United States in the Great War 1917-1918.* New York, NY: W.W. Norton and Company, 1999 pp. 136-139.
7. Cutchins, John A., *An Amateur Diplomat in the World War.* Richmond, VA: The Commanders Committee, The American Legion, 1938. pp. 45-46.
8. Ibid, pp. 45-46. NOTE: Kahn died in 1934 but a high speed boat he helped design and pay for would later be the inspiration for the famous German E-Boats of the Second World War.
9. Cutchins, John A., *History of the Twenty-Ninth Division "Blue and Gray" 1917-1919.* Philadelphia, PA: McCalla and Company, 1921. p.107.
10. *The New York Times.* 18 May 1919.
11. *The New York Times,* 21 June 1921.
12. *The Free Lance Star,* Fredericksburg VA, August 1930.
13. Womer, Jack and Steven DeVito, Fighting with the Filthy Thirteen. Havertown, PA: Casemate Publishers, 2012. pp. 48-52.
14. Ibid, p. 76.
15. Ibid, p. 91.
16. McGeorge, Stephen Chute, *Joining Battle: Mobilization, Training and Leadership of the 29th U.S. Infantry Division February, 1941—September, 1944.* Master's Thesis, Department of History and Faculty of the Graduate School, University of Kansas, 1994. p. 65.

17. Gawne, Jonathan, The 29th Ranger Battalion in *The G.I. Journal*, Vol.1 Number 6. Published in Mar/Apr 1997. pp. 9-11.
18. Ewing, Joseph H., *29 Let's Go*. Washington D.C.: Infantry Journal Press, 1947. p. 25; McGeorge, Stephen Chute, *Joining Battle: Mobilization, Training and Leadership of the 29th U.S. Infantry Division February, 1941—September, 1944*. Master's Thesis, Department of History and Faculty of the Graduate School, University of Kansas, 1994. p. 68.
19. Womer, Jack and Steven DeVito, Fighting with the Filthy Thirteen. Havertown, PA: Casemate Publishers, 2012. pp. 109–111.
20. Botting, Douglas, *The Second Front*. Time-Life Books Inc, 1978, pp. 172-181.
21. Slaughter, John Robert, *Omaha Beach & Beyond: The Long March of Sgt. Bob Slaughter*. Minneapolis, MN: Zenith Press, 2009, p. 110.
22. Barnes, John J., *Fragments of My Life with Company A, 116th Infantry Regiment*. Holland Patent, NY: Steffen Publishing Company, 2000, pp. 65-66.
23. Cawthon, Charles R. *Other Clay. A Remembrance of the World War II Infantry*. Niwot, CO: University Press of Columbia, 1990. p. 71.
24. Cooper, John P., Jr., *The History of the 110th Field Artillery with Sketches of Related Units*. Baltimore, MD: War Records Division, Maryland Historical Society, 1953. pp. 146-147.
25. Ewing, Joseph H.,*29 Let's Go*. Washington D.C.: Infantry Journal Press, 1947. pp. 281-283.
26 Binkoski, Joseph and Arthur Plaut, *The 115th Infantry Regiment in World War II*. Nashville, TN: The Battery Press, Reprinted 1988. pp. 276-277.
27. Cooper, John P., Jr., *The History of the 110th Field Artillery with Sketches of Related Units*. Baltimore, MD: War Records Division, Maryland Historical Society, 1953. pp. 206-212.
28. Ewing, Joseph H., *29 Let's Go*. Washington D.C.: Infantry Journal Press, 1947. pp.263-265; Cooper, John P., Jr., *The History of the 110th Field Artillery with Sketches of Related Units*. Baltimore, MD: War Records Division, Maryland Historical Society, 1953. p. 248; *29 Let's Go Newspaper*. 30 June 1945
29. Cooper, John P., Jr., *The History of the 110th Field Artillery with Sketches of Related Units*. Baltimore, MD: War Records Division, Maryland Historical Society, 1953. p. 30.
30. *Stars & Stripes* 19 Feb 1954

Chapter Fifteen Notes

1. U.S. Department of the Army, *The Army Lineage Book, Volume II: Infantry*. Government Printing Office, Washington D.C., 1953. pp. 315-318; Cutchins, John A., *History of the Twenty-Ninth Division "Blue and Gray" 1917-1919*. Philadelphia, PA: McCalla and Company, 1921. p. 13.
2. U.S. Department of the Army, *The Army Lineage Book, Volume II: Infantry*. Government Printing Office, Washington D.C., 1953. pp. 320-321; Cutchins, John A., *History of the Twenty-Ninth Division "Blue and Gray" 1917-1919*. Philadelphia, PA: McCalla and Company, 1921. p. 13.
3. U.S. Department of the Army, *The Army Lineage Book, Volume II: Infantry*. Government Printing Office, Washington D.C., 1953. pp. 326-328; Cutchins, John A., *History of the Twenty-Ninth Division "Blue and Gray" 1917-1919*. Philadelphia, PA: McCalla and Company, 1921. p. 13; The Institute of Heraldry homepage.
4. U.S. Department of the Army, *The Army Lineage Book, Volume II: Infantry*. Government Printing Office, Washington D.C., 1953. pp. 329-331; Cutchins, John A., *History of the Twenty-Ninth Division "Blue and Gray" 1917-1919*. Philadelphia, PA: McCalla and Company, 1921. p. 13; The Institute of Heraldry homepage. These include from the Revolutionary War: Brandywine, Germantown, Monmouth, Charleston, Cowpens, Guilford Court House, Yorktown, Virginia 1775, Virginia 1776, Virginia 1781, South Carolina 1781, North Carolina 1781, and from The War of 1812: Maryland 1814.
5. U.S. Department of the Army, *The Army Lineage Book, Volume II: Infantry*. Government Printing Office, Washington D.C., 1953. pp. 504-508; *29 Let's Go!1917-1965*. n.p. 1965-dated yearbook for the 29th Infantry Division. pp. 60-63; Cutchins, John A., *History of the Twenty-Ninth Division "Blue and Gray" 1917-1919*. Philadelphia, PA: McCalla and Company, 1921. pp. 13-14)
6. U.S. Department of the Army, *The Army Lineage Book, Volume II: Infantry*. Government Printing Office, Washington D.C., 1953. pp. 504-508; Lewis, Arnold M, *A Brief History of the 176th Infantry*. Fort Benning, Georgia, 1943. pp.8-64; The Institute of Heraldry homepage.
7. Cutchins, John A., *A Famous Command: The Richmond Light Infantry Blues*. Richmond, VA: Garrett and Massie Publishers, 1934; *29 Let's Go!1917-1965*. n.p. 1965-dated yearbook for the 29th Infantry Division. pp. 54-57.
8. Cutchins, John A., *History of the Twenty-Ninth Division "Blue and Gray" 1917-1919*. Philadelphia, PA: McCalla and Company, 1921. p. 13; Cooper, John P., Jr., *The History of the 110th Field Artillery with Sketches of Related Units*. Baltimore, MD: War Records Division, Maryland Historical Society, 1953. pp. 42-83.
9. Cutchins, John A., *History of the Twenty-Ninth Division "Blue and Gray" 1917-1919*. Philadelphia, PA: McCalla and Company, 1921. pp. 13-14; *29 Let's Go! 1917-1965*. n.p. 1965-dated yearbook for the 29th Infantry Division. pp. 106-109; The Institute of Heraldry homepage.
10. Cutchins, John A., *History of the Twenty-Ninth Division "Blue and Gray" 1917-1919*. Philadelphia, PA: McCalla and Company, 1921. pp. 13-14; The Institute of Heraldry homepage.
11. Cooper, John P., Jr. *The History of the 110th Field Artillery with Sketches of Related Units*. Baltimore, MD: War Records Division, Maryland Historical Society, 1953. pp. 251-271; The Institute of Heraldry homepage.
12. Cooper, John P., Jr., *The History of the 110th Field Artillery with Sketches of Related Units*. Baltimore, MD: War Records Division, Maryland Historical Society, 1953.pp. 28-32; Sawicki, James A. *Field Artillery Battalions of the US Army, Volume 1*. Dumfries, Va.: Centaur Pubs, 1977. pp. 417 and 682-683.
13. *29 Let's Go!1917-1965*. n.p. 1965-dated yearbook for the 29th Infantry Division. pp. 110-113; The Institute of Heraldry homepage.
14. Cutchins, John A., *History of the Twenty-Ninth Division "Blue and Gray" 1917-1919*. Philadelphia, PA: McCalla and Company, 1921. p. 13; McGeorge, Stephen Chute, *Joining Battle: Mobilization, Training and Leadership of the 29th U.S. Infantry Division February, 1941—September, 1944*. Master's Thesis, Department of History and Faculty of the Graduate School, University of Kansas, 1994. pp. 175-177; The Institute of Heraldry homepage.
15. The Institute of Heraldry homepage.
16. *29 Let's Go! 1917-1965*. n.p. 1965-dated yearbook for the 29th Infantry Division. p.127; The Institute of Heraldry homepage.
17. *29 Let's Go! 1917-1965*. n.p. 1965-dated yearbook for the 29th Infantry Division. pp. 44-45; The Institute of Heraldry homepage.
18. The Institute of Heraldry homepage.
19. The Institute of Heraldry homepage.

Bibliography

Official Documents and Reports:

American Expeditionary Forces, The General Staff, General Headquarters, *Candid Comment on the American Soldier of 1917-1918 and Kindred Topics by the Germans*. Chaumont, France, 1919.

American Legion. *Source Records of the Great War Volume VII.* Edited by Charles H. Horne. Indianapolis IN: The American Legion, 1931.

Blumenson, Martin, *Breakout And Pursuit*. Center of Military History, United States Army, Washington D.C. 1961.

Dornbusch, Charles Emil, *Histories of American Army Units, World War I and II and Korean Conflict, with some earlier Histories*. Washington D.C.: Department of the Army, Office of the Adjutant General, Special Services Division, Library and Service Club Branch, 1956.

Greenfield, Kent Roberts, Robert R. Palmer and Bell I. Wiley, *United States Army in World War II, The Army Ground Forces: The Organization of Combat Ground Troops*. Washington, D.C.: Center Of Military History, United States Army, (First printed in 1947) 1987.

Harrison, Gordon A, *Cross Channel Attack*. Center for Military History, United States Army, Washington D.C. 1951.

Hylton, Renee, *Citizen Soldiers: An Illustrated History of the Army National Guard*. National Guard Bureau, Historical Services Division, Office of Public Affairs: Washington D.C., 1994.

MacDonald, Charles B., *The Siegfried Line Campaign*. U.S. Department of the Army, Center of Military History, Washington D.C.: Government Printing Office, 1984.

MacDonald, Charles B., *American Military History; Army Historical Series*. Office of the Chief of Military History, United States Army, Washington D.C., 1989.

Melnyk, Les', "Mobilizing for the Storm; The Army National Guard in Operations Desert Shield and Desert Storm." National Guard Bureau Office of Public Affairs, Historical Services Division, 2001.

National Guard Units and Strength, Second Army Area, Headquarters Second Army, Fort George G. Meade, April 1951.

Pershing, General John J., U.S.A. Commander in Chief, American Expeditionary Forces, *Report cabled to the Secretary of War, November 30, 1918*. Corrected January 10, 1919.

Potter, Harold E, *Civil Affairs: Occupation Forces in Europe Series, 1945-46*. (Regraded: Unclassified HQ European Command 11 May 1948) Frankfort-Am-Main, Germany: Office of the Chief Historian, European Command. 1947

Stubbs, Mary Lee and Stanley Russell Connor, U.S. Department of the Army, *Army Lineage Series Armor-Cavalry Part I: Regular Army and Army Reserve*, Office Of The Chief Of Military History, United States Army, Washington, D.C., 1969..

The Infantry Journal. *The Soldier's Handbook*. Revised Edition. Richmond, VA: Garrett & Masse, 1940.

29th Division After Action Report, Month of June 1944, dated 23 July 1944, Commanders Narrative, Section I, "Battle Lessons and Conclusions"

U.S. Department of the Army, *American Military History Vol I*. Richard W. Stewart, Chief Editor, Army Historical Series. Washington D.C., 2005.

U.S. Department of the Army, *American Military History Vol II*. Richard W. Stewart, Chief Editor, Army Historical Series. Washington D.C., 2005.

U.S. Department of the Army, *The Army Lineage Book, Volume II: Infantry*. Government Printing Office, Washington D.C., 1953.

U.S. Department of the Army, Center of Military History, *American Armies and Battlefields in Europe*. Washington D.C.: Government Printing Office, 1995.

U.S. Department of the Army, Historical Division, *United States Army in the World War 1917-1919, American Occupation of Germany*. Washington D.C.: GPO 1948.

U.S. Department of the Army, Historical Division, *United States Army in the World War 1917-1919, Volume 9. Military Operations of the American Expeditionary Forces*. Washington D.C., 1948.

U.S. Department of the Army, Historical Division, *United States Army in the World War 1917-1919, Reports of the Commander-In-Chief, A.E.F, Staff Sections and Services, Volume 12*. Washington D.C., 1948.

U.S. Department of the Army *Medical Department of the United States Army in the World War, Volume II Administration American Expeditionary Forces*. Colonel Joseph H. Ford M.C, Government Printing Office, 1927.

U.S. Department of the Army, *The War with Germany, A Statistical Summary*. Compiled by COL Leonard P. Ayres, Government Printing Office, Washington D.C., 1919 (second edition).

U.S. Department of the Army Quartermaster Corps School, *Operations of the Quartermaster Corps U.S. Army during the World War*, Monograph No 9, Notes on Army, Corps and Division Quartermaster Activities in the American Expeditionary Forces—France. Schuykill Arsenal, Philadelphia Pennsylvania, undated.

United States Military Academy, *Alphabetical Locator of Graduates and Former Cadets.*

Wilson, John B., *Armies, Corps, Divisions and Separate Brigades. Army Lineage Series*, Center of Military History, United States Army, Washington D.C. 1993.

Wilson, John B., *Maneuver and Firepower; The Evolution of Divisions and Separate Brigades.* Army Lineage Series, Center of Military History, United States Army, Washington D.C. 1998.

War Department, *ST-LO (7 July - 19 July 1944).* CMH Pub 100-13, American Forces in Action Series, Historical Division, Center of Military History, United States Army, Washington, D.C. Facsimile Reprint, 1984, 1994, Original 1 August 1946_

Other Published Sources:

Adams, James G., *Review of the American Forces in Germany.* Coblenz, Germany: Adams, 1921.

Balkoski, Joseph M., *Omaha Beach: D-Day, June 6, 1944.* Mechanicsburg, PA: Stackpole Books, 2004.

Balkoski, Joseph M., *Beyond the Beachhead: The 29th Infantry Division in Normandy.* Mechanicsburg, PA: Stackpole Books, 2005.

Balkoski, Joseph M., *From Beachhead to Brittany: The 29th Infantry Division at Brest, August-September 1944.* Mechanicsburg, PA: Stackpole Books, 2008.

Balkoski, Joseph M., "Hardened in Two World Wars, 29th Infantry Division Faces Bright Future as "Light" Force." Published in the *The Freestate Guardian.* June, 1991.

Barkley, Cleve C., "Key to the Normandy Breakout." In *WWII History Magazine.* Published by Sovereign Media in March 2012.

Barnes, Alexander F., *In a Strange Land; The American Occupation of Germany 1918-1923.* Atglen, PA: Schiffer, 2011.

Barnes, John J., *Fragments of My Life with Company A, 116th Infantry Regiment.* Holland Patent, NY: Steffen Publishing Company, 2000.

Blair, Clay, *The Forgotten War, America in Korea 1950-1953.* New York, NY: Time Books, 1987.

Botting, Douglas, *The Second Front.* Second World War Series, Time-Life Books Inc, 1978

Calvert, Brian R, "Virginia Infantrymen Return from 'Troll Duty' in Bosnia." In *National Guard Magazine.* Published by the National Guard Association of the United States in July 1998, Volume 52, Number 7.

Cawthon, Charles R., *Other Clay. A Remembrance of the World War II Infantry.* Niwot, CO: University Press of Columbia, 1990.

Coffman, F. Wilmer, *Rockingham County in the World War.* Bridgewater, VA: Old Dominion Label Co, 1931.

Cole, Merle T., "The Special Military Police at Morgantown Bridge, 1942-1943." in *Military Affairs,* Volume 52, No 1. Published by the Department of History, Kansas State University for the American Military Institute, January 1988.

Cutchins, John A., *An Amateur Diplomat in the World War.* Richmond, VA: The Commanders Committee, The American Legion, 1938.

Dalessandro, Robert J. and Michael G. Knapp, *Organization and Insignia of the American Expeditionary Force 1917-1923.* Atglen, PA: Schiffer, 2008.

Dougherty, Leo, *The Battle of the Hedgerow: Bradley's First Army in Normandy, June- July 1944.* St. Paul, MN: MBI Publishing Company, 2001.

Farwell, Byron, *Over There; The United States in the Great War 1917-1918.* New York, NY: W.W. Norton and Company, 1999.

Faulkner, Richard S., "The Disappearing Doughboys; The American Expeditionary Forces' Straggler Crisis in the Meuse-Argonne" in *Army History,* Spring 2012.

Gaujac, Paul, *U.S. Field Artillery in World War II.* Paris, Franc: Histoire Et Collections, 2009.

Gawne, Jonathan, The 29th Ranger Battalion in *The G.I. Journal,* Vol.1 Number 6. published in Mar/Apr 1997.

Haines, Don, "Bedford's Valiant Boys." In *WWII History Magazine.* Published by Sovereign Media in May 2012.

Harris, Stephen L., *Duffy's War.* Dulles, VA: Potomac Books, 2006.

Irving, David, *The War Between the Generals.* Focal Point Publications, 2010.

Johns, Glover S. Jr., *The Clay Pigeons of St. Lo.* Mechanicsburg, PA: Stackpole Books, 2002.

Kershaw, Alex, *The Bedford Boys: One American Town's Ultimate D-Day Sacrifice.* Cambridge, MA: Da Capo Press, 2003.

Killblane, Richard and Jake McNiece, *The Filthy Thirteen.* Havertown, PA: Casemate Publishers, 2003.

Marshall, George C., *Education of a General 1880-1939.* New York: The Viking Press, 1963.

Marshall, George C., *Memoirs of my Service in the World War 1917-1918.* Boston: Houghton Mifflin Company, 1976.

Mason, Herbert Malloy Jr., *The Great Pursuit.* New York, NY: Random House, 1970.

McGeorge, Major Stephen C., "*Seeing the Battlefield: Brigadier General Norman D. Cota's 'Bastard Brigade' at Omaha Beach*". combatleadership.com, U.S. Army

McGeorge, Stephen Chute, "*Joining Battle: Mobilization, Training and Leadership of the 29th U.S. Infantry Division February, 1941—September, 1944.*" Master's Thesis, Department of History and Faculty of the Graduate School, University of Kansas, 1994.

Mead, Gary, *The Doughboys; America And the First World War.* Woodstock, NY: Overlook Press, 2000.

Miller, Robert A, *Division Commander: A Biography of Major General Norman D. Cota.* Spartanburg, SC: Reprint Company Publishers, 1989.

Miller, Roger G., "Wings and Wheels" in *Air Power History*, Air Force Historical Foundation, Winter 1995.

Milton, Giles, *The Boy Who Went to War*. New York, NY: Thomas Dunne Books, St. Martin's Press, 2011.

Mottley, William W, *A Narrow Strip of World War II: D-Day to the Rhine River in Germany*. Farmville, VA Printing, 1990.

Musicant, Ivan, *The Banana Wars*. New York, NY: MacMillan Publishing Company, 1990.

Ryan, Cornelius, *The Longest Day*. New York, NY: Crest (Fourth Printing), 1962.

Sawicki, James A, *Field Artillery Battalions of the US Army, Volume 1*. Dumfries, Va.: Centaur Pubs, 1977.

Schultz, Steven Patrick, *"'Carry Me Back To Old Virginny': Virginia and the Bonus March of 1932"*. MA Thesis-History Department, University of Richmond, 2008.

Shuey, Theodore G. Jr., *Ever Forward*. Staunton, VA: Lot's Wife Publishing, 2008

Slaughter, John Robert, *Omaha Beach & Beyond: The Long March of Sgt. Bob Slaughter*. Minneapolis, MN: Zenith Press, 2009.

Stallings, Laurence T., *The Doughboys; The Story of the AEF 1917-1918*. New York, NY: Harper and Row, 1963.

Wingfield, Marshall, *A History of Caroline County*. Baltimore, MD: Regional Publishing Company, 1969 reprint

Womer, Jack and Steven DeVito, *Fighting with the Filthy Thirteen*. Havertown, PA: Casemate Publishers, 2012.

Newspapers:

The New York Times, 1918-1922.

Star and Stripes, French edition, 1918-1919.

The Palm Beach Post, 1923.

The Free Lance-Star, Fredericksburg VA, August 1930.

The Nashua New Hampshire Telegraph, November 1930.

29 Let's Go! The 29th Infantry Divisions newspaper printed in Bremen, Germany, June 1945.

Unit Histories:

Binkoski, Joseph and Arthur Plaut, *The 115th Infantry Regiment in World War II*. Nashville, TN: The Battery Press, Reprinted 1988.

Commanding General 88th Division. *The 88th Division in the World War of 1914-1918*. New York, NY: Wynkoop Hallenbeck Crawford, 1919.

Cooper, John P., Jr., *The History of the 110th Field Artillery with Sketches of Related Units*. Baltimore, MD: War Records Division, Maryland Historical Society, 1953.

Cutchins, John A., *A Famous Command: The Richmond Light Infantry Blues*. Richmond, VA: Garrett and Massie Publishers, 1934.

Cutchins, John A., *History of the Twenty-Ninth Division "Blue and Gray" 1917-1919*. Philadelphia, PA: McCalla and Company, 1921.

"Desert Panthers" 4-505 PIR. MFO South Camp, Sinai, Egypt. January—July 1985. Benesh Publishing.

Ewing, Joseph H., *29 Let's Go*. Washington D.C.: Infantry Journal Press, 1947.

Lewis, Arnold M, *A Brief History of the 176th Infantry*. Fort Benning, Georgia, 1943.

Orientation Branch, Information and Education Division, HQs TFSET. *29 Let's Go!* Pocket-sized pamphlet from the Series of G.I. Stories. Published 1945.

Reynolds, Chaplain F.C. and Chaplain William F. McLaughlin, *115th Infantry U.S.A. in the World War*. Baltimore, MD: The Read-Taylor Company, 1920.

Seal, Henry F. Jr., *History of the 111th Field Artillery Regiment 29th Infantry Division 1917-1919*. Richmond, VA: Private publishing by the Virginia Army National Guard, 1953.

Seal, Henry F. Jr., *History of the 116th U.S. Infantry regiment 29th Infantry Division 1917-1919*. Richmond, VA: Private publishing by the Virginia Army National Guard, 1953

Souvenir of Camp McClellan and Anniston Ala (Victory Edition). L.L. Crump & Co, Alabama Paper and Printing Co, 1918

Stars & Stripes. *"These are My Credentials": The Story of the 8th Infantry Division*. G.I. Stories Series published in Paris, France, 1944-1945.

29 Let's Go!1917-1965. n.p. 1965-dated yearbook for the 29th Infantry Division.

Unpublished Sources

Akers, William "Bill". Personal reminiscences of Battery "B" and the D-Day landing during April 2006 Veterans Appreciation Dinner in South Boston, Virginia.

Crawford, Brian G. Personal reminiscences of service in the 29th Infantry Division and his two rotations in Bosnia. 2012

Fritz, Wilber M., Personal reminiscences of service in the 29th Infantry Division provided by his daughter, Teena Gordon

Inge, Richard D. Oral history and Interview in Farmville, Virginia, 2006. Conducted by Chris Calkins.

Koehn, Robert, Collection of Letters 1918-1919. Private collection.

Killblane, Richard, *Manchu Two*. Undated manuscript.

Koon, Chaplain Lewis, Personal Reminiscences of D-Day. Provided by Penny Koon Santilli.

Mills, John "Cam" Cameron, Personal reminiscences of service with the 29th Infantry Division in Bosnia 2001-2002. 2012

Smith, John Henry Sr, Personal memoirs and oral history of service in the 175th Infantry Regiment provided by his children: Jack, Betsy, and Susan Smith

Swanson, Michael, Personal memoirs and oral history of service in Bosnia in 1996. Conducted by Tim Williams, February 2012.

Official Websites

Stafford Soldiers And The Virginia Reserve Militia (VRM) from the staffordhistory.stafford.schoolfusion.us/

The U.S. Naval History and Heritage Command homepage: www.history.navy.mil

The U.S. Army Center of Military History homepage: www.history.army.mil

The U.S. Army Quartermaster Museum homepage: www.qmmuseum.lee.army.mil

The University of Maryland Homepage: (http://digital.lib.umd.edu/archivesum)

The Global Security homepage: www.globalsecurity.org/military/agency/army/arng-history-cold-war.htm

The Virginia Army National Guard History Site: vnghs.org/index.php/virginia-national-guard-history

The Institute of Heraldry homepage (Office of the Administrative Assistant to the Secretary of the Army): http://www.tioh.hqda.pentagon.mil

Photographs:

All color photographs of the artifacts and uniforms, unless otherwise credited, are provided courtesy of Alison Hutton.

A number of other photographs included are courtesy of various governmental, military, or historical organizations. Without their generosity, this work would not be complete. These include:

Special Collections & Archives Division, USMA Library
The Citadel Archives and Museum, Charleston, South Carolina
The Library of Congress
The Institute of Heraldry
The National Archives
The National Guard Educational Foundation
The United States Special Operations Command (USASOC)
The U.S. Army Center of Military History (CMH)
The U.S. Army Military History Institute (USAMHI)
The U.S. Army Quartermaster Museum (USAQM)
Virginia National Guard Historical Collection

Index

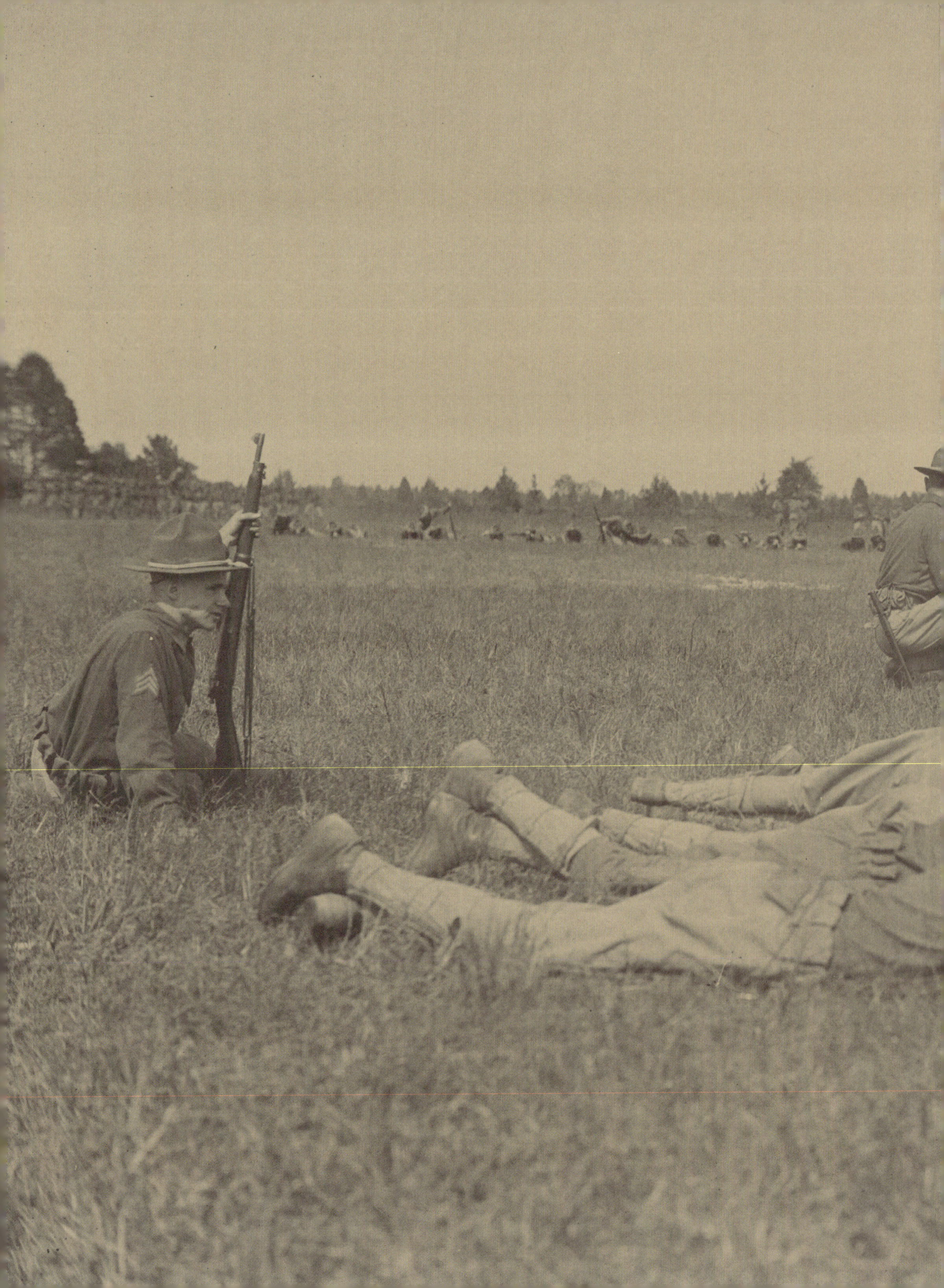